Political Imaginaries in Twentieth-Century India

Critical Perspectives in South Asian History

Critical Perspectives in South Asian History publishes critically innovative scholarship on South Asian history from the ancient world to the present day. It focuses on three broad scholarly developments; a growing engagement with public history in South Asia, a conceptual shift that assigns agency to South Asia as the *generator* of research rather than the *object* of it, and a concerted effort to study histories of neglected regions, peoples, methods and sources.

Forthcoming:

Workplace relations in Colonial Bengal: The Jute Industry and Indian Labour 1870s–1930s, by Anna Sailer

Forms of the Left in Postcolonial South Asia: Aesthetics, Networks and Connected Histories, Edited by Sanjukta Sunderson and Lotte Hoek

Towards a People's History of Pakistan: (In)audible Voices, Forgotten Pasts, Edited by Kamran Asdar Ali and Asad Ali

The YMCA in Late Colonial India: Modernization, Philanthropy and American Soft Power in South Asia, by Harald Fischer-Tiné

The Emergence of Brand-Name Capitalism in Late Colonial India: Advertising and the Making of Middle-Class Conjugality, by Douglas E. Haynes

Political Imaginaries in Twentieth-Century India, by Mrinalini Sinha and Manu Goswami

Political Imaginaries in Twentieth-Century India

Edited by
Manu Goswami and Mrinalini Sinha

BLOOMSBURY
NEW DELHI • LONDON • OXFORD • NEW YORK • SYDNEY

BLOOMSBURY INDIA
Bloomsbury Publishing India Pvt. Ltd
Second Floor, LSC Building No. 4, DDA Complex, Pocket C–6&7,
Vasant Kunj, New Delhi 110070

BLOOMSBURY, BLOOMSBURY ACADEMIC INDIA and the Diana logo are
trademarks of Bloomsbury Publishing Plc

First published in India 2022
First published in Great Britain 2022

Series design by Jade Barnett
Cover image: Crowds watch the cremation of Mohandas Karamchand Gandhi, in 1948.
Photo by Universal History Archive/Universal Images Group via Getty Images

British Library Cataloguing-in-Publication Data
A catalogue record for this book is available from the British Library.

Library of Congress Cataloging-in-Publication Data
A catalog record for this book is available from the Library of Congress

ISBN: 978-93-54351-97-6

For sale in the Indian subcontinent only

Series: Critical Perspectives in South Asian History
Typeset by Integra Software Services Pvt. Ltd.

Digitally printed and bound in India by Replika Press Pvt. Ltd.

For Toshi Goswami and Premini Sinha

Contents

List of Illustrations ix
Notes on Contributors x

1 Political Imaginaries: A Program for Twentieth-Century Political History *Manu Goswami and Mrinalini Sinha* 1

Part 1 Genealogies of the Political

2 Anatomy of a Politics of the People *Mrinalini Sinha* 31
3 Mass Satyagraha and the Problem of Collective Power *Karuna Mantena* 51
4 Conspicuous Communism *Manu Goswami* 73
5 National Wealth or National Poverty? The Politics of Economic Measurement in Late Colonial India *Eleanor Newbigin* 99
6 Law and the Political Imaginary in Mid-Twentieth-Century Southern India *Kalyani Ramnath* 121

Part 2 Democratic Imaginaries

7 Institutionalizing Democratic Uncertainties: "Election Time(s)" in the Life of Indian Democracy *Anupama Roy and Ujjwal Kumar Singh* 141
8 Voting and the Visual: Electoral Symbols, Legal Discourse, and the Sovereign People *David Gilmartin* 159
9 Representations of Electoral Politics: Notes on the Conceptual Career of the "Vote Bank" *Satish Deshpande* 181
10 Dispossession and Democracy: The Land Acquisition Act and the Future of India's Land Wars *Michael Levien* 199

Part 3 Political Commentaries

11 Remembering the Emergency and the Question of Politics *Mary E. John* 223
12 Radicalizing Democracy in India: Three Political Imaginaries *Partha Chatterjee* 241

13 Democracy and the Moment of Politics *Aditya Nigam* 259
14 The New Conjuncture *Nivedita Menon* 277

Index 299

Illustrations

1 Election Commission of India. Report on the First General Election in India 1951–1952. vol. I (New Delhi: Government of India Press, 1955), between pp. 84–85 164

2 Image I created from text of 1957 Congress election pamphlet included in Sangappa *v*. Shivamurthiswamy (In the High Court of Mysore at Bangalore), 23 ELR 51 (1968), with the image of Congress election symbol (from Figure 1) added 167

3 Photograph of EC Workers Covering Elephants in UP, by REUTERS/ Parivartan Sharma (Alamy Stock Photo), January 10, 2012, Noida. The added image of the BSP Election Symbol is from Wikimedia Commons: Furfur, CC BY-SA 3.0 <https://creativecommons.org/licenses/by-sa/3.0>, via Wikimedia Commons 173

Contributors

Partha Chatterjee is a Senior Research Scholar in Anthropology and Middle Eastern, South Asian, and African Studies at Columbia University, USA. He is the past director of the Center for Studies in Social Sciences, Kolkatta, India.

Satish Deshpande is Professor of Sociology at the University of Delhi, India.

David Gilmartin is Distinguished Professor of History at North Carolina State University, USA.

Manu Goswami is Associate Professor of History at New York University, USA.

Mary E. John is Professor at the Centre for Women's Development Studies, New Delhi, India.

Michael Levien is Associate Professor of Sociology at Johns Hopkins University, USA.

Karuna Mantena is Associate Professor of Political Science at Columbia University, USA.

Nivedita Menon is Professor of Political Theory at Jawaharlal Nehru University, Delhi, India.

Eleanor Newbigin is Senior Lecturer in History and Gender Studies at SOAS, University of London, UK.

Aditya Nigam is Professor of Social and Political Theory at the Center for Developing Societies, Delhi, India.

Kalyani Ramnath is Prize Fellow in Economics, History, and Politics at the Center for History and Economics and Lecturer at Harvard University, USA.

Anupama Roy is Professor of Political Science, Jawaharlal Nehru University, Delhi, India

Mrinalini Sinha is Alice Freeman Palmer Professor of History at the University of Michigan, USA.

Ujjwal Kumar Singh is Professor of Political Science, University of Delhi, India.

1

Political Imaginaries: A Program for Twentieth-Century Political History

Manu Goswami and Mrinalini Sinha

This volume reconsiders India's twentieth century through a specific focus on the concepts, conjunctures, and currency of its distinct political imaginaries. It represents a first attempt at grasping the shifting modes and meanings of the "political" in India with specific relation to the twentieth century, understood in qualitative terms as inaugurating new conjunctures and forms of the political rather than in the more familiar sense of a neutral chronological period. This conceptual ambition, of linking "the political" to shifts in historical temporality, extends the volume's reach beyond the interdisciplinary arena of South Asian studies to cognate late colonial and postcolonial formations in the twentieth century.

The impetus behind this volume, which is based on papers that were presented at two conferences held in New Delhi, India, and in Ann Arbor, United States, in 2014, comes from the convergence of certain historical conjunctures.[1] The first conjuncture relates to a revival of academic interest in histories of politics and in genealogies of the political that warrant claims of a "political turn" or the "return of politics" in scholarship.[2] The revival has been fueled in part by the global financial crisis of 2008 and by the explosion of popular protests and struggles across the world, often indexed under the shorthand "Arab Spring moment," which in India came in the form of the Anti-Corruption Movement of 2011. It has brought renewed attention to the remit of both politics *and* Politics—with a capital "P" (to do with matters of the state). In the intervening years, between the conferences in Delhi and Ann Arbor and the ushering of this volume to press, this renewed interest has only become more urgent: as the rise of right-wing and left-wing populisms across the world has brought the relationship between liberal democracy and late capitalism into question.

The scholarly currency of the term "political"—an adjective that was transformed into a noun and entered English-language scholarship at least since the 1980s and 1990s—had already signaled this renewal with a growing interest in the distinctiveness of politics as a sphere, albeit one that extended beyond the once-dominant state-, institution-, male-, and elite-centric focus of an erstwhile political history.[3] Indeed, the pluralization of the conception of politics has been ongoing for a very long time, at least, since the popularity of social history, the contributions of feminist theory and practice, and the reconceptualization of power associated with such figures as Michel Foucault. The multiple histories of politics that followed gave us, as in the case of India, some very fine studies of previously marginalized groups: peasants, adivasis ("tribals"), dalits (formerly referred to as "untouchables"), workers, the poor, women, religious and sexual minorities, and others likewise typically absent from conventional political histories.[4] To this, however, is now added a return, but in a different form, to some of the traditional questions about the nature and constitution of the polity that had once animated political history. The moment is thus ripe for reconstructed political histories, or histories of the political, that come after, and are informed by, the contributions of social history, feminism, and the so-called "cultural" and "linguistic" turns: seeking, in effect, to combine symbolic meanings and representations with governmental and institutional processes; "high politics" with social movements; the public with the private; and momentous events with the everyday. The domain in which politics happens is recognized, by this token, as both expansive and diffuse, exceeding and, at the same time, not excluding institutionalized power relations. This conception of politics traverses a scholarly terrain in South Asian studies that has extended from concerns with demonstrating that the so-called "prepolitical" and "nonpolitical" are inherently political to recent attempts at delineating the specificity of politics itself and its relation to the "extrapolitical."[5] Our focus on the distinctness of "political" imaginaries comes out of this particular conjuncture of thinking about politics.

Second is the opening created for a reorientation of twentieth-century history, especially now looking from the vantage point of almost two decades into the new millennium, beyond what still remains a largely Eurocentric and a North Atlantic frame of reference. The story of the twentieth century, once famously characterized by Henry R. Luce, the American publishing magnate, as the "American century," has been long overdue, especially from the perspective of the present, for a revision.[6] To be sure, the arc of the twenty-first century so far is not quite that of the "decline of the West" (an inverse of the "rise of the West" that ubiquitous, but also incomplete, framing of the nineteenth century). Yet without doubt there has been an acceleration of the shift that had begun in the twentieth century from the economic dominance of the West to the East, more specifically, in recent years, to China. Even as the full implications of this shift remain hard to predict, the recognition of Western domination as contingent has gained wider traction in both popular and academic literature.[7] This, combined with the late-twentieth- and early-twenty-first-century context when the host of contemporary transformations identified broadly under the umbrella of "globalization" still enjoyed considerable legitimacy, prompted a renewal of interest in world history (retooled for our times under the rubric of the "global" and the transnational).[8] Historians in particular contributed by tracing the deeper and longer histories of some of the processes associated with contemporary globalization. One contribution of this scholarship was to modify and nuance earlier accounts of global interactions largely premised on the assumption, "first in the west, then in the rest." The latter had entailed simplistic accounts of a unilateral Western domination over, or impact on, the rest of the world and of the unilinear diffusion of "Western" technology, institutions, goods or ideas to different parts of the world. By contrast, the focus of current scholarship has been both on the mutual constitution of the west-and-the-rest and on the multidirectional nature of processes of exchange as embodied in the popularity in scholarly literature of such terms as "networks" and "circulations."[9]

As a result, even histories of the classical eras of European imperialism, the eighteenth and nineteenth centuries, have begun to look quite different: what once looked like a one-way transplantation of ideas, institutions, goods, and technology from an expansionist West to other parts of the world is now being increasingly rewritten as the outcome of more complicated and uneven processes. But the history of the twentieth century, when many of these imbricated processes were arguably stretched beyond recognition or became so discontinuous as to have embarked on a trajectory of their own, still poses something of a challenge to scholars.[10] The larger story of the twentieth-century world, indeed, is still in need of rewriting to accommodate the ways in which seemingly familiar "Western" forms in formerly colonized or marginalized spaces developed new historical trajectories that could no longer be assimilated as pale copies or derivatives of some European/Western originals. The argument has been made forcefully in relation to the trajectory of democracy in independent India: now recognized increasingly to be neither a hothouse import from Europe nor an aberration of a "modular" form, but itself generative of new forms of comparative scholarship.[11] The economist and philosopher Amartya Sen, writing at the end of the last century, identified the widespread acceptance of democracy as the preeminently acceptable or "default" form of governance as the most significant development of the century—more even than such momentous events as the onset of decolonization, the World Wars, the containment of fascism and Nazism, and the rise, fall, and modification of communism.[12] Whether one agrees with this assessment or not, it raises some interesting possibilities for rewriting the history of the twentieth century from beyond the North Atlantic to the once-colonized regions of the world—not least, in this case, to India the home, as the oft-repeated cliché goes, of the world's largest democracy. What might such a shift in optic mean for the currently dominant narratives of the twentieth century?[13] The potential of a new accounting of the twentieth century, as is our ambition in this volume, lies precisely in the opening it provides for decentering Europe and the North Atlantic from their privileged position as the authors and arbiters of the norms and frameworks that shape the present.

Finally, there is no question that decolonization, which is justly recognized as an axial event of the twentieth century, continues to shape the evolution of scholarship on India's twentieth century.[14] From this vantage, India's place in social science had once resided in its relatively early achievement of the status of a nation-state and its illustration of the dilemmas of a conjoined commitment to democracy and development. Yet a range of empirical and theoretical developments have now converged to transform India from an object of received social science to itself an instigator of new concepts and analytical categories. Consider here the contribution of the interdisciplinary scholarship on India to what has now come to be identified with a broader "postcolonial" critique of the falsely universalizing categories of Eurocentric scholarship.[15] This volume builds upon and extends this consequential shift in thinking conceptually with and through the scholarship on India.

One of the persistent features of Indian studies, especially in its mid-century incubation across the Anglo-American academy, was a hard-and-fast divide between social science and history. A formal temporalization had helped secure empire and colonialism as the preserve of disciplinary history and relegated the post-1947 trajectory of the nation-state as the domain of the social sciences figured, more or less, as a timeless present. The assumptions that underwrote this scholarly division of labor were complexly tied to a cold-war geopolitical order that yoked together developmental historicism and nation-state centrism.[16]

All histories are horizonal. And it is not an exaggeration to say that the dominant horizon of modern histories of India, however divergent their specific thematic focus, have tended to cluster on the 1947–48 moment, anchoring either independence or the partition as *the* decisive political junctures of India's twentieth century. There are many good reasons why the problematic of nationalism and the birthing of the nation-state in spectacular violence has so long preoccupied historical and social scientific debates about modern India. But among its effects has been to drown out competing conceptions of the political. This formal temporal partitioning of disciplinary labor has secured the near-exclusive sourcing of post-1947 democratic institutions and practices in the archive of anticolonial nationalism. There are many individual works and collective projects that have effectively unworked in practice these organizing assumptions, transforming political history into a history of politics. We are thinking, in particular, of the forging of a historical anthropology paradigm that helped constellate colonial and postindependence practices and epistemic frames; the cumulative force of feminist scholarship, subaltern studies, and allied modes of postcolonial inquiry that expanded what was deemed as properly political; and the critical engagement by scholars across the academy of the volatile and viscerally experienced collision of disciplinary history with conjured fantasies in the public domain.[17] Indeed, one of the distinctive features of South Asian studies has been the robust presence of thematics and analytics produced by scholars across the Indian academic field, an illustration of a reciprocal intellectual geography less Atlantic-centered than many other "area" studies formations.[18] We are beneficiaries of these vital traditions within South Asian scholarship, one that this volume builds upon.

Scholarly re-evaluations of India's twentieth century are being prompted in relation to both new contemporary realities and new historical research. Even from within the discipline of history, which was once reluctant to cross the Rubicon of 1947 (independence and partition), there is an increasing interest in joining the game.[19] If the initial impetus for historians to venture beyond 1947 had rested on tendentious claims about the origins of many of the postindependence transformations in India in the late colonial period, then the contribution of current scholarship has been precisely to break out of the tired constraints of colonialism versus nationalism that lay behind such claims. The year 1947, punctuating the century almost exactly in the middle, acquires a rather different valence when it stands as neither the naturalized end point nor the start point of historical narratives about India. Putting 1947 in its place, indeed, has greatly expanded the contours of the political in India's twentieth century.

This new scholarship has resulted in, at least, two critical reappraisals. The first is the challenge to the still dominant nation-state imaginary that informs studies of this period. The latter had resulted in drowning out, or rendering anachronistic, other political formations. Nowhere, perhaps, is this more apparent than in the naturalized equation of decolonization with the creation of the nation-state or in the subsuming of all nationalisms and critiques of colonialism within the single form of anticolonial nationalism.[20] One set of questions that we explore, therefore, is the variegation of political imaginaries of empire and nation and of citizenship and subject that animated politics in the twentieth century.

The second major reappraisal comes, as has already been hinted above, from an appreciation of the expanded forms of democratic politics in India that sit uneasily with the genealogy of liberal democracy in the West. Studies of India's "democratic experiment" have understandably constituted a major theme of India's twentieth-century scholarship. Scholarly evaluations of India's democracy have been as contentious as the phenomenon in question.[21] Our purpose, however, is neither to adjudicate existing disciplinary debates or definitions of democracy as such nor to privilege India's particular experiment with the democratic form. It is rather to foster a consideration of India's democracy as a transdisciplinary object, tracking its formations across distinct institutions (from the social life of caste to juridical discourse to election cycles) and conjunctures. Moreover, our attempt to think of the political and of the twentieth century in relation to India makes no claim about a special place for India. Rather, it is meant to present the Indian case as what Pierre Bourdieu, drawing on Gaston Bachelard called, a "particular case of the possible:" that is, as an exemplary case in a finite universe of possible configurations.[22]

A key aim of the volume, signaled in the subtitle, is foregrounding the twentieth century as a distinct historiographical terrain. Our aim is neither affirming the twentieth century as a "ready-made chronological framework" nor supplanting extant unilineal schemas of periodization (whether from Empire to nation-state; Nehruvian development to Neoliberal populism; or, in Mukul Kesavan's prescient warning about the scope of the changes wrought by the majoritarian Hindu-nationalist government in power since 2014, from the First Republic to the Second Republic)[23] with other single-stranded timelines.[24] Instead, we take as given that historical periodization raises substantive challenges of interpretation and explanation that are not confined to (re)contouring timelines, that is, establishing or emending the irregular beginnings and endpoints of sociopolitical phenomenon.[25] The critical task is attending to the dynamic flourishing of competing political modes *within* distinct conjunctures and the relational constellation of concepts of the political *across* conjunctures. This analytic joining of histories of politics with considerations of historical temporality—both the objective and subjective temporal apprehensions of specific conjunctures and "eventful" crises—is impelled by a long overdue acknowledgment of the coexistent multiplicity and complex sedimentation of conceptions of the political.

Political Imaginaries is divided into three parts. The first, *Genealogies of the Political*, offers a portal into the multiplicity of the political in the twentieth century. It contains essays that challenge received narratives of sovereignty and decolonization, imperial crisis, and mass politics on empirical and conceptual grounds. This rethinking has crucial implications for how we understand the constitution of the Indian nation-state and genealogies of democratic practice. The second half, *Democratic Imaginaries*, reconsiders the infrastructures and everyday practice of democracy. The final section, *Commentaries*, offers some pointed reflections on the politics of the twentieth century from an acute awareness of the urgency of the present moment. Taken together, the essays trace the complex sedimentation of practices, concepts, and institutions of the political across and within specific junctures of India's twentieth century.

This volume gathers together scholars from across disciplinary sites and transnational academies. Making sense of politics as a historically mediated practice and the political formation of historical time is necessarily a transdisciplinary endeavor. Individual essays take up different points of entry into what we might call the dynamic triage or trialectic between consequential conjunctures (eventful junctures on multiple scales), the lived time of politics (experiential and anticipatory), and the complex relations (e.g., competing, coexistent, disjunctive) between political forms. The democratic transformation wrought by a new politics of the "people" is the focus of historian Mrinalini Sinha's exploration of the relatively understudied mobilization against the indentured-labor system. The issue at stake in political scientist Karuna Mantena's study of Gandhi's political mobilization is precisely the efficacy of different forms of mass protest and action for a democratic politics. For the historian Manu Goswami the multiverse worlds of early communism in India, as revisited through the anticommunist Meerut trial, exhibit the "explosion of the political" in the late-imperial landscape. Historian Eleanor Newbigin explores the figuration of the poor in anticipatory debates about national wealth during the 1930s through the work of the socialist political economist K. T. Shah. The historian Kalyani Ramnath charts a long history of civil rights organizing in India by communists and radicals to reflect on the intersection of the languages of the law and of politics in India. The political scientists Anupama Roy and Ujjwal Kumar Singh illuminate the regulated time cycles of electoral institutions that help frame the experience of democracy for the vast majority of India's population. The historian David Gilmartin and the sociologist Satish Deshpande are interested, from different vantages, in the figure of the voter. Gilmartin, through a study of the regulation of visual electoral symbols, explores the construction of the fiction of the voter as a "free" person; for Deshpande the public career, both popular and academic, of the category "vote bank" serves as a symptom of the different phases in the modes of representing politics from the 1970s to the present. The sociologist Michael Levien explores the politics and political economy of mass-scale land dispossessions today, highlighting its departure from prior regimes of development and state capacity. The feminist scholar Mary John explores the unexpected enunciation of new political subjectivities in the emergence of a radical women's politics amidst the "Emergency" of the 1970s. The essay by the political scientist and historian Partha Chatterjee explores temporally coeval yet ideologically distinct movements in contemporary India, oriented toward radicalizing democracy. The essay by political scientist Aditya Nigam analyzes moments of democratic upsurge in the 1990s and 2006 in India to argue against extant notions of politics and democracy and to pose the question of political practice anew. Nivedita Menon, a political scientist, concludes the volume with an argument for a "new conjuncture" in India in the twenty-first century. An analytical leitmotif shared across these essays is a refigured notion of political imaginaries and the imprint of specific temporal politics in their articulation, elaboration, and subsequent imperilment or flourishing. But before elaborating this usage, and the wider stakes of the term, some clarifications are in order.

Political Imaginaries: Anchoring Histories of the Political

A history of politics requires, as individual essays demonstrate, a robust empirical fidelity to the actual course of politics. At the same moment, histories of politics must break from the idealized, ideal-typical, and *a priori* typologies and treatments of political forms enshrined in conventional political history. This doubled commitment to analytical reflexivity and empirical realism neither implies a single disciplinary vantage nor presumes adherence to a single theoretical scaffold. But it does require continual adequation of analytical categories and objects of analysis. Toward this end, we turn to a central keyword of this volume, *Political Imaginaries*.

Given the freight of prior interpretations and their lingering hold, we must clarify our own summoning of the term. The most widely influential elaboration of the term "imaginary" derives, as is well known, from Cornelius Castoriadis, a heterodox Marxist philosopher, a Greek émigré to France, and the co-founder in 1948 of the influential independent left journal *Socialisme ou Barbarie*.[26] This initial coinage, which emerged within a volatile mid-century French communist *milieu*, was intended as a frontal repudiation of the unrelenting economism of the Marxism endorsed by the Stalinist French Communist Party (PCF). The trajectory of the term in the Anglo-American academy has paid relatively little heed to this partisan contextual genesis or its post-1968 alliance with such cognate projects as "autogestion" (associated with the heterodox social philosopher Henri Lefebvre) and "autopoeisis" that sought to foster forms of decentralized political and economic self-management distinct from both Leninist models of the dictatorship of the proletariat and emergent neoliberal utopia.[27] During the 1990s, the term was often deployed in Anglophone social sciences to entrench extant methodological oppositions between ideas versus institutions, norms versus practices, culture versus economy. The deployment of the category in South Asian studies—with the exception of the anthropologist Arjun Appadurai's work on the cultural dimensions of "globalization"—issued less from a direct engagement with Castoriadis or the psychoanalytical elaboration of the imaginary in Jacques Lacan.[28] It broadly followed the retooling offered by the philosopher Charles Taylor in his magisterial synthesis of the philosophical foundations of modern social imaginaries.[29] This imprinting was especially evident during the 1990s and 2000s when debates about modernity and globalization, colonialism and cultural forms, politics and civil society raged across disciplinary sites.[30] Our revisiting of the term departs from this admittedly thumbnail sketch of these prior usages of the concept, imaginary. It is weighted instead toward a more circumscribed and concretely historical purpose.

The concept of the political imaginary, as elaborated by Susan Buck-Morss via the Russian philosophers Valerii Podoroga and Elena Petrovskaia, pluralized here to accommodate the difference and range of postcolonial forms, is our point of entry for a re-evaluation of India's twentieth century. The Russian concept, in contrast to other contemporary invocations of the "imaginary" as primarily a logic of discourse, has a more concrete topographical implication: "not a political *logic*," as Buck-Morss elaborates, "but a political *landscape*, a concrete visual field in which political actors are positioned."[31] These concrete political landscapes, shaped by the intertwining of materiality and human praxis, are the basis for our attempt at rethinking the twentieth century in India.

A topographical conception pushes against the commonplace conflation of imaginary with imagination. Reducing politics to acts of individual imagination and discursive invention returns us, however unwittingly, to the thralldom of political historical narratives about great "thinkers/leaders." More crucially, it brackets the specifically collective (if not always collectivist) mode of twentieth-century politics. We are thinking here of the centrality of new mass collectivities acting in concert in the shaping of modes of sovereignty and representation, directing and displacing development schemas, socializing liberal constitutions, and the like. The essays in the volume emphasize the *collective*, *transpersonal*, and *dynamic* genesis and signification of political imaginaries.

Received conceptions of the imaginary, following Castoriadis and Taylor, have linked it with the "positing of new forms," the "unmotivated" enunciation of radical novelty.[32] Yet this emphasis has so often been pitched as a transhistorical precept, as a kind of philosophical anthropological axiom that guts any specific historical purchase. Political imaginaries are best understood as artifacts and infrastructures of historical change, part and parcel of the temporal weave of contradiction and convergence that mark off particular historical moments as consequential conjunctures. Instead of a lineal succession of absolute ruptures, set apart from or unintelligible to one another, the making of political imaginaries is rooted within the multiple, cumulative, and irreversible "logics of history."[33] They are neither conjured by individual thinkers and activists nor guaranteed by some "cunning of history." The chapters in this book illustrate the topographical concreteness of Political Imaginaries as dynamic tangible forms more persuasively than any schematic methodological injunction could. From this vantage, political imaginaries instantiate the everyday stuff of collective politics, a topography shaped by the durable and lived interdisciplinarity of materiality and ideology, infrastructures, and templates. Political Imaginaries are historical formations, creatures of temporal politics and a temporalized political, "all the way down."

A few words as well on the politics/political distinction.[34] While we invoke this distinction, which entered Anglophone scholarship relatively late compared to its Continental counterpart, we do so not in any prescriptive or doctrinaire way. Carl Schmitt's *The Concept of the Political* ([1932]1976) and Claud Lefort's *The Political Forms of Modern Society: Bureaucracy, Democracy, Totalitarianism* (1986) are arguably the most cited texts for bringing the distinction into the Anglo-American academy.[35] But the sources upon which this distinction draws, including the work of Hannah Arendt that stands as an exception to the belatedness of its entry into the Anglophone tradition, and the work it does in the arguments of individual contributors are, in fact, extremely varied.[36] We, nevertheless, find the distinction useful to signal some of the following. First, a reconceived and expanded understanding of the field of politics, beyond merely a competition for political power, which lies at the basis for an integrative and renewed political history. Second, the specificity or distinctiveness of politics as a field, which is not simply explained away in terms of something else, economics, society, law, psychology, and so on. Third, a recognition of the element of contingency that haunts even the most seemingly necessary social order, making it vulnerable to the potential of ruptures and new beginnings. The latter, especially, has animated some recent humanities and social science scholarship that makes a case for the novel and distinctive contours of politics in India's twentieth century, from new ideas about freedom, equality, justice, and democracy to the role of disciplinary history versus philosophy as sites for thinking about politics as such.[37] We draw loosely on the politics/political distinction primarily to gesture toward these new histories.

The Trouble with the Twentieth Century

Our effort to rethink "India's twentieth century" is necessarily enmeshed with other cognate temporalizations across regional historical fields. We do not assume that India has a unique claim on the twentieth century and are wary of the intensified regional and national narcissisms that saturate global mediascapes. The speculative attribution of fixed temporal endowments—protracted stasis, endemic crisis, or unbounded futurity—to specific regions and geocultural formations was a commonplace of the cold-war era. This kind of temporal reckoning has returned or redoubled in neoliberal market creeds, exclusionary discourses of "civilizations" a la Samuel Huntington, and nativist fantasies of bounded "pure" nations.[38] As recent critical works by Africanists have forcefully demonstrated, the differential rationing of historical time to specific world regions has centered, in particular, on the scarce resource of "futurity."[39] Popular narratives of India in relation to either its dramatic market emergence or its putative status as a rising global power have helped fuel, rather than fell, the merger of market-disciplinary models with authoritarian populism.

The twentieth century is less an objective *chronotope* (to borrow the interwar Soviet linguist Mikhail Bakhtin's phrase) than a dynamic historiographical construct.[40] Even a cursory glance at major efforts to historicize the "twentieth century"—across disciplinary domains—makes this clear. There is little consensus about how to configure the twentieth century, much less what constellation of events, practices, and institutions impart it with an internal structural unity that coheres across world regions. So even as histories of major events, struggles, and artifacts of the twentieth century proliferate—from mass revolution and total war to liberal internationalism and human rights discourses—basic temporal and spatial considerations remain contested.[41] Consider, for instance, three widely influential and conceptually ambitious reckonings of the twentieth century, all rooted within a broadly left-leaning perspective and drawn respectively from political economy, history, and philosophy. Are the temporal logics of the twentieth century best conceived as long, as Giovanni Arrighi's magisterial historical sociology of successive hegemonic regimes and attendant cycles of accumulation argued? In this large-scale Braudelian narrative, the shifting contours of hegemonic regimes and cycles of accumulation, that began in the long sixteenth century, culminated in a twentieth-century variation of intensive financialization and hegemonic fracturing, pointing toward both a terminal crisis of US hegemony and the corresponding rise of East Asia.[42] Or is the duration of twentieth century better understood as short, commencing in 1914 and closing in 1989, to follow Eric Hobsbawm's widely influential plotting of the relatively brief systemic challenge posed by socialism to the apparently irresistible march of liberal capitalism?[43] Alternatively, does the particularity of the twentieth century reside in the incubation of a universal philosophical principle, as Alain Badiou's diagnostic suggests, that joined together collectivity, historical time, and political subjectivation, rendering the century thinkable to itself?[44] The conceptual coherence of the twentieth century as a legible marker of historical time does not lie, he argues, in some "objective datum." It proceeds from the ways divergent political formations were shaped by a distinctive and subjective conviction that "every authentic subjectivation is collective, and that every vigorous and intellectuality implies the construction of a 'we.'"[45] The twentieth century became thinkable in and through this reflexively constituted *collective* understanding of the political.

These distinct, and temporally arrhythmic, versions of the twentieth century offer profound insights into the *longue-durée* interlock of imperial hegemons and cycles of capital accumulation, the abbreviated dramaturgy of communism and liberal capitalism, and the historical novelty of models of politics that enshrined collectivity as both ground and figure. None of them fall prey to the usual sins of unilineal teleology or single-stranded causation. Nor do they revive the cold-war genre of historian-as-commissar compiling dossiers of the wrecked utopias, the totalitarian horrors, the specious avant-gardes, and false illusions exuded by the twentieth century.[46] They share considerable conceptual ground. Badiou and Hobsbawm alike center collective anticapitalist politics—in its differential scales, valence, and modalities—as a historically novel phenomenon of the twentieth century. Even scholars opposed to the explicitly left orientation of Arrighi, Hobsbawm, and Badiou (and we might add, Buck-Morss) would find little empirical bases to contest their shared conviction that novel articulations of the political are what set the twentieth century apart. Yet this shared consensus *only* underlines the manifest absence of decolonization as a world-historical event. All three narratives short-change the reverberations unleashed by successive waves of mid- and late-century imperial dissolution across Asia, Africa, and the Middle-East from the restructuring of the political-economic space of capitalism to new experiments with universality encoded in postindependence sovereignty, citizenship, and democratic representation.[47] This elision underscores how even the most wide-ranging analyses—and globally scaled periodizations—are beholden to a stubbornly persistent logic of presenting the regional as the worldwide, of territorializing politics in self-evident containers that reflect rather than interrogate geopolitical hierarchies.

The challenge of adjudicating what concepts and cartographies might anchor accounts of twentieth-century politics remains a live, unresolved question. Postcolonial scholars have long alerted us to the danger of conflating regional dynamics with the worldwide, of creating a false homology between modernity and Europe. Dipesh Chakrabarty's call to "Provincialize Europe" was, among other things, a lament about the Euro-American coordinates of twentieth-century social science.[48] There is no disputing the inordinate historiographical and normative import of Europe serving as referent and resource in major assessments of the twentieth century from debates about the holocaust and fascism to widely influential genealogies of totalitarianism and terror. It has remained, until quite recently, the default region, the "Ur" space, to think the twentieth century.

A wave of recent works on twentieth-century politics from other world regions have offered fresh, arresting, and new historical insights. Alongside works previously mentioned by Africanist scholars, works grounded in the archive of twentieth-century Latin America and the Caribbean (and the long reverberations of the Haitian revolution) have helped forge a capacious understanding of the political.[49] Historians, political theorists, and anthropologists have highlighted the interplay between geopolitical shifts and local political subjectivation across the cold war era of the twentieth century. Scholars of the Middle-East, following the "new materialism" associated with Bruno Latour, have foregrounded the mid-century moment of the global economic transition from coal to oil, facilitated by imperial expansion in the Middle-East, as a central axis for thinking twentieth-century politics. Timothy Mitchell has called attention to the dynamics of "carbon democracy" or the codependent consolidation of mass democracies across the Atlantic and authoritarian regimes across the Middle East and Gulf states, paving the way for proliferating works on material infrastructures as the crucible of collective social and political life.[50] A new wave of revisionist histories of the Soviet Union and Eastern Europe has, more recently, begun to dismantle the freight of ambient anticommunist cold war narratives.[51] There is no settled consensus, however, on how best to historicize the political across the twentieth century. Much like the "political lives of dead bodies" that emerged as a perverse existential predicament in postsocialist Eastern Europe in the last third of the twentieth century, there is no self-evident analytic to encompass the twentieth century.[52] Charles Maier, the historian of Germany and Europe, has provocatively argued that the longer-run consolidation of "territoriality"—the produced alignment of governance and collective identity—should be the bases for periodizing the twentieth century.[53] For the prominent Chinese scholar Wang Hui the unforeseen dialectic between revolution and the retreat from revolution is the defining dimension of China's twentieth century, while other historians of China, such as Prasenjit Duara and Elizabeth J. Perry, have queried the purchase of regime types as a sufficient basis for differentiating contemporary "democratic" India and "authoritarian" China.[54] In this proliferating genre (scholarly and popular) of comparison, other scholars of ancient India and China have asserted a through line between their ancient pasts and anticipated futures, effectively rendering the place of the twentieth century ambiguous.[55] Juxtaposing these developments in other world regions underscores, for us, the conundrums that beset all efforts at placed temporalization, not just a particular trouble with India's twentieth century.

There is no single all-purpose fix to these vexed questions. An analytic of Political Imaginaries offers, as we suggest above, a potentially useful conceptual anchor to think *through and with* twentieth-century conjunctures of the political. But we fully expect the twentieth century—both "what happened and what was said to have happened" to borrow the Caribbean historical anthropologist Michel Rolph-Trouillot's distilled definition of historical practice—to continually mutate.[56]

Our aim in initiating an interdisciplinary conversation on India's twentieth century is prompted by a desire to think across that great mid-century divide—Independence, Partition, or the Transfer of Power—that still, in our view, carves up the century too neatly and has for long sustained our disciplinary division of labor. And it is also prompted by the desire to take stock of our contemporary conjuncture that has been too quick, perhaps, to consign the twentieth century to a Past, supposedly hived off by a variety of endings, the end of the Cold War, the end of ideology, the end of history, the end of socialism, the end of nations and nation-states, the end of modernity, and so on or as what one scholar has called the "'post'-condition."[57] The question of the beginning as much as of the end of the twentieth century in India—other than as fixed points on a calendar—are very much at play in our efforts to rethink the twentieth century. For a better understanding of our times as well as of the century that has passed we could do no better than to take stock of India's twentieth-century history of politics, with its particular experience of the contradictory pulls of late colonialism; its reconstituted national liberation and anti-imperial mass movements; its anomalous and precocious emergence on the international stage; its contested and fitful experiments with planned development and social change; its swings between the poles of political centralization and decentralization; its long and invidious record around the politics of caste, of religion, of gender, and of economic and social marginality; its proliferation of forms and uneven pace of cultural change; its range of new social and people's movements and their myriad forms of resistance and contestation; and its unmistakable transformations under all that we have come to know today by the shorthand of "globalization" with its accompanying discontents.

Democratic Contradictions

A genealogical parsing of democracy corrects against a lineal teleology that sees the achievement of the nation form—that is, the postpartition era of nation-state consolidation—rather than the multiplicity of struggles within and over empire as well as the continual churning of popular social mobilizations, as its singular source.[58] Our intention here is to challenge the disciplinary parochialism that undergirds many accounts of democracy outside the North Atlantic. We are equally concerned with the wider arena of "democracy studies" that flourished in the post-1989 era.[59] Propelled by cold war triumphalism and the ascendancy of neoliberal market, the dizzying spread of democracy as an analytic construct across scholarly and public spheres was deeply equivocal.

As political scientists rushed to elaborate definitional criteria based, more often than not, on a highly idealized North Atlantic regional model, other groups—from NGOs to transnational institutions—devised and sought to codify such formalistic criteria. Coupled with the revival of "civil society," it was codified in formalistic models and political actors across international organizations (the IMF, the WTO, the World Bank) that helped contain its compass to contested elections and the rolling forward of economic freedom.[60] A voluminous literature has tied this ideological overdetermination to the wider "neoliberal turn" that gathered pace following the collapse of inherited developmental models across postindependence states and the dismantling of "embedded liberalism" in the Euro-American zone.[61]

We thus do not intend with our attention on democracy to join the clamorous paeans of praise for liberal democracy as a political form that has fired a certain public and academic discourse ever since what Samuel Huntington called the "third wave" of global democratization, which began in Southern Europe in the 1970s, climaxed with the collapse of Soviet communism and the fall of apartheid in South Africa and continued unabated with glowing hopes of the spread of political and economic freedoms beyond the so-called developed world.[62] That this effervescent rhetoric, which at its height had confidently proclaimed the arrival of the "end of history," at least in a moral sense, has since been knocked off its perch in the wake of global financial crises and democratic "people's" movements as well as by the stubborn persistence of a purportedly alternative model exemplified by a powerful China, has not necessarily dimmed faith in the future of liberal democracy.[63] The recent concern, especially in the North Atlantic, over the undermining of the middle classes of the developed world—and the emergence of a new public discourse on growing inequality that is emanating from several different quarters—registers a beleaguered sense of the future and is accompanied by numerous calls for renewal.[64] The stakes of our attention to democracy are decidedly different from either the celebration or the handwringing about the future of liberal democracy that are both, in effect, premised on a certain colonization of our thinking about the possibilities of imagining different futures. We wish to invoke democracy here in a more open-ended way.

By the same token, then, we also distinguish our focus from three debates, by now quite tired, to our mind, that are prompted by discussions around democracy in relation to India. The first, and oldest, of these, of course, is centered around the very viability and wisdom of the experiment with democracy as an arguably borrowed political form—measured inevitably by its deviation from its supposed "original" actualized elsewhere—in the inhospitable conditions of a postindependence India.[65] Fortunately, both history on the ground and a considerable body of scholarship since, has rendered this particular question moot. Consider, for example, work that points to the peculiarities of postindependence forms of democracy in India. This is best captured, perhaps, in Partha Chatterjee's re-reading of democracy not as "government of the people," as republican cliché would have it, but, rather, as "the politics of the governed."[66] By this token, then, squatters on public lands or illegal users of water and electricity are not tangential to the understanding of proper democratic politics; but, rather, in making use of democratic politics to make their demands heard, these groups represent examples of the different forms that democratic politics takes in a formerly colonized society. We think it is now safe, indeed, to say that we may have eventually laid this ghost to rest. We take this moment in the scholarship as the starting point for our own effort at recalling democracy.

A second, and related, debate that has long bedeviled talk of democracy in India is the extent to which it is or is not a "real" democracy to be measured by any number of yardsticks. The gap between the myth and reality of democracy in India has also a long history in the scholarship. While the dominant view has tended to share the verdict of the Indian jurist and economist Nani A. Palkhivala that India has "a first class constitution and a third class democracy" others have been far more scathing both about the founding document and the actual performance of Indian democracy.[67] In his door-stopper of a book, *India after Gandhi: The History of the World's Largest Democracy*, Ramachandra Guha tries, among other things, to produce a consensus—in the midst of an unusually raucous disagreement—both within and beyond the walls of the academy—about the score card of Indian democracy at midlife. The verdict, in Guha's largely panegyric account, is that the glass is only half-empty or, in Guha's more colorful borrowing from the Hindi movie comedy actor, Johnny Walker, "phipty-phipty" or 50-50.[68] Our aim is not to march down this well-worn path and get bogged down in the task of drawing up a balance sheet of the successes and failures of Indian democracy, in effect, to endorse seeing like a state. We understand democracy as wider and deeper than a state-centric focus alone can allow.

And, finally, discussions of Indian democracy now—in relation to much of the so-called developing world and certainly the subcontinent—cannot seem to avoid the distorting glint of Indian exceptionalism: not only the world's largest democracy, as we are repeatedly told, but also the exception in terms of its durability and stability, against all odds, in the developing world. The late Sir Christopher Bayly, for example, spoke of an "Indian *Sonderweg*"—special path—in terms of the country's ability to "cling to the values of representative government and later, broad democratic values, in the face of colonial oppressions, populist mass murder, endemic corruption, the restrictive implications of caste 'reservations' [affirmative action] and gross economic inequality."[69] The emphasis on an Indian exceptionalism—that often goes hand in hand, unsurprisingly, with a flexing of India's economic muscle—is not what we wish to signal toward in this volume.

Through a focus on democracy, instead, we put stress on the implications of its suffix ***cracy***, that is power or rule.[70] And, as such, we hope it allows tracking changes and continuities in the configurations of "rule" across the twentieth century, from the late colonial through the postindependent to the present. Democracy, as understood thus, also enables an exploration of the political in myriad social relations that includes the state as an especially charged field of politics but as not necessarily the primary one. And, finally, with an interest in democracy we hope to bring into greater focus the role of institutions, of the law, of political economy, among others, that must continue to be a part of thinking about the political in the twentieth century.

Our aim in this volume is to clear the ground for more robust engagements with the political in India's twentieth century. A propulsive politics of negation has taken hold across many formal representative democracies. The widespread crisis of democratic legitimation is nowhere more visible than in the stark confluence across world regions of revanchist authoritarian populisms.[71] Buoyed by corporatist oligarchies from above yet self-understood as plebian expressions from below, such movements are evident from Poland to the United States, Hungary to Brazil, Turkey to India.[72] Declining or recessionary growth has made the staggering inequalities bequeathed by neoliberal governance and economic creeds both more visible and acute, prompting the label "Billionaire Raj."[73] The many-sided convergence of economic crisis, ecological ruin, and exclusionary nationalisms has dramatically unspooled the organizing axioms of democratic legitimation across world regions. These principles, broadly construed for democracies in the global south, included a calibrated bargain between economic growth and democratic representativeness, a state either set apart from or, as in the Indian constitutional maxim, equivalently distant to religion. These now seem to many citizens of the global south more akin to undeliverable promissory notes. The subordination of "the political" to the "economic" within India has proceeded apace with daily enactments of the outsized fantasy of a unitary Hindu nationhood. Anthropologists and sociologists have provided a richly detailed record of the routinization of actual and symbolic violence against vulnerable citizens in this juncture—a category that exceeds the enduring hierarchical placement of Muslims, Dalits, and Adivasis to casual "footloose labor" in the so-called informal economy, indebted farmers and "rivers of debt," the urban unemployed, the targets of "pharmocracy," dissenting students, among others.[74] This manifest lived record has fueled a vertiginous sense of the terminus of collective political life, of the once keenly sought "power of the multitude."[75] An expansive literature within and beyond South Asia has sought to demonstrate, and account for, what Wendy Brown, the political theorist, has aptly phrased as an "undoing of the demos."[76] While her account focuses broadly on the tortured tangle of neoconservatism and neoliberalism in the United States, the asserted link between "logics of economization" and the denudation of democratic politics has acquired broad purchase.[77]

This volume, like other collective projects, was born in a specific constellation. But our aim is less to inventory the manifold misery of the present than to refigure the shifting modes and meanings of the political across India's twentieth century. The overt recession of the political today demands a broadening and deepening of historical modes of reckoning with politics. The volume shows that questions about historical temporality—from the lived experience of possibility as the nodal condition of collective politics, the recurrence of political concepts across junctures, the dynamics of temporal consciousness—are at the core of collective political experience and intellection. The essays in the volume serve, individually and together, as an argument for and an illustration of how to write new histories of politics across and within major junctures of India's twentieth century.

Notes

1 The first conference was held on January 10–11, 2014 at the India International Center and the Nehru Memorial Museum and Library in New Delhi. It was sponsored by the American Institute of Indian Studies in commemoration of its fiftieth anniversary. The second conference at Ann Arbor, MI, was held on September 4-6, 2014. The conference at Michigan was made possible with generous support from Ranvir and Adarsh Trehan, the Center for South Asian Studies, and the College of Literature, Science, and the Arts at the University of Michigan. We are very grateful to our sponsors for funding and organizational support. We also acknowledge with deep gratitude the contributions of the participants at the conference, some of whom were unable to contribute to the volume, and of the audience at both events.

2 For some examples of this interest, see Chantal Mouffe, *The Return of the Political* (London: Verso Book, 2005); and Pierre Rosanvallon, *Democracy: Past and Future*. Ed. Samuel Moyn (New York: Columbia University Press, 2006). The status of the field of political history, however, remains hotly contested. See, for example, the recent debate on the state of political history in the field of U.S. history that was provoked by Fredrik Logevall and Kenneth Osgood's article "Why Did We Stop

Teaching Political History?" *New York Times*, August 29, 2016. https://www.nytimes.com/2016/08/29/opinion/why-did-we-stop-teaching-political-history.html. Accessed June 15, 2018; for a sample of the debate that ensued, see, Marc Stein, Logevall and Osgood, "Political History: An Exchange," *Perspectives on History*, January 2017. https://www.historians.org/publications-and-directories/perspectives-on-history/january-2017/political-history-an-exchange. Accessed June 15, 2018.

3 See Susan Pedersen, "What Is Political History Now?" in David Cannadine, ed., *What is History Now?* (New York: Palgrave Macmillan, 2002), pp. 36–56; and the special issue on Political History Today in the American Historical Association's *Perspectives on History*, May 2011, especially Steven Pincus and William Novak, "Political History after the Cultural Turn," *Perspectives on History*, May 2011. https://www.historians.org/publications-and-directories/perspectives-on-history/may-2011/political-history-after-the-cultural-turn. Accessed January 24, 2016.

4 For an accounting of such an expanded domain of politics from within the field of South Asian historiography, see Vinayak Chaturvedi, "Histories of Politics after Political History: Reflections from South Asian Historiography," *Perspectives on History*, May 2011. https://www.historians.org/publications-and-directories/perspectives-on-history/may-2011/histories-of-politics-after-political-history. Accessed January 24, 2016; and also Durba Ghosh, "Optimism and Political History: A Perspective From India," *Perspectives on History*, May 2011. https://www.historians.org/publications-and-directories/perspectives-on-history/may-2011/optimism-and-political-history. Accessed January 24, 2016.

5 This terrain has been mapped out in Prathama Banerjee, *Elementary Aspects of the Political: Histories from the Global South* (Durham, NC: Duke University Press, 2020). Unfortunately, this introduction was completed before we were able to engage with the book substantively. The Subaltern Studies Collective was especially instrumental in criticizing the conflation of the political with the domain of elites and the consequent designation of subaltern politics as prepolitical, see Ranajit Guha, *Elementary Aspects of Peasant Insurgency in Bengal* (Delhi: Oxford University Press, 1983); and "On Some Aspects of the Historiography of Colonial India," in Guha, ed., *Subaltern Studies 1: Writings on South Asian History and Society* (Delhi: Oxford University Press, 1982). For some useful critiques of this historiographical initiative, especially the early tendency to conceive of the elite and subaltern domains of politics as autonomous, see individual essays in David Ludden, ed., *Reading Subaltern Studies: Critical History, Contested Meaning and the Globalization of South Asia* (London: Anthem Press, 2002); and Vinayak Chaturvedi, *Mapping Subaltern Studies and the Postcolonial* (London: Verso, 2000).

6 Henry R. Luce, "The American Century," *Life Magazine* (February 17, 1941): 61–5. For a requiem of Luce's famous phrase, see Andrew J. Bacevich, "Farewell, The American Century," *The Nation*, May 11, 2009. https://www.thenation.com/article/farewell-american-century/. Accessed June 24, 2018.

7 Martin Jacques, *When China Rules the World: The End of the Western World and the Birth of a New Global Order* (New York: Penguin, 2009); and Ho-fung Hung, *The China Boom: Why China Will Not Rule the World* (New York: Columbia University Press, 2015).

8 See Bruce Mazlish, "Comparing Global History to World History," *Journal of Interdisciplinary History* 28, no. 3 (Winter 1998): 385–95; Diego Olstein, *Thinking History Globally* (New York and London: Palgrave Macmillan, 2014); and C. A. Bayly et al., "AHR Conversation: On Transnational History," *The American Historical*

Review 111, no. 5 (December 2006): 1441–64. For some arguments from the field of South Asia, see Anupama Rao, "India and Global History," *History and Technology* 26, no. 1 (March 2010): 77–84; and Gopal Balachandran, "Claiming Histories Beyond Nations: Situating Global History," *Indian Economic and Social History Review* 49, no. 2 (2012): 247–72. The more recent disillusionment with "globalization" has also begun to sound a requiem for "global" history, see Jeremy Adelman, "What is Global History Now?" *Aeon*, March 2, 2017. https://aeon.co/essays/is-global-history-still-possible-or-has-it-had-its-moment. Accessed December 22, 2018.

9 For some examples from the history of science in South Asia, where these concepts have been most fully elaborated, see, David Arnold, *The Tropics and the Traveling Gaze: India, Landscape, and Science,1800–1856* (Seattle: University of Washington Press, 2006); and Kapil Raj, *Relocating Modern Science: Circulation and the Construction of Knowledge in South Asia and Europe* (Delhi: Palgrave Macmillan, 2006). For questions arising out of the popularity of the idea of "networks," drawn from the work of Bruno Latour, see Sujit Sivasundaram, "Sciences and the Global: On Methods, Questions, and Theory," *Isis: A Journal of the History of Science Society* 101, no. 1 (March 2010): 146–58; and Kapil Raj, "Networks of Knowledge or Spaces of Circulation?: The Birth of British Cartography in Colonial South Asia in the Late Eighteenth Century," *Journal of Global Intellectual History* 2, no. 1 (2017): 49–66.

10 This case for the twentieth century, for example, is made by Shruti Kapila, "Global Intellectual History and the Indian Political," in Darrin M. McMahon and Samuel Moyn, eds., *Rethinking Modern European Intellectual History* (New York: Oxford University Press, 2014), pp. 253–74.

11 For a succinct case for this argument, see Gurpreet Mahajan, *India: Political Ideas and the Making of Democratic Discourse* (London: Zed, 2013). The initiative itself may be traced back much earlier, see Rajni Kothari, *Politics in India* (New Delhi: Orient Blackswan, 1970).

12 Amartya Sen, "Democracy as a Universal Value," *Journal of Democracy* 10, no. 3 (1999): 3–17.

13 This is suggested by Madhav Khosla who sees India as the paradigmatic democratic experience of the twentieth century in the same way that Tocqueville saw the model of nineteenth century democracy in the United States, see Khosla, *India's Founding Moment*: *The Constitution of a Most Surprising Democracy* (Cambridge: Harvard University Press, 2020).

14 Key works in the rapidly proliferating literature on decolonization across the British Empire include; Frederick Cooper, *Decolonization and African Society: The Labor Question in French and British Africa* (Cambridge: Cambridge University Press, 1996); Jordana Bailkin, *The Afterlife of Empire* (Berkeley, CA: University of California Press, 2012); John Darwin, *Britain and Decolonization: The Retreat from Empire in the Post-War World* (New York: Palgrave,1988); Prasenjit Duara, ed., *Decolonization: Perspectives from Now and Then* (London: Routledge, 2004); A. G. Hopkins, "Rethinking Decolonization," *Past and Present* 200, no. 1 (August 2008): 211–47; Dietmar Rothermund, *The Routledge Companion to Decolonization* (Hoboken, NJ: Routledge 2006); James Le Seur, *The Decolonization Reader* (New York: Routledge, 2003); Vijay Prashad, *The Darker Nations: A People's History of the Third World* (New York: New Press, 2007); Dane Kennedy, *Decolonization: A Very Short Introduction* (Oxford: Oxford University Press, 2016); Jan Jensen and Jürgen Osterhammel, *Decolonization: A Short History* (Princeton, NJ: Princeton University Press, 2017).

15 For a classic statement of this case, see Dipesh Chakrabarty, *Provincializing Europe: Postcolonial Thought and Historical Difference* (Princeton, NJ: Princeton University Press, 2000). Also see the following, Bernard Cohn, *Colonialism and Its Forms of Knowledge: The British in India* (Princeton, NJ: Princeton University Press, 1996); Nicholas B. Dirks, ed., *Colonialism and Its Culture* (Ann Arbor, MI: University of Michigan Press, 1992); Ranajit Guha, *Dominance without Hegemony: History and Power in Colonial India* (Cambridge, MA: Harvard University Press, 1997); Partha Chatterjee, *Nationalist Thought and the Colonial World: A Derivative Discourse?* (New Delhi: Oxford University Press, 1986); Homi Bhabha, *Nation and Narration* (London and New York: Routledge, 1990); Gyan Prakash, "Subaltern Studies as Postcolonial Criticism," *The American Historical Review* 99, no. 5 (1994): 1475–90; Gayatri Chakravorty Spivak, "Subaltern Studies: Deconstructing History," in R. Guha, ed. *Subaltern Studies IV: Writings on South Asian History and Society* (Delhi: Oxford University Press, 1985): 330–63; and her "Can the Subaltern Speak?" in Cary Nelson and Lawrence Grossberg, eds., *Marxism and the Interpretation of Culture* (Urbana, IL: University of Illinois Press, 1992): 271–313; and Gauri Viswanathan, *Masks of Conquest: Literary Study and British Rule in India* (New York: Columbia University Press, 1989). For recent, sharply divergent, assessments by sociologists of this historical literature see Gurminder Bhambra, *Rethinking Modernity: Postcolonialism and the Sociological Imagination* (London: Palgrave Macmillan, 2007); Vivek Chibber, *Postcolonial Theory and the Specter of Capital* (London: Verso, 2013); Julian Go, *Postcolonial Thought and Social Theory* (Oxford: Oxford University Press, 2016). On the practice and meaning of postcolonial theory in Indian scholarship see Elleke Boehmer and Rosinka Chaudhuri, eds., *The Indian Postcolonial: A Critical Reader* (London and New York: Routledge, 2010).

16 Critical genealogies and assessments of "area studies" in mid-century United States abound. Although there is no single volume for South Asian studies, see Nicholas B. Dirks, "South Asian Studies: Futures Past," in David L. Szanton, ed., *The Politics of Knowledge: Area Studies and the Disciplines* (Berkeley, CA: University of California Press, 2004): 341–85. For cognate regional reckonings see, William Glover and Ken Kollman, eds., *Relevant/Obsolete? Area Studies in the U.S. Academy* (Ann Arbor, MI: University of Michigan Press, 2012); Masao Miyoshi and Harry Harootunian, ed., *Learning Places: The Afterlives of Area Studies* (Durham, NC: Duke University Press, 2002); Benedict Anderson, *Specters of Comparison: Nationalism, Southeast Asia and the World* (London: Verso, 1998); Zachary Lockman, *Field Notes: The Making of Middle East Studies in the United States* (Stanford, CA: Stanford University Press, 2016); and Immanuel Wallerstein, "The Unintended Consequences of Cold War Area Studies," in Andre Schiffrin, ed., *The Cold War and the University: Toward an Intellectual History of the Postwar Years* (New York: New Press, 1997): 195–232.

17 For engagement with the fraught "public" life of disciplinary history in India, see Neeladri Bhattacharya, "Teaching History in Schools," *History Workshop Journal* 67 (2009): 99–110. Also see, Sarvepalli Gopal, ed., *Anatomy of a Confrontation: The Babri Masjid Ramjanmabhoomi Issue* (New Delhi: Viking, 1991); Romila Thapar, *Somanatha: The Many Voices of a History* (London: Verso, 2005); Cynthia Talbot, *The Last Hindu Emperor: Prithviraj Chauhan and the Indian Past, 1200–2000* (Cambridge: Cambridge University Press, 2016): and Shahid Amin, *Conquest and Community: The Afterlife of Warrior Saint Ghazi Miyan* (Chicago: University of Chicago Press, 2016).

18 Future scholars might well trace the precise conjunctures when scholarship generated from within the Indian Academy helped shape Indian studies elsewhere. Examples of collaborative work across themes and disciplines include, Veena Das, ed., *Mirrors of Violence: Communities, Riots, and Survivors in South Asia* (New Delhi: Oxford University Press,1990); Ania Loomba and Ritty A. Lukose, ed., *South Asian Feminisms* (Durham, NC: Duke University Press, 2012); Raka Ray and Amita Baviskar, *Elite and Everyman: The Cultural Politics of India's Middle Class* (New Delhi: Routledge India, 2015); Kumkum Sangari and Sudesh Vaid, ed., *Recasting Women: Essays in Indian Colonial History* (New Delhi: Kali for Women, 1989); and David Ludden, ed., *Making India Hindu: Religion, Community and the Politics of Democracy in India* (New Delhi: Oxford University Press, 1996).

19 Among the most prominent are the recent volumes by Ramchandra Guha, especially *India after Gandhi: The History of the World's Largest Democracy* (New York: HarperCollins, 2007); and *Makers of Modern India* (New Delhi: Penguin, 2010). Also see Madhav Khosla, *India's Founding Moment*; Oliver Godsmark, *Citizenship, Community, and Democracy in India: From Bombay to Maharashtra, c. 1930–1960* (London: Routledge, 2018); Gyan Prakash, *Emergency Chronicles: Indira Gandhi and Democracy's Turning Point* (New Delhi: Penguin 2018); Benjamin Robert Siegal, *Hungry Nation: Food, Famine, and the Making of Modern India* (Cambridge: Cambridge University Press, 2018); Rohit De, *A People's Constitution: The Everyday Life of Law in the Indian Republic* (Princeton, NJ: Princeton University Press, 2018); Ornit Shani, *How India Became Democratic: Citizenship and the Making of the Universal Franchise* (Cambridge: Cambridge University Press, 2017); Eleanor Newbigin, *The Hindu Family and the Emergence of Modern India: Law, Citizenship and Community* (Cambridge: Cambridge University Press, 2013); Gyanendra Pandey, *A History of Prejudice: Caste and Difference in India and the United States* (Cambridge: Cambridge University Press, 2013); Sumathi Ramaswamy, *Barefoot across the Nation: Maqbool Fida Hussein and the Idea of India* (London: Routledge, 2010); Anupama Rao, *The Caste Question: Dalits and the Politics of Modern India* (Berkeley, CA: University of California Press, 2009); Vasudha Dalmia, *Poetics, Plays, and Performances: The Politics of Modern Indian Theatre* (New Delhi: Oxford University Press, 2008); Charu Gupta and Mukul Sharma, *Contested Coastlines: Fisherfolk, Nations, and Borders in South Asia* (New Delhi: Routledge, 2008); Joya Chatterji, "Of Graveyards and Ghettos: Muslims in West Bengal, 1947–67," in Mushirul Hasan and Asim Roy, eds., *Living Together Separately: Cultural India in History and Politics* (New Delhi: Oxford University Press, 2005): 224–49; Ayesha Jalal, *Democracy and Authoritarianism in South Asia: A Comparative and Historical Perspective* (Cambridge: Cambridge University Press, 1995); and K. Lalitha, V. Kannabiran, and R. Melkote, "*We Were Making History*": *Women and the Telangana Uprising* (London: Zed Books, 1989). For a historically informed effort by a literary scholar see Leela Gandhi, *The Common Cause: Postcolonial Ethics and the Practice of Democracy, 1900–1950* (Chicago: University of Chicago Press, 2014).

20 The naturalized narrative of the transition from empire to nation-state has been questioned most pointedly by scholars of the French empire; see, for example, Frederick Cooper, *Citizenship between Empire and Nation: Remaking France and French Africa, 1945–1960* (Princeton, NJ: Princeton University Press, 2014); and Gary Wilder, *Freedom Time: Negritude, Decolonization and the Future of the World* (Durham, NC: Duke University Press, 2015). This narrative has always been an especially vexed one for scholars of the Ottoman empire, see Hasan Kayali, *Arabs*

and Young Turks: Ottomanism, Arabism, and Islamism in the Ottoman Empire, 1908–1918 (Berkeley, CA: University of California Press, 1997); and Michelle U. Campos, *Ottoman Brothers: Muslim, Christians, and Jews in Early Twentieth Century Palestine* (Redwood City, CA: Stanford University Press, 2010). For efforts at questioning this narrative from within the scholarship of the British empire, see Luise White, *Unpopular Sovereignty: Rhodesian Independence and African Decolonization* (Chicago: University of Chicago Press, 2015); and Daniel Gorman, *Imperial Citizenship: Empire and the Question of Belonging* (Manchester: Manchester University Press, 2006). And for examples within the scholarship on South Asia, see Sukanya Bannerjee, *Becoming Imperial Citizens: Indians in the Late Victorian Empire* (Durham, NC: Duke University Press, 2010); Mrinalini Sinha, "The Strange Death of an Imperial Ideal: The Case of *Civic Britannicus*," in Saurabh Dube, ed., *Modern Makeovers: Oxford Handbook of Modernity in South Asia* (New Delhi: Oxford University Press, 2011): 29–42; and "Premonitions of the Past," *Journal of Asian Studies* 74, no. 4 (2015): 821–41; Manu Goswami, "Imaginary Futures and Colonial Internationalisms," *The American Historical Review* 117, no. 5 (2012): 1461–85; Karuna Mantena, "Popular Sovereignty and Anti-Colonialism," in Richard Bourke and Quentin Skinner, eds., *Popular Sovereignty in Historical Perspective* (Cambridge: Cambridge University Press, 2016): 297–319; Kavita Saraswathi Datla, "Sovereignty and the End of Empire: The Transition to Independence in Colonial Hyderabad," *Ab Imperio* 3 (2018): 63–88; and Rama Sundari Mantena, "Anticolonialism and Federation in Colonial India," *Ab Imperio* 3 (2018): 36–62.

21 The literature on this is very vast. Manas Ray, "State of Democracy," *Seminar* 674 (2015). https://www.india-seminar.com/2015/674.htm. Accessed June 15, 2018; Niraja Jayal Gopal, *Citizenship and Its Discontents: An Indian History* (Cambridge, MA: Harvard University Press, 2013); and her *Democracy and the State: Welfare, Secularism and Development in Contemporary India* (New Delhi: Oxford University Press,1999); Ashutosh Varshney, *Battles Half-Won: India's Improbable Democracy* (New Delhi: Penguin, 2013); Perry Anderson, *The Indian Ideology* (London: Verso 2012); Gopal Guru, "Liberal Democracy in India and the Dalit Critique," *Social Research* 78, no. 1 (2011): 99–122; Rochana Bajpai, *Debating Difference: Group Rights and Liberal Democracy in India* (New Delhi: Oxford University Press, 2011); Christine Keating, *Decolonizing Democracy: Transformation of the Social Contract in India* (University Park, PA: Pennsylvania State University Press, 2011); Rajeev Bhargava, *The Promise of India's Secular Democracy* (New Delhi: Oxford University Press, 2010); Meghnad Desai, *The Rediscovery of India* (Delhi: Penguin, 2009); Lucia Michelutti, *The Vernacularization of Democracy: Politics, Caste and Religion in India* (New Delhi: Routledge, 2008); Guha, *India after Gandhi*; Amrita Basu and Srirupa Roy, *Violence and Democracy in India* (Kolkata: Seagull Books, 2006); Amartya Sen, *The Argumentative Indian: Writings on Indian History and Culture* (London: Allen Lane, 2005); Rajni Kothari, *Rethinking Democracy* (New Delhi: Orient Longman, 2005); Rajeshwari Sunder Rajan, *The Scandal of the State: Women, Law, and Citizenship in Postcolonial India* (Durham, NC: Duke University Press, 2003); Amrita Basu, Niraja Gopal Jayal, Martha Nussbaum, and Yasmin Tambiah, *Essays on Gender and Governance* (New Delhi: UNDP, 2003); Pratap Bhanu Mehta, *The Burden of Democracy* (New Delhi: Penguin 2003); Rajeev Bhargava, Amiya Kumar Bagchi, and R. Sudarshan, eds., *Multiculturalism, Liberalism, and Democracy* (Delhi: Oxford University Press, 1999); Sunil Khilnani, *The Idea of India* (New Delhi: Penguin,

1997); Atul Kohli, *Democracy and Discontent: India's Growing Crisis of Governability* (Cambridge: Cambridge University Press,1990).

22 Pierre Bourdieu, *Distinction: A Social Critique of the Judgement of Taste*. Translated by Richard Nice (Cambridge, MA: Harvard University Press, 1984 [1979]), p. xi; and *The Logic Of Practice*. Translated by Richard Nice (Stanford, CA: Stanford University Press, 1990 [1980]), p. 63.

23 Mukul Kesavan, "Arguing about India: Assam and Citizenship," *The Telegraph*, February 25, 2018. https://www.telegraphindia.com/opinion/arguing-about-india/cid/1463910. Accessed November 3, 2019. Also see Yogendra Yadav, *Making Sense of Indian Democracy* (Ranikhet, India: Permanent Black, 2020).

24 For debates about periodizing the twentieth century, see Charles Maier, "Consigning the Twentieth Century to History: Alternative Narratives for the Modern Era," *The American Historical Review* 105, no. 3 (2000): 807–31; Manu Goswami, Gabrielle Hecht, Adeeb Khalid, Anna Krylova, Elizabeth F. Thompson, Jonathan R. Zatlin, Andrew Zimmerman, "*AHR* Conversation: History after the End of History: Reconceptualizing the Twentieth Century," *The American Historical Review* 121, no. 5 (2016): 1567–607. Also see Aijaz Ahmad's multipart essay, especially "A Century of Revolutions: Whose Century? Whose Millennium? A Reflection On Our Times," I, *Frontline* 17, no. 2 (2000); and "India in the 20th Century: A Reflection on Our Times," VI, *Frontline* 18, no. 5 (2001). The complete set of essays can be found in *A Reflection on our Times: Revolution, Restoration and Resistance* (New Delhi: Prajasakti Bookhouse, 2004).

25 On the theoretical stakes of historical periodization, from different vantages, see Francois Hartog, *Regimes of Historicity: Presentism and Experiences of Time*. Translated by Saskia Brown (New York: Columbia University Press, 2015 [2003]); Katherine Davis, *Periodization and Sovereignty: How Ideas of Feudalism and Secularism Govern the Politics of Time* (Philadelphia, PA: University of Pennsylvania Press, 2008); Reinhart Koselleck, *The Practice of Conceptual History: Timing History, Spacing Concepts*. Translated by Todd Presner (Palo Alto, CA: Stanford University Press, 2002); and *Futures Past: On the Semantics of Historical Time*. Translated by Keith Tribe (Cambridge, MA: MIT Press, 1985); Jacques Rancière, *The Names of History: On the Poetics of Knowledge*. Translated by Hassan Melehy (Minneapolis, MN: University of Minnesota Press,1994); and "The Concept of Anachronism and the Historian's Truth," *Inprint* 3, no. 1 (2015): 21–48. For influential critical engagements from within modern South Asian history, see Dipesh Chakrabarty, *Provincializing Europe;* and Ranajit Guha, *History at the Limit of World-History* (New York: Columbia University Press, 2002). The problem of periodization has re-animated debates among scholars of the early modern and ancient era. See, for instance, Uma Chakravarti, "Whatever Happened to the Vedic Dasi?: Orientalism, Nationalism, and a Script for the Past," in Kumkum Sangari and Sudesh Vaid, eds., *Recasting Women*, pp. 27–87; Velecheru Narayana Rao, David Shulman, Sanjay Subrahmanyam, *Textures of Time: Writing History in South India, 1600–1800* (New Delhi: Permanent Black, 2001); Sheldon Pollock, "Pretextures of Time," *History and Theory* 46, no. 3 (2007): 366–83; and Rama Mantena, *The Origins of Modern Historiography in India: Antiquarianism and Philology, 1780–1880* (New York: Palgrave Macmillan, 2012).

26 Cornelius Castoriadis, *The Imaginary Institution of Society* (Cambridge, MA: MIT Press, 1998 [1975]); "The Greek and the Modern Political Imaginary," *Salmagundi*

100, no. 1 (1993): 102–29; *World in Fragments: Writings on Politics, Society, Psychoanalysis, and the Imagination* (Stanford, CA: Stanford University Press, 1997).

27 Henri Lefebvre, *State, Space, World: Selected Essays*. Edited by Neil Brenner and Stuart Elden. Translated by George Moore (Minneapolis, MN: University of Minnesota Press, 2009); *Metaphilosophy*. Edited by Stuart Elden. Translated by David Fernbach (London: Verso, 2016).

28 Jacques Lacan, *The Four Fundamental Concepts of Psycho-Analysis*. Translated by Alan Sheridan (London: Karnac,1977).

29 Charles Taylor acknowledges his debt, in turn, to Benedict Anderson's singular usage in his influential recasting of nationalism. Charles Taylor, "Modern Social Imaginaries," *Public Culture* 14, no. 1 (2002): 91–124; *Modern Social Imaginaries* (Durham, NC: Duke University Press, 2004).

30 Arjun Appadurai, *Modernity at Large: Cultural Dimensions of Globalization* (Minneapolis, MN: University of Minnesota Press, 1996); C. A. Bayly, *The Birth of the Modern World, 1780–1914: Global Connections and Comparisons* (Malden, MA: Wiley, 2004); Sudipta Kaviraj and Sunil Khilnani, *Civil Society: History and Possibilities* (Cambridge: Cambridge University Press, 2001); Jürgen Osterhammel and Niels P. Petersson, *Globalization: A Short History*. Translated by Dona Geyer (Princeton, NJ: Princeton University Press, 2005); Manuel Castells, *The Rise of the Network Society* (Malden, MA: Wiley, 2000), Jürgen Habermas, *The Postnational Constellation: Political Essays*. Translated and edited by Max Pensky (Cambridge, MA: MIT Press, 2001); and Michael Hardt and Antonio Negri, *Empire* (Cambridge, MA: Harvard University Press, 2001).

31 Susan Buck Morss, *Dreamworld and Catastrophe: The Passing of Mass Utopia in the East and West* (Cambridge, MA: MIT Press, 2000), p. 11.

32 Cornelius Castoriadis, "The Greek and the Modern Political Imaginary," p. 102.

33 William H. Sewell, *Logics of History: Social Theory and Social Transformation* (Chicago: University of Chicago Press, 2005).

34 For discussions of some of the theoretical foundations for this distinction, see James Wiley, *Politics and the Concept of the Political: The Political Imagination* (London: Routledge, 2016); and Oliver Marchart, *Post-Foundational Political Thought: Political Difference in Nancy, Lefort, Badiou and Laclau* (Edinburgh, UK: Edinburgh University Press, 2007).

35 Carl Schmitt, *The Concept of the Political*, expanded ed. Translated by G. Schwab (Chicago: University of Chicago Press, 2007 [1932]); and Claud Lefort, *The Political Forms of Modern Society: Bureaucracy, Democracy, Totalitarianism* (Cambridge: Polity Press, 1986).

36 See Hannah Arendt, *The Origins of Totalitarianism* (New York: Harcourt Brace and World, 1973); and Richard Shorten, "Conceptions of 'the Political': A Note on Contrasting Motifs In Hannah Arendt's Treatment of Totalitarianism," Hannah Arendt, *Journal for Political Thinking* (2006). http://www.hannaharendt.net/index.php/han/article/view/92/150. Accessed December 22, 2018. Also see Hanna Fenichel Pitkin, *The Attack of the Blob: Hannah Arendt's Concept of the Social* (Chicago: University of Chicago Press, 1998); Seyla Benhabib, *The Reluctant Modernism of Hannah Arendt*, new ed. (Lanham, MD: Rowman & Littlefield Publishers, 2003);Patchen Markell, "The Rule of the People: Arendt, Arche, and Democracy," *American Political Science Review* 100, no. 1 (2006): 1–14. For a brilliant reading of politics/political from within the scholarship on India, see Banerjee, *Elementary Aspects of the Political.*

37 For some attempts to historicize the domain of "politics" and the "political" from within South Asian scholarship, see Jan-Peter Harlung, "Appropriations and Contestations of the Islamic Nomenclature in Muslim North India: Elitism, Lexicography and the Meaning of the Political," *Contributions to the History of Concepts* 12 (2017): 76–110; Sudipta Kaviraj, "On the Historicity of 'the Political': *Rajniti* and Politics in Modern Indian Thought," in Michael Freeden and Andrew Vincent, eds., *Comparative Political Thought: Theorizing Practices* (London: Routledge, 2013): 24–39; Partha Chatterjee, "The Movement against Politics," *Cultural Critique* 81 (2012): 117–22; Prathama Banerjee, "Chanakya/Kautilya: History, Philosophy, Theatre and the 20th Century Political," *History of the Present* 2, no. 1 (2012): 24–51; "Between the Political and the Non-Political: The Vivekanand Moment and the Critique of the Political in Colonial Bengal, 1890–1910s," *Social History* 39, no. 3 (2014): 323–39; "The Subaltern: Political Subject or Protagonist of History," *South Asia: Journal of South Asian Studies* 38, no. 1 (2015): 39–49; and *Elementary Aspects of the Political*; Uday S. Mehta, "The Social Question and the Absolutism of Politics," *Seminar* 615 (2010): 23–7; V. N. Rao and Sanjay Subrahmanyam, "Notes on Political Thought in Medieval and Early Modern South India," *Modern Asian Studies* 43, no. 1 (2009): 175–210; and "An Elegy for *Niti*: Politics as a Secular Discursive Field in the India Old Regime," *Common Knowledge* 14, no. 3 (2008): 396–423; Anthony J. Parel, "Gandhi and the Emergence of the Modern Indian Political Canon," *The Review of Politics* 70, no. 1 (2008): 40–63; and Dipesh Chakrabarty, "'In the Name of Politics': Sovereignty, Democracy, and the Multitude in India," *Economic and Political Weekly* 40, no. 30 (2005): 3293–301.

38 Samuel Huntington, *The Clash of Civilizations and the Remaking of World Order* (New York: Simon and Schuster, 1996).

39 James Ferguson, *Global Shadow: Africa in the Neoliberal Order* (Durham, NC: Duke University Press, 2006); Jane Guyer, "Prophecy and the Near Future: Thoughts on Macroeconomic, Evangelical, and Punctuated time," *American Ethnologist* 34 (2007): 409–21; Jean Comaroff and John L. Comaroff, *Theory from the South or, How Euro-America Is Evolving toward Africa* (Boulder, CO: Paradigm Publishers, 2012); Brian Goldstone and Juan Obarrio, eds., *African Futures: Essays on Crisis, Emergence, and Possibility* (Chicago: University of Chicago Press, 2017).

40 Mikhail M. Bakhtin, *The Dialogic Imagination: Four Essays*. Translated by Caryl Emerson and Michael Holquist (Austin, TX: University of Texas Press, 1981 [1937]).

41 See Bayly, *The Birth of the Modern World, 1780–1914*; Sheila Fitzpatrick, *The Russian Revolution* (Oxford: Oxford University Press, 2017); Mark Mazower, *Governing the World: The History of an Idea, 1815 to the Present* (New York: Penguin, 2013); Samuel Moyn, *The Last Utopia: Human Rights in History* (Cambridge, MA: Harvard University Press, 2012); and Susan Pedersen, *The Guardians: The League of Nations and the Crisis of Empire* (Oxford: Oxford University Press, 2015).

42 Giovanni Arrighi, *The Long Twentieth Century: Money, Power, and the Origins of Our Times* (London: Verso, 1994).

43 Eric Hobsbawm, *The Age of Extremes: The Short Twentieth Century, 1914–1991* (London: Michael Joseph, 1994).

44 Alain Badiou, *The Century*. Translated by Alberto Toscano (Cambridge, MA: Polity, 2007).

45 Ibid., 98.

46 For some examples, see Francois Furet, *The Passing of an Illusion: The Idea of Communism in the Twentieth Century* (Chicago: University of Chicago Press, 1999);

and John V. Fleming, *The Anti-Communist Manifestos: Four Books That Shaped the Cold War* (New York: W. W. Norton and Company, 2009).

47 By contrast, see Prashad, *The Darker Nations*; Ahmad, *A Reflection on Our Times*; and Adom Getachew, *Worldmaking after Empire: The Rise and Fall of Self-Determination* (Princeton, NJ: Princeton University Press, 2019).

48 Chakrabarty, *Provincializing Europe*.

49 Greg Grandin and Gil Joseph, eds., *A Century of Revolution: Insurgent and Counterinsurgent Violence during Latin America's Long Cold War* (Durham, NC: Duke University Press, 2010); Barbara Weinstein, *The Color of Modernity: Sao Paulo and the Making of Race and Nation in Brazil* (Durham, NC: Duke University Press, 2015). The influence of revisionist histories of the Haitian Revolution in contemporary histories of politics is hard to overstate. See C. L. R. James, *Black Jacobins: Toussaint L'Ouverture and the San Domingo Revolution* (New York: Vintage Books, 1989 [1938]); Michel-Rolph Trouillot, *Silencing the Past: Power and the Production of History* (Boston: Beacon Press, 1995); Laurent Dubois, *Avengers of the New World: The Story of the Haitian Revolution* (Cambridge, MA: Harvard University Press, 2004); and *A Colony of Citizens: Revolution and Slave Emancipation in the French Caribbean, 1787–1804* (Chapel Hill, NC: University of North Carolina Press, 2004); Ada Ferrer, "Haiti, Free Soil, and Anti-Slavery in the Revolutionary Atlantic," *The American Historical Review* 117 (2012): 40–60; and *Freedom's Mirror: Cuba and Haiti in the Age of Revolution* (Cambridge: Cambridge University Press, 2014). Also see Ernesto Laclau, *On Populist Reason* (London: Verso, 2005); Susan Buck-Morss, *Hegel, Haiti, and Universal History* (Pittsburgh, PA: University of Pittsburgh Press, 2009); and Adom Getachew, "Universalism after the Post-Colonial Turn: Interpreting the Haitian Revolution," *Political Theory* 44, no. 6 (2016): 821–45.

50 Timothy Mitchell, *Carbon Democracy: Political Power in the Age of Oil* (London: Verso, 2011). Also see Brian Larkin, "The Politics and Poetics of Infrastructure," *Annual Review of Anthropology* 42, no. 1 (2013): 327–43.

51 Anna Krylova, "Bolshevik Feminism and Gender Agendas of Communism," in Silvio Pons and Stephen Smith, eds., *World Revolution and Socialism in One Country* (Cambridge, UK: Cambridge University Press, 2017); Kristen Ghodsee, *Red Hangover: Legacies of 20th Century Communism* (Durham, NC: Duke University Press, 2017); and *The Left Side of History: WW II and the Unfulfilled Promise of Communism in Eastern Europe* (Durham, NC: Duke University Press, 2015).

52 Katherine Verdery, *The Political Lives of Dead Bodies: Reburial and Postsocialist Change* (New York: Columbia University Press, 1999). For an animated effort to compare the predicaments of post-socialism and post-colonialism, see Sharad Chari and Katherine Verdery, "Thinking between the Posts: Postcolonialism, Postsocialism, and Ethnography after the Cold War," *Comparative Studies in Society and History* 51, no. 1 (2009): 6–34.

53 Charles Maier, "Consigning the Twentieth Century to History."

54 Wang Hui, *China's Twentieth Century: Revolution, Retreat and the Road to Equality* (London: Verso, 2016); Prasenjit Duara and Elizabeth J. Perry, eds., *Beyond Regime: China and India Compared* (Harvard, MA: Harvard University Press, 2018).

55 Benjamin Elman and Sheldon Pollock, eds., *What China and India Once Were: The Pasts That May Shape the Global Future* (New York: Columbia University Press, 2018).

56 Trouillot, *Silencing the Past*, p. 5.

57 Aijaz Ahmad, "Postcolonial Theory and the 'Post'-Condition," *The Socialist Register* 33 (1997): 353–81. For further elaborations of the term, see Ranjit Kaur Kapoor and

Manjit Inder Singh, eds., *The Post-Condition: Theory, Texts, and Contexts* (Patiala, Punjab: Punjabi University Press, 2000); and Makarand R. Paranjape, *Debating the "Post" Condition in India: Critical Vernaculars, Unauthorized Modernities, Post-Colonial Contentions* (New Delhi: Routledge India, 2017).

58 See Sumit Sarkar, "Indian Democracy: The Historical Inheritance," in Atul Kohli, ed., *The Success of India's Democracy* (Cambridge: Cambridge University Press, 2001), pp. 23–46; Yogendra Yadav, "Understanding the Second Democratic Upsurge," in Francine Frankel et al., ed., *Transforming India: Social and Political Dynamics of Democracy* (New Delhi: Oxford University Press, 2000); Christophe Jaffrelot, *India's Silent Revolution: The Rise of the Lower Castes in North India* (New York: Columbia University Press, 2003); and Partha Chatterjee, *Lineages of Political Society: Studies in Democracy* (New York: Columbia University Press, 2011).

59 An influential example from Political Science is Adam Przeworski, Michael E. Alvarez, Jose Antonio Cheibub and Fernando Limongi, *Democracy and Development: Political Institutions and Well-Being in the World, 1950–1990* (Cambridge: Cambridge University Press, 2000). The authors rely upon "minimalist" and formalistic definition of democracy as "a regime in which those who govern are selected through contested elections," p. 15. Juan J. Linz and Alfred Stepan, *Problems of Democratic Transition and Consolidation: Southern Europe, South America, and Post-Communist Europe* (Baltimore, MD: Johns Hopkins University Press, 1996); and Guillermo O'Donnell and Philippe C. Schmitter, *Transitions from Authoritarian Rule: Tentative Conclusions about Uncertain Democracies* (Baltimore, MD: Johns Hopkins University Press, 1986).

60 Jean Cohen and Andrew Arato, *Civil Society and Political Theory* (Cambridge, MA: MIT Press, 1992); John Keane, *Civil Society: Old Images, New Visions* (Stanford, CA: Stanford University Press, 1998). For dissident approaches see John Comaroff and Jean Comaroff, eds., *Civil Society and the Political Imagination in Africa: Critical Perspectives* (Chicago: University of Chicago Press, 1999); Nancy Fraser, "Rethinking the Public Sphere: A Contribution to the Critique of Actually Existing Democracy," *Social Text* 25/26 (1990): 56–80; Charles Taylor, "Modes of Civil Society," *Public Culture* 3, no. 1 (1990): 119–32; and Partha Chatterjee, "A Response to Taylor's Modes of Civil Society," *Public Culture* 14, no. 1 (2002): 21–47.

61 Jean and John Comaroff, *Millennial capitalism and the culture of neoliberalism* (Durham, NC: Duke University Press, 2001); Michael Hardt and A. Negri, *Multitude: War and Democracy in the Age of Empire* (New York: Penguin, 2004); David Harvey, *A Brief History of Neoliberalism* (Oxford: Oxford University Press, 2005); William Robinson, *Promoting Polyarchy: Globalization, US Intervention, and Hegemony* (Cambridge: Cambridge University Press,1996). The now commonplace coinage "embedded liberalism" derives from John Gerard Ruggie, "International Regimes, Transactions, and Change: Embedded Liberalism in the Postwar Economic Order," *International Regimes* 36, no. 2 (1982): 379–415.

62 Samuel Huntington, *The Third Wave: Democratization in the Late Twentieth Century* (Norman, OK: University of Oklahoma Press, 1991).

63 Francis Fukuyama, *The End of History and the Last Man* (New York: Free Press, 1992); and with some modifications of the "end of history" thesis, *Our Posthuman Future: Consequences of the Biotechnology Revolution* (New York: Farrar, Strauss & Giroux, 2002).

64 Francis Fukuyama, "The Future of History: Can Liberal Democracy Survive the Decline of the Middle Class?" *Foreign Affairs* 91, no. 1 (2012): 53–61; and Yascha

Mounk, *The People vs Democracy: Why Our Freedom Is in Danger and How to Save It* (Cambridge, MA: Harvard University Press, 2018).

65 Arend Lijphart, "The Puzzle of Indian Democracy? A Consociational Interpretation," *American Political Science Review* 90, no. 2 (1996): 258–68. For a discussion of this literature, see Ashutosh Varshney, "Why Democracy Survives?" *Journal of Democracy* 9, no. 3 (1998): 36–50; and *Battles Half-Won*.

66 Partha Chatterjee, *The Politics of the Governed: Reflections on Popular Politics in Most of the World* (New York: Columbia University Press, 2004).

67 Quoted in R. Guha, *Patriots and Partisans* (New Delhi: Allen Lane, 2012). For the Constitution, see Granville Austin, *The Indian Constitution: The Cornerstone of a Nation* (Oxford: Clarendon Press, 1966); and *Working a Democratic Constitution: The Indian Experience* (New Delhi: Oxford University Press, 2003); Madhava Khosla, *The Indian Constitution* (New Delhi: Oxford University Press, 2012); and Sujit Choudhury et al., eds., *The Oxford Handbook of the Indian Constitution* (New Delhi: Oxford University Press, 2016).

68 Guha, *India after Gandhi*, p.749. For his subsequent re-evaluation of the score, see "India's Descent from a 50–50 to a 30–70 Democracy," *The Hindustan Times*, March 21, 2020, https://www.hindustantimes.com/columns/india-s-descent-from-a-50-50-to-a-30-70-democracy/story-CBlmSCCeaxXpO8rPL7nycI.html. Accessed December 18, 2020. The contested nature of the relationship of several of the North-Eastern States and of the Kashmir Valley with "India," however constituted, would be a case in point.

69 C. A. Bayly, *Recovering Liberties: Indian Thought in the Age of Liberalism and Empire* (Cambridge: Cambridge University Press, 2012), p. 344.

70 The etymology of demo+cracy takes us to the Greek *kratia*, which means power or rule; but it also carries a secondary meaning that refers to "healing," see Manas Ray, "Who is the People?" *Seminar* 674 (2015): 68–76. Jean-Luc Nancy develops the etymology of the word differently to argue that since demo+cracy derives from the root "cracy," and not "archy" (as in "monarchy" or "oligarchy"), it has no grounding principle and, as such, refers to no concrete configuration of government: the rule of the people, then, is not so much any specific form of government as it is a general disposition toward being in common. See "On the Meanings of Democracy," *Theoria* 111 (2006): 1–5; and *The Truth of Democracy*. Translated by Pascale-Anne Brault and Michael Naas (New York: Fordham Press, 2010).

71 Jurgen Habermas, *Legitimation Crisis*. Translated by Thomas McCarthy (Boston: Beacon Press, 1975).

72 See, Pankaj Mishra, *The Age of Anger: A History of the Present* (New York: Farrar, Strauss & Giroux, 2017); and Jan-Werner Müller, *What Is Populism* (Philadelphia: University of Pennsylvania, 2016).

73 Branko Milanovic, *Global Inequality: A New Approach for the Age of Globalization* (Cambridge, MA: Belknap Press of Harvard University Press, 2016); Lucas Chancel and Thomas Piketty, "Indian Income Inequality, 1922–2014: From British Raj to Billionaire Raj?" October 2017, CEPR Discussion Paper No. DP12409; SSRN. https://ssrn.com/abstract=3066021

74 Abhay Kumar Dubey, *Hindu-Ekta Banam Gyan Ki Rajniti* [*Hindu Unity vis-à-vis Politics of Knowledge*] (New Delhi: Vani Prakashan, 2019); Nikhil Anand, *Hydraulic City: Water and the Infrastructures of Citizenship in Mumbai* (Durham, NC: Duke, 2017); Amita Baviskar, *In the Belly of the River: Tribal Conflicts over Development in the Narmada Valley* (New Delhi: Oxford University Press, 2004); Laura Bear,

Navigating Austerity: Currents of Debt along a South Asian River (Stanford, CA: Stanford University Press, 2015); Jan Breman, *Footloose Labour: Working in India's Informal Economy* (Cambridge: Cambridge University Press, 1996); Akhil Gupta, *Red Tape: Bureaucracy, Structural Violence, and Poverty in India* (Durham, NC: Duke University Press, 2012); Aloysius Irudayam, Jayshree P. Mangubhai, and Joel G. Lee, *Dalit Women Speak Out: Caste, Class and Gender Violence in India* (New Delhi: Zubaan Books, 2011); Craig Jeffrey, *Timepass: Youth, Class, and the Politics of Waiting in India* (Stanford, CA: Stanford University Press, 2010); Craig Jeffrey, Patricia Jeffrey, Robin Jeffrey, *Degrees without Freedom?: Education, Masculinities, and Unemployment in North India* (Stanford, CA: Stanford University Press, 2007); Nandini Sundar, *Burning Forest: India's War in Bastar* (New Delhi: Juggernaut Books, 2016); Kaushik Sundar Rajan, *Pharmocracy: Value, Politics, and Knowledge in Global Biomedicine* (Durham, NC: Duke University Press, 2017); and *Biocapital: The Constitution of Postgenomic Life* (Durham, NC: Duke University Press, 2006); Sukhadeo Thorat, Harsh Mander, Ghanshyam Shah, Amita Baviskar, and Satish Deshpande, *Untouchability in Rural India* (New Delhi: Sage Publications, 2006); and Amartya Sen and Jean Drèze, *An Uncertain Glory: India and Its Contradictions* (London: Penguin, 2013).

75 Arjun Appadurai, "Deep Democracy: Urban Governmentality and the Horizon of Politics," *Public Culture* 14, no. 1 (2002): 21–47; Dipesh Chakrabarty, "'In the Name of Politics.'"

76 Wendy Brown, *Undoing the Demos: Neoliberalism's Stealth Revolution* (New York: Zone Books, 2015). Also see Adam Tooze, *Crashed: How a Decade of Financial Crises Changed the World* (New York: Penguin Books, 2018).

77 For recent sharp evaluations of the state of democracy see Nadia Urbinati, *Democracy Disfigured* (Cambridge, MA: Harvard University Press, 2014); Giorgio Agamben et al., *Democracy in What State?* (New York: Columbia University Press, 2012); and Jacques Ranciere, *Hatred of Democracy* (London: Verso, 2006).

Select Bibliography

Appadurai, A. "Deep Democracy: Urban Governmentality and the Horizon of Politics," *Public Culture* 14, no. 1 (2002): 21–47.

Arrighi, G. *The Long Twentieth Century: Money, Power, and the Origins of Our Times* (London: Verso, 1994).

Badiou, A. *The Century*. Translated by Alberto Toscano (Cambridge, MA: Polity, 2007).

Banerjee, P. *Elementary Aspects of the Political: Histories from the Global South* (Durham, NC: Duke University Press, 2020).

Bayly, C. A. *Recovering Liberties: Indian Thought in the Age of Liberalism and Empire* (Cambridge: Cambridge University Press, 2012).

Buck-Morss, S. *Dreamworld and Catastrophe: The Passing of Mass Utopia in the East and West* (Cambridge, MA: MIT Press, 2000).

Castoriadis, C. *The Imaginary Institution of Society* (Cambridge, MA: MIT Press, 1998 [1975]).

Chakrabarty, D. "'In the Name of Politics': Sovereignty, Democracy, and the Multitude in India," *Economic and Political Weekly* 40, no. 30 (2005): 3293–301.

Chatterjee, P. *The Politics of the Governed: Reflections on Popular Politics in Most of the World* (New York: Columbia University Press, 2004).

Duara, Prasenjit and J. Perry Elizabeth, eds. *Beyond Regime: China and India Compared* (Harvard, MA: Harvard University Press, 2018).

Elman, B. and Sheldon Pollock, eds. *What China and India Once Were: The Pasts That May Shape the Global Future* (New York: Columbia University Press, 2018).

Guha, R. *India after Gandhi: The History of the World's Largest Democracy* (New York: HarperCollins, 2007).

Hobsbawm, E. *The Age of Extremes: The Short Twentieth Century, 1914–1991* (London: Michael Joseph, 1994).

Jaffrelot, C. *India's Silent Revolution: The Rise of the Lower Castes in North India* (New York: Columbia University Press, 2003).

Kapila, S. "Global Intellectual History and the Indian Political," in Darrin M. McMahon and Samuel Moyn, eds., *Rethinking Modern European Intellectual History* (New York: Oxford University Press, 2014), pp. 253–74.

Kaviraj, S. "On the Historicity of 'the Political': *Rajniti* and Politics in Modern Indian Thought," in Michael Freeden and Andrew Vincent, eds., *Comparative Political Thought: Theorizing Practices* (London: Routledge, 2013), pp. 24–39.

Khosla, M. *India's Founding Moment: The Constitution of a Most Surprising Democracy* (Cambridge: Harvard University Press, 2020).

Maier, C. "Consigning the Twentieth Century to History: Alternative Narratives for the Modern Era, " *The American Historical Review* 105, no. 3 (2000): 807–31.

Mehta, U. S. "The Social Question and the Absolutism of Politics," *Seminar* 615 (2010): 23–7.

Mitchell, T. *Carbon Democracy: Political Power in the Age of Oil* (London: Verso, 2011).

Mouffe, C. *The Return of the Political* (London: Verso Book, 2005).

Pedersen, Susan, "What Is Political History Now?" in David Cannadine, ed., *What Is History Now?* (New York: Palgrave Macmillan, 2002).

Ranciere, Jacques, *Hatred of Democracy* (London: Verso, 2006).

Ray, M. "Who Is the People?" *Seminar* 674 (2015): 68–76.

Rosanvallon, P. *Democracy: Past and Future*. Ed. Samuel Moyn (New York: Columbia University Press, 2006).

Sarkar, S. "Indian Democracy: The Historical Inheritance," in Atul Kohli, ed., *The Success of India's Democracy* (Cambridge: Cambridge University Press, 2001), pp. 23–46.

Sen, Amartya and Jean Drèze, *An Uncertain Glory: India and Its Contradictions* (London: Penguin, 2013).

Taylor, C. *Modern Social Imaginaries* (Durham, NC: Duke University Press, 2004).

Part One

Genealogies of the Political

2

Anatomy of a Politics of the People

Mrinalini Sinha

On March 12, 1917, the Government of India, with the approval of the Secretary of State for India in London, announced the termination of recruitment for indentured labor in India for plantations in colonies overseas. The announcement was made on the grounds that labor recruitment would purportedly interfere with recruitment for the army that was an imperial priority during the war. This temporary wartime stoppage, subsequently regularized with the passage of the Indian Emigration Act of 1922, was an anticlimactic ending for a vigorous and multi-layered popular movement in India for the abolition of the century-old-indentured labor system.[1] Between 1834, in the aftermath of the abolition of Atlantic slavery, and March 1917, some 1.3 million workers—a small fraction of the total number of workers exported from India under a variety of coercive conditions—had been transported under government-sanctioned indenture contracts, with draconian penal provisions, to substitute for emancipated Africans as cheap labor on plantations across the British empire and beyond.[2] The "second abolition," so named in the wake of the prior abolition of Atlantic slavery, has not been the subject of anything like the voluminous historiography that characterizes the abolition of Atlantic slavery.[3] This is especially surprising because the second abolition, unlike its more famous predecessor, was the first empire-wide change in the British Empire that was prompted by a shift in public opinion not in metropolitan Britain but in colonial India.[4] The popular public protest that brought down the indentured labor system, despite its prosaic official termination, is long overdue for a reappraisal and a place in the annals of the democratization of anticolonial national politics in twentieth-century India.

The historiography of the anti-indenture movement has tended to obscure how the demand for abolition helped produce a new political subject, the people or the *demos*, in late colonial India. Too often, for example, scholars identify the entire anti-indenture movement only with what the colonial bureaucracy insisted was the "sentimental" objections of a small elite nationalist leadership in India. The indenture system, in this elite Indian discourse, was an affront to the nation's "honor:" it was held responsible for the fact that *all* Indians—and not just the class of Indians from which the indentured workers came—were stigmatized abroad in the plantation colonies as "*coolies*"

My thanks to Clement Hawes and William Glover for comments on an earlier draft.

[derogatory term for indentured workers] and thus subject to racist discrimination.[5] Even when the more popular dimension of the movement is acknowledged, it is too often folded into the narrative of an exclusively Gandhian politics in which it appears merely as an extension of the South African phase of his movement, most notably of his last mass civil disobedience or *satyagraha* [nonviolent resistance] in South Africa in 1913. Scholars have thus largely followed M. K. Gandhi, who in his book *Satyagraha in South Africa*, alludes only briefly to the broader anti-indenture movement in India and, then, only as a potential opportunity for transplanting onto Indian soil his novel weapon of satyagraha.[6] While these characterizations accurately describe certain aspects of the movement, they do not capture the novel mobilization of the people as the political subjects of the movement.

The subjects whose voices were mobilized during the movement have thus been denied their status as *political* subjects—that is, as subjects produced out of the working of the politics of abolition rather than as subjects belonging to already "given" or pre-existing identity categories and social groups in India. It is, indeed, the nature of the *political* subjects so constituted that gives Indian abolitionism an important place in the genealogy of twentieth-century democratic politics in India. The democratizing significance of Indian abolitionism does not lie in the involvement of this or that hitherto marginalized group—peasants, ex-indentured workers, middle-class women, dalits [formerly called "untouchables"]—in the campaign against indenture. Rather, and more crucially, it lies in the constitution of a "people," or a *demos*, as the collective political subject of anticolonial national politics in India.

Central to abolition's novel articulation of a *demos* was the ways in which anti-indenture activists *generalized* the cause of the indentured workers as the cause of the whole of society: enabling, in effect, a *sarvasadharan junta* [ordinary public][7] to represent or stand in for the nation as a whole.[8] The circulation of the experience of the indentured worker Kunti, which became a *cause célèbre* of the anti-indenture movement, offers a glimpse into what was entailed in generalizing the anti-indenture cause.[9] On August 1, 1913, the abolitionist newspaper, the *Bharat Mitra*, a leading Hindi-language daily published in Calcutta, carried a letter purportedly written by an obscure woman called Kunti.[10] She was identified in the press as a married woman belonging to the "untouchable" Chamar caste from Gorakhpur in the erstwhile United Provinces of eastern India, the chief labor-exporting region under the indentured labor system. In her letter, Kunti recounts in harrowing detail her escape from a sexual assault by a white overseer on a plantation in Fiji where she was indentured.

The account of Kunti's resilience or, if you will, of her good fortune, was subject to multiple appropriations in India within several different narratives. It was duly picked up by most of the major pro-abolition English-language and vernacular newspapers of the time. Stock versions of the threat that female indentured workers faced from sexual assault on the plantations, with its often problematic reliance on notions of female sexual purity, entered the broader popular culture of abolitionism, which included vernacular poems, newspaper reports, tracts, plays, folk songs, and public performances, including the migration-inspired folk genre of eastern India called the "bidesiya," literally meaning the foreigner, in the years leading up to abolition.[11] Even though the outsized focus of abolitionist propaganda on sexual assaults on women workers reflected a paternalist and sexist logic, a focus on Kunti as a historical figure offers the possibility of a different understanding of the apotheosis of her story within abolitionist propaganda.

The process of the publication of Kunti's letter in the *Bharat Mitra* reveals the existence of an extensive network of obscure and ordinary men and women in the colonies and in India who toiled behind the scenes to change the elitist Indian opposition to indenture: from an initial concern about the affront to the nation's honor in the misrecognition of all Indians in the colonies as "coolies" to the subsequent identification of the plight of indentured workers themselves as the *real* affront to the honor of the nation or the community as a whole. Once only a fringe demand, abolition had emerged as a shared demand of all the major political parties and established factions in India, from the Indian National Congress to the Muslim League, the Home Rulers to the Non-Brahmin movement, the Moderates to the Extremists, and the long-established political classes to the emerging class of big industrialists and capitalists. But it was largely an army of obscure men and women—those who had had no prior part in national political deliberations—who helped transform abolitionism in India.

The official investigations that followed the publication of Kunti's letter reveal the backstory that went into its circulation in India. The Government of India, nervous about the potential of a public relations disaster around Kunti's allegations, issued a secret directive to the Government of Fiji to investigate the case so as to establish, as R. E. Enthoven, Secretary of the Government of India, wrote, the "falsity" of the case before it had a chance to cause more damage in India.[12] The Fiji government's investigations, in an effort to discredit the story, succeeded in getting recantations from all those named by Kunti as agents in her escape, but it failed to deter Kunti from the facts narrated in her letter. The investigation summarily concluded that "it was absolutely untrue that female indentured immigrants are violated or receive hurts or cruel treatment at the hand of their plantation managers."[13] It further noted that two known "political agitators" in the islands, the ex-indentured worker, Totaram Sanadhya, and a recently arrived Arya Samajist missionary from India, Manoharram Saraswati, had orchestrated Kunti's letter to the press in India. The question of whether Kunti was really sexually assaulted or whether she had concocted the story either for personal gains or to further the cause of abolition remains unclear.

Yet the investigation into her story reveals something about the abolitionist networks that extended from Fiji to India and back that were responsible for publicizing her story. Sanadhya, the ex-indentured worker, who was identified both in the Fiji government's investigations and in a public testimonial from indentured and ex-indentured workers in Fiji on his departure for India in 1914, as the person responsible for the publication of Kunti's letter in the *Bharat Mitra*, was a veteran of the anti-indenture cause by the time Kunti's letter was published. Sanadhya had encountered the Calcutta-based pro-abolition Indian newspaper *Bharat Mitra* while he was still in Fiji where he was already involved in a variety of activities to draw attention to the situation of indentured workers. On behalf of the recently formed British Indian Association (1911) of Fiji, he had written a letter to Gandhi in South Africa (published in the latter's newspaper, the *Indian Opinion*) requesting him to send an Indian barrister to Fiji who would take up the cause of the indentured workers in the law courts.[14] Sanadhya's call in the

Indian Opinion was answered by one Manilal Maganlal Doctor, a Gujarati barrister like Gandhi, who on the latter's advice was practicing in Mauritius where he provided legal aid to the Indians on the plantations.[15] In moving to Fiji, Manilal started what was, perhaps, Fiji's first Hindi paper, a cyclostyled sheet, in 1913, that became a precursor for the English-language *Indian Settler* that he launched subsequently in 1917. Sometime during this period, however, the focus of Sanadhya's own activism shifted from Fiji to India where he hoped to make the condition of indentured workers more widely known. Here he planned both to influence public opinion on indenture as well as to take the struggle against the indentured system directly to the small towns and villages in India from where the workers for the overseas plantations were recruited.

Sanadhya prepared for his role in India by documenting and archiving the hardship of Indians on the plantations. His first attempt to do so was with a camera, which he had learned to use especially for the purposes. This was stymied when his collection of photographs was confiscated by the Fijian authorities. When Sanadhya finally left Fiji, somewhat unexpectedly, in 1914, in the aftermath of his involvement in bringing Kunti's letter to the *Bharat Mitra*, he did so with a trunk full of papers, with stories presumably similar to Kunti's, to bring before an Indian public. This time, however, he managed to smuggle the trunk past the inspectors on the ship by switching his trunk with that of another returning worker; when the authorities, already suspicious of his activities in Fiji, opened his trunk they found nothing "objectionable."[16]

On his return to India, Sanadhya published *Fiji Mein Mere Ekkis Varsh* (1914) [*My 21 Years in Fiji*], with the help of his amanuensis, the as-yet-unknown government schoolteacher and aspiring Hindi-language journalist Benarsidas Chaturvedi, who had read some of the latter's writings in the *Bharat Mitra*. The book, the closest thing produced by the second abolition to the "slave narratives" made famous during the movement for the abolition of Atlantic slavery, reproduced Kunti's story along with other stories of men and women in Fiji whose "*kasht*" or hardship Sanadhya had seen first-hand.[17] Back in India, Sanadhya continued speaking out against "*kuli-pratha*" or the indentured labor system in speeches and pamphlets in small towns, villages and *melas* (fairs) as the Agra-based representative of the Anti-Indenture Emigration League and Coolie Protection Society.[18] The impact that village-level abolitionists, like Sanadhya, were beginning to have on recruitment in the districts was noted by the Colonial Officer in charge of recruitment in Benares, A. Marsden. Marsden lodged a formal complaint with the Colonial Office in London in which he submitted as proof leaflets that he had confiscated from the area. At least one of the leaflets, after warning people against volunteering for indentured labor, urged them specifically to read Sanadhya's book to get accurate information, as opposed to the falsehoods spread by recruiters, about indenture.[19] Another of Sanadhya's submissions to the press, not unlike Kunti's letter in the *Bharat Mitra*, drew the attention once again of the Government of India. The August 16, 1915, issue of the Hindi-language paper, *Pratap*, carried a letter from Sanadhya about a Muslim woman, Bachi, the wife of one Mohammed Beg in Fiji.[20] Bachi, Sanadhya claimed, had sent him a written declaration from Fiji accusing a Mr. Stafford, of the Vunisei plantation in Rewa, of raping her. The Government of India, as in the case of Kunti's letter, deliberated whether to request the Fiji government again for a refutation. While nothing came out of the government's request to refute

Bachi's case, Sanadhya had clearly positioned himself through a network of abolition activists in India as an important conduit through which the accounts of indentured workers could be disseminated to an Indian public.

The insertion of indentured workers themselves in the national debate on the indentured labor system did not go unnoticed. Even Kunti, on her return to India with her husband and two daughters in 1915, and having faced the consequences of her notoriety in the hostility toward her from government officials in Fiji and India, had a brief moment in public. She shared a platform with Bhupendranath Basu, a member of the Imperial Legislative Assembly, at a large public meeting against indenture in Calcutta in August 1915.[21] In the meantime, Sanadhya's activism on behalf of overseas Indians, which was carried on first from Shantiniketan in Bengal and later from Gandhi's *ashram* [retreat] in Sabarmati, continued to draw national visibility to the plight of ex-indentured workers. The abolition of indenture was the only political movement with which Gandhi associated himself in 1915, at a time when he had otherwise taken a hiatus from politics to educate himself about India after his long sojourn in South Africa.[22] At a February 1916 protest meeting in Bombay, he even threatened the government with a satyagraha—preventing emigrant ships with indentured workers from leaving the ports of Calcutta—if indentured recruitment in India was not halted by May 31, 1917.[23] The imprint of Sanadhya's work was also felt on the famous 1916 Report on Indentured Labor in Fiji by Gandhi's lieutenants the Reverends C. F. Andrews and W. W. Pearson that is widely credited with having single-handedly converted the then Viceroy, Lord Hardinge, and his government to abolition.[24] The report, based substantially on the testimony of workers, was something of a landmark in being the first citizen-led inquiry into the indentured labor system—an early precursor to what would become a tradition of civil society activism in late colonial India with the appointment of nonofficial inquiry commissions by the Congress and other political parties to examine a variety of issues.[25] Kunti's letter in the *Bharat Mitra*, indeed, was the tip of the iceberg of an extensive propaganda war that was waged by an army of anti-indenture activists—indentured and ex-indentured workers as well as their supporters, who were largely outside the established political circles in India and were often impatient with the latter's more pusillanimous stand on indenture.[26]

The apotheosis of Kunti's story, against this background, represents more than a ubiquitous elite nationalist discourse of patriarchal chivalry. Neither Kunti, identified unambiguously in the *Bharat Mitra* as a low-caste Chamar, nor Bachi, the indentured Muslim woman worker, who became widely known through abolitionist propaganda, were the kind of women who were typically made the objects of reverence and recognized as deserving of chivalric protection in discourses of national honor. By representing Kunti and other women indentured workers as a direct reproof to Indian society as a *whole*, which had hitherto tolerated the system of indenture, abolitionists were not merely critiquing the system of indenture, but they were also staking a broader claim to equality: making a marginalized population stand in for the entire nation. They were, in effect, showing up or upending the hitherto partial conception of the "common" that had allowed the sectional interests of the powerful and privileged classes to be identified with the nation or the whole of society.

The democratic achievement, and the roots of the success, of this ragtag army of Indian abolitionists lay precisely in articulating their cause not as a sectional demand affecting only a part of society, but in the universalist claim of equality that affected all of society. By the 1910s, only a very small proportion of the population in India—no more than 8,000 to 10,000 annually were recruited on indentured labor contracts overseas—and a very localized area—only two districts in the United Provinces, for example, provided more than 80 percent of annual recruitment—were directly affected by the indentured labor trade.[27] It was by generalizing the demand for abolition to the entire nation that the anti-indenture movement, within a relatively short period, came to upend politics-as-usual: the *sarvasadharan junta* [ordinary public] and the *aam admi* [common person] could now come to stand in for the nation as a whole.

A second contribution of the movement was that the newly reconstituted national community was conceived not in terms of an already existing *ethnos* but in the expansive terms of a *demos*. Those who became newly politicized by the story of Kunti and of others like her, and who went on to become the real foot soldiers of the abolitionist movement, did not necessarily do so by asserting a pre-existing identification with the potential victims of the indentured labor system. To be sure, there were numerous Hindu activists and Hindu religious organizations, especially the Arya Samaj whose missionaries were actively involved in the anti-indenture movement, and who criticized the indentured system as endangering Hindu beliefs and practices: most notably the difficulty of maintaining intercaste interdictions under the conditions of indenture. Yet the experience of the Marwaris of Calcutta, one of the most active supporters of the anti-indenture cause and who formed the backbone of the support for abolition in India, complicates any simple identitarian explanation of the anti-indenture movement. For several groups newly politicized by the demand for abolition, the movement served self-consciously as a vehicle for going beyond their own narrow or sectional interests to make common cause, without necessarily claiming an identity, with persons directly affected by the indentured labor system.

The example of the Marwaris of Calcutta, an immigrant community of Hindu and Jain businessmen from western India, with a reputation for being orthodox and clannish or aloof, is especially apposite.[28] Calcutta Marwari organizations provided the bulk of the funds as well as the infrastructure and activists for the village-level anti-indenture movement in northern and eastern India even though Marwaris did not constitute the typical recruit for indentured labor. Yet it was the Marwari paper, *Bharat Mitra*, whose circulation extended to the Indian communities in Fiji and in other colonies, that had first published Kunti's letter, and the Marwari Relief Society of Calcutta had set up the Anti-Indenture Emigration Leagues and Coolie Protection Societies in Calcutta, Madras, Bombay, Allahabad, and small towns across northern India to coordinate the nationwide protest against indenture. The port city of Calcutta from where ships departed and returned with indentured workers to and from the colonies, and where the governments of the various colonies had established holding "depots" to collect and quarantine workers who were recruited "up-country" (northern districts) before they embarked on their journey to the colonies, was a natural hub for abolition activities. The Marwaris of Calcutta were thus well placed to play a pivotal role in bankrolling the anti-indenture movement as well as providing it with its army of ordinary foot soldiers.

The account that the Marwaris give about the origin of their involvement in the anti-indenture movement, which is repeated in the 1916 Andrews-Pearson report on indenture, is one about the community's evolution as a consequence of their newfound activism: a move away from an exclusive focus on parochial or community-based concerns toward a broader solidarity with vulnerable human beings. The incident that purportedly made Marwaris into abolitionists begins with the wrongful confinement of a rich Marwari lady, Lakshmi, in a coolie depot in Calcutta.[29] While on a trip from her home in Agra to her business interest in Ajmer, she was, through a series of lies, waylaid and brought to the Calcutta depot where she was bound under indenture for the West Indies. Even though Lakshmi knew no one in Calcutta, she was confident, on the basis of the close-knit nature of Marwari communities, that someone from the community in Calcutta would come to her rescue. In a remarkable display of resourcefulness, she managed one day through the bars of the coolie depot to attract the attention of a young boy selling newspapers on the harbor. She gave him a note for a made-up person, a Hiralal Motilal (a common name among Marwaris). The boy brought the note to the attention of some people in Barabazar, an area of the city dominated by Marwaris. The local Marwari leaders, including Babu Onkarmull Shroff, the Honorary Secretary of the Marwari Sahayak Samiti [Marwari Relief Society], agreed that the community ought to come to Lakshmi's help. They formed a delegation and sought permission from the Protector of Emigrants in Calcutta, R. W. Banks, to visit the depot to check out Lakshmi's story. The involvement of the Marwaris in the inequities of the indentured-labor system, according to this account of the origins of Marwari abolitionism, was initiated, in keeping with common stereotypes of the Marwaris, on the basis of a narrow community or sectional interest: the fate of a fellow Marwari woman.

From this small beginning, however, would grow the expansive politics of the Marwaris. When the Marwari delegation arrived at the depot, they found Lakshmi and her daughter there. But it was what they saw in the depot—thousands packed together in miserable conditions—that apparently caught their attention. They were beseeched from all sides for help. Since they were aware that the law would not allow them to petition for the release of any individual from a contract without providing specific names, the delegates quickly "began to take down in pencil, unperceived by the depot officers, the names of all those who were not willing to emigrate."[30] Before leaving with Lakshmi and her daughter, along with a Brahmin woman who Lakshmi had managed to rescue by claiming that she was her servant, the Marwari delegates were able to get the names of fourteen other women whom they also agreed to rescue after getting all the proper paperwork. The pull of community feeling—what, in the first place, had prompted Lakshmi to be able to count on support from the local Marwari community as well as the willingness of the local Marwari leaders to organize a delegation on her behalf—had expanded, upon seeing the plight of the ordinary recruits, especially women, to a wider concern for all those caught in similarly desperate circumstances.

The difficulties of rescuing these other women had their own lesson to teach. Shroff immediately instituted proceedings for the release of the fourteen women, but this time he was rebuffed by the Protector of Emigrants. The latter, who had been willing to give permission to rescue a "respectable" woman to avoid drawing unfavorable attention to recruitment practices, already the subject of much controversy in India, presumably saw nothing to be gained by allowing Marwari do-gooders to interfere with the general population of recruits. Shroff, enlisting the support of Bhupendranath Basu, the prominent Bengali lawyer and politician, managed to get a police sub-inspector to escort his own lawyer to the depot to collect the women's evidence. When Banks refused them permission to enter, Basu directed the Marwaris to seek the help of the District Magistrate to override Bank's orders. Since it was the Durga Puja holidays, one of the most important holidays for Bengalis, all the offices were closed. The emigrant ships, however, were due to sail with the first tide after the holidays: time, therefore, was of the essence. Drawing upon all the official influence they could muster, the Marwaris and their lawyer somehow managed to get the requisite permission to enter the depots with orders to have the women released on a Rupees 50 bail until their cases could be heard in the court. But they arrived at the depot too late to save all the women: the first ship had already sailed, leaving only five of the original fourteen in the depot. The ease with which Lakshmi, a "respectable" woman, was released and the difficulties in the case of the average recruit was not lost on the Marwaris. The experience revealed the gulf that separated those like the stray members of the privileged classes who were caught by accident from the ordinary emigrant, the typical recruit, who had no such clout to count upon. This was the need that the Marwaris now stepped in to fulfil.

In seeking the release of the five remaining women through the magistrate's court, and of repatriating those who still had homes to which to return, the Marwari abolitionists were further stretched to put aside their own conservative social views about women. Of the five women, the experience of only one fit the trope of the helpless woman victim popularized in abolitionist propaganda: this woman had gone to bathe at the confluence of the Ganga and Jamuna at Allahabad, but in the crush of the crowds at the train station she got separated from her party and was taken away by an unscrupulous *arkati* [unlicensed recruiter]. The stories of the other women revealed the complexity of the conditions under which women volunteered or were recruited for indenture. Two of the women were lured to volunteer by the false promise of high wages by an *arkati*; one was promised marriage, only to be abandoned at the depot; and the fifth, an eighteen-year-old girl married off to a nine-year-old boy, had rejected her marriage and run away from her home. Having become actually involved in the rescue of recruits, and thereby exposed to the complexity of individual circumstances under which people became involved in the process, the Marwari abolitionists had to learn to set aside their own caste, gender, religious, or class prejudices, even if temporarily, in order to continue their rescue efforts. The origin story of the abolitionism of Calcutta Marwaris, as they themselves recounted it, was one of gradually learning to extend their community of concern.

Whatever the actual reasons that had prompted the Marwaris to become abolitionists, the fact that they chose to tell this through a conversion to a new kind of politics—not based on any sectional or pre-given identities—is itself significant. There were certainly alternative explanations—on, say, the preservation of religious and caste prejudices or economic self-interest—for the Calcutta Marwaris to get involved in the anti-indenture movement: these self-interested arguments, indeed, never entirely disappeared from the repertoire of the broader movement for abolition. But the Marwaris chose to ground their own self-understanding of abolition upon the contours of a wider concern beyond mere self-interest: legitimizing, in effect, the redirection of the resources and networks at their disposal for a purpose beyond immediate community interests. The beneficiaries of the Anti-Indenture Emigration League and Coolie Protection Society, indeed, included a broad spectrum of persons: Hindus, of all castes, dalits, Muslims, men and women, both respectable and those whose morals were likely perceived by many, like the Marwaris, as beyond the pale. By the same token, later community histories of the Marwaris have been eager to note that the Marwari stalwarts of the movement, such as Rambihari Tandon and Ramdev Chokhani, were motivated neither by caste nor religious prejudices in becoming champions of abolition.[31] The experience of Marwari abolitionism, at least by its own reckoning, had produced a trajectory for the community in which it gradually shed its earlier focus only on parochial or community concerns to engage, through abolition, with the concerns of a wider humanity.

The anti-indenture activism of some other groups, like the elite and middle-class women's organizations, especially the Prayag Mahila Samiti [Allahabad Ladies Club] of the United Provinces, served a similar function of broadening the community of concern. Abolitionism allowed women activists to stake a claim for themselves in public politics beyond the limits of the "woman's question" that was still defined largely in elite and upper-caste terms. This did not necessarily produce an identification between middle-class women activists and the class of women who were typically subject to indentured labor. To be sure, women activists saw women workers largely through the limiting figure of "victims." But they also created an opening for transforming them into potential "sisters": whose dishonor, albeit as seen largely through the lens of middle-class sexual respectability, ought to be a matter of concern to all.[32] The relationship that women activists asserted with women workers, indeed, did not depend upon complete identification; their relationship, instead, to use Jean-Luc Nancy's terms, represented "contiguity but not continuity."[33] Women activists, on the basis of this contingent connection, were extending their activism beyond the particularities of their own class interests in support of, and in solidarity with, others who were not, by a simple sleight of hand, rendered the same as themselves.

The anti-indenture cause, indeed, had called into being a specific kind of political subject—one that was not simply reducible to any existing social groups or identities in the established social order of late colonial India. As such, it produced a "supernumerary subject," an excess or a supplement, over and above the existing units of society, who demanded recognition as equal stakeholders in society.[34] This was the sense in which the collective political subject of abolitionism—not reducible to any pre-existing groups or identities—represented a genuinely democratizing moment: the coming into being of a *people* not on the basis of any logic of sameness, or of a shared ethnos, but through a willingness to stand shoulder-to-shoulder as a demos.

Finally, and perhaps most importantly, certain abolitionist strategies served to teach disparate groups, despite their continuing differences, to be and act in common as a people. This helps explain what was, perhaps the most mystifying, and seemingly baffling, strategy adopted by abolitionists: the publishing of affidavits from ex-indentured workers returning to India in vernacular newspapers. Starting in 1912, the *Bharat Mitra* and other pro-abolition Hindi-language newspapers began printing affidavits from returning indentured workers that testified to their experience of injustice under the system.[35] The affidavit, a legal term from medieval Latin, formed through a combination of *affidaire* "to trust oneself" and *fidus* or faithful, literally means "he has stated on oath."[36] As a legal genre, it was certainly not unfamiliar in India. The affidavit, as a written statement of fact made voluntarily, confirmed by oath or affirmation of the party making it, and signed before a notary or other officer empowered to administer such oaths, was for long admissible in a court of law in colonial India. The point of repurposing affidavits, beyond their recognizable use in the legal-juridical realm, for public circulation in newspapers appears to be an innovation of the anti-indenture movement.

The Anti-Indenture League and Coolie Protection Society employed an army of activists, who were themselves either former indentured workers or low-level local social activists, to meet returning workers at the Calcutta docks and walk them through the process of supplying affidavits for the use of abolitionists. By 1914, the project of collecting affidavits from returning workers had swelled sufficiently for the organization to hire accommodations at 167 Harrison Road in the Garden Reach area near the Docks—close to its own offices at 160 Harrison Road—to house workers temporarily. This way workers could stay back in Calcutta to provide affidavits before they were dispersed to their former homes either in the north or to the districts around Madras in the south.[37] The co-editor of the *Bharat Mitra*, Ambika Prasad Vajpeyi, apparently took a personal interest in this project: his signature, for example, appears as a witness in the affidavit provided by Sanadhya on his return to India.[38]

The purpose behind the *publication* of these affidavits remains opaque. They appear to have had no purpose in the arsenal of legal strategies adopted by abolitionists to free recruits wrongfully recruited and confined in depots.[39] The public circulation of workers' affidavits in newspapers functioned outside the adversarial process of cross examination in the courts—there was no way, therefore, to vouch for the veracity of the information in the affidavit or to account for the role of the various interlocutors and intermediaries who had a hand in translating and making visible the affidavit before the public. The publications of the affidavits, likewise, did not contribute to the fact-finding mode on indenture. The latter was dominated by the numerous official commissions of enquiry periodically instated by the government in response to the abuses associated with the system.[40] The official consensus, at least in the India Office and in the Colonial Office in London, was that the system, despite some isolated problems that could be ameliorated, was basically sound. This official consensus was not the primary audience for the affidavits. Only thirty-nine of the total number of affidavits that were presumably originally published in newspapers like the *Bharat Mitra* eventually reached the attention of British officials. The publication of the affidavits in vernacular-language newspapers clearly operated apart from, and in contrast to, the domain in which the official facts about indenture were debated. If workers' affidavits functioned beyond the legal-juridical and fact-finding realms, they also exceeded the desire for simply publicizing workers' experiences, given that there were a wide variety of genres for narrating these experiences. On the eve of abolition there was already an accumulating popular archive of the experiences of indentured workers recorded in folk songs and in the letters and reports that were published in the press. What did the affidavit, a more obviously mediated genre than firsthand accounts from workers, add to this building archive of indentured-workers' experiences?

The affidavits, arguably, functioned differently from the more sensationalized popular accounts of indenture. So, for example, Kunti, despite having her story told and retold several times since her letter to the *Bharat Mitra* in 1913, chose to reiterate her story upon her return to India in an affidavit sworn before one Amalendu Sen, a Calcutta Police Magistrate, on January 8, 1916.[41] Her affidavit not only confirmed the details of the allegations that she had made in her original letter to the *Bharat Mitra* but also provided further details of her and her husband's experiences in Fiji. That Kunti, along with several other returning indentured workers, submitted affidavits for publication, despite the multiplicity of genres in which the experiences of indentured workers were now being circulated, suggests that something more than publicity was at stake in the choice of collecting affidavits and publishing them in newspapers.

The published affidavits, unlike the ubiquitous petitions from subordinated groups addressed to those in power, were directed pointedly to a general public. They carried therefore something of the dialogic implications of what Kelly Oliver identifies as "testimonial exchange." To testify, in this context, was "to address another, to impress upon a listener, to appeal to a community."[42] The publication of the affidavits, from this perspective, may be seen as a performance that called upon a public to bear witness to the injustice of the indenture system. The "witness" was both the person who had given testimony, in this case the returning indentured workers, and the secondary witness, the broader reading public in India, that received it. The pedagogic function of the affidavit in this case may be seen as an attempt to produce an altered public through the solemn act of witnessing.

The act of witnessing entailed in the publication of the steady stream of affidavits from former indentured workers serves as a quiet staging of equality: a call to reconfigure existing subject positions, of both the workers and the readers, to be and act in common. Witnessing, as Kelly Oliver reminds us, goes beyond the familiar politics of recognition, which underwrites certain forms of contemporary discourses of multiculturalism, diversity, and inclusion that leave the essential hierarchy between subject and object intact.[43] By contrast, witnessing offers a more radical politics of recognition by entailing a transformative intersubjective investment in the call both to see and to believe the other. The project of witnessing opens possibilities for new ways of being and acting in common without necessarily erasing the situated differences between differing social positions.

Consider what is at stake between a mere politics of recognition and the more radical act of witnessing.[44] Kunti's original letter to the *Bharat Mitra* in 1913 about her sexual assault provoked widespread public sympathy and outrage in India, spurring the popular demand for abolition. The letter worked ostensibly by eliciting sympathy for Kunti and inviting even upper caste and elite readers to try and identify with her—conferring, in effect, a recognition to Kunti of her essential sameness across their myriad differences. Here the subject–object relationship, the party conferring recognition and the party seeking recognition, remains essentially unchanged. Kunti's affidavit, by contrast, makes a somewhat different demand on her readers. To bear witness to her testimony, to believe it without any guarantee of its truth, the hypothetical upper-caste and elite readers are being called upon, beyond the realm of pure reason, to trust Kunti and to thereby open themselves up to her. The reader's decision whether to accept Kunti's testimony or not is ultimately an emotional or an affective one, calling upon the reader to take a leap of faith and to extend beyond themselves toward the person submitting the affidavit. The transformation that is called for on the part of the readers includes confronting their own implication in Kunti's situation: a failure, until now, to have seen or heard a countless other Kuntis. By the same token, Kunti as herself witness, whose testimony sets in motion this chain of reciprocity with her reader, also stands transformed: no longer just a poor dalit woman worker (dependent upon the reader's recognition of her humanity), but, as evident in the levels of mediation that went into the making of her affidavit, transformed into the generalizable and universal subject of a collective protest. The act of witnessing, in effect, creates an opening for an altered relationship between Kunti and her readers. In short, the dialogic work of witnessing that is suggested by the publication of workers' affidavits in newspapers creates the possibility of learning, despite differences, of new more egalitarian ways of being and acting in common as a people.

While we may never know for certain the purpose behind the publication of the workers' affidavits, nor the impact they may have had on the reading public, we find some traces of the subjective transformation that was being called upon those who were being mobilized for the cause in the content of some of the abolitionist texts and speeches. We see it, for example, in Gandhi's stump speeches at protest meetings attended by elite and middle-class men and women, both Indian and British, reminding them of both his and their complicity in the indentured labor system: "for fifty years and more," he declared at a meeting in Madras in November 1915, "we have allowed this practice to continue. We must no longer be silent."[45] The immediate goal of the abolition movement, of course, was the termination of indenture, but in that demand was also a call for a different conception of the common: one in which the powerful would acknowledge, and unlearn, their privilege to invest in more shared and equitable ways of being. Abolitionism laid the foundations for that possibility of a radically transformed conception of society.

Those who were hitherto excluded from the exercise of power and had no fixed part in the social order—Jacques Rancière's *les sans-part*—were mobilized in the anti-indenture movement not only to protest a wrong—the indenture system—but to also make a "usurpatory claim" to be heard on an equal footing. And, even more, perhaps, the once excluded articulated their demands in a way that identified them as representatives of the Whole of society, as identical to the Nation, as such. This identification of a nonpart with the Whole, or the part of society with no properly defined place in it (or resisting their allocated subordinated place in it) with the Universal is, what Rancière, among others, identifies as an elementary act of politicization that is discernible in all great democratic events.[46] Popular abolitionism in India was just such a democratic event: an authentic political opening in which an excluded "part of no part" came to stand for the true universality of society. Here, unlike those who stand only for their particular privileged interests, a new political subject appeared as a representative or a stand-in for the Universal, thereby bringing the supposedly natural functioning of the social order into question. The democratic and egalitarian impulse of this moment had produced, in effect, a novel representation of the common or the community as a whole. The threat, in the wake of abolition, lay in the containment of this rupture when the *sarvasadharna janta* or the *aam admi*, the ordinary person, as it were, had become the subject for the reconstitution of the national collectivity.

What would follow would be precisely attempts to tame the implications of this new political subject—the *people* or the *demos*—by reassigning it a fixed part, a particular designated place, in an elite reappropriation of the common: the part, that is, of the pre-given sociological category of the masses, the peasants, the workers, the poor, or the plebian. The Indian Emigration Act of 1922, which provided legislative imprimatur to the termination of indenture and shifted the locus of action to a largely unrepresentative body comprising British officials and Indian politicians in the Imperial Legislative Assembly in Delhi, sought to redesignate the newly constituted people to a fixed and established place in society.[47] The Act, which was passed with only a few dissenting voices, made any scheme of assisted migration of unskilled labor from India illegal, except for the hugely lucrative labor market in Ceylon and the Federated States of Malaya, without a special act of exemption made by the legislature. The Act was justified in the name of both protecting the ignorant masses of India from exploitation abroad and of securing within India an adequate and cheap supply of labor for the good of the nation. The "people" who had presented themselves during the movement as a stand-in for the Universal, were now being put in their place—as the "ignorant poor" or the masses either in need of protection or to be valued as workers for the good of the nation—to perform designated functions and play particular parts in society. This rival conception of the common in which the poor played their designated part under elite tutelage was, in effect, an attempt to reverse that democratizing moment in which the excluded (the people) had put forward their claim to a common that was reconstituted in their name. The Act attempted to roll back this political opening by disaggregating the people into already established social groups with their predesignated functions in society.

The antagonistic visions of the common, which lies at the heart of the transformation of the political in twentieth-century India, is what is disavowed when the history of Indian abolitionism is excised from its legitimate place as an inaugural moment in the democratizing of anticolonial national politics. The moment of Indian abolitionism—despite its subsequent excision from histories of the advent of mass anticolonial politics in India—provides an opportunity to reflect on the nature of the "political" itself. The "political," to quote Ernesto Laclau, is "not an internal moment of the social but, on the contrary, that which shows the impossibility of establishing the social as an objective order."[48] And, as such, Indian abolitionism was an exemplary moment of the *political*: the challenge it represented, however tenuous, had called the hitherto dominant vision of society into question. The political imaginary of abolition, even more than the legendary anticolonial mass campaigns of the post-1919 period, captures the potential of the democratic transformation of nationalist politics in India's twentieth century.

Notes

1 The most detailed account of the abolition movement in India remains Karen A. Ray, "The Abolition of Indentured Emigration and the Politics of Indian Nationalism, 1894–1917" (Ph.D. dissertation, McGill University, 1980). This Indian movement, of course, built upon the prior labor actions undertaken by workers in the plantation colonies themselves. See, Radica Mahese, "'Abolish Indenture' and the Indian Nationalist Discourse in the Early 20th Century," https://www.academia.edu/4094172/ABOLISH_INDENTURE_AND_THE_INDIAN_NATIONALIST_DISCOURSE_IN_THE_EARLY_20TH_CENTURY. Accessed November 17, 2019.

2 The classic study on the indentured labor system, is Hugh Tinker, *A New System of Slavery*: The *Export of Indian Labor Overseas, 1830–1920* (London: Hansib, 1993 [1974]); for an updating of this account, see Ashutosh Kumar, *Coolies of Empire: Indentured Indians in the Sugar Colonies, 1830–1920* (New Delhi: Cambridge University Press, 2017).

3 For an attempt to place both abolitions within the same frame, see Seymour Drescher, *Pathways from Slavery: British and Colonial Mobilizations in Global Perspective* (London: Routledge, 2018).

4 The point is made in Tinker, *A New System of Slavery*, p. 288.

5 Even more comprehensive recent histories of the movement have seen it largely as reflecting elitist concerns and biases; see, Ashutosh Kumar, "Indian Nationalists and End of the Indentured Emigration," *Occasional Paper Series No. 48, Nehru Memorial Museum and Library*, New Delhi, 2014; and Charu Gupta "'Innocent' Victims/'Guilty' Migrants: Hindi Public Sphere, Caste and Indentured Women in Colonial North India," *Modern Asian Studies* 49, no. 5 (2015): 1345–77.

6 M. K. Gandhi, *Satyagraha in South Africa*. Trans from Gujarati by Valji Govind Desai (Ahmedabad: Navjivan Trust, 1968 [1928]). For a reappraisal of some dominant trends in interpreting Gandhi's relation to indentured workers in South Africa, see Anil Nauriya, "Representing Indian Toilers in Natal: Some Explorations with Gandhi," *Natalia* 46 (2016): 31–53.

7 For a discussion of the tropes of the "sarvasadharan junta" and of the "aam admi" [common person] during abolitionism, see Mrinalini Sinha, "Totaram Sanadhya: *Fiji Mein Mere Ekkis Varsh*: A History of Empire and Nation in a Minor Key," in Antoinette Burton and Isabel Hoffmeyr, eds., *Ten Books That Shaped the British Empire: Creating an Imperial Commons* (Durham, NC: Duke University Press, 2014), pp. 168–89. For a longer history of the idea of the "common people" in the Hindi-speaking sphere, see Sikandar Maitra Kumar, "Hindi and the Struggle for the Democratic Commons (1857–1965)," forthcoming Ph.D. dissertation, Department of History, University of Michigan, Ann Arbor, United States.

8 I am drawing this formulation from the work of Jacques Rancière. See especially Todd May, *The Political Thought of Jacques Rancière*: *Creating Equality* (State College, PA: Pennsylvania State University, 2008). On contradictory ideas of the people, also see Alan Baidou et al., *What Is a People?* (New York: Columbia University Press, 2016).

9 For the context for Kunti's letter, the classic study is Brij V. Lal, "Kunti's Cry: Indentured Women on Fiji Plantations," *Indian Economic and Social History Review* 22 (1985): 55–71. For further details of the case, see John D. Kelly, *A Politics of Virtue: Hinduism, Sexuality and Counter Colonial Discourse in Fiji* (Chicago: University of Chicago Press, 1992); Karen A. Ray, "Kunti, Lakshmibhai and the 'Ladies': Women's Labor and the Abolition of Indentured Emigration from India," *Labour, Capital and Society* 29, no. 1, 2 (April–November 1996): 1226–52; and Margaret Mishra "The Emergence of Feminism in Fiji," *Women's History Review* 17, no. 1 (2008): 39–55. Also see Prem Misir, ed., *The Subaltern Indian Woman: Domination and Social Degradation* (London: Palgrave Macmillan, 2018).

10 See *Commerce and Industry Department, Emigration, March 1914, nos 8–12, Part B* & *Nov. 1914, nos. 17–20, Pt. B*, National Archives of India, New Delhi [NAI].

11 For some of this literature, see Ved Prakash Vatuk, "Protest Songs of East Indians in British Guiana," *American Folklore* 77, no. 35 (July–September 1964): 220–35; Mousumi Majumdar, ed., *Kahe Gaile Bides? Where Did You Go? On Bhojpuri Migration Since the 1870s and Contemporary Culture in Bihar, Uttar Pradesh, Suriname and the Netherlands* (Amsterdam: KIT Press, 2010); Ashutosh Kumar, "Anti-Indenture Bhojpuri Folk Songs and Poems from Northern India," *Man in India* 93, no. 4 (2013): 509–19; and his "Songs of Abolition: Anti-Indentured Campaigns in Early Twentieth Century India," in P. Pratap Kumar, ed., *Indian Diaspora: Socio-Cultural and Religious Worlds* (Leiden: Brill Publishers, 2015), pp. 38–51.

12 *Commerce and Industry Department, Emigration, March 1914, nos 8–12, Part B*; & *Nov. 1914, nos. 17–20, Pt. B* NAI.

13 Ibid.

14 See B. Chaturvedi, "Totaram Sanadhya," in *Sansmaran* (Kashi: Bharitya Gnanpith, 1958), pp. 180–9; and Jaganath Lahiri, *Janam Shatabdi Ke Punya Avsar Par, Sri Totaram Sanadhya Samarika (1876–1976)* (Ferozabadh: Ferozabad Sandesh Press, n.d.); and Brij V. Lal and Yogendra Yadav, "Hinduism under Indenture: Totaram Sanadhya's Account of Fiji," *Journal of Pacific History* 30, no. 1 (1995): 99–111. For Sanadhya as an abolitionist, see Sinha, "Totaram Sanadhya's *Fiji Mein Mere Ekkis Varsh*."

15 For the career of Manilal, see Hugh Tinker, "Odd Man Out: The Loneliness of the Indian Colonial Politician—The Career of Manilal Doctor," *Journal of Imperial and Commonwealth History* 2, no. 2 (1974): 226–43; and Dharmendra Prasad, *Public Life of Manilal Doctor* (Bombay: Rite Print-Pak, 1992).

16 Chaturvedi, "Totaram Sanadhya;" and Sanadhya, "Prastavna," in "Ek Bharitiya Hriday," in *Fiji Mein Bharatiya Pratibandh:Kuli-Pratha* (Kanpur: Pratap Press, 1919), pp. 1–54.

17 For a history of the book's publication, see Sinha, "Totaram Sanadhya's *Fiji Mein Mere Ekkis Varsh*." Scholars have also used the genre of "testimonio" to talk of this book, see Vijay Mishra, *Writing Indenture Histories through Testimonios and Oral Narratives* (New York: Routledge, 2017); and Frederik Schröer, "Of Testimonios and Feeling Communities: Totaram Sanadhya's Account of Indenture," *Südasien-Chronik-South Asia Chronicle* 6 (2016): 149–74.

18 Sanadhya's collection of speeches was published by the Abhyudaya Press of Allahabad and was titled, *Kuli-Pratha* [The Coolie-System], see *Statement of Books, during the Quarter Ending March 1915*, Uttar Pradesh Archives, Lucknow, India [UPA].

19 See *Commerce and Industry, Emigration, May 1916, nos. 10–16, Pt. B;* and *Commerce and Industry, Emigration, Dec. 1915, nos. 43–54, Pt. A*, NAI. The Government of

India instituted an inquiry in all the provinces to determine the impact of the village-level movement against indenture; the Government of Bihar and Orissa reported evidence of the movement in certain districts, see "Reported Movement in India to Secure the Termination of Indentured Labour" -June -10-20- Em – 15 of 1915—Part A, *Proceedings of the Govt of Bihar & Orissa Municipal Dept, Commerce Branch, 1915*, India Office Records [IOR] Asian and African Collections, British Library, London.

20 *Commerce and Industry, Emigration, May 1916, nos. 10–16, Pt. B*, NAI.

21 *Bharat Mitra*, vol. 11, nos. 11–12, May–July 1916, p. 43.

22 Judith Brown, *Gandhi's Rise to Power: Indian Politics 1915–1922* (Cambridge: Cambridge University Press, 1972). This point is made in Ray, "The Abolition of Indentured Emigration."

23 See Ray, "The Abolition of Indentured Emigration."

24 C. F. Andrews and W. W. Pearson, *Report on Indentured Labour in Fiji* (Calcutta: Star Printing, 1916). For Sanadhya's influence on Andrews, see Sinha, "Totaram Sanadhya's *Fiji Mein Mere Ekkis Varsh*."

25 For the origins of civil society activism in late colonial India, see Kalyani Ramnath, "*ADM Jabalpur's Antecedents*: Political Emergencies, Civil Liberties, and Arguments from Colonial Continuities in India," *American University International Law Review* 31 (2016).

26 For Sanadhya's impatience with the professions of sympathy from national political parties and political leaders, see Sinha, "Totaram Sanadhya's *Fiji Mein Mere Ekkis Varsh*."

27 From the 1880s to the end of indenture, the United Provinces provided 80 percent of the migrants, Bengal and Bihar provided 13 percent, and the rest came from Central India and the Punjab; See Pradipta Chaudhury, "Labour Migrations from the United Provinces, 1881–1911," *Studies in History*, n.s., 8, no. 1 (1992): 13–41; and Brij V. Lal, "The Odyssey of Indenture: Fragmentation and Reconstitution in the Indian Diaspora," *Diaspora: A Journal for Transnational Studies* 5, no. 2 (1996): 167–88.

28 For the Marwaris, see Thomas A. Tinberg, *The Marwaris: From Traders to Industrialists* (Delhi: Advent Books, Div, 1978); and Anne Hardgrove, *Community and Public Culture: The Marwaris in Calcutta, 1897–1997* (New York: Columbia University Press, 2004). For Marwari involvement in the abolition movement, see Ray, "Kunti, Lakshmibhai and the 'Ladies.'"

29 Statement of Lakshmi, included in memorial from Marwari Association, Calcutta to the Government of India, February 7, 1916, *Commerce and Industry Department, Part B, 30–33, April 1916*, NAI.

30 Ibid.

31 See, *Sri Ram Dev Chokhani,* ed. Radhakrishna Nivatiya et al. (Calcutta: All Indian Marwari Samelan, c 1950s [59?]); and Balchandra Modi, *Desh Ke Itihas Mein Marwari Jati Ka Sthan* (Calcutta: New Rajasthan Press, 1942), especially p. 655. This moment, I suggest, stands out in contrast to the more familiar story of Marwari involvement in Hindu sectarian politics in India both before and after abolition; for Marwari involvement in the nineteenth-century cow-protection movement in the U.P., see Gyanendra Pandey, *The Construction of Communalism in Colonial North India* (Delhi: Oxford University Press, 1990), esp. Ch. 5; and for the community's subsequent role in Hindu propaganda, see Akshaya Mukul, *The Gita Press and the Making of Hindu India* (Noida, UP: HarperCollins, 2015).

32 For elite women's activism around indenture, see Shobhna Nijhawan, "Fallen through the Nationalist and Feminist Grids of Analysis: Political Campaigning of

Indian Women against Indentured Labour Emigration," *Indian Journal of Gender Studies* 20, no. 1 (2014): 111–33.

33 Jean Luc Nancy, *Being Singular Plural*. Translated from French by Robert Richardson and Anne O'Byrne (Stanford, CA: Stanford University Pres, 2000), p. 10.

34 The terms is Rancière's, see May, *The Political Thought of Jacques Rancière*.

35 I have so far found several references to the publication of the affidavits in the *Bharat Mitra* as well as in other vernacular papers, see *Marwari Association Papers*, Reel 4, NMML; also see Affidavit of one Baldeo Thakur, published in the *Dainik Chandrika*, 3/7/1915 in *Report on Native Newspapers, Bengal, 1915*, p. 961, West Bengal State Archives, Kolkata [WBA]. I have been able to locate only a handful of actual affidavits, primarily those included with "Agitation in India against Indentured Emigration 1915," *L/PJ/6/1420 file 4279*, IOR.

36 https://www.etymonline.com/word/affidavit. Accessed November 12, 2019.

37 See Letter No. 322, dated Darjeeling, October 14, 1915, from James Donald, secretary to the Government of Bengal, Financial Department to the Secretary to Government of India, *Commerce and Industry Department*, NAI.

38 For Sanadhya's affidavit, see *Revenue, Emigration, File no. 3E- 6, Proceedings*, nos. 5–7, Nov. 1915, WBA.

39 For the legal activism of the Marwaris, see Karen Ray, "Marwari Politicization to Counter Village Victimization: The Anti-Indenture Struggle," *Shodhak* 17, no. 8 (1988): 85–92.

40 See Radhika Mongia, "Impartial Regimes of Truth: Indentured Indian Labor and the Status of Inquiry," *Cultural Studies* 18, no. 5 (2004): 749–68.

41 *Revenue, Emigration, File no. 3E- 6, Proceedings*, nos. 5–7, November 1915.

42 See Kelly Oliver, *Witnessing: Beyond Recognition* (Minneapolis, MN: University of Minnesota Press, 2001). There has been a growing body of scholarship on the colonial petition; but the "public" dimension of these affidavits gave them a very different function. See Rosalind O'Hanlon, "In the Presence of Witnesses: Petitioning and Judicial 'Publics' in Western India," *Modern Asian Studies* 53, no. 1 (2019): 52–88.

43 Ibid.

44 I am drawing here from Oliver, *Witnessing*.

45 Gandhi, *CWMG*, vo.13, p. 247.

46 See Rancière, "Ten Theses on Politics." *Theory and Event* 5, no. 3 (2001). Project Muse (accessed February 13, 2015); and Oliver Davis, *Jacques Rancière* (Cambridge: Polity, 2010), pp. 55–6.

47 For the debate on this legislation, see *Legislative, Assembly & Council, July 1922, nos. 1–19*, Pt. A, NAI; and *India Office, Judicial and Public Department*, L/PJ/7/2093: 1922; and L/P/J/6/1744: 1922, IOR.

48 Ernesto Laclau, "Letter to Aletta," in his *New Reflections on the Revolution of Our Time* (London: Verso, 1990), pp. 159–60.

Select Bibliography

Baidou, A., et al. *What Is a People?* (New York: Columbia University Press, 2016).

Buck-Morss, S. *Dreamworld and Catastrophe: The Passing of Mass Utopia in the East and West* (Cambridge, MA: MIT Press, 2000).

Drescher, S. *Pathways from Slavery: British and Colonial Mobilizations in Global Perspective* (London: Routledge, 2018).

"Ek Bharitiya Hriday," in *Fiji Mein Bharatiya Pratibandh: Kuli-Pratha* (Kanpur: Pratap Press, 1919).

Gandhi, M. K. *Satyagraha in South Africa*. Trans from Gujarati by Valji Govind Desai (Ahmedabad: Navjivan Trust, 1968 [1928]).

Gupta, C. "'Innocent' Victims/'Guilty' Migrants: Hindi Public Sphere, Caste and Indentured Women in Colonial North India," *Modern Asian Studies* 49, no. 5 (2015): 1345–77.

Hardgrove, Anne. *Community and Public Culture: The Marwaris in Calcutta, 1897–1997* (New York: Columbia University Press, 2004).

Kelly, John D. *A Politics of Virtue: Hinduism, Sexuality and Counter Colonial Discourse in Fiji* (Chicago: University of Chicago Press, 1992).

Kumar, A. "Anti-Indenture Bhojpuri Folk Songs and Poems from Northern India," *Man in India* 93, no. 4 (2013): 509–19.

Kumar, A. "Indian Nationalists and End of the Indentured Emigration," *Occasional Paper Series No. 48, Nehru Memorial Museum and Library*, New Delhi, 2014.

Kumar, A. "Songs of Abolition: Anti-Indentured Campaigns in Early Twentieth Century India," in P. Pratap Kumar, ed., *Indian Diaspora: Socio-Cultural and Religious Worlds* (Leiden: Brill Publishers, 2015), pp. 38–51.

Kumar, A. *Coolies of Empire: Indentured Indians in the Sugar Colonies, 1830–1920* (New Delhi: Cambridge University Press, 2017).

Laclau, E. *New Reflections on the Revolution of Our Time* (London: Verso, 1990).

Lal, B.V. "Kunti's Cry: Indentured Women on Fiji Plantations," *Indian Economic and Social History Review* 22 (1985): 55–71.

Mahese, Radica. "Abolish Indenture' and the Indian Nationalist Discourse in the Early 20th Century," https://www.academia.edu/4094172/ABOLISH_INDENTURE_AND_THE_INDIAN_NATIONALIST_DISCOURSE_IN_THE_EARLY_20TH_CENTURY

Majumdar, Mausomi, ed. *Kahe Gaile Bides? Where Did You Go? On Bhojpuri Migration Since the 1870s and Contemporary Culture in Bihar, Uttar Pradesh, Suriname and the Netherlands* (Amsterdam, NE: KIT Press, 2010).

May, T. *The Political Thought of Jacques Rancière: Creating Equality* (State College, PA: Pennsylvania State University, 2008).

Mishra, M. "The Emergence of Feminism in Fiji," *Women's History Review* 17, no. 1 (2008): 39–55.

Mishra, Vijay. *Writing Indenture Histories through Testimonios and Oral Narratives* (New York: Routledge, 2017).

Misir, Prem, ed. *The Subaltern Indian Woman: Domination and Social Degradation* (London: Palgrave Macmillan, 2018).

Mongia, Radhika. "Impartial Regimes of Truth: Indentured Indian Labor and the Status of Inquiry," *Cultural Studies* 18, no. 5 (2004): 749–68.

Nauriya, Anil. "Representing Indian Toilers in Natal: Some Explorations with Gandhi," *Natalia* 46 (2016): 31–53.

Nijhawan, S. "Fallen through the Nationalist and Feminist Grids of Analysis: Political Campaigning of Indian Women against Indentured Labour Emigration," *Indian Journal of Gender Studies* 20, no. 1 (2014): 111–33.

Oliver, K. *Witnessing: Beyond Recognition* (Minneapolis, MN: University of Minnesota Press, 2001).

Rancière, J. "Ten Theses on Politics," *Theory and Event* 5, no. 3 (2001). https://muse-jhu-edu.proxy.lib.umich.edu/article/32639. Accessed February 13, 2015.

Rancière, J. *Dissensus: On Politics and Aesthetics*. Translated by Steven Corcoran (London: Bloomsbury, 2010).

Ray, K. A. "The Abolition of Indentured Emigration and the Politics of Indian Nationalism, 1894–1917," (Ph.D dissertation, McGill University, 1980).

Ray, K. A. "Kunti, Lakshmibhai and the 'Ladies': Women's Labor and the Abolition of Indentured Emigration from India," *Labour, Capital and Society* 29, no. 1, 2 (April–November 1996): 1226–52.

Ray, K. A. "Marwari Politicization to Counter Village Victimization: The Anti-Indenture Struggle," *Shodhak* 17, no. 8 (1988): 85–92.

Schröer, Frederik, "Of Testimonios and Feeling Communities: Totaram Sanadhya's Account of Indenture," *Südasien-Chronik-South Asia Chronicle* 6 (2016): 149–74.

Sinha, M., "Premonitions of the Past," *Journal of Asian Studies* 74, no. 4 (November 2015): 821–41.

Sinha, M. "Totaram Sanadhya: *Fiji Mein Mere Ekkis Varsh*: A History of Empire and Nation in a Minor Key," in Antoinette Burton and Isabel Hoffmeyr, eds., *Ten Books That Shaped the British Empire: Creating an Imperial Commons* (Durham, NC: Duke University Press, 2014), pp. 168–89.

Tinker, H. *A New System of Slavery: The Export of Indian Labor Overseas, 1830–1920* (London: Hansib, 1993 [1974]).

3

Mass Satyagraha and the Problem of Collective Power

Karuna Mantena

I The Perils and Possibilities of Mass Satyagraha

Gandhi's first attempts at political mobilization against British rule were understood to be experiments in *mass* satyagraha. In his words, "*satyagraha* was being brought into play on a large scale on the political field for the first time."[1] Gandhi had been developing satyagraha as a new style of political action on behalf of Indian migrants in South Africa, and more recently in local campaigns in Champaran, Kheda, and Ahmedabad. By 1919, Gandhi was poised to amplify satyagraha on an unprecedented scale, culminating in the Non-Cooperation/Khilafat Movement (1920–2).

Scaling up was driven by Gandhi's understanding of the political project of swaraj or Indian self-rule. In respect to the goal of swaraj, numerical size mattered tactically, strategically, and morally. Political action, especially disruptive protest, will always prove most potent when large numbers are involved. This has been confirmed especially strongly in the most recent empirical studies of nonviolence. Chenoweth and Stephan's *Why Civil Resistance Works*, for example, argues that what lends nonviolence its political potency is precisely its "participation advantage;" simply put, nonviolence mobilizes significantly more people than armed rebellion.[2] Tactics like noncooperation work by staging mass disaffection, large-scale withdrawal, and nonparticipation, and make visible the illegitimacy of a regime. For Gandhi, mass dissent became the practical demonstration that political power resides in the people's consent.

That nonviolence works via "people power", or a consent theory of power, also gives it a democratic valence.[3] When masses assemble to contest authority, in that very moment they also constitute an alternative *demos*; they seemingly actualize popular sovereignty. Moreover, there was a distinct populism to Gandhi's call for mass satyagraha. In *Hind Swaraj*, he had contended that Indian swaraj was only truly achieved as an analogue to individual swaraj. Swaraj was something that had "to be experienced, by each one for himself."[4] Indian freedom therefore depended on the freedom of the vast majority and the realization of their political agency, which in practice meant the direct action of the rural masses. The ends of such a movement would be a fundamentally village-centered swaraj. This is perhaps the deepest sense of why mass satyagraha was the necessary means to swaraj; it was poised to realize true swaraj, or what Gandhi called "swaraj *in terms of the masses*."[5]

Gandhi thus appeared on the Indian political scene as the champion of direct, popular mass action in a manner than was meant to challenge imperial authority as well as disrupt the existing patterns of elite politics. But almost immediately these experiments in mass satyagraha became imbricated with violence. This ranged from the riots and property destruction of the short-lived Rowlatt Satyagraha to the infamous killing of police constables at Chauri Chaura, which effectively ended the Non-Cooperation movement (hereafter referred to as NCO). In Chauri Chaura, constables, after firing upon NCO protesters, had been chased into the police thana which was then set alight, leaving twenty-three dead. In response, Gandhi announced the immediate cessation of mass civil disobedience and began a five-day fast of purification.

It was an extraordinary moment in the history of popular politics, of a leader calling off a movement at the height of its momentum. Gandhi's decision remains one of the most confounding of a long and contentious political career. For radical activists, it occasioned a real disillusionment with Gandhian politics. But even those closest to Gandhi—like Jawaharlal Nehru—never fully reconciled themselves to Gandhi's reasoning. What neither could fathom was why Gandhi seemed so quick to quell what looked to be a cascading revolution toward independence. After all Gandhi himself had been campaigning on the promise that sustained nationwide mobilization would bring about—as the slogan went—"swaraj in one year."[6]

In this moment, two connected lines of criticism emerged that are still at play in contemporary assessments of Gandhi, and of nonviolent politics. One critique perceives an arbitrary moralism in the heart of Gandhian politics. This involves concerns that the spiritual demands of Gandhian *satyagraha* might work to undermine its political usefulness. The second line of criticism—and the one I focus on in this essay—viewed Gandhi's decision as a denigration of popular agency, the betrayal of mass politics as such. This is a core element of left critique of Gandhian politics, a critique that coalesced in the aftermath of Chauri Chaura. The suspension was seen as a concerted attempt by Gandhi (and the Congress coalition) to reign in a radicalizing mass movement; the plea for nonviolence merely a cover for a conservative and/or reactionary ideology.

In this essay, I focus on how Chauri Chaura shaped Gandhi's evolving understanding of the perils and possibilities of mass satyagraha. I will attend to competing interpretations of NCO and its end to foreground a collision between Gandhian and Marxist models of collective action. Gandhi referred to Chauri Chaura, and more broadly the incidents of violence concomitant with these first experiments in mass satyagraha, as his "Himalayan miscalculations."[7] The need to rethink satyagraha in their wake was so urgent that it would be nearly a decade before Gandhi led another all-India campaign of mass civil disobedience. In this respect, the end of NCO was a crucial moment of reckoning and conceptual clarification, out of which Gandhi refashioned satyagraha itself. I argue that what Gandhi rejected at Chauri Chaura was not mass action as such but forms of action that were premised on the display of collective power. From this angle we see more clearly how unusual satyagraha would be as a model of collective action, one that was disturbed by and suspicious of its collective or corporate nature.

After revisiting the debate on Chauri Chaura, I will explore more fully Gandhi's critique of collective power, especially in its connection to his skepticism of mass democracy. Chauri Chaura revealed to Gandhi that even ostensibly nonviolent mass action could function as a pure demonstration of power. That is, when mass satyagraha relies on numerical superiority to pressure, intimidate, and coerce, it was akin to violence in purpose and effect. Gandhi became deeply concerned that these forms of political action—political action as the demonstration of collective power—would not only be tactically fraught, they portended a false or dangerous swaraj, a kind of freedom that was more akin to domination. From our contemporary vantage point, there is in Gandhi's diagnosis of NCO a prescient attunement to the imbrication of power and freedom in democratic politics, a problem we face perhaps most urgently today in the guise of majoritarianism.

II Satyagraha as Mass Action

The recent renaissance in studies of Gandhi's political thought has positioned Gandhi as a powerful critic of conventional political ideologies and concepts, from liberalism, sovereignty, to democracy. This critical distance is seen to stem partly from the unusual and provocative ways Gandhi's politics were deeply imbricated in ethical and theological frames.[8] In these new engagements, however, there is less focus on reevaluating, or situating Gandhi's ideas within his political campaigns and, more generally, the theory and practice of satyagraha. In my view, Gandhi's significance as a political thinker is closely tied to his understanding of the nature of political action. Hence, I focus on reconstructing Gandhi as an important theorist of mass action, and of satyagraha as a novel form of politics.

In this endeavor, I am tracing the evolution of Gandhi's political thinking over time. It was in the context of ongoing debates with his Congress colleagues, as well as opponents and critics, that we can see Gandhi working out the meaning and structure of nonviolent action. These debates often occurred in moments of political crises, during which Gandhi reflected publicly on the causes of failure and how satyagraha could be improved.

As a theory of action, nonviolence does not imply passivity or a negative turning away from politics. Nor would it be a purely aspirational or exemplary form of politics, in which one is acting "as-if" the ideal world you want to shape already exists. For Gandhi, satyagraha was oriented towards political efficacy; it sought to disrupt and overcome opposition and positively shape political outcomes. A theory of action implies a theory of politics, a set of background assumptions about the nature of political conflict, where the main practical impediments to political change lay, and how they manifest themselves. It then posits a range of action that would be most successful at transforming them to effect progressive change. *Violence* was very often the name that Gandhi gave for a whole series of impediments to constructive politics.

Gandhi's theory of politics hinges on a distinct understanding of the sources of violence and domination. What I have termed Gandhi's *realism* stems from a view of politics as a realm of recurring violence and of political action as a peculiarly hazard-bound activity.[9] I want to suggest that Gandhi understood political action to be a precarious activity wrought with difficulty, always subject to failure, and one that carried within it the potential for violence. The burdens of political action are made more dangerous—action is further subject to escalation, and harder to manage—because political contestation enables and is enabled by negative passions and egoistic dispositions. When left unchecked, the logic of political contestation leads to polarization and enflames feelings of indignation and resentment, which, in turn, feed the temptation towards violence. Provocative or violent tactics would only exacerbate these given political dynamics and dispositions.

Nonviolence, by contrast, would be the correlative force and orientation that seeks to limit and mitigate the negative, affective dynamics of political action. To be sure, there are ethical elements at play here—ideas of moral integrity, self-discipline, and self-mastery. But importantly integrity is tied to a political—that is, a strategic and tactical—account of the efficacy of nonviolent action. Here, the self-disciplining of action, the inward work of satyagraha, is linked to its outward effects that aim to abate recurring obstacles to political change.

These concerns about the negative entailments of political action place Gandhi in interesting proximity to a critical and skeptical strand amongst theorists of action. The problem of action was a central topic of political debate throughout the twentieth century. Indeed, it came to the fore in a new and pressing way in Gandhi's era as a whole range of Marxist, existentialist, progressive, anarchist, and anticolonial thinkers and activists wrestled with the legitimacy and efficacy of new forms of mass political action—such as the boycott, the general strike, etc.—as well as the specific question of the use of violence in politics and revolution. From Tolstoy, Lenin, Sorel, Weber, Gramsci, Trotsky, Dewey, Niebuhr up through Camus to Fanon, important strands of twentieth-century political thinking were centrally concerned with techniques of mass mobilization, questions of popular agency, and their relation to political and social change. Indian nationalist debate was also profoundly shaped by, and often riven apart by, these questions, such as the relationship between political action and social reform and the utility and necessity of exemplary violence. Political action was also the terrain for some of the most generative modern philosophical interpretations of the *The Gita*, and the revisionary reading of karma yoga as detached, worldly action.[10]

Within this broad debate on political action, we can distinguish three guiding concerns about the moral, strategic, and tactical purposes of popular action. A first set of questions revolved around how to bring people into the political sphere. From Gandhi to Lenin, Sorel, and Fanon, radical activists and thinkers were concerned with how to inspire and sustain popular action and argued about which forms of action could work best to recover a person's dignity, autonomy, and agency. A second set of concerns revolved around how popular movements and collective action ought to be organized so as to prefigure and embody the collective ends of popular mobilization, i.e. the future shape of anarchist, socialist, or democratic self-government.

But there also existed a third and often overlooked strand, what I term a skeptical or critical strand. This line of thinking foregrounds the excesses of political action, tendencies toward enthusiasm, hubris, and overextension that could undermine or overwhelm sought-after political ends. This skepticism was most apparent in the voices of critics of violent revolution as the strategy and goal of popular mobilization—such as Tolstoy, Camus, Weber, and Arendt. All of these thinkers, in different ways, like Gandhi, were concerned with the moral psychology of action, of how to reckon with the psychological burdens of unintended consequences, of escalation and polarization.

Marxism and Gandhian satyagraha were comprehensive theories of action; they engaged with, and were implicated in, all three kinds of questions. But the inclusion of a strong skeptical element in Gandhian satyagraha has seemed, especially to his Marxist critics, to be evasive. As noted above, one prominent criticism in the aftermath Chauri Chaura was that though Gandhi seemed to venerate mass popular agency in his call to direct action, in practice, Gandhism involved disciplining it in the negative sense of trying to dampen its revolutionary potential. What I hope to show is that Gandhi's position was less contradictory than it may at first appear, and attending to its seeming duality reveals something distinctive about mass satyagraha as a form of political action.

III Interpreting Chauri Chaura

There are many enduring differences between Gandhism and Marxism, most importantly at the level of ideology. Marxists often presented Gandhian ideas as a loose mix of medievalism and mysticism, which were implicated in conservative and reactionary ideals.[11] Above all, they rejected Gandhism's anti-modern elements—the critique of industrialism and the modern state—and its overtly moral and religious orientation. Alongside this wariness, however, was also consistent praise of Gandhi's populism and emphasis on the necessity of mass action. In R. P. Dutt's words, Gandhi's great feat in NCO was that he "brought before the masses a policy of action, of action of the masses."[12] That is, most Marxists saw Gandhi as capable of being a genuine mass leader and considered his ability to "awaken" the masses to be his unique historical role.

But the suspension of NCO after the events of Chauri Chaura provoked doubts about Gandhi's commitment to mass action. Gandhi's professed aim was to recover the power of action of ordinary people through mass satyagraha. And yet, he seemed to call off the movement just as ordinary people—in this case, the peasants of UP—were realizing their power and beginning to undertake independent action. Marxists, already wary of the moral-religious language of nonviolence, came to suspect that nonviolence was being used as a pretext to constrain popular agency. But to what end? It was in answer to this puzzle that Marxist criticism of Gandhian politics would take on its most characteristic form.[13]

The most prominent line of interpretation, one that coalesced in the immediate aftermath of Chauri Chaura, was inaugurated by M. N. Roy and R. P. Dutt.[14] For both, Gandhi's vacillation stemmed from the class character of his leadership and, more generally, of the Congress coalition. Roy and Dutt differ in their characterization of this class as primarily bourgeois or feudal but what mattered was that, for both, Gandhi and the Congress party were beholden to landed and propertied elites and their interests. In tactical terms, it meant that the national movement had to reign in any popular initiatives that threatened those interests; in effect, they had to disavow mass action that was building towards popular revolution.[15] Marxist critics also differed as to whether this class leadership was intentional—i.e. that Gandhi was insincere and intentionally duplicitous when he mobilized the masses—or objective, a feature of the broad-based nationalist coalition that necessarily included elite classes, which, for strategic reasons, could not be directly attacked. In either case, it implied that Gandhi was willing to encourage mass discontent but only so long as he could direct it from above. This exposed the ideological limitations of the movement, but also made the movement susceptible to political compromise and imperial cooptation since it could not risk a truly revolutionary awakening of the masses.

This general line of criticism has been surprisingly tenacious, and has been recapitulated in comparable terms throughout the twentieth century, as part of both polemical and scholarly evaluation.[16] An important restatement of this criticism can be found Ranajit Guha's seminal essay, "Discipline and Mobilize."[17] In line with the subaltern studies project of revising the historiography of Indian nationalism, Guha foregrounds what he sees as the authoritarian elements in Gandhi's varied attempts to impose discipline and order on mass action. In the essay Guha pulls together wide-ranging evidence of Gandhi's frustration with unruly crowds and mob-like behavior to give substance to this claim. For Guha, Gandhi's repeated displays of aesthetic revulsion of the crowd were signs of elite anxiety and contempt for the spontaneity, immediacy, and autonomy of subaltern agency. What aligns this to the earlier Marxist line of interpretation is that, like Dutt, Guha registers the moral and spiritual language of nonviolence as a form of "soul control,"[18] a way to harness the power of the masses and at the same time to demobilize an awakening mass consciousness.[19] The philosophy of nonviolence serves to keep the masses in a condition of paternalistic subjection, a deeply authoritarian paternalism that is meant, I think, to also throw suspicion on the idea that Gandhi held any serious commitment to popular agency, equality, or democracy.

In this line of criticism Gandhi's decision to suspend NCO is taken to be such an outright contradiction that analytic focus turns toward unearthing implicit ideological commitments. But in trying to pinpoint these underlying causes, these accounts tend to ignore Gandhi's own reasoning for the suspension of NCO. It seems to me that this becomes something of a closed hermeneutic: the assumption and conclusion is that Gandhi's logic had no internal coherence. But attending to Gandhi's understanding of the violence at Chauri Chaura reveals a more immediate, straightforward, and important divergence at play between Marxist and Gandhian models of mass action. Marxist critique of Gandhian politics is premised on a model of mass action as the accretion of collective agency, and popular revolution as the cascading effervescence of that power and energy. Gandhi's formulation of mass satyagraha was always at odds with that model and, in the aftermath of Chauri Chaura, became more explicitly an immanent critique of it.

As we saw, a common feature of Marxist critique—and one especially emphasized in accounts like Guha's—is a view of Gandhi's insistence on discipline in action as the counterpart to a disapproving view of popular initiative and spontaneous agency, and the suggestion that such disavowals were the motivating cause of the suspension of NCO. Though Guha is surely right to note the often paternalistic logic of Gandhi's understanding of, and relationship with, the masses, it is not at all clear that Gandhi diagnosed the violence at Chauri Chaura as a problem of mass psychology or mass indiscipline. For one, Gandhi did not see the violence as either spontaneous or as driven by something like mob frenzy. This becomes more evident when we look at the debate and criticism that ensued in the wake of the suspension of NCO.

The most common critical refrain was that Gandhi was imposing impossibly high standards for mass resistance. Critics contended that outbreaks of popular violence were the expected risks of popular awakening, especially under conditions of colonial repression. In response, Gandhi argued that the issue was not violence per se; in his words, "Violence there always will be, and I should not be perturbed by stray cases of violence."[20] The problem of Chauri Chaura was the specific kind of violence enacted, a violence he characterized as "political violence."[21] Neither unruly crowds nor spontaneous outrage in response of state violence were sufficient grounds for halting the movement. Gandhi noted several instances of violence, including the more serious Malabar Rebellion—known at the time as the Moplah Revolt—that did not interrupt the movement or require atonement. The reason that Chauri Chaura elicited such a severe reaction was that it was *political* in three overlapping senses. Firstly, in the contrast to the violence in Malabar, the event was sparked by public-political activity that was intimately connected with Gandhi and the Congress movement; in terms of ideology, organization, and personnel, the demonstration was openly allied to their political aims. Secondly, the demonstration was *organized* and the violence *foreseeable*, neither the cause nor the intended effect was spontaneous. And, finally, the tactics were political in a third sense, the demonstration that ended in violence was undertaken to cause a political effect through the display of power.

In numerous reflections on his so-called Himalayan "miscalculations" of the period, including the culminating blunder of Chauri Chaura, Gandhi conspicuously emphasized the non-mob-like character of this violence. From the most determined *mea culpa* and to his varied admonishments after violent outbreaks, Gandhi punctuated these meditations with reminders of, and praise for, the capacity of workers and peasants to show restraint in the face of provocation. Moreover, he used this to direct attention to the responsibility of Congress workers, that is, the elite and middle classes for failing to understand the necessity of discipline for satyagraha. That is, in Gandhi's view, Congress demonstrations, instead of displaying a strength and courage borne of self-constraint and self-mastery, became occasions for the testing and display of a newly found and threatening power. In correspondence with Nehru, Gandhi noted that with the success of NCO as a movement, "our people were becoming aggressive, defiant and threatening."[22] At Chauri Chaura, this was evident in the purpose of the demonstration. It was intended to stage a particular kind of confrontation and, in that sense, the violence that erupted was a foreseeable, perhaps even desired end. The political procession—led and organized by Congress volunteers—was purposely taken in the direction of the police station, knowing full well that it would instigate a collision between the police and the people. That is, the violence followed from a structure of protest that was meant to demonstrate power and provoke a response.

In this sense, Gandhi's reckoning of Chauri Chaura was neither simply a display of moral outrage with a violence with which he felt himself complicit, nor an aesthetic revulsion of unruly, mob behavior but rather the "discovery that very few understand the nature of non-violence." What he saw at Chauri Chaura was the intimation of a seductive sense of power and an idea that displays of power can be politically effective. In a long and particularly revealing letter to Konda Venkatappayya—the leader of the provincial Andhra Congress and the only officially sanctioned no-tax campaign of NCO—Gandhi argued that in Chauri Chaura, as well as previous events in Bombay and Madras, Congress workers showed that they "liked and loved excitement, and underneath these vast demonstrations was an idea unconsciously lurking in the breast that it was a kind of demonstration of force, the very negation of non-violence."[23] In correspondence with Nehru, Gandhi reiterated this concern when he spoke of how NCO demonstrations had everywhere become ever more "politically minded."[24] They capitalized on "a vague sense of political wrong" to show strength through acts of intimidation.[25]

To be sure, in these outbursts of violence there were issues of popular discipline at play. And, of course, the emphasis on discipline was a recurrent chorus of all of Gandhi's speeches and writing. But here the source of indiscipline was tied to a conceptual confusion of strength with displays of force, especially in terms of the power of large numbers. To Gandhi, this underscored not a lack of spiritual resolve but a mistaken understanding of the political logic of nonviolence. The aim of nonviolence as a form of politics was to persuade the opposition rather than to coerce or force it into compliance. The confusion of nonviolent strength with force and provocation demonstrated that "the workers did not understand the full purpose of non-violence nor its implications."[26] They seemed "to believe that violence can run parallel to non-violence and the two together accelerate the progress of the country towards its goal."[27] With this mistaken understanding, what workers seemed to want was "to deliver 'non-violent' blows" and through a "show of force" win swaraj.[28]

At issue then was the very purpose and logic of nonviolent action, of how nonviolence is supposed to do its political work. R. P. Dutt was closer to the mark when he noted that throughout the NCO movement rival understandings of the purpose and form of effective mass action were at play. Gandhi envisioned mass satyagraha to be a form of noncoercive persuasion—a "spiritual" weapon and argument—whereas Marxists understood that NCO was primarily "a question of *power*" and its "whole political importance" was "the attempt to *force* the Government to submit, by the use of the power of the united action of the masses."[29] Dutt did not feel the need to elaborate this distinction, for he viewed Gandhi's alternative reasoning to be disingenuous and confused. But as I have tried to show, these differences did not simply turn on the morality of violence nor were they symptoms of ideological divergence. What looked like moralism or confusion was in fact a dispute about how mass action worked as a lever of political change. For Dutt, for Marxist theories of collective action more generally, and—more surprisingly—for most contemporary advocates of nonviolence, the logic of mass political action is understood to work as the assertion of a nonviolent but nevertheless coercive collective power.[30] For Gandhi, by contrast, nonviolent persuasion—especially in its mass form—works through the disruptive dramatization of discipline and self-mastery. The performative dynamics of discipline distinguish the logic of nonviolence from *both* the pure violence of armed rebellion as well as the "nonviolent coercion" at work in collective power.

Chauri Chaura forced a clarification of the logic of mass satyagraha, of how to retool satyagraha in such a way as to avoid the generation and implications of collective power. Before outlining some aspects of this retooling, I want to explore the nature of Gandhi's critique about collective power. Collective power was associated with a particular moral psychology; the excitement of action was linked to the experience of acting in numbers. Mass action in this sense was bred by a collective egoism, a moral hubris grounded in a sense of corporate power—we might even say a democratic conception of power. Gandhi's worries about collective power track well his better-known critique of mass democracy. In addition to strategic and tactical concerns about the efficacy of coercive collective power, as crucial were moral and political conundrums about freedom's potential affiliation with mastery.

IV Gandhi's Critique of Collective Power

One of the earliest sources of Gandhi's critical account of collective or corporate power can be discerned in his well-known aversion to mass democracy. My contention is that there are instructive analogies between the critique of mass democracy and the critique of mass action. In his critique of mass democracy, Gandhi was participating in a radically individualist strand of nineteenth-century thought, which included thinkers and interlocutors he most admired such as Thoreau, Emerson, Tolstoy, and Tagore.[31] All of them worried about the effects of modern politics—and the principle of majority rule therein—on individuality. One overarching concern was the threat posed by conformity to moral integrity. This threat could take the form, as Gandhi expressed in *Hind Swaraj*, of unreflective deference to public opinion at the expense of genuine public spiritedness and right judgement.[32] Majority rule held no special moral standing and might even work to confuse questions of moral right. This was majority opinion as "brute force,"[33] where the power of numbers imposes a kind of false truth. Gandhi therefore would insist that "in matters of conscience, the Law of Majority had no place."[34]

When modern political institutions engendered conformity they exemplified a general problem of external imposition, of how institutions come to impinge upon moral conscience and hinder the possibility of self-realizing truth. Gandhi's model of self-mastery praised internally generated action as an answer to externally imposed forms—from practices of social boycott to the very structures of legitimation of the modern state and law. Here, we may also add, Gandhi also viewed egoistic attachment as functioning as an extrinsic force that compromised the integrity of the self.

Most alarmingly, the coercive implications of majority rule were becoming exacerbated in the age of mass democracy, which bestowed a new authority to the power of numbers. The democratic celebration of majority-rule legitimates and puts into play a new kind of power politics, a new and dangerous logic of "might over right."[35] As we know, in the colonial world, the numbers game became a central and particularly fraught political logic. The moral claim to popular rule became seductively entwined with the demographic superiority of numbers, pitting groups against one another in an open competition for power. In our own time, we are beginning to recognize that this is a recurring feature of modern democracy. Democratic claims necessarily braid moral-ethical claims to legitimacy with claims to power, and it is that mingling that makes them especially hard to restrain. In plural societies especially, this dual logic becomes a recipe for majoritarian assertion and minority vulnerability.

Gandhi was remarkably prescient in his attunement to the dangers of majoritarianism in India. This was especially prominent in the ways in which he conceptualized Hindu-Muslim conflict and the mechanisms for mitigating it. He laid emphasis on legitimate Muslim fear of Hindu dominance in a future swaraj government and therefore insisted that it was incumbent upon Hindus as the numerically advantaged community to actively work to mitigate these fears. Gandhi also discerned the majoritarian turn at Chauri Chaura, as a claim to power within the context of protest. The democratic logic of numbers imbues collective protest with a double logic of enacting democratic sovereignty—the greater the crowds the closer you concretize popular will—as well as asserting sheer power.

The conjoined critique of collective power and of mass democracy never implied the abandonment of democracy, nor was it inherently elitist in orientation. Gandhi accepted the principle of majority rule, even parliamentary government, as the basic frame of a swaraj government. Moreover, in his ideal version of a decentralized village democracy, universal suffrage was the rule.[36] As a decision rule, Gandhi considered "the principle of majority rule" to be just and necessary in "ordinary matters;" it was "justice as the world understands justice."[37] To be sure, Gandhi was attuned to the potential for ignoring the interests of the politically weak, and so suggested that a government that was "perfectly democratic" would look beyond "the rule of the majority" and protect "the interests of even the smallest limb of the realm."[38] There was always a "subtle violence implicit in the very fact of a majority."[39] The real danger was when this latent coercion becomes overt assertion, when empowered majorities become intolerant of minority interests. "Swaraj necessarily means the rule of the majority. If, however, a large mass of people get more power and misuse their increased power, that will not be swaraj, that will be oppression or tyranny."[40]

Gandhi understood majoritarianism as a problem of moral psychology to be related less to conformity than the temptations of power. He feared that "in the consciousness of strength we are daily acquiring," lay a risk of repeating "the mistakes of the rulers in an exaggerated form in our relations with those who happen to be weaker."[41] Indeed, it would lead to "a worse state" than British rule. The danger was of awakening a kind of political freedom that in overcoming slavery instantaneously reveled in mastery, hence becoming a form of domination.

British rule was a minority rule, the rule of a "bureaucratic" minority, and as such required coercion to secure the obedience of the many. But Indian tyranny would be a "terrorism imposed by a majority,"[42] its coercion would be of a wholly excessive kind. For Gandhi, NCO was marred by instances in which noncooperators sought to impose their views on "cooperators"—by forcing people to wear khadi caps, forcibly shuttering foreign cloth and liquor shops, or imposing social boycott. Chauri Chaura was a stark illustration of this intolerance, stemming from an eagerness to demonstrate power. In the aftermath of NCO, Gandhi began to insist that this was the greatest obstacle to attaining swaraj. No longer a problem of British power, true swaraj had to forestall the internal aspiration to unconstrained power. He noted this problem in relation to communal tensions but also in relationship to the caste question. Gandhi's refrain was that if caste Hindus "came into power, with the stain of untouchability unfazed, I am positive that the untouchables would be far worse under that 'swaraj' than they are now, for the simple reason that our weakness and our failings would then be buttressed by the accession of power."[43] A Hindu majority would feel morally justified by the logic of democracy to impose its will on others.

Again, Gandhi's worry is different from an anxiety about mob frenzy. It was aimed at the self-certainty brought on by feelings of power, and in this respect, is closer to what Reinhold Niebuhr called collective or group egoism. Collective egoism was most dangerous when its claim to power is tethered to a sense of moral altruism or rectitude. This overlap in the analysis of group egoism in collective conflict is what made Niebuhr one of Gandhi's earliest interpreters.[44] One of Niebuhr's great insights was how group egoism was itself premised on a paradoxical melding of altruism and selfishness. Collectives allow a distinct opportunity for self-denial, i.e. in the willingness to sacrifice for the group, but this self-denial is tied to an egoism on a larger scale. Patriotism is the most vivid example of the transmutation of individual unselfishness into collective egoism, an egoism whose fervor yields dangerous forms of self-delusion, which in turn enable unconstrained politics. While Niebuhr had in mind racism, nationalism, and imperialism as his examples of collective egoism, we might now want to add to that list the problem of democratic majoritarianism, which also uneasily veils its claims of power with moral ideals.[45]

My reading of Chauri Chaura as a problem of collective power, and majority rule, aligns with the emerging consensus amongst scholars of Gandhi who present him as a champion of the minority. The idea of the minority is also connected in interesting ways to alternative visions of freedom, especially nonsovereign models of agency that try to undo the association of freedom with mastery. Uday Mehta, for example, has powerfully argued that Gandhi fundamentally rejected the category of "the people" as a collective moral and political agent. Faisal Devji has articulated this worry about sovereignty in Gandhi's interest in the minority as the pure agent of nonviolence, where the majority represents tendencies towards domination. With similar resonance, Ramin Jahanbegloo associates nonviolence with a plural or shared sovereignty in contrast to unitary sovereignty. Dustin Howes also formulates the grounds of a nonviolent conception of freedom, for the uncoupling of freedom from violence, through an ambitious re-reading of narratives of liberation in the Western political tradition. Finally, Ajay Skaria's work disrupts the traditional figure of freedom as the sovereign warrior by contrasting the warrior's self-mastery with that of the satyagrahi's. The satyagrahi, like the warrior, overcomes fear through the display of self-discipline but also enacts *abhaydan*, the gift of fearlessness.[46]

Satyagraha as Disciplined Action

If I have a quibble with these subtle and persuasive philosophical accounts of Gandhian nonviolence is that they tend to stop short of describing what these intimations of nonsovereign freedom looked like in the context of political action. Gandhi was primarily driven by the question of how to translate ideas into practical action. Indeed, it might be more accurate to say he strove to experiment in the sphere of action. Given Gandhi's suspicion of collective power—the worry that an orientation towards dominance seemed conjoined with its expression—the challenge was to recalibrate mass satyagraha so as to mitigate these troubling aspects. The period between Chauri Chaura and the Salt Satyagraha can be seen as a moment of satyagraha's reformulation. Gandhi would continue to defend the controversial Bardoli decision to call off aggressive civil disobedience in the near term. It was in part the very success of NCO that had shifted the tasks of the national movement. NCO was meant to bring people into consciousness of their individual power and to break the hypnotic hold of British authority. Even if the program of total withdrawal was never fully realized, for Gandhi, NCO was nevertheless successful in both these tasks, in teaching people to realize agency and to call into question the government's legitimacy. But the problem was—as suggested in the previous section—the consciousness of power as agency had become aligned to the assertion of power as mastery, and it was this braiding that Gandhi needed to disrupt. Power once recovered had to be properly organized and, most importantly, disciplined. Only through disciplined shows of strength would the power of the nonviolent action be realized.

To repeat, Gandhi's challenge was to develop forms of collective action that could temper collective egoism and, at the same time, be effective without relying upon sheer force. The key mechanism of self-limitation was *tapasya* or disciplined suffering.[47] In *Satyagraha in South Africa*, which was written in this period as an object lesson in the kind of patience and discipline needed for successful satyagraha, Gandhi described satyagraha as "a force containing within itself seeds of progressive self-restraint."[48] The idea of self-suffering in satyagraha is often associated with the paradigm of sacrifice, and conjures up images of extreme self-abnegation like the fast unto death. But suffering in Gandhi's conception of it was less concerned with physical distress per se but something more along the lines of self-discipline in action. Moreover, in conceptual terms, *discipline* more readily conveys important aspects of self-constraint

Sacrifice was for Gandhi a much more fraught political practice. It was by nature double-edged, it could easily take more negative, egoistic, vain forms. This was the case with the violent revolutionary as much as the ill-advised hunger striker.[49] The problem of the patriotic sacrifice is that though it is selfless in form it is often tied to an unconscious desire to display one's commitment and, at worst, to garner fame. In the context of political conflict, its consequences are also double-edged; while they may show commitment, they also escalate conflict. Moreover, sacrifice and self-denial when tied to and subsumed by patriotism and sovereignty become vehicles for the accretion of power—a point made eloquently and differently by Uday Mehta and Ajay

Skaria.[50] For Mehta this is the basic paradigm of modern politics, part of its "inherent idealism," in which all action is subsumed by and only given meaning in terms of greater purposes.[51] For Skaria this is part of the paradox of the self-mastery, especially in the form of the sovereign warrior.[52] Sacrifice can convey a mastery deeply tied to moral self-certainty which is what makes the politics its drives hard to contain. By contrast, Gandhian politics more consistently aims for a discipline that can moderate the compulsions of collective political mobilization.

This is why I argue that discipline is the defining feature of satyagraha and the orientation towards "progressive self-restraint" becomes especially central in mass satyagraha. Moreover, discipline is something that needed to be built into the very structure of nonviolent protest; practices of self-discipline and ascetic self-mastery are *staged* in mass nonviolent protest and action. The dramatization of *tapasya* was vital to its success as nonviolent protest. Comportment and discipline also appeared to serve a second function, one especially crucial in mass satyagraha, namely, the reinsertion of individuation into the dynamics of mass action. Mass satyagraha would then function not through the power of numbers per se but by the coordinated activity of disciplined individuals whose individuality would be maintained and expressed in their comportment and detachment. If mass action could be given such an individuating structure, it would neither depend on nor incite collective egoism.

Arguably, the best exemplification of the centrality of discipline—in the organization of action and the bearing of satyagrahis—would be the Salt Satyagraha, Gandhi's next major campaign of mass disobedience and the campaign that garnered global acclaim. The tight scripting of the campaign from the ritualized discipline of the salt march to the escalation following Gandhi's arrest became the exemplary model in the global diffusion of nonviolent action. In the early phase of global adoption, in the antinuclear campaigns in UK to the US civil rights movement, nonviolent discipline were likewise dramatized and staged in directed actions like sit-ins, marches, and freedom rides.

Before the famous renewal of mass civil disobedience, in the interregnum between NCO and the Salt Satyagraha, Gandhi also pushed for another kind of disciplined satyagraha in the form of the constructive program. In its own way, constructive satyagraha was also a response to the dilemmas of mass action and the problem of collective power as they appeared in the aftermath of NCO. The constructive program would eventually become a permanent campaign of rural reform and rejuvenation. Its central pillars would be Hindu-Muslim unity, the eradication of untouchability, as well as various campaigns for promoting literacy, hygiene, and temperance. For Gandhi, the *ends* of nonviolent action—the moral, tactical, and strategic ends—had to be built into and expressed via the *means* of nonviolent action. If the goal is true swaraj—a swaraj that did not end in majoritarian tyranny—the intertwining of means and ends meant that satyagraha had to model a different horizon of democracy, one in which toleration, equality, and the defense of the weakest would be central.[53] The constructive program's focus on identification with the poor and excluded was precisely a way of cultivating these moral values, most radically entailed in Gandhi's call for educated, urban, elite Congress workers to go to the villages and take up the work of service.

Constructive satyagraha was the mode by which Gandhi sought to privilege internal reform rather than resistance to British power as the main fulcrum of national political activity. For Gandhi, what looked like a social program was necessarily political. It simultaneously built the collective capacity for self-rule by its power of self-organizing and its determination to solve the most pressing social and economic issues of the day. Gandhi argued that if the movement could neither model democratic values in its political action, nor begin to make self-rule a reality through the enactment of genuine social change, then it was not deserving of swaraj. Finally, the "silent work of construction" was contrasted to the exuberant assemblies and protests as better training in and for politics. Service cultivated patience; the day-to-day focus of practical work was to "steady and calm us" and counteract cycles of enthusiasm and despair, hope, and disappointment.[54]

Above all else, khadi and the practice of spinning were the symbolic and material heart of the constructive programme. It was right after his release from jail in 1924, that Gandhi begins his most expansive and relentless push for khadi. Famously, Gandhi partially implemented and then withdrew a strict khadi franchise in Congress, which in its most expansive form made spinning the basis of membership and, most controversially, a prerequisite for office-holding in Congress. The failure led to the eventual creation of the All-India Spinning Association (AISA). Khadi was important for its "universal" quality, for promoting the identification of rich and poor, undoing privilege, and the problem of rural poverty. Moreover, spinning was the practice that best modeled the discipline of an inward-directed practice. But khadi was also an example of individuation within the context of mass collective action, maybe even Gandhi's ideal model of dispersed, individuated-collected action. Recall, the khadi system was a large-scale, decentralized system of cooperative cloth production. It was a mode of cooperation that was collective in nature but also premised on the patient work of radically *isolated* individuals, where each individual—in the act of spinning—would separately cultivate inward discipline, let go of egoism, calm their passion, and experience a kind of individual self-rule.[55]

Disciplined conduct and individuated comportment would become core features of Gandhian nonviolence in its classic mold, displayed in the ritualized form of the directed campaign, or the slow march, or strike. Here silence, calmness, slowness, and repetition over time might be usefully contrasted to crowds gathering in public spaces more readily associated with collective nonviolence today. Over the course of his long career and evident in his writings, Gandhi devised a set of rules of nonviolent action, for how specific actions like pickets and hartals could be organized so as to avoid coercion. These rules of action register how discipline is to be performed. Rules reconcile what often appear to be nonviolence's exacting ethical demands with Gandhi's insistence that satyagraha did not require "saints for its working."[56] That is, rather than thinking of discipline as a prior condition of action—or a set of virtues cultivated outside political action—we can conceive of discipline as cultivated in and through specific forms of nonviolent action. Gandhi's expectation was not that everyone had to be pure in order to act or had to adopt nonviolence as a creed as he had, but that people consistently "carry out the rules of non-violent action."[57]

The Politics of Nonviolence Today

In a 1936 meeting with the African-American theologian Howard Thurman, Gandhi famously suggested that "it may be through the Negroes that the unadulterated message of nonviolence will be delivered to the world."[58] He implied that only minority movements could offer a pure demonstration of nonviolence since majoritarian movements—like the anticolonial movement in India—would always be "adulterated" in the sense that their seeming success may be attributable more to collective power than disciplined satyagraha. The basic conceptual confusion Gandhi identified between mass satyagraha as the assertion of power versus mass satyagraha as the public display of self-mastery was neither resolved nor clarified within the nationalist movement. On the one hand, in memorializing the independence struggle, it became common to pay lip service to Gandhian nonviolence and, in the same breadth, celebrate the revolutionary violence of Bhagat Singh or Subhas Chandra Bose and the Indian National Army. (More recently and most alarmingly, the pantheon has been extended to include Gandhi's assassins.) The veneration of martyrs as well as the more violent episodes is indicative of the fact that there existed no clear disavowal of violence, let alone a reckoning with the coercion of nonviolent forms of political action.

On the other hand, in a kind of inverse mirror, there were concerns expressed about the place of satyagraha in independent India, warnings that mass protest would undermine the moral and political habits needed to sustain India's precarious experiment with democracy. This was Ambedkar's famous admonition that the "method of civil disobedience, non-cooperation and satyagraha" was the "Grammar of Anarchy" and must be abandoned in favor of constitutional methods.[59] Indeed, some of Gandhi's closest comrades, from Vallabhbhai Patel, Vinoba Bhave, and later Nehru, similarly worried that the resort to mass disobedience in everyday politics was a dangerous legacy of the independence movement.[60] This uneasiness was echoed more recently in the debate about Anna Hazare's hunger strikes during the India Against Corruption campaign. Many public intellectuals highlighted the coercive character of ostensibly nonviolent tactics—like the fast unto death—and argued that their use threatened democratic institutions.[61]

I want to suggest that all of these views are symptomatic of the conceptual confusion between the two ways to view mass satyagraha I have been exploring. It is a slippage that makes visible a central puzzle about contemporary Indian politics. Gandhian forms of action—the political fast, the hartal (a work stoppage), etc.—have been persistent features of Indian politics, practiced by politicians and activists across the ideological spectrum. But the recourse to forms of political action whose semiotic reference is Gandhi is coupled with a lack of clarity in what would define these practices as Gandhian in a conceptual sense. I tried to show that in his own time Gandhi took great pains to distinguish between nonviolent forms of protest and coercive forms, and insisted that any action—even ostensibly nonviolent action—could become coercive depending on the context within which it was enacted. But these distinctions often appeared to critics as sophistries.

Instead, the wider contestation over who or what Gandhi represents tends to overdetermine questions about the nature and specificity of nonviolent action. Most often *satyagraha* and nonviolence are taken as symptoms of Gandhian ideology, his underlying philosophy, or deeper political commitments. For critics from the left, as we have seen, nonviolence cannot be disentangled from these ideological commitments and is seen to be aligned to a conservative and/or reactionary agenda. For the right, nonviolence is equally compromised but more often as a deeply enervated and/or emasculated nationalism. But even defenders of Gandhi tend to tie nonviolence very tightly to Gandhian philosophy, for instance, insisting that nonviolence is best practiced as a way of life which can only be disfigured when treated as political tactic.

Gandhian satyagraha offered an alternative to cascading models of revolution. The need for such alternatives might be even more urgent for democratic politics. In democracy, political antagonists are also recalcitrant fellow citizens, with whom one has to find a means of coexisting in peace. Gandhi's emphasis on discipline and individuation, and more generally the attempt to formulate rules and models of action, was meant to navigate the demanding path of political persuasion, a project that has only become more vital today.

Notes

1 M.K. Gandhi, "The Duty of Satyagrahis (6-7-1919)," *The Collected Works of Mahatma Gandhi*, vol. 18: 183. References to *The Collected Works of Mahatma Gandhi* (Electronic Book), 98 vols. (New Delhi, 1999) and are cited hereafter as *CWMG*, followed by volume and page number.

2 Erica Chenoweth and Maria J. Stephan's, *Why Civil Resistance Works: The Strategic Logic of Nonviolent Conflict* (New York: Columbia University Press, 2011), pp. 3–61.

3 On nonviolence and a consent theory of power, see Dustin Ells Howes, "The Failure of Pacifism and the Success of Nonviolence," *Perspectives on Politics* 11, no. 2 (June 2013) and Gene Sharp, *The Politics of Nonviolent Action, vol. 1* (Boston: Sargent, 1973), pp. 10–16. It is also referred to as a social theory of power or the "pluralistic" view of power. On the association of nonviolence with democracy, see Jonathan Schell, *The Unconquerable World: Power, Nonviolence, and the Will of the People* (New York: Metropolitan Books, 2003).

4 M.K. Gandhi, *Hind Swaraj*, *CWMG* 10: 282.

5 M. K. Gandhi, "In Fulfilment of Promise (24-7-1924)," *Young India*, *CWMG* 28: 345. Italics in original. Also M. K. Gandhi, "Speech at Meeting of Deccan Princes (28-7-1946)," *CWMG* 91 (1946): 372.

6 M. K. Gandhi, "Swaraj in One Year (22-9-1920)," *Young India*, *CWMG* 21 (1920): 278–81.

7 See M.K. Gandhi, "Speech at Mass Meeting, Ahmedabad (14-04-1919)," *CWMG* 17 (1918–19): 420–4; "The Duty of Satyagrahis," pp. 182–5; "Gandhi Old and New (4-05-1920)," *CWMG* 23 (1921): 112–13; "A Confession of Error (18-08-1921)," *CWMG* 24 (1921): 109–12; "The Crime of Chauri Chaura (16-02-1922)," *CWMG* 26 (1922–23): 177–82; "A Revolutionary's Defence (12-02-1925)," *CWMG* 30 (1924–25): 243–9; "Notes (10-09- 1925)," *CWMG* 32 (1925): 390; "The Truth is One (24-04-1927)," *CWMG* 38 (1927): 295–6; "A Himalayan Miscalculation," *The Story of My Experiments with Truth*, *CWMG* 44 (1929): 441–2.

8 Akeel Bilgrami, *Secularism, Identity, and Enchantment* (Cambridge, MA: Harvard, 2014); Faisal Devji, "Morality in the Shadow of Politics," *Modern Intellectual History* 7, no. 2 (2010): 373–90; Faisal Devji, *The Impossible Indian: Gandhi and the Temptations of Violence* (Cambridge, MA: Harvard University Press, 2012); Leela Gandhi, *The Common Cause: Postcolonial Ethics and the Practice of Democracy* (Chicago: University of Chicago Press, 2014); Farah Godrej, "Ascetics, Warriors, and a Gandhian Ecological Citizenship," *Political Theory* 40, no. 4 (2012): 437–65; "Gandhi, Foucault, and the Politics of Self-Care," *Theory & Event* 20, no. 4 (2017): 894–922; Ashwary Kumar, *Radical Equality: Ambedkar, Gandhi, and the Risk of Democracy* (Palo Alto: Stanford, 2015); Uday Mehta, "Gandhi on Democracy, Politics, and the Ethics of Everyday Life," *Modern Intellectual History* 7, no. 2 (2010): 355–71; Uday Mehta, "Gandhi and the Common Logic of War and Peace," *Raritan* 30, no. 1 (Summer 2010): 134–56; Uday Mehta, "Gandhi and the Burden of Civility," *Raritan* 33, no. 1 (Summer 2013): 37–49; Ajay Skaria, "Gandhi's Politics: Liberalism and the Question of the Ashram," *The South Atlantic Quarterly* 101, no. 4 (2002): 955–86; "Relinquishing Republican Democracy: Gandhi's *Ramrajya*," *Postcolonial Studies* 14, no. 2 (2011): 203–29; Ajay Skaria, *Unconditional Equality: Gandhi's Religion of Resistance* (Minneapolis: University of Minnesota Press, 2016).

9 K. Mantena, "Another Realism: Gandhi and the Politics of Nonviolence," *American Political Science Review* 106, no. 2 (2012): 455–70.

10 Nagappa Gowda, *The Bhagavadgita in the Nationalist Discourse* (New Delhi: Oxford University Press, 2011); Shruti Kapila and Faisal Devji, eds., *Political Thought in Action: The Bhagavad Gita and Modern India*; Sanjay Palshikar, *Evil and the Philosophy of Retribution: Modern Commentaries on the Gita* (London: Routledge, 2014).

11 S. G. Sardesai, "Gandhi and the CPI," in M. B. Rao, ed., *The Mahatma: A Marxist Symposium* (New Delhi: People's Publishing House, 1969).

12 R. Palme Dutt, *Modern India* (Communist Party of Great Britain, 1927), p. 72.

13 Subrata Mukherjee, *Marxist Interpretations of Gandhi* (PhD Thesis, Indiana University, 1976); M. B. Rao, ed., *The Mahatma: A Marxist Symposium*.

14 M. N. Roy, *India in Transition* and "Mahatmaji and Bolshevism"; Dutt, *Modern India*.

15 In this case, the main evidence for the claim was the substance of the Bardoli resolution that ended NCO which emphasized the necessity of revenue payment to landlords. Dutt analyzes these Bardoli clauses in detail. Dutt, *Modern India*, pp. 75–80.

16 For a recent endorsement of the thesis, see Perry Anderson, *The Indian Ideology* (Delhi, 2015). For a longer history, see especially Mukherjee, *Marxist Interpretations of Gandhi*. There have been a few notable exceptions to this consensus. S.A. Dange's *Gandhi vs Lenin* (1921), perhaps the earliest comparison of Marxism and Gandhism, assessed with subtlety the potentialities of NCO as a novel form of mass mobilization that targeted the ideology of state authority. Consider also Philip Spratt's 1939 work, *Gandhism: An Analysis*, which explicitly disputed the Marxist account of Gandhi's condemnation of the events of Chauri Chaura as driven by the need to placate the zamindars of UP. Indeed, Spratt went so far as to argue that the policy of nonviolence was more realistic than revolution under Indian conditions. Finally, Partha Chatterjee's tour-de-force chapter on Gandhi characterizes his leadership as the "the moment of manoeuvre," of genuine popular awakening, in *Nationalist Thought and the Colonial World: A Derivative Discourse?* (Minneapolis: University of Minnesota Press, 1993), Chapter 4.

17 Ranajit Guha, "Discipline and Mobilize: Hegemony and Elite Control in Nationalist Campaigns," in *Dominance without Hegemony: History and Power in Colonial India* (Princeton, 1998), pp. 100–51.

18 Ibid., pp. 143–50.

19 Shahid Amin's important exploration of the varied, rival accounts of Chauri Chaura and its political meaning approvingly cites Guha on the ugliness of Gandhi's disdain for the mob. He likewise highlights Gandhi's obsessive emphasis on the need for discipline and organization but does not read it as a strategy of demobilization as much as one of attempted control. Here Amin aligns himself with Partha Chatterjee's assessment that the question of discipline emerged out of the practical exigencies of organizing a national movement. Chatterjee views Gandhism as having incorporated contradictory elements but nevertheless a genuine moment of popular mobilization. Shahid Amin, *Event, Metaphor, Memory: Chauri Chaura 1922–1992* (London: Oxford University Press, 1995); Chatterjee, *Nationalist Thought and the Colonial World.*

20 M. K. Gandhi, "Interview to 'The Bombay Chronicle' (15-2-1922)," *CWMG* 26: 169.

21 "It is political violence which *must* stop civil disobedience." M. K. Gandhi, "Notes (9-3-1922)," *CWMG* 26: 299. On this point, see also Amin, *Event, Metaphor, Memory*, pp. 49–50.

22 M. K. Gandhi, "Letter to Jawaharlal Nehru (19-2-1922)," *CWMG* 26: 197.

23 M. K. Gandhi, "Letter to Konda Venkatappayya (4-3-1922)," *CWMG* 26: 271.

24 Gandhi, "Letter to Nehru," 26, 196.

25 Gandhi, "Interview to 'The Bombay Chronicle'," 26, 169.

26 Gandhi, "Letter to Venkatappayya," 26, 270.

27 M. K. Gandhi, "Violence in the Camp (9-2-1922)," *Young India, CWMG* 26: 134.

28 M. K. Gandhi, "The All-India Congress Committee (2-3-1922)," *Young India, CWMG* 26: 261–2.

29 Dutt, *Modern India*, p. 73.

30 I critically explore contemporary invocations of nonviolence as collective power in Karuna Mantena, "Competing Theories of Nonviolent Politics," in Melissa Schwartzberg, ed., *Protest and Dissent: NOMOS LXII* (New York: New York University Press, 2020), Chapter 4.

31 Perhaps best characterized as a Romantic liberal strand. Marxists like Dange and Spratt were quick to pick up on this individualist aspect of Gandhi. Dange linked it to Tolstoy, while Spratt implied an affiliation to bourgeois individualism. Dange, *Gandhi vs Lenin*; Spratt, *Gandhism*.

32 M. K. Gandhi, *Hind Swaraj* (1909 in Gujarati/1910 in English), *CWMG* 10: 255–8.

33 "Europe, which we are so impatient to imitate, also worships brute force or, which is the same thing, majority opinion, and the majority, surely, does not always look after the interests of the minority." M. K. Gandhi, "Insanity (30-5-1920)," *Navajivan, CWMG* 20: 375.

34 M. K. Gandhi, "The Congress and Non-Co-Operation (4-8-1920)," *Young India, CWMG* 21: 114.

35 The idea of "might over right" is echoed in Thoreau's essay, "Resistance to Civil Government" where he argues that in popular government "the practical reason the majority are permitted, and for a long period continue, to rule, is not because they are most likely to be in the right, nor because this seems fairest to the minority, but because physically they are the strongest."

36 Strikingly, his two conditions to qualify for suffrage was a specific age qualification (between 18–50) and the bread labor principle. Neither of these, especially the latter, can easily be cast as elitist.

37 Gandhi, "Insanity," 20, 375. See also Ajay Skaria's discussion in "Relinquishing Republican Democracy: Gandhi's *Ramrajya*," *Postcolonial Studies* 14, no. 2 (2011): 203–29.

38 Gandhi, "Insanity," 20, 375.
39 M. K. Gandhi, "My Notes (29-1-1922)," *Navajivan, CWMG* 26: 37.
40 M. K. Gandhi, " (2-2-1922)," *Navajivan, CWMG* 26: 45.
41 M. K. Gandhi, "Fraught with Danger (26-1-1922)," *Young India, CWMG* 26: 15.
42 M. K. Gandhi, "The Secret of It (27-10-1921)," *Young India, CWMG* 25: 12.
43 M. K. Gandhi, "Speech at Ahmedabad (2-8-1931)," *CWMG* 53: 168.
44 Reinhold Niebuhr, *Moral Man and Immoral Society: A Study in Ethics and Politics* (New York: Harvard University Press, 1932).
45 Ibid., especially Chapter 4.
46 See Uday Mehta, "Gandhi on Democracy, Politics, and the Ethics of Everyday Life." Faisal Devji, *The Impossible Indian*; Ramin Jahanbegloo, *The Gandhian Moment* (Cambridge: Harvard University Press, 2013); Dustin Howes, *Freedom without Violence: Resisting the Western Political Tradition* (Oxford, 2016); Ajay Skaria, *Unconditional Equality*.
47 The term *tapas* or *tapasya* was variously translated by Gandhi as "self-discipline," "self-suffering," "voluntary suffering," or "sacrifice." It was also translated as "power." See M. K. Gandhi, "Speech on Non-Co-Operation, Calcutta (22-12-1920)," *Young India, CWMG* 20: 89.
48 M. K. Gandhi, "Satyagraha in South Africa," *CWMG* 34 (1925): 174.
49 On the "false exultation" of the revolutionary's sacrifice, see M. K. Gandhi, "A Revolutionary's Defence (12-2-1925)," *Young India, CWMG* 30: 249.
50 This point is also echoed in Niebuhr, Moral Man, and Immoral Society.
51 Mehta, especially 363–9.
52 Skaria, *Unconditional Equality*.
53 Gandhi, "Insanity," 20, 375; M. K. Gandhi, "Definitions of Swaraj (14-8-1921)," *Navajivan, CWMG* 24: 88–9; "The Moral Issue (24-11-1921)," *Young India, CWMG* 25: 147–9. [Add citations]
54 Gandhi, "Notes," 26, 254; also Gandhi, "Letter to Venkatapayya," 26, 272.
55 M. K. Gandhi, "Interview to Nirmal Kumar Bose (9/10-11-34)," *CWMG* 65: 317.
56 "To follow out non-violence as a policy surely does not require saints for its working, but it does require honest workers who understand what is expected of them." Gandhi, "Letter to Venkatappayya," *CWMG*, 26, 270.
57 " … for my movement I do not at all need believers in the theory of non-violence, full or imperfect. It is enough if people carry out the rules of non-violent action" Gandhi (1943), quoted in Sharp, *Gandhi as a Political Strategist*, p. 279.
58 M. K. Gandhi, "Interview to American Negro Delegation (1936)," *CWMG* 68: 237–8.
59 B. R. Ambedkar, "Speech at the Closing of the Constituent Assembly (25-11-1949)," in Vasant Moon, ed., *Dr. B.R. Ambedkar: Writings and Speeches* (Govt of Maharashtra, 1994), vol. 13, p. 1215.
60 On Nehru's worry about disruptive protest, see Dipesh Chakrabarty, "'In the Name of Politics': Democracy and the Power of the Multitude in India," *Public Culture* 19, no. 1 (2007): 35–57.
61 See especially, Pratap Bhanu Mehta, "Of the few, by the few," *Indian Express* (April 7, 2011) and "Time to Step Back," *Indian Express* (August 16, 2011); and Aradhana Sharma, "Epic Fasts and Shallow Spectacles: The 'India against Corruption' Movement, Its Critics, and the Re-Making of 'Gandhi,'" *South Asia: Journal of South Asian Studies* 37, no. 3 (2014): 365–80; Mitu Sengupta, "Anna Hazare and the Idea of Gandhi," *The Journal of Asian Studies* 71, no. 3 (2012) and "Anna Hazare's Anti-Corruption Movement and the Limits of Mass Mobilization in India," *Social Movement Studies* 13, no. 3 (2014): 593–601 & 406–13.

Select Bibliography

Amin, Shahid, *Event, Metaphor, Memory: Chauri Chaura 1922–1992* (Delhi: Oxford University Press, 1995).

Anderson, Perry, *The Indian Ideology* (Delhi: Three Essays Collective, 2015).

Bilgrami, Akeel, *Secularism, Identity, and Enchantment* (Cambridge, MA: Harvard University Press, 2014).

Chakrabarty, Dipesh, "'In the Name of Politics': Democracy and the Power of the Multitude in India," *Public Culture* 19, no. 1 (2007): 35–57.

Chatterjee, Partha, *Nationalist Thought and the Colonial World: A Derivative Discourse?* (Minneapolis, MN: University of Minnesota Press, 1993).

Chenoweth, Erica and Maria J. Stephan's, *Why Civil Resistance Works: The Strategic Logic of Nonviolent Conflict* (New York: Columbia University Press, 2011).

Dange, S. A. *Gandhi vs Lenin* (Bombay: Loksevak Press, 1921).

Devji, Faisal, *The Impossible Indian: Gandhi and the Temptations of Violence* (Cambridge, MA: Harvard University Press, 2012).

Dutt, R. Palme, *Modern India* (London: Communist Party of Great Britain, 1927).

Gandhi, Leela, *The Common Cause: Postcolonial Ethics and the Practice of Democracy* (Chicago: University of Chicago Press, 2014).

Gandhi, M. K. *The Collected Works of Mahatma Gandhi* (Electronic Book), 98 vols. (New Delhi: Electronic, 1999).

Godrej, Farah, "Ascetics, Warriors, and a Gandhian Ecological Citizenship," *Political Theory* 40, no. 4 (2012): 437–65.

Godrej, Farah, "Gandhi, Foucault, and the Politics of Self-Care," *Theory & Event* 20, no. 4 (2017): 894–922.

Gowda, Nagappa, *The Bhagavadgita in the Nationalist Discourse* (Delhi: Oxford University Press, 2011).

Guha, Ranajit, "Discipline and Mobilize: Hegemony and Elite Control in Nationalist Campaigns," in *Dominance without Hegemony: History and Power in Colonial India* (Princeton: Princeton University Press, 1998).

Howes, Dustin, "The Failure of Pacifism and the Success of Nonviolence," *Perspectives on Politics* 11, no. 2 (June 2013).

Howes, Dustin, *Freedom without Violence: Resisting the Western Political Tradition* (New York: Oxford University Press, 2016).

Jahanbegloo, Ramin, *The Gandhian Moment* (Cambridge, MA: Harvard University Press, 2013).

Kapila, Shruti and Faisal Devji, eds., *Political Thought in Action: The Bhagavad Gita and Modern India* (Cambridge: Cambridge University Press, 2013).

Kumar, Aishwary, *Radical Equality: Ambedkar, Gandhi, and the Risk of Democracy* (Palo Alto, CA: Stanford University Press, 2001).

Mantena, Karuna, "Another Realism: Gandhi and the Politics of Nonviolence," *American Political Science Review* 106, no. 2 (2012): 455–70.

Mantena, Karuna, "Competing Theories of Nonviolent Politics," in Melissa Schwartzberg, ed., *Protest and Dissent: NOMOS LXII* (New York: New York University Press, 2020), Chapter 4.

Mehta, Uday, "Gandhi and the Common Logic of War and Peace," *Raritan* 30, no. 1 (Summer 2010): 134–56.

Mehta, Uday, "Gandhi and the Burden of Civility," *Raritan* 33, no. 1 (Summer 2013): 37–49.

Mehta, Uday, "Gandhi on Democracy, Politics, and the Ethics of Everyday Life," *Modern Intellectual History* 7, no. 2 (2010): 355–71.

Mukherjee, Subrata, *Marxist Interpretations of Gandhi* (PhD Thesis, Indiana University, 1976).

Niebuhr, Reinhold, *Moral Man and Immoral Society: A Study in Ethics and Politics* (New York & London: C. Scribner & Sons, 1932).

Palshikar, Sanjay, *Evil and the Philosophy of Retribution: Modern Commentaries on the Gita* (New Delhi & New York: Routledge, 2014).

Rao, M. B., ed. *The Mahatma: A Marxist Symposium* (New Delhi: People's Publishing House, 1969).

Roy, M. N., *India in Transition* (Geneva: J.B Target, 1922).

Schell, Jonathan, *The Unconquerable World: Power, Nonviolence, and the Will of the People* (New York: Henry Holt, 2003).

Sharp, Gene, *The Politics of Nonviolent Action, vol. 1* (Boston: Sargent, 1973).

Skaria, Ajay, "Gandhi's Politics: Liberalism and the Question of the Ashram," *The South Atlantic Quarterly* 101, no. 4 (2002): 955–86.

Skaria, Ajay, "Relinquishing Republican Democracy: Gandhi's *Ramrajya*," *Postcolonial Studies* 14, no. 2 (2011): 203–29.

Skaria, Ajay, *Unconditional Equality: Gandhi's Religion of Resistance* (Minneapolis, 2016).

Spratt, Philip, *Gandhism: An Analysis* (Madras: Huxley Press, 1939).

4

Conspicuous Communism

Manu Goswami

Some eighty years after its publication, Karl Marx's *Communist Manifesto* was designated a "co-conspirator" by imperial authorities in a legal trial held in a north Indian garrison town.[1] The Manifesto, a foundational text of political modernism, had sought to render visible the contradictions within bourgeois society and to inaugurate what became the first international within Europe. A central irony of communism, in its nineteenth-century European incarnation, was that a programmatic for making manifest the contradictions of a prevailing bourgeois order had to proceed—with the great exception of the Paris Commune—in a veiled manner.[2] The Russian Revolution upended this clandestine world and animated the Manifesto's legendary specter on a worldwide scale. More than a decade following the global shock of the Russian Revolution, the summoning of Marx's *Manifesto* in a trial waged against colonial communists and trade unionists highlights the quixotic quest by imperial authorities to return communism to the nineteenth-century order of a secret society. But in order to sequester the dreaded specter to an opaque realm of criminality, it had to first make it public.

Communism was summoned to the bars of juridical conviction relatively early in twentieth-century colonial India. Commencing in 1929 and ending some four-and-a-half years later, the infamous Meerut Trial targeted some thirty-two communists, trade union leaders, and peasant organizers. It was both the longest and largest of the proliferating genre of conspiracy trials in 1920s.[3]

Conducted amidst a catastrophic depression, Meerut has the dubious distinction of being the most expensive trial ever prosecuted by a modern European colonial state, costing some 150,000 pounds.[4] The trial's proceedings were massive and literally international—from the 320 witnesses summoned by the prosecution across the British Empire to the 62 organizations and texts it indicted as co-conspirators. The list of organizations included the Comintern-funded *League against Imperialism* centered in Weimar Berlin and presided over by the entrepreneurial "red millionaire" Willi Munzenburg alongside Virendranath Chattopadhyaya, a leading Bengali communist, a chief rival of M. N. Roy, who would disappear in Stalin's purges.[5] And it included the

This paper was first presented at the Delhi Conference in January, 2014. A version of this essay has appeared as "A Communism of Intelligence: Early Communism in Late-Imperial India" in Erag Ramizi eds., Anachronism and its Histories, Special issue, Diacritics, *Vol 48*, 2, 2020, 90–109.

London-based *Worker's Welfare League* of India, co-founded by Shapurji Saklatvala (1874–1936), a member of the Tata industrial family who sent to manage a Manchester plant fled his oligarchic inheritance to become the first arrest during the 1924 General Strike in London and the first Communist member of the British Parliament.[6] At the very center of the prosecution's case was a Borgesian labyrinth of 3,500 works, the textual "co-conspirators" that escorted Marx's Manifesto. The prosecution exhibits spanned Bengali, Urdu, Punjabi, and Marathi journals, pamphlets, posters, intercepted correspondence, routine trade union memoranda alongside the works of Karl Marx and Vladimir Lenin, Nikolai Bukharin and Josef Stalin, Harold Laski and Richard Tawney, Leonard Woolf and H. G. Wells, John Hobson and G. D. H. Cole.

Scholarship on the trial has highlighted its legal excess, and more recent works have carefully charted the transnational linkages of trade unions and organizations it implicated.[7] Yet this scholarship scants the ideological substance of the trial and its "eventful" status in relation to a new global conjuncture of politics.[8] Three intersecting arguments anchor the analysis that follows.

First, the Meerut Trial was the first time in the twentieth-century history of the British Empire, that communism was officially reckoned with as a large-scale concept, collective practice, and an existential threat to a political-economic order. It was where the cosmological reading of communism as a worldly religion congealed and acquired unprecedented publicity, presaging its subsequent entrenchment as an enduring fundament of Cold War ideology. Second, what the state's first prosecutor Langford James grasped in ways subsequent historical accounts have failed to fully appreciate is that the exceptional character of the trial resided not simply in its legal excess. Rather it issued from the commitment of communists to a transformative politics, their effort to establish communism as a "working rule of life." It was for them, he thundered, not an "abstract philosophy" but a visceral matter of everyday being.[9] The trial set forth in stark relief the intensifying antagonism between an imperial order that could only conform, in the sense provided by the French political philosopher Jacques Rancière, to a model of politics *as police*, that is, the daily iteration of systemic hierarchy and an expansive program of self- and collective emancipation.[10] Third, the actions of the accused broke the monopoly of both imperial and nationalist claims on a collective postimperial future. They broadcast a veritable "explosion" of the political, signifying the new sensibilities and sympathies that altered a late-imperial landscape.[11] The Meerut Trial, and more precisely the mass-scale mobilizations that had preceded it, was crucial for the consequential emergence of the demand for complete political independence by the Indian National Congress at its Lahore conference in 1929. The Congress was forced to abandon its aim of achieving a negotiated dominion status within the empire and fashion modalities of collective action more militant in intensity and scope. What this sequence underlined was an entrenched dialectic of codependence, alternately conflicting and cooperative, between communist and nationalist imaginaries in forging twentieth-century political modernism.

But before plunging further into this "eventful" juncture of early communism, I will briefly sketch some of the wider stakes of revisiting early communism in late-imperial India.

It is hard to think of a political imaginary other than Communism that has occasioned such opposed assessments from the radical futurity proclaimed by Karl Marx's *Communist Manifesto* to the triumphal endism that marked its conclusion, following the breakup of the Soviet Union, in the post-1989 era.[12] The significance of the recent philosophical revival of communism resides in the breaching of the temporal containment wall that had sought to keep it as part of the ruin and rubble of the twentieth century.[13] Yet the philosophical return has proceeded apace with the relative retreat of communism from critical historical inquiry.[14] What is more, new philosophical debates like older histories remain North Atlantic centered. There has been little revision of the historical-geographic templates through which early communism has been vantaged, especially for worlds outside the former Soviet Union and beyond official communist regimes. Despite a boom in global histories of twentieth-century politics and institutions—e.g., the institutions and ideas of liberalism—the discrepant global arc of communism across world regions has yet to be fully explored.[15]

There is an enormous literature on early twentieth-century communism, as well as on the principal Soviet vector of its circulation—the Comintern.[16] Much of this scholarship has centered either on the organizational modes, shifting strategies, and ideological inflections of the Comintern upon state- and nation-centered accounts of communist parties, with subsequent debates hinging upon the degree of relative autonomy fashioned by the latter in relation to the former. But this line of inquiry, which cuts across regional fields of historical inquiry, has bracketed the logically prior question of its purchase across heterogeneous social terrains.[17] How did a philosophical programmatic associated with an implacable universality obtain adherence across a highly differentiated world order in divergent colonial peripheries from India to Indonesia? How might we address the dizzying pace through which this political imaginary became a worldwide phenomenon?

Beginning with the transmissibility of communism rather than the topography of its conduction uncovers, I suggest, the peculiar combinatory power of early twentieth-century communism-in-motion. Jacques Ranciere notion of collective emancipation as rooted in a "communism of intelligence," or the "capacity of anybody to be where she can't be and do what she cannot do" carries unexpected empirical warrant in colonial locales.[18] The emergence of communism in colonial worlds, from India to Indonesia, resided neither in a marriage of the October revolution with an extant organized national left nor in the splitting off of existing social democratic parties. These two general pathways, identified by Eric Hobsbawm for the post-1917 institution of communist parties in Europe, has little purchase for the British Empire where party systems were absent or confined to nationalist organizations.[19] Put differently, the thesis of a "communism of intelligence" on an imperial terrain foregrounds the multitudinous pathways of becoming and being a communist and the dynamic processes through which particular social forms came to be articulated universally.

These general claims will, I hope, become more concrete in the Meerut Trial where imperial authorities confronted with the novelty of mass-scale communist action rendered it in cosmological terms, as a revealed religion—not unlike Islam, as we shall see.

What set apart the Meerut Trial from other early 1920s conspiracy trials in colonial India was the singular conjuncture wrought by mass scale labor militancy *and* political organization. The trial was a concerted effort to stall the transformative political and social activity that the accused had orchestrated. These encompassed the first general strikes in colonial India across the textile industry—cotton mills in Bombay and Sholapur and Kanpur, jute factories in Calcutta—industrial work sites in Jamshedpur and across major railway companies from 1927–9.[20] This upsurge across industrial sectors and concentrated infrastructural sites was accompanied by the first-ever expansion of collective organizing by urban scavengers and sanitation employees in Calcutta where, as Tanika Sarkar shows, Dalit workers led.[21] Among the unions established was the worker-organized communist *Girni Kamgar Union* (red flag) in Bombay whose membership swelled from an initial 384 to some 54,000 by 1929.[22] This wave of labor struggles was, from an empire-wide vantage, unprecedented as a *political* mode of anti-imperial resistance. It preceded the labor militancy that fueled decolonization across British African colonies following the Second World War.[23] And it stood apart from other contiguous movements within colonial India—especially those that recent histories of "revolutionary" violence have recovered—for its resolutely nonviolent character.[24] The combination of mass-scale mobilization with organized nonviolence was a distinctive feature of communist and radical trade union action across urban sites from Bombay to Calcutta to Kanpur. It preceded the Gandhi-led civil disobedience movement that would fill colonial jails *en masse* by the early 1930s. This temporal succession of mass-scale labor action followed by mass-scale nationalist action—has been obscured partly because of a long-standing separation between labor and political history, a partition that owes as much to the methodological nationalism of political history as it does to the actual institutional subordination of the labor question to a national dispensation. The rationale of this organized nonviolence was tied to a political modernism that centered land ownership, labor rights, and distributive justice as the substance of a future postimperial society. It was distinct from the concerns—whether rooted in a political realist consequentialism (as Mantena argues in this volume), an ethical commandment, or pragmatic concerns about civil war—that, as scholars continue to debate, anchored Gandhi's delimitation about the legitimate conduct and character of mass action.[25]

A network of dispersed communists, trade union radicals, and peasant leaders had established a raft of worker and peasant parties whose manifestoes voiced the demand for complete independence against the dominion status pursued by the Indian National Congress.[26] This multifronted program of social transformation enunciated, as the prosecutor Langford James ventured, a new kind of politics and the constitution of a discrete political subjectivity. James drew out the distinction among anti-imperial movements:

> The revolution which these accused have conspired for, which they have visualized, is indeed a revolution that lives long. It is a continuing and almost perpetual revolution … It is an anti-national revolution. ….the object in fact which these accused had is, I repeat, anti-nationalist. They would, I think, say it was international, but the two words are really the same.[27]

This opening sought to fracture any potential alliance between communists, radical trade union leaders, and members of the Congress. For among the most alarming correspondence intercepted by intelligence agents was the extended debate between the Berlin based office of the League against Imperialism, through its chief emissaries Virendranath Chattopadhyay and Willi Munzenberg, with Jawaharlal Nehru pushing the Congress towards full independence.[28] In February 1927, Nehru had attended the Congress of the Oppressed Nationalities held in Brussels as the representative of the Indian National Congress, and was elected to its executive committee.[29] This conference launched the Comintern-allied association, the *League Against Imperialism and for National Independence.*[30] Nehru drafted the Congress's resolution hoping that the "Indian nationalist movement" would fashion a "programme on the full emancipation of the peasants and workers of India, without which there can be no real freedom."[31] Nehru noted astonishment that the independence resolution and an alliance with the LAI were "all almost unanimously adopted" by the Congress. But he could not shake "an uncomfortable feeling that the resolutions were either not understood for what they were, or were distorted to mean something else. That this was so became apparent soon after the Congress, when a controversy arose on the meaning of the Independence resolution."[32]

The Secretary of the Home Department, H. G. Haig's urgent missive to Langford James made clear that "from the political point of view it would be an advantage to be able to convince in general as early as possible that Communism is not the kind of movement that should receive the sympathy of Nationalists."[33] James assured Haig that the "public" would view the impending trial as a "Moscow case and nothing to do with Nationalism."[34] Haig counseled a "juridical pronouncement" that would "enable us to deal with further manifestations of Communism and to prevent the Communist movement recovering from the blow which the arrest of the leaders has dealt it."[35] This correspondence pulsed with the paradox that while absolute sovereignty was first proclaimed by the new worker and peasant parties they sought it neither as a simple telos nor as absolute value. The stakes of this political imaginary was a transformation of the ways and means of everyday collective life—the overhauling of imperial capitalism by a Workers and Peasants Republic—rather than political sovereignty alone. The collective future envisioned by communists, as James correctly surmised, was bound neither to the nation-state nor liberal constitutionalism. They sought a new collective condition, beyond both empire and capitalism and their cognate modes of sovereignty.

Confronted with a new kind of political subject, imperial authorities struggled to improvise a new kind of criminal. The charge of "seditious speech" had been leveled against *all* nationalist leaders from Tilak to Gandhi. In those cases the specific clause summoned, namely, 124-A from the articles of sedition decreed "whosoever by words, either spoken or intended to be read or by signs or by visible representations or otherwise excite or attempts to excite feelings of disaffection to the Government established by law in British India."[36] The Meerut accused were charged under the more repressive 121-A of the Indian Penal Code with "waging war against the sovereignty of the King-Emperor." This clause became law in colonial India in 1870 and was modeled on the English Act of 1848–that sought to contain the contagion of European popular uprisings—promulgated the same year Marx's Manifesto was published.[37] It had been deployed in colonial India against violent actions but its usage in the Meerut case overturned precedent.

Since establishing reading circles, registering trade unions, and organizing strikes were lawful, the prosecution had to show that simply becoming and being a communist comprised agreement to waging war against the empire. Section 121-A was expedient because of its attendant sub-clause: "to constitute a conspiracy under this section it is not necessary that any act or illegal omission shall take place in pursuance thereof."[38] A charge of conspiracy could be mounted through illustrating agreement—a shared premise—rather than an illegal act. The "whole burden" was "proving that there was such an agreement between the accused, and between the accused and their co-conspirators in and outside India" to "deprive the King-Emperor of his sovereignty of British India."[39] Depriving sovereignty was defined capaciously—as "bringing about by methods other than constitutional of the cessation of the existing form of Government of British India."[40] In this improvised miasma of counterinsurgent power there could be no distinction between thought and action. Indeed, the judge claimed that the precise content of sovereignty did not matter as such, for after a diligent "study of the statements of the accused and of numerous Communist writings," it was evident no distinction existed between "Imperial Government," the "Kings Sovereignty," or "British Imperialism."[41] The logical entailment of reading communists texts, then, was a permanent sedition against an actually existing political order.

All varieties of anti-imperial struggle were not, from the standpoint of imperial authorities, alike. Nationalists were figured as normal civic opponents of the state, whose activity described as the "excitement of disaffection" positioned them internally, as dissident subjects within an imperial polity. Communists, in contrast, were designated as extraordinary enemies of imperial sovereignty—as an existential imperilment.

The Meerut Trial codified this structural inequality among modes of anti-imperial opposition on an empire-wide terrain. Consider here the subsistence of the Communist Party of Great Britain. The 1924 trial in Britain against J.R. Campbell, the Scottish communist editor of the *Worker's Weekly*, for a seditious editorial inciting soldiers to mutiny had precipitated the fall of the first short-lived Labour Government. And the later 1925 Tory-initiated trial against twelve communists in Britain also focused on seditious libel, placing them in the same juridical category as colonial nationalists.[42]

Among the constitutive ironies of the Meerut Trial was that while the mass arrests of the accused were steered by a Tory government, the trial, was prosecuted under a Labour regime with a self-avowed socialist, Wedgewood Benn (father of Tony Benn), serving as the secretary of state for India. Benn had been a fierce critic of the Campbell trial on the ground that "this type of prosecution was as practically inexpedient as it was vicious in principle" and had queried whether all "active Republicans" in Britain would be deemed criminals.[43] But a stance assumed in relation to the imperial center was deemed incommensurable for its periphery. Writing in 1935 about the Meerut trial, the political theorist Harold Laski described it as "a prosecution scandalous in its inception and disgraceful in its continuance. If the responsibility for undertaking it lies at the door of a Tory viceroy, that for its continuance belongs to a Socialist Secretary of State."[44] British socialism ceased, Laski suggested, at the frontier of the empire.

The historic assumption of the British Labour party had not varied its incapacity, as Victor Kiernan wryly observed, to "see class conflict in Britain and India in the same perspective."[45] Once in power again it actively sought to prosecute communists in colonial India. The Meerut Conspiracy case was a "grand demonstration" of the racial paternalism that made the Labour party a bulwark for, not against, empire:

> Everything Indian was perpetually in a state of being under active consideration by the Labour Party. What the party did do was co-operate heartily, when in office, in jailing Indian trade union organizers, who either were Communists, or—merely by being active unionists—laid themselves open to suspicion of being such. … It was proper that Indian workers should not be duped by the patriotic claptrap of their bosses, but highly improper that they should think of doing anything against these bosses. The Indian working class was to be encouraged to stand on its own feet, so long as it stood perfectly still.[46]

Kiernan's status as a founding member of the Communist Party Historians Group and the journal *Past and Present* is widely known.[47] But his intimacy with the Meerut Case has been forgotten. Kiernan arrived in colonial India in 1936 as the immediate successor to Ben Bradley and Phillip Spratt–the two British subjects amongst the Meerut accused who were members of the British Communist party. While working as an agent of the CPGB, he established a welter of Marxian reading circles across northern colonial India, and married Shanta Gandhi, a founding member of the communist-inspired Indian People's Theater Association (IPTA) established in 1943. Staying on till the blood-soaked misery of 1948, Kiernan also undertook luminous translations of Urdu poets, including the communist colossus Faiz Ahmad Faiz.[48]

The Meerut Trial elaborated a view of communism that would become common sense in the postwar decades and settle by century's end into a fixed dogma. Communism was, in this view, a structure of belief formally akin to revealed religions. It was an ensemble of original and fixed prescriptions that, however redescribed, restated, and reimagined under varying times and locales, were essentially unchanged and unchangeable. This textualization was at once dehistoricizing and overdetermined.

The construal of communism as a static cosmology was partly shaped by a viscerally felt immediacy—the panic roused by the preponderance of Muslim colonial subjects, many of whom were former Pan-Islamists, across various inflection points of early communism in motion in colonial India, including key defendants at the trial. In the wake of the collapse of the Ottoman Empire and the abolition of the Sultan as Caliph, thousands of Pan-Islamists had fled colonial India as a *dar-ul-harb* (a terrain of war), into the new Soviet Union, and in a stunning ramification many joined the Bolshevik army.[49] Another smaller stream of Muslim Indian soldiers had undertaken a separate path to radicalization. Balking at the idea of killing coreligionists during Britain's Mesopotamia campaign, many hundreds joined the *Ghadr* movement and later became the rank and file of Punjab's multiple communist groups.[50]

The philosophical analogy drawn between religion and Communism is easily sourced. In 1920 Bertrand Russell asserted an "elective affinity" between Islam and communism: "Among religions, Bolshevism is to be reckoned with Mohammedanism rather than with Christianity and Buddhism. Christianity and Buddhism are primarily personal religions, with mystical doctrines … Mohammedanism and Bolshevism are practical, social, unspiritual, concerned to win the empire of this world."[51] It is hard to overstate the obduracy of this analogy, and its barnacle-like accretions, that simultaneously reified two distinct histories. In the Meerut Trial, the temptation of seeing communist godlessness as yet another Islamic artifact overwhelmed legal reason. The prosecutor Langford James summoned this hallucinatory presence at the outset: "there is no god at all in the Mecca to which these gentlemen look."[52]

The precocious conflation of Islam and Communism in the Meerut Trial was shaped by a specific place-bound phenomenology. Anxious that a jury trial held in the provincial capitals of Bombay or Calcutta would result in an acquittal, given popular sympathy for the strikes, imperial authorities constituted a special sessions court presided by a Magistrate in Meerut. The trial was conducted not in the Magistrate's court office but in the bungalow (Garden House) of General William Edmund Ironside, who had led the British section of the Allied Expeditionary force in northern Russia against the Bolsheviks in 1917 and was sent to command the Meerut district from 1928 till 1931. The Urdu coinage of *mofussil* is an apt descriptor of the mix of infrastructure and collective sensibility (neither wholly urban nor wholly rural) that defined such provincial outposts. But Meerut, recall, had played an outsized role on a world stage, as the originating scene of the great rebellion of 1857, the largest mass-scale revolt against the British Empire in the nineteenth century. That the "Mutiny" originated in Meerut is among the few stable facts about the events of 1857–8, set against its split interpretative status in the nineteenth century. Early official histories saw it as an outcome of an invariant religious fanaticism, sparked by the "cartridge" affair (paper cartridges greased with pork and beef fat) and folded into an elite Muslim plot seeking to restore the Mughal Empire. Marx heralded it as a mass nationalist uprising supplanting the "cartridge thesis" with a more sublime dialectic: "There is something in human history like retribution: and it is a rule of historical retribution that its instrument be forged not by the offended, but by the offender himself."[53] In the twentieth century, the events of 1857 were parsed as an agrarian revolt led by recently dispossessed peasants turned colonial soldiers still innocent of the "imagined community" of the nation form. But by century's end it was framed, once more, as a millenarian *jihadi* movement.[54] The association between Meerut and the Mutiny endured because of an ambient analogy between provincial sensibility and religious fervor, of north Indian *Mufassils* and Muslims.

If the sedimented allusion between Meerut and Muslim insurrection haunted the trial, the conjecture of Islam and Communism seemed to acquire plausibility by the late-1920s. British imperial intelligence agents had monitored the mass-scale communist uprising in 1926–7 in West Java and West Sumatra, both Muslim majority rural provinces of the Dutch East Indies.[55] A dissident faction of communists had sought an Islamic communism akin to the early heterodox vision of Mirsaid Sultan Galiev.[56] The severity of the Dutch imperial response resulted in the absence of the Communist party as a political force for the remainder of Dutch colonial rule. It reemerged in the 1950s and 1960s when the dynamics of the "global Cold War" unleashed a brutal massacre of communists in postcolonial Indonesia.[57]

The Russian Revolution had struck where it was not supposed to have, in a peasant society under an oppressive imperial yoke. Precisely because it was seen as ectopic—a phenomenon both untimely *and* outside its proper place—its extroverted universalism became an obsessive concern for imperial authorities. The "metaphysics of communist hating," was rooted in a paranoiac response to an imagined confluence of Bolshevism, Islam, and insurrectional equality. This confluence crystallized, for the Crown, in the Meerut Trial. The prosecution and the two-volume 676-page judgment sought to congeal and condemn Communism as a cohesive mega-entity. But the actual proceedings of the trial—that is, the defense—pushed the other way.

While the point of the Moscow show trials of the 1930s was public penitence, the dramaturgy at Meerut resided elsewhere. Its dramaturgy stemmed from the collective decision announced by Muzzafar Ahmad, a Bengali communist, to "transform the court room into a political forum."[58] In a remarkable act of solidarity the three British subjects accused did not avail a separate jury trial. Of all the trials prosecuted across the British Empire from India to Malaysia, Kenya to Jamaica, it is the only documented instance of British subjects voluntarily giving up the racial privilege of a separate jury trial. Demanding access to proscribed literature and their private collections of books and papers seized during the arrests, the accused provided lovingly detailed accounts of their activities and aspirations. Theirs was a conspicuous communism.

This conspicuousness mocked the legal construal of communism as a clandestine conspiracy. It reversed the ambient disgust expressed towards communists as embodying what Phillip Spratt—among the three British accused and especially niggling as a Cambridge educated CPGB emissary—called a "moral obliquity."[59] Correctly anticipating extended press coverage, the accused proceeded to appropriate what time they could, juridical time, to amplify the specter that imperial authorities sought to stamp out. Their long imprisonment yielded the first vernacular translations of Marx's *Communist Manifesto* into Marathi (by G. Adhikhari) and Hindi (by A. Prasad).[60]

Taken individually and together, the individual statements belie the homogenizing composite of communism conceived by the prosecution and enshrined in the voluminous judgment. Apart from Benjamin Bradley and Phillip Spratt, who were CPGB agents, most of the Meerut accused did not conform to the disciplined, full-time cadres that were the cellular units of Lenin's single-most consequential invention—the vanguard party. Even Bradley's radicalization occurred not in the working-class milieu of an Essex childhood, but through witnessing the "oppression" of Indian railway workers when he was a civil engineer in Rawalpindi in 1921–2. His disgust at the hysterical racism exhibited during and after the Amritsar Massacre led him to resign his civilian contract and return to London. He joined the Communist Party in 1923, and returned to colonial India, five years on, as a CPGB emissary. Only a few of the accused held formal party membership. Gautam Adhikari was a communist with a doctorate in chemistry. While a doctoral student in Weimar Berlin he had joined the ranks of the German Communist party or KPD. His imprisonment prompted a strong letter of protest by Albert Einstein to the British Authorities. Amir Haidar Khan, a former Pan-Islamist from rural Punjab whose only formal education had been in a Madrassa, joined the Communist party of the United States while working at a Detroit car assembly plant. This was a diverse assortment of disparate communist party members confined together in a colonial prison. But the majority of the accused were communists not by official membership but by conviction. And others were trade unionists sympathetic to socialism.

Even a selective précis underscores the immensely variegated points of entry into early communism. Shaukat Usmani and Abdul Majid elaborated the initial pan-Islamist inspiration of many of the first recruits into Indian communism who later became the entering class of the University of the Toilers of the East established in Moscow in 1921. While in prison, Usmani wrote a testimonial of his conversion from a pan-Islamic activist to a Communist and contested the Spen Valley election as a candidate for the CPGB in 1929.[61] His opponent Sir John Simon had fiercely opposed the 1926 General Strike in Britain and would head the eponymous commission on India's constitutional status. Ayudhya Prasad detailed his own radicalization in relation to anarchic peasant traditions in northern India. We are "repeatedly told," he argued, that Communism "Is foreign to this land and it is an imported Utopia which can never get roots in this country. This is a land of religions. Such people are not perhaps aware that the first idea of Communist society was taken from the collective production and distribution which prevailed in primitive society similar to those of Indian village commune."[62] But "even today," he continued, "the scattered bones of primitive communities can be seen. In India communism is not a foreign question but a matter of reestablishing the old relations on the basis of the advanced mode of production of today.. it is about smashing the capitalist relations imported in the last century."[63] For Prasad the contemporaneity of these "primitive communities" with imperial capitalism anchored the possibility of alternate paths, suggesting the regenerative capacity of apparently archaic and anachronistic forms—much as the late-nineteenth-century Russian Marxist Vera Zasulich had sought assurance of from Karl Marx in an insightful exchange.[64] Lester Hutchinson, who was elected vice president of the *Girni Kamgar* Union (Red Flag), the communist workers union in Bombay, and the Great Indian Peninsular Railway (whose membership had swelled to 41,000 by 1929), was a radical Scottish journalist.[65] The only British subject not a formal member of the CPGB, Hutchinson's commitment to internationalism refracted the tradition of revolutionary socialism that made Scotland and Wales the predominant regions of communist and radical left political influence during 1920s Britain.[66] Sohan Singh Josh elaborated the many Punjabi texts authored by rank-and-file members of the ideologically promiscuous *Ghadr* movement who saw communism in the likeness of the militant egalitarianism espoused by the fifteenth-century warrior-prophet Guru Nanak.[67]

In the course of the trial, communism emerged less as a monolithic universalism than a dynamic pluriverse. The defense statements of the accused orchestrate the fateful jostling of distinct strands within colonial India—pan-Islamic, agrarian-utopian, urban proletarian, Sikh egalitarian—that coalesced to animate early communism. This jostling underscores the temporal and social variegation of communism as a lived political imaginary—the simultaneous reference to a radically other noncapitalist future and its perception as an ancient precept, one that preceded industrial capitalism and was understood as broadly congruent with the martial egalitarianism of Sikhism or the abstract universality of an Islamic *Ummah*.

Shaukat Usmani who opened his statement by identifying as a "communist, in no other than a Marxist-Leninist sense" recounted his route from a pan-Islamist who had "joined the army of Hijrat" in 1919 during the early Khilafat/Non-Cooperation movement to a fateful encounter with Bolshevism.[68] What he saw in the new Soviet Union, he claimed, was a new egalitarian federation beyond "Rajas or Nawabs, Landlords or Money Lenders, capitalists or big merchants." Instead, "the working and peasant masses of Tartars and Turkomans, Uzbegs and Tajaks, Bashkars and Cossacks, Kirghiz and Kalmock, Armenians and Georgians, Daghastanis and Azerbaijanians, Ukrainians and Russians" were recomposed as federated Soviets. And it was this socialist federation that had seized his allegiance.[69] Usmani was the first candidate to stand in British Parliamentary elections from "within prison walls"; and warmly acknowledged the "brave class-consciousness of the workers of Spen Valley" who had selected him as their candidate against Sir John Simon.[70] This was, Usmani well understood, an extraordinary phenomenon, a "long-distance" electoral internationalism conducted across an unequal imperial terrain. It suggested a mode of solidarity rooted neither in communitarian confluence nor liberal toleration, but in an antisystemic overturning what Usmani, in a rhetorical flourish, called the "sovereignty of British Finance-capital."

Bristling at the framing of Marxism as a religion, Gautam Adhikhari indicted the court for miming the "inquisitions for heresy" that had pockmarked medieval Europe.[71] Against the reading of communism as a revelatory doctrine with a permanent message, he countered that as a scientist he had embraced Marxism precisely because it was a "perspective not a prophecy."[72] His familiarity with the limits of liberal empire enabled a rare differentiation of distinct social philosophical currents across "Europe." On the "continent of Europe," Adhikari observed the

> [L]iberal sections of the bourgeoisie which is opposed to the conclusions of Marxism, recognizes it as one of the achievements of human thought. In the thoroughly bourgeois University of Berlin you find a course of lectures on the materialist conception of history being included in the official list of the summer term of 1931. In India you imprison people for being Marxists ....you seize classical works on Marxism which you find in their possession. You file well-recognized philosophical works on Materialism as incriminating evidence against them.[73]

Beyond the lineal stagism of third international Marxism, he offered an alternate archaeology of imperial capitalism. Its temporal origins in a hierarchical feudal order were most evident in its farthest spatial reaches. While capitalism was worldwide in scope, its cultural and political forms were not unitary. The "British bourgeois rule in India" was "of a feudal-absolutist character," dissimilar from the wider "world of bourgeois ideas."[74] It is fair to assume that as a doctoral student and as a communist activist in Weimar Berlin, Adhikhari had a keen vantage on imperial provincialism—or, what he called the "chambers of the Meerut Civilian Club with the Whisky and Soda, Havana Cigars and Race Course atmosphere." These mundane spaces of the civic life of empire incubated, he implied, a solipsistic autocracy.

Given this "feudal-absolutist" stamp, it was not surprising that imperial authorities presented the actions and thoughts of the accused as originating not with themselves but "by a little body of men like the Moscow clique." Given an absolutism preserved in aspic, the prosecution could only proceed on self-referential grounds. The hermeneutic obstacles faced by the court were rooted, he argued, in its originating mercantilist foundations. Perhaps, he queried to the laughter of his fellow accused, the prosecution perceived the Soviet Union as "huge joint-stock company, the bulk of whose shares are concentrated in the hands of a clique and perhaps in the hands of Mr. Stalin himself."[75]

One of the distinguishing features of historical materialism is that formal epistemological questions are reckoned as intrinsically political. Questions about volition and determinism, about when and how collective action might intersect with objective conditions, about the mutuality between social worlds and generalized practice have a concrete political significance. Against the mechanical materialism of the second international, the early communism of the post-Bolshevik era was alight in a rediscovery of purposive collective activity. The Meerut accused were commanded, through a liberal juridical formalism, to articulate what had been for them an experiential renewal of the question of consciousness.

Defense statements are a regulated mode of "truth-telling," constrained by institutional norms and anchored within the speech-act conventions of the law. Yet given the charges the accused faced their statements were less what Judith Butler calls "giving an account of one self" where individual self and performance stand in a continuous iterative relationship.[76] These were not performative utterances in the restricted individualist sense of speech-act theory than a kind of intellectual and political history fashioned *in extremis*. They showcase the kind of theorizing on the hoof that characterized early communism. The German playwright and communist Bertolt Brecht affirmatively named this big-brush thinking, "*plumpes denken,*" or literally rough-hewn thought.[77]

Plumpes Denken, Brecht's self-avowed communist aesthetic, was a complex distillation of 1920s Bolshevik agitprop. Brechtian theater would exercise a rare sway upon the vernacular theatre of northern India in the 1940s and 1950s, virtually dominating, as Vasudha Dalmia shows, a generation of Hindi theatre.[78] In the late-imperial era, it emerged as the aesthetic monogram of the British Workers Theater Movement from 1928–36 that eschewed formal party allegiance and exhibited an unruly and "exuberant revolutionism."[79] Embraced by working-class communists in northern industrial cities and in London by "clerks, school-teachers and East End Jewish proletarians," this worker-led theater focused on "specific agitations" and particular mobilizations.[80] Mixing montage and mime the performances were distinguished by intricate choreography and fast-paced declamations presented by and to factory and dockworkers, lascars, and the rising numbers of unemployed. The sketch *Meerut* was regarded as a standard bearer of the repertoire of the worker-theatre movement. Performed by the men and women of the London *Hammer and Sickle Players* and the northern Salford based *Red Megaphones* it was performed outside docks, factories, and public baths, with the actors forced to play a furtive dance with the police. Conceived amidst the trial in solidarity with the Meerut accused its production notes specified a calibration of rhythm, gesture and pace. The opening was a collective declamation, paced from a whisper to a crescendo, "Murder, Murder, **Murder, Murder,**" indicting imperial "police and troops" for crushing "the rising tide of revolt against our vile conditions" in British India.[81] The production notes detail the measured sarcasm with which the performers were to conclude the opening statement "The average wage for all workers and peasants is less than a shilling a day—the brightest jewel in Britain's Crown."[82] In a rapid register shift, the sketch continued:

> The Government denies us education, and when, as in England, in Germany, and France, in America—in every capitalist state in the world—they sought to drive us harder by wage-cuts and speed-up, throwing more and more of us on to the streets, We revolted! They foster our religious differences in order to divide us … they send you here with arms … They tell you we are religious maniacs.

Detailing the strike wave of 1928 from the 20,000 workers who struck on the East India Railway to the heroism of the 60,000 strong *Girni Kamgar* Union the sketch changed voices, once more, to herald "the comrades who showed us how to fight, how to organize, how to break the bonds of British tyranny." The sketch's finale had performers stretching their hands across the upright bars into the audience, urging them to dissuade their brothers and sons and fathers from imperial employment, instructing them to extend their "arms across the sea" and recognize that "This is your fight," an enactment of a commensurability wrought yet simultaneously denied by empire. For "those who have jailed the workers in India" were the same as those "who cut wages and enforce the Means Test in Britain." The large expenses for the defense were overwhelmingly on small-scale subscriptions solicited from such performances and unions and worker organizations.[83] The Meerut Trial elicited a response within Britain—the Spen Valley voters who chose the accused Usmani as their candidate, northern working-class theatre groups in Lancashire, the Manchester Labor Councils and east-London radical Jewish organizations that protested the trial, and even a joint labor and communist demonstration held in Hyde Park on May 7, 1933—unique for its working class density and regional range.[84]

The trial prompted letters of protest from a cast of interwar international public intellectuals: the French intellectual Romain Rolland, the German-Jewish Physicist and communist Albert Einstein who wrote an open letter to Ramsay Macdonald protesting the arrests; the Calcutta-born economic historian R.H Tawney; the Archbishop of York; the socialist writer H.G. Wells, and Bertrand Russell.[85] In a pamphlet produced to help raise defense funds, titled, *For the Meerut Prisoners*, Romain Rolland condemned a world order comprising a "narrow circle of the privileged nations" for generating a "terror which now weighs on every part of earth delivered over to capitalist exploitation" and that had "assumed gigantic proportions in the great territories of India and the Far East."[86] Harold Laski had vigorously campaigned for the Meerut accused, even discussing the trial with Franklin Delano Roosevelt during a visit to the United States.[87] He lodged its meaning within a grotesque global sequence of trials: "The Meerut Trial belongs to the class of cases of which the Mooney trial and Sacco-Vanzetti trial in America, the Dreyfuss trial in France, and Reichstag Fire trial in Germany, are the supreme instances." A state that was "capable of such folly" effectively "indicts itself," for the Meerut Trial had become iconic of a government that "acts in fear; it operates by terror" and therefore lies beyond "justifiable power."[88]

Writing in 1935, Jawaharlal Nehru claimed the trial had steered "the younger men and women of the Congress" away from a prior more narrowly liberal and nationalist cannon. After Meerut, they no longer "read Bryce on Democracies and Morley and Keith and Mazzini," but sought "when they could get them books on socialism and communism and Russia." The actions of the accused "helped greatly in directing minds to the new ideas" of socialism and economic democracy that Eleanor Newbigin explores in this volume in relation to K. T. Shah, Harold Laski's protégée and an influential socialist.[89]

The Meerut Trial's judgment anticipated the conceptual and political closures imposed with the commencement of the third "ultra-leftist" period in the Comintern. This was apparent in the gap between the general statement authored by sixteen of the accused against the official judgment, under the formal direction of CPGB, and individual defense statements.[90] For all its polemic ferocity, the general statement adhered to a straitened historical stagism. It envisioned revolution as engraved in the infrastructure of capitalism, as a mechanical reflex of a unitary historical process, in that fusion of an exaggerated objectivism and extreme subjectivism that would become a fixture of regime communism. By the mid-1930s, the criminalization of communism enacted relatively early in late colonial India would become the norm in much of East Asia, Southeast Asia, and Latin America. As Communist Parties were forced to go underground, the exigencies of resistance and clandestinity re-enforced Stalinist modes of leadership and organization across regional contexts. Field manuals replaced the more egalitarian testimonial literature that had flourished under the dispensation of dispersed communists. There were, of course, exceptions within colonial India, clustering mostly in the late-1940s and early 1950s, from the Tehbhaga movement in Bengal to the armed rebellion by Dalit communist coir workers in the princely state of Travancore in 1946, and the radical peasant insurgency in Telangana in Hyderabad where women played a leading role.[91] But these were also self-organized insurgencies by rank-and-file subjects, aided rather than directed by communist parties-on-high.

The repression in Meerut disaggregated powerful collective movements into individual survival strategies and extracted labor and trade union leaders from their communities during a savage depression. It consolidated the hegemony of the Congress and nation-centered mass mobilizations. It was, in this sense, a consequential juncture through which a nation-centered framing of "the social" rather than an internationalist imaginary of a robustly socialist or communist collective future came to prevail in late 1930s and 1940s India. It pushed aside, an enabling insight of early twentieth-century communism, namely, that common ground was found less in simple convergence than a mobile "practice of insurgent comparisons."[92] Early communism was grounded in particular social forms that came to be articulated universally on trans-regional scales. The subsequent trajectory of communism was distinct, taking the form of a universality differently articulated.

The capacious notion of conspiracy as "belief" that took place in Meerut, amid a convulsive clinging to empire, prefigures the global expansion of conspiracy law following 9/11. The repressive laws of sedition brought against the Meerut accused are enshrined in the Indian Penal Code. The longest serving criminal code in the common law world it is still operative across former British colonies.[93] In February 2016, a communist student leader, Kanhaiya Kumar, from New Delhi's prestigious Jawaharlal Nehru University (JNU)—whose father belongs to a communist farmer organization and whose older brother serves as a soldier in the contested region of Kashmir—was charged with "seditious speech" for demonstrating solidarity with Kashmiri dissidents.[94] This response by a Hindu Nationalist regime spurred the renovation of JNU into an open-air seminar where public figures queried the meanings of freedom or "Azaadi." What this temporal rhythm—an autocratic decree by a Hindu-majoritarian regime and counterdemonstrations mounted by secular students and a middle-class intelligentsia—verified was the synergetic alliance between concurrent and competing political imaginaries that had first emerged in the late imperial era and which continue, even in recession, to haunt India's political landscape. What the vast scholarship on India's serrated experiment with democracy has yet to fully consider is the influence of communism as movement, ideology, and experiential horizon in quotidian democratic practice and ideals. This inheritance has more often been treated as a regional electoral phenomenon then a *differentia specifica* of India's democracy where a plurality of communist movements persisted across the cold war era. The relational coevalness of communism and nationalism in the late imperial era ceded a robust legitimacy to socialist and communist movements across postcolonial junctures of the political.

In the global conjuncture opened by 9/11, the clause summoned in Meerut has, in fact, been used much more forensically against contemporary Indian Maoists and suspected *jihadis*. The metaphysics of communist hating persists, then, well beyond the conclusion of the short twentieth century.

Notes

1 A chapter of the judgment was devoted to a reading of Marx's Manifesto and his 1847 *The Poverty of Philosophy*. Adhir Chakravarti ed., *Judgment on the Meerut Communist Conspiracy Case: Delivered by R.L. Yorke*, Volume 1, State Archives of West Bengal, Education Department, Govt. of West Bengal, Calcutta, 1991, pp. 16–36.

2 Eric Hobsbawm, ed., *The History of Marxism. Vol. 1: Marxism in Marx's Day* (London: Harvester, 1982).

3 Between 1922 and 1927, some 5 trails were held across northern colonial India from Peshawar to the textile mill-town of Kanpur in the United Provinces. Older histories of communism in India include Ross Mallick, *Indian Communism: Opposition, Collaboration and Institutionalization* (Delhi: Oxford University Press, 1994); G. D. Overstreet and M. Windmiller, *Communism in India* (Berkeley, CA: University of California Press, 1959); T. R. Sareen, *Russian Revolution and India: A Study of Soviet Policy towards Indian National Movement, 1922–29* (New Delhi: Sterling Publishers, 1978); Saumyendranath Tagore, *Historical Development of the Communist Movement in India* (Calcutta: Red Front Press, 1944).

4 Home Department, Political, November 10, 1932, National Archives of India.

5 Nirode K. Barooah, *Chatto: The Life and Times of an Indian Anti-Imperialist in Europe* (Oxford: Oxford University Press, 2004); Sean McMeekin, *The Red Millionaire. A Political Biography of Willi Münzenberg, Moscow's Secret Propaganda Tsar in the West* (New Haven: Yale University Press, 2003); Fredrik Petersson, "Hub of the Anti-Imperialist Movement: The League against Imperialism and Berlin, 1927–33," *Interventions: International Journal of Postcolonial Studies* 16, no. 1 (2014): 49–71.

6 Susan Pennybacker, *From Scottsboro to Munich: Race and Political Culture in 1930s Britain* (Princeton: Princeton University Press, 2009), pp. 146–99.

7 Pramita Ghosh, *The Meerut Conspiracy Case and the Left Wing in India* (Calcutta: Papyrus, 1978); Sobhanlal Datta Gupta, *The Comintern and the Destiny of Communism in India, 1919–1943* (Calcutta: Seribaan, 2006); A. G. Noorani, *Indian Political Trials*, 1775–1947 (Oxford: New York, 2007). For recent works see Michele Louro, "Where National Revolutionary Ends and Communist Begins': The League against Imperialism and the Meerut Conspiracy Case," *Comparative Studies of South Asia, Africa and the Middle East* 33, no. 3 (2013): 331–44; Carolien Stolte, "Trade Unions on Trial: The Meerut Conspiracy Case and Trade Union Internationalism, 1929–32," *Comparative Studies of South Asia, Africa and the Middle East* 33, no. 3 (2013): 345–59; Ali Raza, "Separating the Wheat from the Chaff: Meerut and the Creation of 'Official' Communism in India," *Comparative Studies of South Asia, Africa and the Middle East* 33, no. 3 (2013): 316–30.

8 William Sewell, "Historical Events as Transformation of Structures: Inventing Revolution at the Bastille," *Theory and Society* 25, no. 6 (1996): 841–81.

9 Langford James, Opening Address of the Special Public Prosecutor before R. Milner White in the Emperor v. Phillip Spratt and Others, June 12, 1929, Meerut: Saraswati Machine Printing Press, 1929.

10 Jacques Rancière and R. Bowlby, "Ten Theses on Politics," *Theory & Event* 5, no. 3 (2001).

11 On antisystemic politics as "explosion" see Henri Lefebvre, *The Explosion: Marxism and the French Upheaval* (Boston: Monthly Review, 1968).

12 Jacques Derrida, *Spectres of Marx: The State of the Debt, the Work of Mourning and the New International*. Translated by Peggy Kamuf (London: Routledge, 1994); Francois Furet, *The Passing of an Illusion: The Idea of Communism in the Twentieth Century* (Chicago, IL: University of Chicago Press, 1999).

13 Alain Badiou, *The Communist Hypothesis*. Translated by D. Macey and S. Corcoran (London: Verso, 2015/2010); Susan Buck-Morss, *Dreamworld and Catastrophe: The Passing of Mass Utopia in East and West* (Cambridge, MA: MIT Press, 2000); Costas Dousinaz and Slavoj Zizek, eds., *The Idea of Communism*, volume 1 (London: Verso, 2010).

14 Recent revisionist works include Kristen Ghodsee, *Red Hangover: Legacies of 20th Century Communism* (Durham, NC: Duke University Press, 2017); Kristin Ross, *Communal Luxury: The Political Imaginary of the Paris Commune* (London: Verso, 2015).

15 C. A. Bayly, *Recovering Liberties: Indian Thought in the Age of Empire and Liberalism* (London: Cambridge University Press, 2011); Mark Mazower, *Governing the World: The History of an Idea* (London: Penguin, 2013); Susan Pedersen, *The Guardians: The League of Nations and the Crisis of Empire* (London: Oxford University Press, 2015). For treatments of liberal internationalism in South Asian history see, Sunil Amrith and Glenda Sluga, "New Histories of the United Nations," *Journal of World History* 19, no. 3 (2008): 251–74; Manu Bhagavan, *The Peacemakers: India and the Quest for One World*

(London: Palgrave Macmillan, 2012); Sugata Bose and Kris Manjapra, *Cosmopolitan Thought Zones: South Asia and the Global Circulation of Ideas* (London: Palgrave Macmillan, 2010).

16 E. H. Carr, *The Bolshevik Revolution 1917–1923, Volume 1* (London: Penguin, 1977); Kevin McDermott and Jeremy Agnew, *The Comintern: A History of International Communism from Lenin to Stalin* (New York: St Martin's press, 1997).

17 New works in communist history rooted in different questions include Chitra Joshi, *Lost Worlds: Indian Labor and Its Forgotten Histories* (Delhi: Permanent Black, 2004); Dilip Menon, *Caste, Nationalism and Communism in South India: Malabar, 1900–1948* (London and Cambridge: Cambridge University Press, 1994); Vijay Prashad, ed., *Communist Histories*, Volume 1 (Delhi: Left World Books, 2016); Ali Raza, *Revolutionary Pasts: Communist Internationalism in Colonial India* (Cambridge, 2020); Ania Loomba, *Revolutionary Desires: Women, Communism, and Feminism in India* (London: Routledge, 2018).

18 Jacques Ranciere, "Communists without Communism," in Costas Douzinas and Slavoj Zizek, eds., *The Idea of Communism*, Volume 1 (Cambridge), pp. 169, 171.

19 Eric Hobsbawm, *Revolutionaries* (New York: New Press, 2001).

20 Rajnarayan Chandavarkar, *Imperial Power and Popular Politics: Class, Resistance and the State in India, c.1850–1950* (London: Cambridge University Press, 1997); Meena Menon and Neera Adarkar, *One Hundred Years, One Hundred Voices: The Millworkers of Girangaon: An Oral History* (Calcutta: Seagull Books, 2004); Gyan Prakash, "From Red to Saffron," in *Mumbai Fables* (Princeton, NJ: Princeton, 2010), pp. 204–50; H. Van Wersch, *The Bombay Textile Strike* (London: Oxford University Press, 1992).

21 Tanika Sarkar, "'Dirty Work, Filthy Caste': Calcutta Scavengers in the 1920s," in Ravi Ahuja, ed., *Working Lives and Working Militancy: The Politics of Labour in Colonial India* (Chennai: Tulika Books, 2013), pp. 174–206; Anna Sailer, "'Various Paths Are Today Opened': The Bengal Jute Mill Strike of 1929 as a Historical Event," in Ravi Ahuja, ed., *Working Lives and Working Militancy* (Chennai: Tulika Books) pp. 207–55.

22 "Events and Developments in the Communist Situation in India from September 1928 to January 1929," National Archives of India, Home/Political/1928, F. 1/28; David Petrie, *Communism in India, 1924–1927*, Calcutta, 1927, Home Department, Intelligence Bureau.

23 Frederick Cooper, *Decolonization and African Society* (London and Cambridge: Cambridge University Press, 1996).

24 Proliferating works include Durba Ghosh, *Gentlemanly Terrorists: Political Violence and the Colonial State in India, 1919–1947* (Cambridge and London: Cambridge University Press, 2017); Peter Heehs, *The Bomb in Bengal: The Rise of Revolutionary Terrorism in India, 1900–1910* (New Delhi: Oxford University Press, 1993); Shruti Kapila, "A History of Violence," *Modern Intellectual History* 7, no. 2 (2010): 437–57; Kama Maclean, *Revolutionary History of Interwar India: Violence, Image, Voice, and Text* (London: Hurst & Co, 2015); Chris Moffat, *India's Revolutionary Inheritance: The Promise and Politics of Bhagat Singh* (Cambridge and London: Cambridge University Press, 2019); Maia Ramnath, *Decolonizing Anarchism: An Antiauthoritarian History of India's Liberation Struggle* (Chico, CA: AK Press, 2012).

25 Shahid Amin, "Gandhi as Mahatma: Gorakhpur District, Eastern UP, 1921–2," in Ranajit Guha, ed., *Subaltern Studies III: Writings on South Asian History and Society* (Delhi: Oxford University Press, 1984); Partha Chatterjee, *Nationalist Thought and the Colonial World* (Minnesota: University of Minnesota Press, 1993), 85–130; Faisal Devji, *The Impossible Indian: Gandhi and the Temptation of Violence* (Cambridge,

MA: Harvard University Press, 2012); Ajay Skaria, *Unconditional Equality: Gandhi's Religion of Resistance* (Minnesota: University of Minnesota, 2016); Uday Singh Mehta, "Gandhi on Democracy, Politics, and the Ethics of Everyday Life," *Modern Intellectual History* 7, no. 2 (2010): 355–71.

26 Sukhbir Choudhary, *Peasant's and Worker's Movement in India, 1905–1929* (New Delhi: People's Publishing House, 1971). *Swadeshi* radicals had demanded independence, but the Congress had balked.

27 Langford James, Opening Address of the Special Public Prosecutor before R. Milner White in the Emperor v. Phillip Spratt and Others; Indian Annual Register, 1929, 1.

28 Govt of India, Home Department, Communism in India, 1924–1927, pp. 47–8, National Archives of India, New Delhi. For early discussions of this correspondence see Michael Brecher, *Nehru: A Political Biography* (London: Oxford University Press, 1959), p. 109; John Callaghan, "Jawaharlal Nehru and the Communist Party," *Journal of Communist Studies* 7, no. 3 (1991): 350–6. On Nehru's internationalism see Michelle Louro, *Comrades against Imperialism: Nehru, India, and Interwar Internationalism* (Cambridge: Cambridge University Press, 2018). On Nehru's relationship to communists, especially M. N. Roy, see Sanjay Seth, *Marxist Theory and Nationalist Politics* (Delhi: Sage, 1995).

29 Jawaharlal Nehru, *An Autobiography: With Musings on Recent Events in India* (Bombay: Allied Publishers, 1962), pp. 82–3.

30 Govt of India, Home Department, Communism in India, 1924–1927, National Archives of India, New Delhi.

31 Indian Annual Register, 1927, 1, 207, Nehru Memorial and Museum, New Delhi.

32 Jawaharlal Nehru, *An Autobiography*, 167.

33 "H.G. Haig, Secretary, Home Department, Govt of India, to Langford James, the Chief Prosecutor, April 29, 1929" in Subodh Roy ed., *Communism in India: Unpublished Documents, 1925–1934* (Delhi: Ganasahitya Prakash, 1972), p. 95.

34 Ibid., p. 96.

35 Ibid., pp. 94–5.

36 Walter Russell Donogh, *The History and Law of Sedition and Cognate Offences in India*. 2nd ed. (Calcutta: Thacker Spink and Co., 1914), p. 9. For trials against prominent nationalist figures see A.G. Noorani, *Indian Political Trials.*

37 Adhir Chakravarti ed., *Judgment on the Meerut Communist Conspiracy Case*, p. 10.

38 Ibid., p. 10.

39 Ibid., p. 11.

40 Ibid.

41 Ibid.

42 James Klugmann, *History of the Communist Party of Great Britain: Volume One: Formation and Early Years, 1919–1924* (London: Lawrence and Wishart, 1968), pp. 366–8.

43 Free Speech in India, *Manchester Guardian*, December 9, 1929.

44 Harold Laski, Preface, in Lester Hutchinson, *Conspiracy at Meerut* (New York: Arno Press, 1972 [1935]), p. 7.

45 Victor Kiernan, "India and the Labour Party," *New Left Review* 1, no. 42, (March–April 1967): 47.

46 Ibid., p. 53.

47 Eric Hobsbawm, "Victor Kiernan," *Past & Present* 208, no. 1 (August 1, 2010): 3–8.

48 See Tariq Ali, "Victor-Kiernan," *Independent*, February 20, 2009.

49 M. Hasan and M. Pernau, *Regionalizing Pan-Islamism: Documents on the Khilafat Movement* (New Delhi: Maohar, 2005); Maia Ramnath, *Haj to Utopia: How the Ghadar Movement Charted Global Radicalism and Attempted to Overthrow the British Empire* (Berkeley, CA: University of California Press, 2011).

50 Radhika Singha, "Finding Labor from India for the War in Iraq: The Jail Porter and Labor Corps, 1916–1920," *Comparative Studies in Society and History* 49, no. 2 (2007): 412–45; "Front Lines and Status Lines: Sepoy and 'Menial' in the Great War, 1916–1920," in H. Liebau, K. Bromber, K. Lange, D. Hamzah, and R. Ahuja, eds., *The World in Wars, Experiences, Perceptions and Perspectives from the South* (Leiden: Brill, 2010).

51 Bertrand Russell, *The Practice and Theory of Bolshevism* (London: Allen, 1920), 106.

52 Langford James, Opening Address of the Special Public Prosecutor before R. Milner White in the Emperor v. Phillip Spratt and Others, June 12, 1929, Meerut: Saraswati Machine Printing Press, 1929.

53 J. Kaye and G. Malleson, *Kaye's and Malleson's History of the Indian Mutiny of 1857*, 8 vols (London: Cambridge University Press, 2010 [1890]); Karl Marx and Freidrich Engels, *The First Indian War of Independence 1857–1859* (Moscow: Foreign Languages Publishing House, 1959).

54 Eric Stokes, *The Peasant and the Raj: Studies in Agrarian Society and Peasant Rebellion in Colonial India* (London: Cambridge University, 1978); Rudranghu Mukherjee, *Awadh in Revolt: A Study of Popular Resistance* (London: Anthem Press, 1984); Seema Alavi, *The Sepoys and the Company: Tradition and Transition in Northern India* (Delhi: Oxford University Press, 1995); William Dalrymple, *The Last Mughal* (London: Bloomsbury, 2006).

55 Harry J. Benda and Ruth T. McVey, *The Communist Uprisings of 1926–27 in Indonesia, Key Documents* (Ithaca: Cornell University Press, 1960).

56 Maxime Rodinson, "Sultan-Galiev: A Forgotten Precursor," in *Marxism and the Muslim World*. Translated by Jean Matthews (London: Zed Press, 1979).

57 Odd Arne Westad, *The Global Cold War: Third World Interventions and the Making of Our Times* (Cambridge, UK: Cambridge University Press, 2007).

58 Muzzafar Ahmad, *Communists Challenge Imperialism from the Dock* (Calcutta: National Book Agency, 1967), p. ii. Also see Suchetana Chattopadhyay, *An Early Communist: Muzaffar Ahmed in Calcutta 1913–1929* (Chennai: Tulika Books, 2011).

59 Meerut Conspiracy Case 1929–32, National Archives of India, Private Collection, Statement of Accused, File 212, vol. 3/2, 362.

60 Prakash Karat, ed., *A World to Win: Essays on the Communist Manifesto* (Delhi: Leftworld Books, 1999). For a fine account of the vexed submergence of caste as class see, Juned Shaikh, "Translating Marx: Mavali, Dalit and the Making of Mumbai's Working Class, 1928–1935," *Economic and Political Weekly* XLVI, no. 31 (2011): 65–73.

61 Shaukat Usmani, *Peshawar to Moscow: Leaves from an Indian Muhajireen's Diary* (Benares: Swarajya Publishing House, 1927); *Historic Trip of a Revolutionary Sojourn in the Soviet Union* (New Delhi: Sterling, 1977).

62 Meerut Conspiracy Case 1929–32, National Archives of India, Private Collection, Statement of Accused, File 212, vol. 3/2, 536.

63 Ibid.

64 Teodor Shanin, "Letters of Vera Zasulich and Karl Marx," *The Journal of Peasant Studies* 45, no. 7 (2018): 1183–202.

65 Meerut Conspiracy Case 1929–32, Private Collection, National Archives of India, Statements of Accused, File 224.

66 Kevin Morgan, *Bolshevism and the British Left, Part One: Labour Legends and Russian Gold* (London: Lawrence and Wishart, 2007).
67 Meerut Conspiracy Case 1929–32, National Archives of India, Private Collection, Statement of Accused, File 224, 3/2; Sohan Singh Ghosh, *The Great Attack: Meerut Conspiracy Case* (Delhi: People's Publishing House, 1979).
68 Meerut Conspiracy Case 1929–32, National Archives of India, Private Collection, Statement of Accused, File 225, 840–1.
69 Ibid., p. 846.
70 Ibid., p. 844.
71 Meerut Conspiracy Case 1929–32, National Archives of India, Private Collection, Statement of Accused, File 220, 1242.
72 Ibid., p. 1269.
73 Ibid., p. 1284.
74 Ibid., p. 1188.
75 Ibid., p. 1233.
76 Judith Butler, *Giving an Account of Oneself* (New York: Fordham Press, 2005).
77 Walter Benjamin, *Understanding Brecht*. Translated by Anna Bostock (London: Verso, 2003).
78 Vasudha Dalmia, *Poetics, Plays and Performances: The Politics of Modern Indian Theatre* (New Delhi: Oxford University Press, 2006, pp. 153–70).
79 Raphael Samuel and Tom Thomas, "Documents and Texts from the Workers' Theatre Movement, 1928–1936," *History Workshop Journal* 4 (1977): 108.
80 Ibid., p. 106.
81 Meerut: Workers Theatre Movement Play, Working Class Movement Library, Salford, Org/Unity/2/1/45, n.d. emphasis in original.
82 Samuel and Thomas, "Documents and Texts from the Workers' Theatre Movement, 1928–1936," pp. 135–6.
83 Lester Hutchinson, *Conspiracy at Meerut*, p. 91; Amar Farooqui, ed., *Remembering Dr. Gangadhar Adhikari* (New Delhi: People's Publishing House, 1998), pp. 36–7.
84 On the joint demonstration see Patricia Cockburn, *The Years of the Week* (London: MacDonald & Co., 1968), 71.
85 *The Meerut Prisoner's Reply* (India: Pamphlet and Oriental Office Records, 1931), 96–7; Manchester Guardian, December 8, 1929.
86 Romain Rolland, "For the Meerut Prisoners: Against Imperialist Terror" in Meerut Conspiracy Case, March 1929–July 1933, pp. 3–4; L/PJ/12/337, India and Oriental Office Records, New British Library (see photo 6).
87 Muzzaffar Ahmad, *Communists Challenge Imperialism*, p. xiii.
88 Harold Laski, preface, *Conspiracy at Meerut*, p. 8.
89 Jawaharlal Nehru, *Toward Freedom: An Autobiography*, pp. 231–2.
90 Muzzaffar Ahmad, ed., *Communists Challenge Imperialism from the Dock* (Calcutta: National Book Agency, 1967).
91 Robin Jeffrey, "India's Working Class Revolution: Punnapra-Vayaler and the Communist 'conspiracy' of 1946," *Indian Economic and Social History Review* xviii, no. 2 (1981); K. Lalitha, V. Kannabiran, and R. Melkote, "*We Were Making History*": *Women and the Telangana Uprising* (London: Zed Books, 1989); Peter Custers, *Women in the Tebhaga Uprising: Rural Poor Women and Revolutionary Leadership, 1946–1947* (Calcutta: Naya Prokash, 1987).
92 Manu Goswami, "Imaginary Futures and Colonial Internationalisms," *The American Historical Review* 117, no. 5 (2012): 1484.

93 Barry Wright, ed., *Codification, Macaulay and the Indian Penal Code: The Legacies and Modern Challenges of Criminal Law Reform* (London: Routledge, 2016).

94 Kanhaiya Kumar, *Bihar to Tihar: My Political Journey* (Delhi: Juggernaut Books, 2016).

Select Bibliography

Ahmad, Muzzafar, *Communists Challenge Imperialism from the Dock* (Calcutta: National Book Agency, 1967).

Alavi, Seema, *The Sepoys and the Company: Tradition and Transition in Northern India* (Delhi: Oxford University Press, 1995).

Ali, Tariq, "Victor-Kiernan," *Independent*, February 20, 2009.

Amin, Shahid, "Gandhi as Mahatma: Gorakhpur District, Eastern UP, 1921–2," in Ranajit Guha, ed., *Subaltern Studies III: Writings on South Asian History and Society* (Delhi: Oxford University Press, 1984).

Amrith, Sunil and Glenda Sluga, "New Histories of the United Nations," *Journal of World History* 19, no. 3 (2008): 251–74.

Badiou, Alain, *The Communist Hypothesis*. Translated by D. Macey and S. Corcoran (London: Verso, 2015/2010).

Barooah K., Nirode, *Chatto: The Life and Times of an Indian Anti-Imperialist in Europe* (Oxford: Oxford University Press, 2004).

Bayly, C. A., *Recovering Liberties: Indian Thought in the Age of Empire and Liberalism* (London: Cambridge University Press, 2011).

Benda, Harry J. and Ruth T. McVey, *The Communist Uprisings of 1926–27 in Indonesia, Key Documents* (Ithaca: Cornell University Press, 1960).

Benjamin, Walter, *Understanding Brecht*. Translated by Anna Bostock (London: Verso, 2003).

Bose, Sugata and Kris Manjapra, *Cosmopolitan Thought Zones: South Asia and the Global Circulation of Ideas* (London: Palgrave Macmillan, 2010).

Brecher, Michael, *Nehru: A Political Biography* (London: Oxford, 1959).

Buck-Morss, Susan, *Dreamworld and Catastrophe: The Passing of Mass Utopia in East and West* (Cambridge, MA: MIT Press, 2000).

Butler, Judith, *Giving an Account of Oneself* (New York: Fordham Press, 2005).

Carr, E. H., *The Bolshevik Revolution 1917–1923*, vol. 1 (London: Penguin, 1977).

Callaghan, John, "Jawaharlal Nehru and the Communist Party," *Journal of Communist Studies* 7, no. 3 (1991): 350–56.

Chakravarty, Adhir, ed., *Judgment on the Meerut Communist Conspiracy Case: Delivered by R.L. Yorke*, vol. 1 (State Archives of West Bengal: Education Department, Govt. of West Bengal, Calcutta, 1991).

Chandavarkar, Rajnarayan, *Imperial Power and Popular Politics: Class, Resistance and the State in India, c.1850–1950* (Cambridge, UK: Cambridge University Press, 1997).

Chatterjee, Partha, *Nationalist Thought and the Colonial World* (Minnesota: University of Minnesota Press, 1993).

Chattopadhyay, Suchetana, *An Early Communist: Muzaffar Ahmed in Calcutta 1913–1929* (Chennai, India: Tulika Books, 2011).

Choudhary, Sukhbir, *Peasant's and Worker's Movement in India, 1905–1929* (New Delhi: People's Publishing House, 1971).

Cockburn, Patricia, *The Years of the Week* (London: MacDonald & Co., 1968).
Cooper, Frederick, *Decolonization and African Society* (Cambridge, UK: Cambridge University Press, 1996).
Custers, Peter, *Women in the Tebhaga Uprising: Rural Poor Women and Revolutionary Leadership, 1946–1947* (Calcutta: Naya Prokash, 1987).
Dalmia, Vasudha, *Poetics, Plays and Performances: The Politics of Modern Indian Theatre* (New Delhi: Oxford University Press, 2006).
Dalrymple, William, *The Last Mughal* (London: Bloomsbury, 2006).
Datta Gupta, Sobhanlal, *The Comintern and the Destiny of Communism in India, 1919–1943* (Calcutta: Seribaan, 2006).
Derrida, Jacques, *Spectres of Marx: The State of the Debt, the Work of Mourning and the New International*. Translated by Peggy Kamuf (London: Routledge, 1994).
Devji, Faisal, *The Impossible Indian: Gandhi and the Temptation of Violence* (Cambridge, MA: Harvard University Press, 2012).
Donogh, Walter Russell, *The History and Law of Sedition and Cognate Offences in India* (Calcutta: Thacker Spink and Co, 1914).
Dousinaz, Costas and Slavoj Zizek, eds., *The Idea of Communism*, Volume 1 (London: Verso, 2010).
Farooqui, Amar, ed., *Remembering Dr. Gangadhar Adhikari* (New Delhi: People's Publishing House, 1998).
Furet, Francois, *The Passing of an Illusion: The Idea of Communism in the Twentieth Century* (Chicago, IL: University of Chicago Press, 1999).
Ghodsee, Kristen, *Red Hangover: Legacies of 20th Century Communism* (Durham, NC: Duke University Press, 2017).
Ghosh, Durba, '*Gentlemanly Terrorists*': *Political Violence and the Colonial State in India, 1919–1947* (Cambridge, UK: Cambridge University Press, 2017).
Ghosh, Pramita, *The Meerut Conspiracy Case and the Left Wing in India* (Calcutta: Papyrus, 1978).
Ghosh, Sohan Singh, *The Great Attack: Meerut Conspiracy Case* (Delhi: People's Publishing House, 1979).
Goswami, Manu, "Imaginary Futures and Colonial Internationalisms," *The American Historical Review* 117, no. 5 (2012): 1461–85.
Hasan, M. and M. Pernau, *Regionalizing Pan-Islamism: Documents on the Khilafat Movement* (New Delhi: Maohar, 2005).
Heehs, Peter, *The Bomb in Bengal: The Rise of Revolutionary Terrorism in India, 1900–1910* (New Delhi: Oxford University Press, 1993).
Hobsbawm, Eric, ed., *The History of Marxism. Vol. 1: Marxism in Marx's Day* (London: Harvester, 1982).
Hobsbawm, Eric, *Revolutionaries* (New Press, NY, 2001).
Hobsbawm, Eric, "*Victor Kiernan*," *Past & Present* 208, no. 1 (August 1, 2010): 3–8.
Hutchinson, Lester, *Conspiracy at Meerut* (New York: Arno Press, 1972 [1935]).
James, Langford, *Opening Address of the Special Public Prosecutor before R. Milner White in the Emperor v. Phillip Spratt and Others, 12 June 1929* (Meerut: Saraswati Machine Printing Press, 1929).
Jeffrey, Robin, "India's Working Class Revolution: Punnapra-Vayaler and the Communist 'conspiracy' of 1946," *Indian Economic and Social History Review* xviii, no. 2 (1981): 97–122.
Joshi, Chitra, *Lost Worlds: Indian Labor and Its Forgotten Histories* (Delhi: Permanent Black, 2004).
Kapila, Shruti, "A History of Violence," *Modern Intellectual History* 7, no. 2 (2010): 437–57.

Karat, Prakash, ed., *A World to Win: Essays on the Communist Manifesto* (Delhi: Leftworld Books, 1999).
Kaye, J. and G. Malleson, *Kaye's and Malleson's History of the Indian Mutiny of 1857*, 8 volumes (London: Cambridge University Press, 2010 [1890]).
Kiernan, Victor, "India and the Labour Party," *New Left Review* 1, no. 42 (March-April 1967): 44–55.
Klugmann, James, *History of the Communist Party of Great Britain: Volume One: Formation and Early Years, 1919–1924* (London: Lawrence and Wishart, 1968).
Kumar, Kanhaiya, *Bihar to Tihar: My Political Journey* (Delhi: Juggernaut Books, 2016).
Lalitha, K., V. Kannabiran and R. Melkote, "*We Were Making History*": *Women and the Telangana Uprising* (London: Zed Books, 1989).
Laski, Harold, Preface, in Lester Hutchinson, *Conspiracy at Meerut* (New York: Arno Press, 1972 [1935]).
Lefebvre, Henri, *The Explosion: Marxism and the French Upheaval* (Boston: Monthly Review, 1968).
Loomba, Ania, *Revolutionary Desires: Women, Communism, and Feminism in India* (London: Routledge, 2018).
Louro, Michele *Comrades against Imperialism: Nehru, India, and Interwar Internationalism* (Cambridge: Cambridge University Press, 2018).
Louro, Michele, "Where National Revolutionary Ends and Communist Begins': The League against Imperialism and the Meerut Conspiracy Case," *Comparative Studies of South Asia, Africa and the Middle East* 33, no. 3 (2013): 331–44.
Maclean, Kama, *Revolutionary History of Interwar India: Violence, Image, Voice, and Text* (London: Hurst & Co, 2015).
Mallick, Ross, *Indian Communism: Opposition, Collaboration and Institutionalization* (Delhi: Oxford University Press, 1994).
Marx, Karl and Freidrich Engels, *The First Indian War of Independence 1857–1859* (Moscow: Foreign Languages Publishing House, 1959).
Mazower, Mark, *Governing the World: The History of an Idea* (New York: Penguin Random House, 2013).
McDermott, Kevin and Jeremy Agnew, *The Comintern: A History of International Communism from Lenin to Stalin* (New York: St Martin's press, 1997).
McMeekin, Sean, *The Red Millionaire. A Political Biography of Willi Münzenberg, Moscow's Secret Propaganda Tsar in the West* (New Haven: Yale University Press, 2003).
Mehta, Uday Singh, "Gandhi on Democracy, Politics, and the Ethics of Everyday Life," *Modern Intellectual History* 7, no. 2 (2010): 355–71.
Menon, Dilip, *Caste, Nationalism and Communism in South India: Malabar, 1900–1948* (Cambridge, UK: Cambridge University Press, 1994).
Menon, Meena and Neera Adarkar, *One Hundred Years, One Hundred Voices: The Millworkers of Girangaon: An Oral History* (Calcutta: Seagull Books, 2004).
Moffat, Chris, *India's Revolutionary Inheritance: The Promise and Politics of Bhagat Singh* (Cambridge, UK: Cambridge University Press, 2019).
Morgan, Kevin, *Bolshevism and the British Left, Part One: Labour Legends and Russian Gold* (London: Lawrence and Wishart, 2007).
Mukherjee, Rudranghu, *Awadh in Revolt: A Study of Popular Resistance* (London: Anthem Press, 1984).
Nehru, Jawaharlal, *An Autobiography: With Musings on Recent Events in India* (Bombay: Allied Publishers, 1962).
Noorani, A. G., *Indian Political Trials*, 1775–1947 (Oxford: New York, 2007).

Overstreet, G. D. and M. Windmiller, *Communism in India* (Berkeley, CA: University of California Press, 1959).

Pedersen, Susan, *The Guardians: The League of Nations and the Crisis of Empire* (London: Oxford University Press, 2015).

Pennybacker, Susan, *From Scottsboro to Munich: Race and Political Culture in 1930s Britain* (Princeton: Princeton University Press, 2009).

Petersson, Fredrik, "Hub of the Anti-Imperialist Movement: The League against Imperialism and Berlin, 1927–33," *Interventions: International Journal of Postcolonial Studies* 16, no. 1 (2014).

Prakash, Gyan, *Mumbai Fables* (Princeton: Princeton University Press, 2010).

Prashad, Vijay, ed., *Communist Histories*, vol. 1 (Delhi: Left World Books, 2016).

Ramnath, Maia, *Decolonizing Anarchism: An Antiauthoritarian History of India's Liberation Struggle* (Chico, CA: AK press, 2012).

Ramnath, Maia, *Haj to Utopia: How the Ghadar Movement Charted Global Radicalism and Attempted to Overthrow the British Empire* (Berkeley, CA: University of California Press, 2011).

Rancière, Jacques, transl D. Panagia and R. Bowlby, "Ten Theses on Politics," *Theory & Event* 5, no. 3 (2001).

Raza, Ali, *Revolutionary Pasts: Communist Internationalism in Colonial India* (Cambridge, 2020).

Raza, Ali, "Separating the Wheat from the Chaff: Meerut and the Creation of 'Official' Communism in India," *Comparative Studies of South Asia, Africa and the Middle East* 33, no. 3 (2013).

Rodinson, Maxime, "Sultan-Galiev: A Forgotten Precursor," in *Marxism and the Muslim World*. Translated by Jean Matthews (London: Zed Press, 1979).

Ross, Kristin, *Communal Luxury: The Political Imaginary of the Paris Commune* (London: Verso, 2015).

Roy, Subodh, *Communism in India: Unpublished* Documents, *1925–1934* (Delhi: Ganasahitya Prakash, 1972).

Russell, Bertrand, *The Practice and Theory of Bolshevism* (London: Allen, 1920).

Sailer, Anna, "'Various Paths are Today Opened': The Bengal Jute Mill Strike of 1929 as a Historical Event," in Ravi Ahuja, ed., *Working Lives and Working Militancy: The Politics of Labour in Colonial India* (Tulika Books, 2013).

Samuel, Raphael and Tom Thomas, "Documents and Texts from the Workers' Theatre Movement, 1928–1936," *History Workshop Journal* 4, no. (1977).

Sareen, T. R., *Russian Revolution and India: A Study of Soviet Policy Towards Indian National Movement, 1922–29* (New Delhi: Sterling Publishers, 1978).

Sarkar, Tanika, "'Dirty Work, Filthy Caste': Calcutta Scavengers in the 1920s," in Ravi Ahuja, ed., *Working Lives and Working Militancy: The Politics of Labour in Colonial India* (Tulika Books, 2013).

Seth, Sanjay, *Marxist Theory and Nationalist Politics* (Delhi: Sage, 1995).

Sewell, William, "Historical Events as Transformation of Structures: Inventing Revolution at the Bastille," *Theory and Society* 25, no. 6 (1996).

Shaikh, Juned, "Translating Marx: Mavali, Dalit and the Making of Mumbai's Working Class, 1928–1935," *Economic and Political Weekly* XLVI, no. 31 (2011): 65–73.

Shanin, Teodor, "Letters of Vera Zasulich and Karl Marx," *The Journal of Peasant Studies* 45, no. 7 (2018): 1183–202.

Singha, Radhika, "Finding Labor from India for the War in Iraq: The Jail Porter and Labor Corps, 1916–1920," *Comparative Studies in Society and History* 49, no. 2 (2007): 412–45.

Singha, Radhika, "Front Lines and Status Lines: Sepoy and 'Menial' in the Great War, 1916–1920," in H. Liebau, K. Bromber, K. Lange, D. Hamzah and R. Ahuja, eds., *The World in Wars*, Experiences, *Perceptions and Perspectives from the South* (Leiden: Brill, 2010), pp. 55–106.

Skaria, Ajay, *Unconditional Equality: Gandhi's Religion of Resistance* (Minnesota: University of Minnesota, 2016).

Stokes, Eric, *The Peasant and the Raj: Studies in Agrarian Society and Peasant Rebellion in Colonial India* (London: Cambridge University, 1978).

Stolte, Carolien, "Trade Unions on Trial: The Meerut Conspiracy Case and Trade Union Internationalism, 1929–32," *Comparative Studies of South Asia, Africa and the Middle East* 33, no. 3 (2013): 345–59.

Tagore, Saumyendranath, *Historical Development of the Communist Movement in India* (Calcutta: Red Front Press, 1944).

Usmani, Shaukat, *Historic Trip of a Revolutionary Sojourn in the Soviet Union* (New Delhi: Sterling, 1977).

Usmani, Shaukat, *Peshawar to Moscow: Leaves from an Indian Muhajireen's diary* (Benares: Swarajya Publishing House, 1927).

Wersch, H. Van, *The Bombay Textile Strike* (London: Oxford University Press, 1992).

Westad, Odd Arne, *The Global Cold War: Third World Interventions and the Making of Our Times* (Cambridge, UK: Cambridge University Press, 2007).

Wright, Barry, ed., *Codification, Macaulay and the Indian Penal Code: The Legacies and Modern Challenges of Criminal Law Reform* (London: Routledge, 2016).

5

National Wealth or National Poverty? The Politics of Economic Measurement in Late Colonial India

Eleanor Newbigin

In 1924 K. T. Shah and K. J. Khambata published a joint work, *Wealth and taxable capacity of India*.[1] Shah was professor of economics at the University of Bombay and Khambata his research scholar. The book comprised two parts: the first, by Khambata, was a computation of India's annual national wealth from 1914 to 1922. Shah offered a study of India's taxable capacity in the second part. The men were able to cooperate well enough to publish the research, but the separate introductions point to some unease. Shah described Khambata's work as dealing "almost exclusively with matters and statements of facts" and explained that, while his own writing "has its share of the basic facts … it has also its share of opinions on some of the most vexed problems of to-day and to-morrow."[2]

Their work received attention from economic specialists outside India, much of which was negative. Several British reviewers praised Khambata's work, but were critical of Shah, who was attacked for his methodology and for his "very strong political feeling" in what "ought to be [a] scientific work."[3] This view seems to have shaped later academic engagement with this text, which has been almost entirely ignored by scholars of Indian economics or economic history.

This chapter sets out a close reading of this more or less unknown work, specifically Shah's half of it, not to "rescue" it as an important economic treatise, but to consider what it tell us about "the political imaginaries" of the early 1920s, both within British India, and at a more global level. Read in conversation with contemporary works deemed more properly "economic," Shah's work allows us to question politics and the political from two different, but interlinked perspectives. On the one hand this chapter seeks to understand the politics that underpinned the claim that Shah's approach to measuring national wealth was not scientific. What was different about Shah's approach

This is a revised draft of an essay that original appeared as "Accounting for the nation, marginalising the empire: taxable capacity and colonial rule in the early twentieth-century" in *History of Political Economy*, May 2020. The author expresses thanks to the editors of this journal, and to the editors of the present volume, for their willingness to allow this reproduction and for their insightful comments on and input into both drafts.

to economic measurement and those of his British and imperial contemporaries? What does this reveal about the "scientific" nature of more properly economic approaches? And what has been the legacy of sidelining these questions, and Shah's work, in later historical analysis of this period? In addressing these questions, the chapter seeks to reconsider supposedly global histories of the economy from the vantage of the Indian subcontinent.

On the other hand, the chapter examines how economic techniques enabled the production of new political topologies and subjectivities in 1920s British India. This entails a flipping of the theoretical framework to ask what global histories of the twentieth-century economy can bring to scholarly debates about politics in late colonial South Asia. Like other chapters in this book, this essay argues that a more properly historical understanding of the economy reveals important moments of shift, not simply between the mutually constructed fields of "economy" and "politics" but also in the qualities that define relationships across these fields. From this basis, the chapter explores how emergent techniques of economic measurement produced new understandings of the national economy and the society to which it was now seen to be connected and how this played out in the context of postwar British India.

That Shah's work, and that of other Indian economists writing in this period, have not been read as significant, either to the history of the economy, or to the history of Indian politics is striking, especially as there have been very productive exchanges between these fields with regards to the long nineteenth century. Scholarship on the history of "the economy," as distinct from economic history, developed in the 1990s. Deeply influenced by the approaches of Susan Buck Morss and Timothy Mitchell, these studies unpacked "the economy" as a historically constructed entity at precisely the moment when arguments about the "natural" state of the free-market economy were beginning to gain powerful traction.[4] This scholarship divided along two rather different understandings of the "chronology" of the economy.[5] For one group of scholars, "the economy" emerged around the eighteenth and nineteenth centuries, as a result of new ideas about the separation of politics, economy and culture.[6] Studies of South Asia have demonstrated the importance of imperial technologies and praxis for this process. They have shown that, far from being the recipient of practices forged in the West, India was a critical staging ground for the production of new ideas of economic and national-political space.[7]

Another group of scholars, however, have argued that the emergence of "the economy" took place much later than this, around the early and middle parts of the twentieth century. Timothy Mitchell, with whom this argument is perhaps most closely associated, has argued that, while the term "economy" was used widely before this period, its meaning underwent a radical transformation between the 1930s and 1950s, from one that referred to specific kinds of relationships to a term that signified a "total process."[8] This transformation produced a conception of the economy as an aggregative, measurable "thing," the governance of which required specific professional and technical expertise. The development of new socio-technocratic practices rendered the economy an object that was both discrete and marked by a capacity to grow, and thus regulated and enumerated, in a manner that the fields from which it was already assumed to be distinct—politics and culture—could not. The nation-state became the central reference point through which to measure and govern "the economy," producing a new global topology of power in which it was the basic unit of global order, in stark contrast to the late-nineteenth-century world of imperial power.[9]

Mitchell's reading of the history of the "modern economy" was developed as a means to understand the imperial(ist) genealogies of development but it is striking that non-Western spaces and actors appear more peripheral in this account than in readings of the economy as a construct of the eighteenth or nineteenth centuries. Mitchell and others agree that the breakup of European empires and the rise of "imperialist nationalism" were central to the emergence of the modern economy.[10] But the primary interest has been in showing how the modern economy was constructed in ways that naturalized the postimperial order rather than in considering how these were enabled by imperial ideologies and practices, as well as those of imperialism's opponents.[11] Writing in the decade before the transformations analysed by Mitchell and others, Shah and Khambata's work provides insight into how the changes in knowledge production, technology, and governance that enabled the emergence of the modern economy worked to disrupt imperial logics and make way for new political claims, both by the colonizer and colonized.

Viewed as a kind of hiatus between the breakup of the nineteenth-century geopolitical order and the emergence of a new macroeconomic order, the decade following the First World War is an underexplored moment in histories of the economy. Many of the theoretical advancements that made it possible to consider "the economy" as a singular, measurable object had not yet taken on a standardized form. As can be seen from Shah's critics, however, some approaches were already being given greater legitimacy than others. The hierarchies of this debate not only selectively elevated certain voices but also particular understandings of and historical approaches to economic practices.

Here scholarship on the formation of "the economy" in nineteenth-century South Asia can bring new insights to our understanding of the emergence of a measurable economy in the twentieth century. Histories of economic measurement more generally, and national accounting in particular, have tended to reify Western experiences in which the problem of measuring national wealth has been tied to the question of war and state resources. Widely celebrated as the first attempt to measure national wealth, William Petty's assessment of the wealth of England in the mid-seventeenth century was an attempt to check the viability of the British Parliament's taxation plans to fund the Anglo-Dutch wars.[12] Adam Tooze has argued that the question of German reparations provided major incentive for more accurate measurement of national wealth.[13] Economic specialists warned that "squeezing Germany until the pips squeaked" would not provide sustainable or positive economic benefits for Britain or France. After the Ruhr crisis of 1923, the Dawes Committee reorganized the reparation schedule around Germany's "capacity to pay." However, the Committee did not resolve how to measure such a capacity and, given the paucity of economic data, the problem of calculating national wealth continued to animate economists and statisticians, including Khambata and Shah, throughout the 1920s.[14] The measurement framework that emerged as the basis of Keynesian macroeconomics was developed within this context.

Studies of the production of "the economy" in nineteenth-century India reveal a different genealogy of economic measurement and national accounting. Uma Kalpagam has shown that, the pressure on the East India Company to ensure that its operations were profitable ensured that accurate accounting was a hallmark of British imperialism from the outset, though the transfer to Crown rule in 1858 brought about a step change in the quantity and range of data collected.[15] An early focus on collecting detailed data about trading practices shaped approaches to governance that saw colonial society and space in highly numerical terms. The Crown's formulation of "Home Charges" in this period, as a contribution to British public debt, added another dimension to this regime of accountancy. It rendered the "cost" of imperialism in clear fiscal terms, as a liability to be shouldered by Indian subjects. This distinct history provided a very different basis for discussions of national wealth as compared to the West. Rather than a means to measure the state's power in wartime, attempts to account for national wealth in a colonial context became the basis for attempts to measure the material impact of British rule on India and its people.[16]

First read to the Bombay Branch of the East India Association in 1876, Dadabhai Naoroji's *Poverty of India* sparked a series of attempts by both Indian and British economic specialists to measure India's wealth.[17] These estimates have been discussed in earlier studies of Indian nationalism and in histories of "the economy" in the long nineteenth century. However, in a division that replicates contemporary criticism of Khambata and Shah's work as "political" and lacking the "objectivity" required to be considered properly "economic," none of these estimates feature in the histories of early national accounting written after the standardization of these accounting practices, a process that reflects the positioning of economics as a state science in the mid-twentieth century.[18]

Drawing insight from a range of economists, in India and the West, Shah and Khambata's text pushes us to rethink accepted views of both Indian economic thought and supposedly "global" histories of national accounting. Khambata referred directly to Naoroji's work in his half of the book but Shah was also clearly inspired by his methodologies and by the strong institutional approach to economics that was common to Naoroji but also Indian economists such as Ramesh Chunder Dutt and Mahadev Govind Ranade. Like these earlier Indian economists, Shah and Khambata were interested not simply in measuring India's wealth but in questions of how much of this wealth was accessible to Indians themselves. In Naoroji's 1876 work, and the responses that followed, this income level was arrived at by dividing the total wealth by the most recent date on population numbers. Shah and Khambata's study engaged more recent works of Edwin Cannan, Josiah Stamp, Arthur Cecil Pigou and Irving Fisher, to ask new questions about income *distribution* in India. In so doing, their work reflects more than a refinement of earlier Indian economists' debates and can be read instead as a powerful reformulation of ideas of Indian poverty and, through this, of India's future political economy.

Manu Goswami has argued that the frameworks of measuring poverty used by late-nineteenth and early-twentieth-century Indian nationalists stressed the unity of Indian society in carrying the financial burden of colonial rule.[19] Their works acknowledged that income was not distributed evenly amongst Indians, but the very methodology of the per capita income approach established poverty as the marker of Indian society as a whole. Shah's emphasis on income distribution and taxable capacity, however, presented Indian society as marked by economic heterogeneity and inequality, even as it remained united by the experience of colonialism. In so doing, his work used economic measurement to bring into being a new imperial subject: that of the poor Indian individual.

Yet, to read Shah's work simply in terms of an "Indian" debate reproduces the Western/Indian divide this chapter seeks to challenge. Before qualifying as a barrister, Shah studied at the London School of Economics, the institutional home of many of the figures driving British discussions about national income and accounting in the early twentieth century. Shah had clearly read these works and drew on them in his own work in taxable capacity, as this chapter explores. However, while Shah may have been able to engage with these ideas and experts as an LSE student, the later historical analysis of his work show that Shah faced strong obstacles to engaging in such scholarly dialogue once he had graduated. This chapter considers why Shah's work was not read, at the time or later by historians, as a text in dialogue with a network of scholars in the UK and beyond, at a critical moment of imperial shift. The conclusion of the chapter considers how reading Shah's work as a dialogue of this kind opens up new possibilities for understanding the history of early-twentieth-century anti-imperial debate in India, and the history of economic thought more globally.

An analysis of Shah and Khambata's work must begin with a discussion of its title: *Wealth and taxable capacity*. Taxable capacity is not a term used by economists today but, understood to refer to the ability of individuals and companies to bear taxation, was the subject of much discussion in the early twentieth century particularly in the aftermath of the First World War and the staggering costs it had entailed. British economic specialists played a prominent role in this debate. Their arguments were often framed in terms of the distinctiveness of Britain's fiscal situation. But the political and economic links between Britain and other major powers, particularly the United States and, after the war, Germany, as well as British economic specialists' access to international networks of economic professionals ensured that British economists' work commanded a more canonical status in global discussions about how to measure national wealth and taxable capacity than studies by economists working outside these networks, such as Shah.[20]

British discussions about taxable capacity were deeply informed by the wartime transformation of the British income tax system. Britain had adopted a system of progressive income tax as early as 1909, though only in relation to a few, large incomes. Over the course of the war, the tax threshold was lowered, from £160 to £130, and the progressive components of the tax increased so that while 1,200,000 people had been assessed for income tax before the war broke out, by 1918–19 this figure had risen to 5,747,000, in a total population of around 40,000,000 people. Of these taxpayers, over two million received a full tax rebate, but the effect of these changes was to make income tax a far more general tax than had been the case previously so that the income taxpayer became a central feature of discussions about the relationship between the state and postwar society.[21]

Taxation, of income and other forms of wealth, had helped to sustain the British war effort but certainly not to cover it. By 1918–19 the British national debt had risen to £7,481 million, a dramatic increase from £706 million in 1913–14.[22] Much of this came from foreign loans, particularly from the United States, but also included money borrowed from British citizens through instruments such as war bonds and securities. The interest on this internal debt rose from £16.7 million in 1913–14 (or 9.6 percent of budget receipts) to £308.7 million (22.4 percent of receipts) in 1920–1.[23] There was considerable fear that this could spark social conflict within British society as the government sought to balance the interests of those who held the national debt against those of the taxpayer and producer. How far the government could use taxation to pay for the war debt without harming either national production or general social welfare became a central topic of public debate.[24]

By the early 1920s, Sir Josiah Stamp put forward what came to be known as the aggregate income method for measuring national wealth and taxable capacity. A civil servant in the British Inland Revenue, Stamp was also a talented economics student working at the London School of Economics around the same time that Shah attended. Stamp received his thesis from the LSE in 1916 which was published as *British Incomes and Property*.[25] He maintained close connections with economic staff at the LSE, publishing a prominent study on national income with Arthur Lyon Bowley, professor of statistics, in 1927.[26]

Stamp's approach was set out most clearly in his 1922 publication *Wealth and taxable capacity*. Writing with the nonspecialist in mind, Stamp invited readers to imagine national income as a "heap" of all the goods and services produced by the national community in a year, piled on top of the capital goods saved from previous years:

> Will you suppose that all the services and goods that are produced by us as a community in a year are all piled in the centre of this room in a great miscellaneous heap. Every one of you, in the work that you do, is putting that work there. It includes the boots and the clothes that are made, the loaves that are baked, the sheep that are reared … everything that can be given by us whereby we have a claim upon the work of our fellow-man who are contributing to the heap, including the services of those who have helped to make the heap larger than it would or could be if we started afresh without the assistance of piled-up capital goods saved from the heaps of former years. Let it be supposed that we have no such thing as money, but that for each contribution we have made to the heap there is given to us a "labour or services ticket" with a claim to draw something out of the heap in return … Now the total of tickets giving titles to the heap will exactly equal the mass in the heap, and when we have all drawn out what we want of other people's products and handed in our tickets, the heap will have vanished.[27]

Stamp's intention in using this metaphor was to turn the seemingly theoretical idea of national income into something that was "living and real … not … a mass of figures."[28] In so doing, he linked the concept of "national income" to that of "national community," or at least a national community of service providers, as Stamp sidestepped the problem of mass unemployment that Britain was experiencing at the time. Stamp's "heap" presented national income as something that was materially tangible, but also something that existed through relationships with those living and working around them.

From national income, Stamp argued, one could begin to consider the problem of taxable capacity. At its most basic level, he explained, taxable capacity could be found by taking the difference between the total quantity of production and the total quantity of consumption by a given community.[29] Yet, Stamp insisted, taxable capacity was not an absolute figure that could be deduced through fiscal arithmetic alone. Taxation was a "moving and dynamic problem," which involved thinking about emotions and sentiments as well as resources.[30]

High tax levels produced greater revenue in the short term, Stamp argued, but

> We have to ask not only how little we can leave [the taxpayer] with, but also how much reduction will he stand before he slackens in work and abstinence? How long will he come up smiling to be taxed in this way? … Thus it is little use thinking of the consumption level only—we have to keep our eye on the production side too, and watch the effects of our action there.[31]

While it was reasonable to ask richer members of society to pay more tax than those who were less well off, Stamp argued, it was important not to burden these taxpayers to the extent that they lost interest in providing the services that made them rich precisely because these services were what made up the shared national heap.[32]

This argument was also intended to address popular calls for Germany to be heavily taxed under the reparation agreement made at the Paris Peace Conferences of 1919. It was not only British taxpayers who were psychologically affected by high levels of taxation, Stamp argued. To use taxation to strip Germans of all but a basic level of subsistence would quickly impact on levels of production and national income, and through that on revenue collection in the longer term. Thus, taxation rested on a number of different, ever shifting factors, including "what the taxation is to be used for … the spirit and national psychology of the people taxed, which may be influenced by patriotism or sentiment … [and] … the distribution of wealth."[33] For Stamp, therefore, the primary aim of modern government was to sustain a cyclical flow of resources between the national community and the "heap." Such a government stood outside both the community and the "heap" but monitored both carefully, using taxation to move the flow of goods and services around the system to allow it to function as sustainably as possible.

Stamp's *Wealth* focused on the questions of taxable capacity facing postwar Britain but, as his discussion of German society shows, he clearly saw his methodology as one that could be applied to other national economies. Yet, as George Findlay Shirras explained in his *Science of Public Finance,* published two years after Stamp's *Wealth,* not all economies produced the type of data required for this method.[34] A prominent statistician and administrator within the Indian colonial administration, Findlay Shirras argued that Stamp's approach was suitable to the case of Britain and other "advanced" economies, but he set out a second approach for measuring national wealth and taxable capacity, which he called the "inventory" or "production method," to be applied to economies without an abundance of financial statistics.

Findlay Shirras's intervention in debates about taxable capacity drew from his professional expertise within the imperial administration. Born in Aberdeen, in 1885,

Findlay Shirras entered the Indian educational service as professor of economics at Dacca College in April 1909, two years after graduating from the University of Aberdeen. He was made director of statistics to the Government of India in 1914 before taking up a seat in the Bombay legislative council in 1921. From this position, he proffered that the Indian economy was the archetype for the production method of national wealth assessment, on the basis that agriculture, the main industry, was not covered under the Indian income tax system.[35] In India, income tax was applied to nonagricultural incomes only, and therefore covered only a small and, in Shirras's argument, unrepresentative section of the Indian economy.

Findlay Shirras sought to establish the taxable capacity of India by calculating annual levels of agricultural income. He did this by tabulating the main crops and source of agricultural produce cultivated in India and setting these against the size of the area as well as the total amount of each good produced. These figures were then multiplied by the average wholesale price of each commodity, worked out on a province-by-province basis. The total sum of India's nonagricultural income, based on income tax returns, was then added to this figure, which was finally divided by the total population to give a rate of per capita income.[36]

From here, Findlay Shirras sought to deduce India's taxable capacity. Like Stamp, he stressed the relative nature of social expectations relating to consumption and living standards.

> The standard of comfort is an elastic term, and taxable capacity will vary with different standards of comfort. In India the standard is low … We take then the standard of living as it is and not what it ought to be.[37]

Findlay Shirras based his figures for Indian living standards not on his own data but on J. C. Jack's 1916 *Economic life of a Bengal District,* which gave Rupees 240 per year as the minimum budget needed to feed an "average" family of five people for a year, or Rupees 48 per head. Adjusting this for postwar price inflation Findlay Shirras suggested that in 1922 this would translate into Rupees 90 per head. On top of this Findlay Shirras added contingency of 10 percent to cover seeds, manure, and replacement of family capital.

These figures were then compared with annual government tax revenue, though Findlay Shirras excluded expenditure on the internal debt on the basis that these transactions did not entail taking money out of the country. He concluded that the total tax burden shouldered by the Indian people was considerably lower than that of their British counterpart. According to his figures, in 1920–1 public authorities absorbed "30 per cent of what might have been taken, i.e. total taxable capacity ….as against 82 per cent in the United Kingdom." He pointed out that this comparison should be considered in relation to the very different level of living in the two countries, so that "ultimately Great Britain can stand much higher taxation. That explains why 82 per cent taken from total taxable capacity did not lead to the same hardships as the same percentage might do in a country with a lower standard of living."[38]

While Findlay Shirras followed Stamp's view that taxable capacity was dictated by national conditions, he spent little time on the particular components of those conditions that Stamp had set out in his study, namely "the spirit and national psychology … which may be influenced by patriotism" as well as the distribution of wealth amongst the people taxed.[39] Indeed, the people played a considerably smaller role in Findlay Shirras's "inventory" method than they did in Stamp's "aggregate income" approach. Stamp's argument began with the figure of the income taxpayer and the "heap" of national income produced by this person. His discussion of the role of services and community showed not only how individuals put into the heap but also what they could take out of it. In other words, the community was at the source of his workings and the "heap" was imagined as their property. In Findlay Shirras's approach, the people only appeared at the final stage of the process and then as highly abstracted individuals, not the more complex, psychologically defined figures set out by Stamp. In contrast to Stamp's emphasis on psychological conditions, Findlay Shirras's calculations read like an account book, focusing on the things produced in India, rather than the people who were doing the producing.

Findlay Shirras's intervention in discussions about taxable capacity, and its measurement in India, was not purely academic. The cost of India's involvement in the First World War had raised questions about revenue and taxable capacity that were distinct to British India. Widely seen as a "reward" for Indian support in the war effort, the 1919 Government of India Act introduced a new system of devolved government. The Act is seen as marking the beginning of representative government in India as it ushered an expansion of the Indian electorate and the state.[40] Through the formation of provincial legislatures, Indian representatives were given new powers over certain "transferred" subjects while the colonial administration dominated the main edifice of government.

Dyarchy involved the division of political powers between the central and provincial governments, but it also brought a new division of fiscal responsibilities.[41] Provincial governments became responsible for public works, education, industry, and agriculture—the so-called "nation-building" activities—while the central government retained control over law, finance, revenue, and home affairs. To help pay for the new services they were expected to provide, provinces were given control over land revenue, liquor excise, irrigation receipts, revenue from the forestry department, general and judicial stamps and registration fees. The central government controlled other forms of revenue including customs and income tax. But this was not an entirely straightforward division. Because land tax constituted the administration's largest single source of revenue it was feared that this division of income would leave the central government in deficit. Provincial governments were required to make regular contributions to the center to reimburse this revenue loss.[42] Dyarchy thus made the monitoring of provincial and national incomes, including the capacity of each layer of government to raise levels of taxation, central to the project of representative government in India. It promised new kinds of service provision to the Indian populace, while putting a heavy financial burden on the wings of government expected to provide it.

Stephen Legg has shown how the triangulation of democracy, autocracy and bureaucracy underpinning the 1919 Act transformed the colonial state but also understandings of what constituted responsible government.[43] The Act's imperial authors had envisaged responsible government in terms of *responsibility for* particular subjects. This seems to have been the way in which Findlay Shirras understood dyarchy.

At several points during the early 1920s, he stressed the importance of raising revenue to pay for the new "nation-building" tasks of government, particularly education.[44] While Indian taxpayers may not be able to shoulder tax burdens of 82 percent of their income, they could, he felt, pay more than the 30 percent he had calculated.

But, as Legg has shown, this was not the only way to interpret the meaning of responsible government as set out in the 1919 Act. For many Indian commentators, the 1919 Act established government in terms of *responsibility to* the people of India.[45] Shah was a prominent advocate of this latter point of view. In the same year as publishing *Wealth and taxable capacity*, Shah published a commentary on the 1919 Act with G. J. Bahadurji which made precisely this argument.[46]

In his own work on taxable capacity, K. T. Shah made no direct reference to Findlay Shirras's *Science* but he was certainly familiar with its author, who, like him, lived and worked in Bombay City.[47] The works that fill his short bibliography suggest that Shah was drawing on his LSE training rather than speaking to provincial government officials. And yet, Shah's study was a wholesale assault not only on Findlay Shirras's methodological approach to measuring taxable capacity, but also the assumptions that underpinned his understandings of the Indian economy and society. An interest in "nation-building" underpinned the discussion of taxable capacity in Shah's work as much as in Findlay Shirras's, but his understanding of the term was very different. Indeed, one of the basic conjectures in Shah's work was that the colonial state's taxation policy was not building the nation but harming it. He agreed that taxation was important for good government, but only if it served the interests of the national populace.

Findlay Shirras had included services in this calculation of national income, and thus in the amount of wealth from which to judge taxable capacity, but Shah and Khambata did not. While acknowledging the long debate amongst economic thinkers about whether services were productive, Shah and Khambata's justification of this omission was firmly in keeping with the broader traditions of Indian national economic thought which also discounted the contribution of services to national wealth.[48] Shah explained that "the only reliable and acceptable estimate of the national wealth can be had only in regard to material commodities." But more than this, Shah argued that "a number of services are really worthless, or even injurious to the community."[49] This argument was presented in general terms, but his position as a colonial subject undoubtedly informed his discussion of the monetary value produced by "the lawyer … the merchant … the Soldier … the Civil Servant, … the Statesman (or politician) and the Teacher," professions whose senior ranks were still dominated by British men in this period.[50] This list of "worthless" and "injurious" professions carries strong echoes of Gandhi's argument in *Hind Swaraj* though Shah made no direct reference to this work and many of his own economic views did not follow those of the Mahatma.

Even excluding services, Khambata's study of national wealth, which made up the first part of the book, identified a general increase in the country's wealth over recent decades. Khambata estimated that the real annual wealth of India had increased by about 10 percent from the prewar years.[51] But while generally optimistic about the progress of national income under British rule, Khambata expressed considerable concern in the closing section of his text about the way this income was distributed amongst India's population. Khambata estimated the gross annual income per capita of the Indian population to be Rupees 74.[52] He pointed out that this was a highly abstract measurement as babies as well as grown adults were included in the population figures. Furthermore, these figures reflected "the gross income of the people, from which charges [taxes and other levies] must be deducted in order to arrive at the total income available for enjoyment to the people of this country."[53] Once this was done, Khambata argued, "the measurement of the Wealth of India, [became]the measurement, rather of the poverty of India's millions."[54]

Shah's discussion of India's taxable capacity proceeded from this point. The first part of his study sought to establish precisely those "taxes and other levies" that were deducted from Khambata's calculation of the gross income of the Indian people. Tabulating duties and charges other than official taxes—which Shah took to include postal, railway, and irrigation charges; payments and interests on foreign capital invested in India; payments for shipping and banking services; and of course, Home Charges—he concluded that the Indian populace was left with a little less than Rupees 1,900 crores from which to pay national taxes—central, provincial, and local—as well as any domestic production costs.[55] Shah included in this latter category not only raw materials and transport, but also a diet adequate to feed a laboring individual.

In his work on taxable capacity Findlay Shirras had argued that the basic level of subsistence was a nationally relative concept. Shah agreed that "The food required by an individual varies not only according to his or her age, height, weight, and constitution in general, but also according to the climate under which the person is living and the work he is doing."[56] But he was interested in establishing a more concrete measure of minimum human need. Drawing on works by Benjamin Seebohm Rowntree, Bernard McFadden, and Frederick William Pavy he sought to determine a level of human sustenance below which a person could not function in even the most basic way. Following Naoroji, Shah analysed contemporary information about the dietary intake of different sections of Indian society including jail inmates, Indian army officers, lascars, and those under the Bombay Famine Relief system.[57] He deduced that "the cost of nourishing a human being on the same scale as a prisoner, that is the lowest scale of comfort consistent with keeping body and soul together" was, in current price terms, approximately Rupees 90 per annum, considerably in excess of the Rupees 74 per capita income calculated by Khambata.[58] Including taxes and deductions of around Rupees 18 per capita per annum, Shah concluded that

> [T]he average Indian income is so small that it is quite insufficient to meet even all the primary wants of man of food, clothing and shelter. Assuming that the last is relatively unimportant under Indian conditions ... the average Indian income is just enough either to feed 2 men in every three of the population (or give all of them 2 in place of every three meals they need) on condition that they all consent to go naked, live out of doors all year round, have no amusement or recreation, and want nothing else but food, and that, the lowest, coarsest, the least nutritious![59]

Such an argument highlighted the difference between basic need and quality of life. Shah's mode of analysis was very different to that of Stamp, but his discussion evoked the Indian population in terms closer to his income taxpaying community than the abstract understanding of population in per capita terms set out by Findlay Shirras. Whereas Stamp called on his audience to imagine themselves as a community, the individuals that Shah described were not people with whom his well-educated, English speaking readers would easily identify. Yet, Shah's key point was that these people *were* like his readers in terms of their physical needs. Of course the force of Shah's argument lay in the fact that, while poor Indians had the same kind of bodies as his wealthier readers, they were not able to maintain them. The condition of poor and lower-caste Indians' bodies had long been the site on which upper-class and upper-caste Indians had staked their nation-building projects, as well as providing moral justification for British rule in India.[60] At other points in his work, Shah seemed to present a more pejorative view of poor Indians as physically weak that echoed this kind of rhetoric.[61] But in using data about dietary consumption to invoke the Indian populace as a collection of embodied individuals he rejected a view of poverty as the inherent physical condition of the poor. All Indians had the physical capacity to be healthy; the problem lay in their ability to access enough food. In other words, Indian poverty arose from the improper distribution of the national "heap" to members of the national "community."

From here Shah turned to the question of India's tax burden. Shah highlighted the impact of dyarchy on taxation levels, breaking down his analysis into a discussion of taxation and expenditure by the various tiers of Indian government: central, provincial, municipal and the local boards. While Khambata's analysis focused only on British India, Shah included tributes to the colonial government from rulers of Native States in his calculation of the tax burden. This followed arguments he had made elsewhere that the political and economic present, as well as the future, of these States was bound up with that of British India, and fueled British critics' claims that Shah's work was more political than economic.[62] From this he proposed that the total tax burden could be rounded up to Rupees 400 crores per annum, or Rupees 12.5 per capita per annum.[63] However, Shah explained, the full significance of the tax burden became clear only when one ascertained the proportion of each taxpayers' *personal* wealth spent on tax.

Shah used the final section of his work to focus on the social distribution of this tax burden. Here, Shah drew heavily on Indian income tax data, in spite of the limited reach of the tax system. The wartime reforms of the British income tax system had triggered some changes in India also. Influenced by British tax legislation, the Government of India moved Indian income tax from a fixed rate to a progressive tax system in 1916, prompting a threefold ride in revenue collection.[64] Yet the number of Indians affected by income tax remained very small. The 1924 Economic Enquiry Committee reported the total number of Indian tax payers for the 1922–3 fiscal year was 238, 212.[65] The 1921 Census put the total population of India at almost 319 million people, meaning that around 0.07 percent of the population paid income tax.[66] Importantly, income tax covered only nonagricultural income, leaving agriculture, India's primary economic sector outside its purview. It was for these reasons that Findlay Shirras had argued the personal aggregate approach to taxable capacity could not be applied to India.

Shah made income tax data central to his methodology but used this information to think about the distribution of wealth across Indian society. Shah began with the information he did have. He calculated the total amount of income tax collected annually and divided this between the total number of taxpayers. He thought it reasonable to assume that if there were about 250,000 people who were officially registered to pay income tax, there were probably three times that number who should be paying the tax but had managed to evade it.[67] He concluded that a million people in India enjoyed a total income of around Rupees 375 crores or an annual average income of Rupees 3,750. If each of these individuals supported four dependents from this income, "we have a per capita income in this class of Rupees 937.5 per annum."[68]

This covered only nonagricultural income. Using census data and land records, Shah estimated that agriculturalists generated around Rupees 175 crores per year. Across all the Indian provinces, Shah identified a little more than 12 million (12,358,550) rent receivers, the group, he argued, which enjoyed this income. Thus Rupees 550 crores (the total of the income collected through agricultural taxes and income tax *plus* Shah's estimate of undeclared income supported roughly 17.5 million people (the 1 million income taxpayers (actual and potential), their 4 million dependents and the (12 million + rent receivers) on an income of roughly Rupees 325 per capita.[69]

But what about the remainder of the population? The vast bulk of Indians drew their livelihood from agriculture. Shah analysed the distribution of the remaining proportion of national income on this basis, subtracting Rupees 550 crores from Khambata's estimate of Rupees 2,364 crores, as well as another Rupees 175 crores, which, he argued, reflected the wealth of landlords and rent receivers. This left around Rupees 1,325 crores which, Shah argued, must be distributed amongst ordinary cultivators of whom 19.31 crores had been recorded under the 1921 Census. This gave a per capita income for this group of Rupees 68.6 per annum.

Shah did not stop here. Within this lower earning group, he argued, "It would … be absurd to assume that this whole amount is distributed equally and equitably among the total population."[70] Using data from income tax records and combining this with speculation about the relative size of different social classes, Shah argued that the distribution of wealth across Indian society could be broken down in the following way:

- 6,000 individuals with an average income per head of Rupees 100,000 per annum absorb [Rupees]600,000,000 among them, and support 30,000 persons.
- 270,000 individuals escaping or exempted from the Income Tax, but having an income liable to that tax, with an average income of Rupees 5,000 per head per annum, absorb among them [Rupees]1,350,000,000 and support 1,350,000.
- 2,500,000 individuals with an average annual income of Rupees 1,000 absorb among them Rupees 2,500,000,000 and support 12,500,000 persons.
- 35,000,000 individuals with an average income of Rupees 200 per annum absorb among them Rupees 7,000,000,000 and support 100,000,000 persons.
- The remainder have an average income of about Rupees 50 per annum and absorb among them 825 crores.[71]

"The result of this calculation" Shah continued

> [I]s that more than a third of the wealth of the country is enjoyed by about one percent of the population, or allowing for … dependents, about 5 percent at most;

> that slightly more than another third, about 35 percent of the annual wealth produced in the country, is absorbed by another third of the population allowing for the dependents, while 60 percent of the people of British India enjoy among them about 30 percent of the total wealth produced in the country.[72]

Framing taxable capacity in this manner, Shah did not simply contest Findlay Shirras's data but transformed the nature of this capacity to produce a fundamentally different understanding of the Indian economy. Findlay Shirras had argued that paucity of data meant that Indian taxable capacity should be measured using the "production inventory method." Yet the inventory method itself was premised on, and thus its findings served to reproduce, an understanding of India as a repository (of goods and labor) from which the colonial state was entitled to draw its wealth.

Shah's understanding of the Indian economy as related to Indian people led him to see and measure taxable capacity quite differently. It was this understanding of the economy that prompted him to ask questions about the distribution of India's wealth, not only between India and Britain as earlier Indian economists had discussed, but amongst Indian people themselves. In this sense, Shah's work connects much more closely to the approaches developed by Stamp in relation to the British context, than with Findlay Shirras's work on India. At the same time, Shah's work did not reproduce the "aggregate income approach" advocated by Findlay Shirras and Josiah Stamp in the British context—the lack of income tax data in India made this impossible. Rather, Shah forced a reversal of the statistics gathering process, using the limited information he possessed about the small number of Indian income taxpayers to give statistical substance to another figure—that of the little- or no-income-earning subject who, Shah argued, made up the majority of the Indian populace.

This act of bringing the poor Indian to statistical life was a clear assault on the political legitimacy of the colonial state in general but particularly in the transition to dyarchy. For Shah, British rule left the vast majority of the Indian people in a material condition in which they were unable to take proper responsibility for their own physical well-being, let alone for their own government. Read alongside his critique of the 1919 Government of India Act, Shah's work on taxable capacity appears as an urgent call for a government more responsible to—and simply capable of seeing—the people of India.

But Shah's study also marked a powerful departure from the more established lines of Indian economic nationalist thought. Shah's analysis made the redistribution of resources and economic uplift of the poor, defined in terms of household income levels, an imperative for a self-governing India. While the taxpayer was the focus of new ideas of national economy emerging in Europe, for Shah, it was the non-tax-paying poor that were the focal point of an emancipated Indian national economy. Within the broader cannon of Indian economic thought, his work on taxable capacity seems to offer an opportunity to imagine Indian society as a united but internally heterogeneous collective, to see the poor not in generalized abstraction, but as discernible individuals with distinct wants and needs.

For Shah, at least, early 1920s debates about the question of taxable capacity represented a moment of possibility to transcend the boundaries of purportedly separate political fields. The problem of postwar taxation was extensive enough to allow for a more imperial, or even global, conversation about measuring national wealth and income distribution; the possibility to use scholarship about British finances to critique imperial possibility; the possibility to use economic praxis to generate data that could reveal what had been made invisible by both imperial and nationalist economists: the material inequality of Indian society itself. How far were these possibilities ever realized? The contemporary reception of this work, and the fact that it has been so resoundingly forgotten, suggests that many people were not willing to accept Shah's ways of seeing Indian economy and society. Yet it is precisely the way in which this work helps us to destabilize the accepted norms of economic and political debate in this period, and beyond, that makes it historically significant.

In 1939, Shah was selected by Subhas Chandra Bose and Jawaharlal Nehru to serve as secretary for the Indian National Congress's National Planning Committee. This body and the series of reports it produced are widely seen as the roots for the Indian experiment in economic planning, even as these debates came, in the mid-1940s, to be dominated by rather different political voices, most noticeably the representatives of Indian capital. The shared language of economic planning in this period was arguably more reflective of a desire to obscure deep rooted fractures in the Indian political landscape than the outcome of any real consensus amongst Indian leaders.[73] There has been significant scholarly interest in showing how and why Indian opponents of socialism came to support economic planning.[74] However, Shah's 1924 work gives new insight to our understanding of the "other side" of this debate, revealing how economic planning could be seen not just as a mechanism through which to raise India to the economic status of other polities, but linked to and informed by a richer and more varied genealogy of debates about how to address economic inequalities and effect more radical social change.

At the same time, Shah's work pushes us to unpack the stability of contemporary scholarship on the history of twentieth-century economics. Shah's work reminds us that the development of modern national accounting involved settling not only questions of methodology, about the means by which to formulate those accounts, but also questions about what constituted the nation that was to be measured in this process. In this sense, Shah's British critics were right: his text was political, but so too was their refusal to engage with his methodology as economic practice. Alain Desrosières and Theodore Porter have shown that for economics to "hold" and be useful in the world, it must work in tandem with the worldviews and "truths" of other social and political power structures.[75] Shah's work was dismissed as unscientific because it disrupted the "account" of Indian society and economy that underpinned British understandings of the "truth" of British colonialism and India's place in the world.

Shah and Khambata's work does not contest existing histories of modern national accounting, as a set of practices that arose from Western debate. Rather, it helps us to see the political parameters of that debate and how economic theory and practices could work to naturalize the early twentieth-century political order. It pushes us to develop more global histories of national accounting and economic practices that reveal, rather than reproduce, the politics of economic knowledge production.

Notes

1 K. T. Shah and K. J. Khambata, *Wealth and Taxable Capacity of India* (Bombay: D.B. Taraporevala Sons & Co., London: P.S. King and Son, Ltd., 1924).
2 Ibid., pp. v–vi.
3 W. S. Thatcher, "Review of *Wealth and Taxable Capacity of India* by K. T. Shah, K. J. Khambata and other books," *The Economic Journal* 35, no. 140 (December 1925): 629.
4 Arguably Karl Polanyi was one of the first scholars to historicize the economy, *The Great Transformation* (Boston: Beacon Press, [1944] 1957), but it was the work of Susan Buck-Morss and Timothy Mitchell around the middle of the 1990s that helped to establish key aspects of the history of the economy. See in particular Buck-Morss, "Envisioning Capital: Political Economy on Display," *Critical Inquiry* 21, no. 2 (Winter 1995): 434–67 and Mitchell, "Origins and Limits of the Modern Idea of the Economy," Advanced Study Center, University of Michigan, Working Papers Series, no. 12, 1995. https://blogs.cuit.columbia.edu/tm2421/files/2018/01/Mitchell-1995.pdf and "Fixing the Economy," *Cultural Studies* 12, no. 1 (1998): 82–101.
5 Daniel A. Hirschmann, "Inventing the Economy or How We Learned to Stop Worrying and Love the GDP," PhD dissertation, University of Michigan, 2016, pp. 22–30.
6 Mary Poovey, *A History of the Modern Fact: Problems of Knowledge in the Sciences of Wealth and Society* (Chicago: University of Chicago Press, 1998); Margaret Schabas, *The Natural Origins of Economics* (Chicago: University of Chicago Press, 2005); Michel Foucault, *Security, Territory, Population: Lectures at the Collège de France 1977–1978* and *The Birth of Biopolitics: Lectures at the Collège de France, 1978–1979* (Basingstoke: Palgrave Macmillan, 2009); Manu Goswami, *Producing India: From Colonial Economy to National Space* (Chicago: University of Chicago Press, 2004).
7 Goswami, *Producing India*; Ritu Birla, *Stages of Capital: Law, Culture, and Market Governance in Late Colonial India* (Durham, NC: Duke University Press, 2008).
8 Timothy Mitchell, "Fixing the economy," *Cultural Studies* 12, no. 1 (1998): 82–101, esp. pp. 88–9; see also J. Adam Tooze, *Statistics and the German state, 1900–1945: The Making of Modern Economic Knowledge* (Cambridge: Cambridge University Press, 2001).
9 Mitchell, "Fixing the Economy,"; Tooze, *Statistics and the German state,* Introduction.
10 Tooze, *Statistics and the German state,* p. 20.
11 The work that comes closest to doing this is Benjamin Zachariah's Developing India but this is framed in terms of discourse analysis and does not engage with the material, socio technocratic developments that drive Tooze and Mitchell's arguments. *Developing India: An Intellectual and Social History* (New Delhi: Oxford University Press, [2005] 2012).
12 Paul Studenski, *The Income of Nations: Part One History* (New York: New York University Press, 1958).
13 J. Adam Tooze, "Imagining National Economies: National and International Economic Statistics," in Geoffrey Cubitt, ed., *Imagining Nations* (Manchester: Manchester University Press, 1998), pp. 218–20.
14 Ibid., pp. 218–19.
15 Uma Kalpagam, *Rule by Numbers: Governmentality in Colonial India* (Lanham, MD: Lexington Books, 2015), pp. 145–51.

16 Manu Goswami, "From Swadeshi to Swaraj: Nation, Economy, Territory in Colonial South Asia, 1870 to 1907," *Comparative Studies in Society and History* 40, no. 4 (1998): 609–36.

17 This paper was published two years later as Naoroji, *Poverty of India* (London: Vincent Brooks Day, 1878).

18 Tooze, *Statistics and the German state,* introduction; Studenski, *The Income of Nations*, pp. 149–55; John W. Kendrick, "The Historical Development of National-Income Accounts," *History of Political Economy* 2, no. 2 (1970): 304–15; Diana Coyle, *GDP: A Brief but Affectionate History* (Princeton, NJ: Princeton University Press, 2014), pp. 7–40.

19 Goswami, "From Swadeshi to Swaraj," pp. 622–3.

20 Josiah Stamp, the key authority on taxable capacity played a major role in shaping British fiscal policy and international policies on taxation as a member of the committee appointed in 1921 by the League of Nations to report on Double Taxation: Stamp's colleagues on the committee hailed from Holland (Prof. G.W.J. Bruins), Italy (Professor Senator Luigi Einaudi) and, America (Prof. Edwin Seligman). *Double Taxation and Tax Evasion: Report and Resolutions Submitted by the Technical Experts to the Financial Committee of the League of Nations* (Geneva: League of Nations, 1925). For some examples to Stamp see reviews by the American economists T. S. Adam and Willford I. King in *Journal of the American Statistical Association* 18, no. 140 (December 1922): 543–5 and *The American Economic Review* 12, no. 3 (September 1922): 531–3 respectively.

21 Martin Daunton, "How to Pay for the War: State, Society and Taxation in Britain, 1917–1924," *English Historical Review* CXI, no. 443 (September 1996): 889; Daunton, *Just Taxes,* especially pp. 103–41.

22 Stephen Broadbery and Peter Howlett, "The United Kingdom during World War I," in Stephen Broadbery and Mark Harrison, eds., *The Economics of World War I* (Cambridge, UK: Cambridge, 2005), p. 219.

23 Daunton, "How to Pay for the War," p. 883.

24 Ibid., pp. 882–919 and *Just Taxes*, pp. 103–41.

25 Josiah Stamp, *British Incomes and Property: The Application of Official Statistics to Economic Problems* (London: P.S. King and son, 1916).

26 A. L. Bowley and Josiah Stamp, *The National Income, 1924* (Oxford: Clarendon Press, 1927).

27 Josiah Stamp, *Wealth and Taxable Capacity: The Newmarch Lectures for 1920–1 on Current Statistical Problems in Wealth and Industry* (London: P. S. King and Sons, 1922), pp. 42–4.

28 Ibid., p. 42.

29 Ibid., pp. 112–13.

30 Ibid., p. 115.

31 Ibid.

32 Ibid., pp. 116–17.

33 Ibid., p. 118.

34 George Findlay Shirras, *The Science of Public Finance* (London: MacMillan and Co., 1924). This book was a huge success for Shirras who revised the book for two further editions, printed between 1925 and 1936.

35 Ibid., pp. 135–49. See also Findlay Shirras's "Taxable Capacity and the Burden of Taxation and Public Debt," *Journal of the Royal Statistical Society* 88, no. 4 (July 1925): 521–2.

36 Findlay Shirras, *The Science of Public Finance*, pp. 138–41.
37 Ibid., p. 147.
38 Ibid., p. 148.
39 Stamp, *Wealth and Taxable Capacity*, p. 118.
40 James Chiriyankandath, "'Democracy' under the Raj: Elections and Separate Representation in British India," *The Journal of Commonwealth & Comparative Politics* 30, no. 1 (1992): 39–63.
41 P. J Thomas, *The Growth of Federal Finance in India: Being a Survey of India's Public Finances from 1833 to 1939* (Madras: Oxford University Press, 1939), pp. 303–57.
42 Neil Charlesworth, "The Problem of Government Finance in British India: Taxation, Borrowing and the Allocation of Resources in the Inter-war Period," *Modern Asian Studies* 19, no. 2 (1985): 535.
43 Stephen Legg, "Dyarchy: Democracy, Autocracy and the Scalar Sovereignty of Interwar India," *Comparative Studies of South Asia, Africa, and the Middle East* 36, no. 1 (May 2016): 44–65.
44 Findlay Shirras, *The Science of Public Finance*, vii; see also Findlay Shirras, *The War and Indian Trade* (1919).
45 Legg, "Dyarchy," p. 45.
46 Ibid., pp. 44–5, 59–61.
47 Shah cites several government papers on Indian finance and Bombay worker household budgets written by Findlay Shirras.
48 see Naoroji, *Poverty and Un-British Rule*, especially pp. 170–3.
49 Shah and Khambata, *Wealth and Taxable Capacity*, p. vii.
50 Ibid.
51 Ibid., p. 196. Khambata calculated that the total net income of the country rose from Rupees 1,106 crores to Rupees 2,364 by 1921–2, but this latter figure had to be adjusted around changing price levels. When this was accounted for it became Rupees 1,182 crores, pp. 196–200.
52 Ibid., p. 201. This was lower than the figures of Rupees 107 and Rupees 116, given by Shirras for the years 1921 and 1922 respectively. Shirras, *The Science of Public Finance*, p. 141.
53 Shah & Khambata, *Wealth and Taxable Capacity*, p. 200.
54 Ibid., p. 203.
55 Ibid., p. 237–8.
56 Ibid., p. 214.
57 Ibid., pp. 243–50. On the history of the Famine Code see Sunil S. Amrith, "Food and Welfare in India, c. 1900–1950," *Comparative Studies in Society and History* 50, no. 4 (2008): 1012–15 and David Arnold, "The 'Discovery' of Malnutrition and Diet in Colonial India," *The Indian Economic & Social History Review* 31, no. 1 (1994): 1–26.
58 Shah and Khambata, *Wealth and Taxable Capacity*, p. 252. There are strong parallels between this emotive language and that used by Naoroji in *Poverty and Un-British Rule in India*, pp. 289–90.
59 Ibid., p. 253. It is worth contrasting Shah's discussion here with that of Radhakamal Mukerjee in his 1916 work *The Foundations of Indian Economics* (London: Longmans, Green and Co.). Mukerjee compiled information from a range of household budget surveys to discuss Indian poverty but was resolute that this question be managed on the basis of familial assessment, and not individual. See pp. 56–9 and pp. 15–46 of this work.

60 See, for example, Nandini Gooptu, *The Politics of the Urban Poor in Early Twentieth-century India* (Cambridge: Cambridge University Press, 2001), pp. 10–18; Anshu Malhotra, "The Body as Metaphor for the Nation: Caste, Masculinity and Femininity in the Satyartha Prakash of Swami Dayananda Saraswati," in Avil A. Powell and Siobhan Lambert-Hurley, eds., *Rhetoric and Reality: Gender and the Colonial Experience in South Asia* (New Delhi, 2006); on the importance of bodily purity for Gandhian anticolonialism see Joseph S. Alter, *Gandhi's Body: Sex, Diet, and the Politics of Nationalism* (Philadelphia: University of Pennsylvania Press, 2000).

61 Shah and Khambata, *Wealth and Taxable Capacity*, pp. x–xii.

62 Ibid., p. 258. See Shah's *Governance of India, Being a Commentary on the "Government of India" Acts 1915 and 1916, with Additional Chapters on the Indian Local Government, Indian Army, Indian Finance and the Native States of India* (Bombay: Ramchandra Govind & Son, 1917), pp. 304–18; this argument was repeated in a revised commentary, published with Bahadurji in 1924, the same year as *Wealth and Taxable Capacity*; Shah and Bahadurji, *Governance of India. A Commentary*, pp. 369–84. The review of Shah's work in the *Journal of the Royal Statistical Society* was scathing of the inclusion of the Native States in these calculations. *Journal of the Royal Statistical Society* 89, no. 2 (March 1926): 346–7.

63 Shah and Khambata, *Wealth and Taxable Capacity*, p. 261.

64 Income tax revenue rose from Rupees 3 crores to Rupees 9.5 crores in 4 years. For more on these changes see Newbigin, *The Hindu Family and the Emergence of Modern Citizenship: Law, Citizenship and Community* (Cambridge: Cambridge University Press, 2013), pp. 58–92.

65 "Report of the Indian Economic Enquiry Committee," (1925) vol. I, 28. V. K. R. V Rao estimated in 1931–2, 913, 582 individuals—as opposed to "legal person" (a term that included companies, firms and Hindu Undivided Families, paid income tax—about 0.25 percent of the population of India according to the 1931 census. V. K. R. V. Rao, *The National Income of British India, 1931–1932* (London: Macmillan, 1940), pp. 125–9.

66 The total figure for population was: 318,942,480. Census Commissioner, "Census of India, 1921," (1922) vol. 1, Part II—Tables, 2–3.

67 Shah and Khambata, *Wealth and Taxable Capacity*, p. 298.

68 Ibid. To put this into perspective, under the second schedule of the 1919 Government of India Act members of the executive council of the governor of Bengal, Madras, Bombay, and the United Provinces were allocated an annual salary of up to Rupees 64,000. The maximum salary of the Governor-General of India was Rupees 256,000. *Government of India Act, 1919*, ch. 101.

69 Shah and Khambata, *Wealth and Taxable Capacity*, p. 302.

70 Ibid., p. 304.

71 Ibid., p. 307.

72 Ibid.

73 Zachariah, *Developing India*, pp. 213–63

74 B. R. Tomlinson, *The Economy of Modern India, 1860–1970* (Cambridge: Cambridge University Press. 1993), Zachariah, *Developing India*.

75 Alain Desrosières, *The Politics of Large Numbers: A History of Statistical Reasoning*. Translated by Camille Nash (Cambridge, MA: Harvard University Press, 1998), esp. pp. 1–13. Theodore M. Porter, *Trust in Numbers* (Princeton and London: Princeton University Press, 1995).

Select Bibliography

Alter, Joseph S., *Gandhi's Body: Sex, Diet, and the Politics of Nationalism* (Philadelphia: University of Pennsylvania Press, 2000).

Arnold, David, "The 'Discovery' of Malnutrition and Diet in Colonial India," *The Indian Economic & Social History Review* 31, no. 1 (1994): 1–26.

Amrith, Sunil S., "Food and Welfare in India, c. 1900–1950," *Comparative Studies in Society and History* 50, no. 4 (2008): 1010–35.

Birla, Ritu, *Stages of Capital: Law, Culture, and Market Governance in Late Colonial India* (Durham, NC: Duke University Press, 2008).

Bowley, A. L. and Josiah Stamp, *The National Income, 1924* (Oxford: Clarendon Press, 1927).

Broadbery, Stephen and Peter Howlett, "The United Kingdom during World War I," in Stephen Broadbery and Mark Harrison, eds., *The Economics of World War I* (Cambridge: Cambridge University Press, 2005), pp. 206–34.

Buck-Morss, Susan, "Envisioning Capital: Political Economy on Display," *Critical Inquiry* 21, no. 2 (Winter 1995): 434–67.

Charlesworth, Neil, "The Problem of Government Finance in British India: Taxation, Borrowing and the Allocation of Resources in the Inter-war Period," *Modern Asian Studies* 19, no. 2 (1985): 521–48.

Chiriyankandath, James, "'Democracy' under the Raj: Elections and Separate Representation in British India," *The Journal of Commonwealth & Comparative Politics* 30, no. 1 (1992): 39–64.

Coyle, Diana, *GDP: A Brief but Affectionate History* (Princeton, NJ: Princeton University Press, 2014).

Daunton, Martin, "How to Pay for the War: State, Society and Taxation in Britain, 1917–1924," *English Historical Review CXI* (September, 1996).

Desrosières, Alain, *The Politics of Large Numbers: A History of Statistical Reasoning*. Translated by. Camille Nash (Cambridge, MA: Harvard University Press, 1998).

Foucault, Michel, *The Birth of Biopolitics: Lectures at the Collège de France, 1978–1979* (Basingstoke: Palgrave Macmillan, 2008).

Foucault, Michel, *Security, Territory, Population: Lectures at the Collège de France 1977–1978* (Basingstoke: Palgrave Macmillan, 2009).

Gooptu, Nandini, *The Politics of the Urban Poor in Early Twentieth-century India* (Cambridge: Cambridge University Press, 2001).

Goswami, Manu, "From Swadeshi to Swaraj: Nation, Economy, Territory in Colonial South Asia, 1870 to 1907," *Comparative Studies in Society and History* 40, no. 4 (1998): 609–36.

Goswami, Manu, *Producing India: From Colonial Economy to National Space* (Chicago: University of Chicago Press, 2004).

Hirschmann, Daniel A., "Inventing the Economy or How We Learned to Stop Worrying and Love the GDP," PhD dissertation, University of Michigan, 2016.

Kalpagam, Uma, *Rule by Numbers: Governmentality in Colonial India* (Lanham, MD: Lexington Books, 2015).

Kendrick, John W., "The Historical Development of National-Income Accounts," *History of Political Economy* 2, no. 2 (1970): 284–315.

Legg, Stephen, "Dyarchy: Democracy, Autocracy and the Scalar Sovereignty of Interwar India," *Comparative Studies of South Asia, Africa, and the Middle East* 36, no. 1 (May 2016): 44–65.

Malhotra, Anshu, "The Body as Metaphor for the Nation: Caste, Masculinity and Femininity in the Satyartha Prakash of Swami Dayananda Saraswati," in Avil A. Powell and Siobhan Lambert-Hurley, eds., *Rhetoric and Reality: Gender and the Colonial Experience in South Asia* (2006): 121–53.

Mitchell, Timothy "Fixing the Economy," *Cultural Studies* 12, no. 1 (1998): 82–101.

Mitchell, Timothy, "Origins and Limits of the Modern Idea of the Economy," Advanced Study Center, University of Michigan, Working Papers Series, no. 12, 1995.

Mukerjee, Radhakamal, *The Foundations of Indian Economics* (London: Longmans, Green and Co., 1916).

Naoroji, Dadabhai, *Poverty of India* (London: Vincent Brooks Day, 1878).

Newbigin, Eleanor, *The Hindu Family and the Emergence of Modern Citizenship: Law, Citizenship and Community* (Cambridge: Cambridge University Press, 2013).

Poovey, Mary, *A History of the Modern Fact: Problems of Knowledge in the Sciences of Wealth and Society* (Chicago: University of Chicago Press, 1998).

Polanyi, Karl, *The Great Transformation* (Boston: Beacon Press, 1957 [1944]).

Porter, Theodore M., *Trust in Numbers* (Princeton and London: Princeton University Press, 1995).

Rao, V. K. R. V., *The National Income of British India, 1931–1932* (London: Macmillan, 1940).

Schabas, Margaret, *The Natural Origins of Economics* (Chicago: University of Chicago Press, 2005).

Shah, K. T. and G. J. Bahadurji, *Governance of India, Being a Commentary on the "Government of India" Acts 1915 and 1916, with Additional Chapters on the Indian Local Government, Indian Army, Indian Finance and the Native States of India* (Bombay: Ramchandra Govind & Son, 1917).

Shah, K. T. and K. J. Khambata, *Wealth and Taxable Capacity of India* (Bombay: D.B. Taraporevala Sons & Co.; London: P. S. King and Son, Ltd, 1924).

Shirras, George Findlay, *The Science of Public Finance* (London: MacMillan and Co., 1924).

Shirras, George Findlay, "Taxable Capacity and the Burden of Taxation and Public Debt," *Journal of the Royal Statistical Society* 88, no. 4 (July 1925).

Stamp, Josiah, ed., *British Incomes and Property: The Application of Official Statistics to Economic Problems* (London: P.S. King and son, 1916).

Stamp, Josiah, ed., *Double Taxation and Tax Evasion: Report and Resolutions Submitted by the Technical Experts to the Financial Committee of the League of Nations* (Geneva: League of Nations, 1925).

Stamp, Josiah, ed., *Wealth and Taxable Capacity: The Newmarch Lectures for 1920–1 on Current Statistical Problems in Wealth and Industry* (London: P.S. King and Sons, 1922).

Studenski, Paul, *The Income of Nations: Part One History* (New York: New York University Press, 1958).

Thomas, P. J, *The Growth of Federal Finance in India: Being a Survey of India's Public Finances from 1833 to 1939* (Madras: Oxford University Press, 1939).

Tomlinson, B. R., *The Economy of Modern India, 1860–1970* (Cambridge: Cambridge University Press, 2013).

Tooze, J. Adam, "Imagining National Economies: National and International Economic Statistics," in Geoffrey Cubitt, ed., *Imagining Nations* (Manchester: Manchester University Press, 1998), pp. 90–105.

Tooze, J. Adam, *Statistics and the German state, 1900–1945: The Making of Modern Economic Knowledge* (Cambridge: Cambridge University Press, 2001).

Zachariah, Benjamin, *Developing India: An Intellectual and Social History* (New Delhi: Oxford University Press, 2012 [2005]).

6

Law and the Political Imaginary in Mid-Twentieth-Century Southern India

Kalyani Ramnath

I

Law and legalities shaped political imaginaries of twentieth-century India. In turn, the contours, ridges, and sharp edges of legal landscapes (to invoke the topographical metaphor of the imaginary) were shaped by emergent political possibilities. This essay provides a historical sketch of mid-twentieth-century India illustrating these dynamics as an account of a collective conversation on imperial pasts and democratic futures. It is peopled by those who traversed the spheres of law and electoral politics with some ease, often buoyed by their professional privileges (and attendant privileges of class, caste, and gender).[1] It maps the worlds they traveled in—courtrooms, collectorates, and conferences; their names inscribed on reports, petitions, and affidavits where their familial, gender, and caste identities lent their voices and opinions greater or lesser authority. In conversation with Partha Chatterjee, Mary John, and Aditya Nigam in this volume, it suggests that rather than dismiss law as complicit in the making of particular (statist) political futures that sought to maintain the status quo, it is instructive to think of it as a terrain that could be reimagined.[2] While scholars have rightly pointed to the limits of law and to its potential to enable epistemic violence, I am interested to show how these limits (and possibilities) were perceived by those who lived and worked at a time when democratic futures, unblemished by imperial rule, seemed within reach.

As the sketches that follow show, one of the preoccupations of the mid-twentieth-century moment (the 1940s and 1950s) was the colonial legacy of legal infrastructures: legislation, legal practices, lawyers, and judges that were intended to serve and preserve colonial power. This was most noticeable in questions over criminal procedure. The initial arguments against retaining colonial-era criminal procedure were to suggest that it had been used to curb dissent: memories of the Rowlatt Act, for instance, used to imprison and censor, were all too fresh in the minds of those who lived through the tumultuous 1940s. So was the widespread use of emergency regulations during the World Wars and their surreptitious continuance in the postwar phase. Activists would deem both less vicious than the preventive detention legislation of the first decade of Indian independence. When the new Indian Constitution came into force in 1950, the debate manifested as a conflict between criminal procedure and constitutional rights. Often, as this essay shows, it coalesced around the question of civil liberties. These conversations took place amongst those with divergent political affinities, which makes it particularly interesting in understanding how the framework of imaginaries can help us rethink histories of the political. As a historical sketch, this essay joins a growing number of scholars who point to the mid-twentieth-century moment as critical in understanding the long arc of state–society relations which has tended to center the 1970s, the declaration of a national emergency and the suspension of constitutional remedies as the first sign of an imperiled Indian democracy. One of the key implications of my argument is that chasms frequently attributed to the 1975–7 Emergency—particularly over a failure of economic democracy—had begun to appear from the earliest days of independent India.[3]

These are interconnected impressionistic sketches, and are by no means, an attempt at capturing the scale of the "national" or indeed, the "regional." As the Introduction notes, one of the ways in which imaginaries rethink the notion of the "political" is by opening up predetermined frameworks such as the nation-state. In these sketches, one might usefully ask what frameworks our historical actors used as they navigated the political transition from empire to nation; there were certainly many (nation, region, world/global, empire, local) for them to choose from. Instead of making any assumptions, here, I follow their itineraries instead of reconstructing one *for* them. The professional lawyers and political workers in this Chapter moved within India, but wherever appropriate, I have also gestured to the broader Indian Ocean worlds of which they were aware of, and engaged with.

I begin with three notable constitutional law cases of the early 1950s began at the Madras High Court: *State of Madras* v. *V. G. Row*, *A. K. Gopalan* v. *State of Madras*, and *Champakam Dorairajan* v. *State of Madras*. Beginning with these cases, but going beyond them, I use examples mentioned in the *Indian Civil Liberties Bulletin*, published by the Servants of India Society between 1949 and 1960 from Pune. The *Bulletin* was edited by R. G. Kakade, S. G. Vaze, N. M. Joshi (until 1955), and Madhu Limaye, all members of the Servants of India Society and prominent political leaders in Bombay, for most of its publication history. K. G. Sivaswamy, the Organizing Secretary of the All India Civil Liberties Council who was based in Madras, was also instrumental in building a wider readership for the *Bulletin*. In its very first issue in October 1949, the editors asserted that it would function as a kind of "news record," not as a commentary on legal and political affairs. Further, it would bear no party affiliation. At first glance, the sketches below bear out these assertions. However, reading beyond the news snippets, each was steeped in, and responded to, the social and economic realities of the time; leading to multiple political imaginaries that were circulated, appreciated, and sometimes discarded. For the purposes of this essay, they invoke a broader history of the political left in southern India, but also suggest directions to think about the relationship between law and political imaginaries in other contexts as well.

II

In 1949, the first Indian Civil Liberties Conference was held in Madras, where the All India Civil Liberties Council was formally inaugurated. State and district level civil liberties unions and committees (which had been formed in the interwar years across colonial India) submitted reports, detailing transgressions of civil liberties that they had documented in their own states. At the 1949 conference, the published Report showed that one of their greatest preoccupations was the rise of public safety legislation, variously termed "public safety acts" or "public order acts" across the country: in the Central Provinces and Berar, East Punjab, Bihar, Saurashtra, and beyond. So rampant were the enactment of public safety laws and the legal challenges to them that the *Indian Civil Liberties Bulletin* carried them under a separate section titled "Public Safety Acts." The Report noted that these laws were being used to conduct statewide sweeps of political workers belonging to opposition parties and noted the many legal challenges decided by courts. For members of civil liberties unions, this signaled the use of colonial-era legal strategies that they believed had no place in a democratic society.

Madras, where the conference was held, had its own variant of a public safety legislation, ostensibly to tide over the uncertainties of the transition from colonial rule to independence. The Madras Maintenance of Public Order Act was first enacted as a provincial legislation in March 1947 that allowed for preventive detention, censorship, and control of essential commodities, ostensibly ensuring "public safety." For six weeks prior, the Madras Government issued it as an ordinance, in order to tide over the time required for the legislature to debate and enact the law. Over these six weeks, according to figures presented in the Madras Legislative Assembly, over 145 people were arrested and 35 warrants issued for searches and seizures.[4] In 1949, it had the highest number of all detainees belonging to the Communist Party. As mentioned earlier, in 1947, the Act was not unusual either in its nomenclature or its substantive provisions. Several other provinces in British India had enacted, or were in the process of enacting, similar legislation.[5] While provisions of the Act came under judicial scrutiny from its very inception, it escaped unscathed and remained on the statute books until 1952. It was supplanted in February 1950 by a central (federal) law, the Preventive Detention Act, 1950. The 1950 Act retained many of the MMPOA's stringent provisions that courts had struck down, beginning a plethora of repressive detention laws in postcolonial India. Peacetime preventive detention was also validated when it was included as a provision in the 1950 Constitution. Its constitutional validity was upheld in *A. K. Gopalan* v. *Union of India*,[6] a case that began at a trial court in Madras.

Going strictly by political chronology, it was a colonial law since it was first brought into force before Indian independence. Its stated intention was to curb the chaos that governments believed would ensue during the partition of the subcontinent into India and Pakistan, a tumultuous, and tragic political transition. In practice, in states like Madras, it was increasingly used against the political opponents of the ruling Indian National Congress Party. For instance, debates in the Madras Legislative Assembly regarding the Act revealed that the government had meant for the Act to replace the Defence of India Rules, a Second World War-era legislation that had expired in 1946.[7]

In its implementation too, during the transitional period from colonial to postcolonial, it mimicked features of earlier repressive colonial-era legislation. But beyond this relatively well-known history, the MMPOA not only authorized preventive detention, but also had several provisions relating to the control and distribution of essential commodities, and various forms of censorship.[8] It mandated the imposition of collective fines and strict limits on the freedom of movement for both people and commodities. Government reports noted that disturbances and riots arising during the harvest season could be curtailed with the help of the MMPOA. Coupled with the food control policy implemented by the Madras Government in the late 1940s (part of the broader move toward the control and permits for commodities in the immediate postwar period), the Act was part of the legal arsenal used to shape the postcolonial economy.[9]

This targeting of the political opposition using the provisions of a public safety legislation perhaps lay precisely in this anxiety over economic production. Statistics from the fortnightly reports submitted to the Madras Government show that while the Act was used against workers across the political spectrum, it was increasingly used against the political Left. The number of Communist Party workers was far greater than those of the Rashtriya Swayam Sevak Sangh, for instance. The Communist Party in the later 1940s had established strong links with peasant movements in all parts of the Madras Presidency, including the important rice producing districts of Thanjavur and Tirunelveli, in addition to the Telangana movement across its territorial borders in Hyderabad. In the city of Madras, it influenced unions at major establishments from the South Indian Railway Company to the Buckingham and Carnatic Mills. The Madras Administration Report 1946 noted that strikes stood at an all-time high of 273, which it attributed to "disruptive elements" and "communists in particular."[10] Across the Palk Strait, in Ceylon/Sri Lanka, left parties including the important Lanka Sama Samaja Party exercised influence over plantation workers. The Madras Government believed that Kisan Sabhas and agricultural unions had been "captured" by the Communist Party. There was a perception (not wholly unsubstantiated) that the post-Second World War resurgence of the political Left in southern India (and in Sri Lanka and Malaya, to some extent) was at odds with the impetus of the politically dominant Indian National Congress.

It is against the background of these electoral, political and social anxieties that the formation of a civil liberties union in Madras becomes important. Since the Madras Civil Liberties Union was formed a few days after the promulgation of the Ordinance that became the Madras Maintenance of Public Order Act, 1947,[11] it is likely that the members of the Union would have been able to observe all of the activity under the Act. The representatives of civil liberties unions in the various districts of Madras were in possession of a legal education, familiar with legal arguments made in similar cases in courts across the country. Their voices were amplified owing to their gender, class, and caste privileges. As I have noted elsewhere, the connections between the Bombay Civil Liberties Union and the chapters of the Indian Civil Liberties Union formed a few years later were significant.[12] For example, N. M. Joshi, the noted trade union leader in Bombay who was one of the editors of the *Bulletin* was in conversation with his counterparts in Madras, including the labor leader V. V. Giri. Not least was a shared interest and experience with law and lawyering, even as the first issue of the

Bulletin noted that "lovers of civil liberty must not build too high hopes on the power of High Courts to restore freedom to detained persons."[13] For instance, P. R. Das, who chaired the first conference of the All India Civil Liberties Council, had formerly been a judge of the Patna High Court. Since they moved between their professional spheres and the world of electoral politics, they were often translators and mediators of social movements and economic realities that they confronted or were petitioned about. In short, they became what historian Mithi Mukherjee has called in the context of the Indian nationalist elite, the "enunciative persona" of political movements.[14]

III

Among the most prominent supporters of the civil liberties movement in Madras in the late 1940s was the law firm of Row and Reddy. V. G. Row and A. Ramachandran had both qualified as barristers in England. Legend has it that they were sent to London to prepare for the Indian Civil Services examination, which was considered the pinnacle of success for young men from well-to-do families at the time. Row and Ramachandran were both influenced by the outspoken criticism by the Communist Party of Great Britain of the British government in India and vowed not to be part of an imperialist institution like the ICS. "In the thirties," Ivor Jennings, the architect of Ceylon's 1948 Constitution would later write of men like Row, "it was fashionable for the England educated to turn Communist."[15] Most of the *habeas corpus* applications filed by the MMPOA detainees in 1949 were filed by Row and Reddy, who were approached because of their links to the party as well as organized labor movements in the city.

Unlike the Communist Party in India at the time, which had come under the influence of the ultraleft Ranadive line, Row and Ramachandran were communists who returned to set up a law firm to represent labor. Row also represented the interests of the working class in the Madras Legislative Council (of which he was a member) through his championing of workers' rights under the Shops and Establishments Act, where nonindustrial workers could go to court against dismissals from their places of employment.[16] When the 1950 Constitution came into force, Row continued to exhibit his communist sympathies by filing a test case challenging the ban on the People's Education Society, a semi-legal front floated by the party when the ban was in force from 1947. Later, he would petition the courts challenging provisions of the Indian Passport Act for not allowing him and S. B. Adityan (a fellow Communist member of the Madras Legislative Council) to travel to Russia.[17] Row and Reddy's involvement shaped legal precedent on the nature of transitional preventive detention laws, and the fates of thousands of political prisoners under the MMPOA. Among the many habeas corpus applications that Row and Reddy filed challenging the detention orders against their clients, this paragraph employs the language of civil liberty to issue a stinging rebuke of the use of the Act:

> [T]he alleged activities of the Communist Party is an unwarranted and uncalled for slanderous attack on a legally existing political party by the Congress Party in power today. This only shows that the Public Safety Act is used to lock up

> arbitrarily and indefinitely without trial persons of opposite political convictions. This is nothing up vindictive persecution of political opponents and amounts to a negation of all democratic rights and a wholesale violation of accepted civil liberties in any civilized country. I state that these false allegations against the Communist Party are put in only to justify my illegal detention somehow.[18]

Only a few of these habeas corpus applications, demanding the release of illegally detained political workers, were ever successful. The *Bulletin*, which recorded the filing of some of the petitions, is unlikely to have had the readership that a sensational reporting of a high-profile trial would have had. In perusing the scholarship on the rise of political Left(s) in colonial India, we either find a number of accounts of the Meerut Conspiracy Case held in the 1920s which was widely covered in the newspapers at this time or institutional histories of the Communist Party and the ideological differences amongst its membership in India. In contrast, here, there are no grand acts of political imagination or the use of the courtroom as theatre. Note that lawyers with communist sympathies like Row and Reddy did not dismiss the use of law, courts or legislatures to support their colleagues. Although "civil liberty" formed part of the legal and political vocabulary during the earliest days of British colonial rule, in the extract from the affidavit above, Row and Reddy claim it for democratic citizens rather than for colonial subjects. Similar instances of lawyers and political workers working together to preserve freedom of association, speech and movement through habeas corpus applications in the United Provinces, Bombay, Bihar, Orissa, and elsewhere were extensively documented in the *Bulletin.*

The courtroom or the legal trial as the scene of competing political ideas is not a new trope in modern Indian history. Take again, for instance, Mithi Mukherjee's discussion of the Warren Hastings's impeachment trial in the eighteenth century.[19] She suggests that there were two competing visions of justice at stake in the trial: that of colonial justice and imperial justice. Tracing the long arc of these two competing visions—with equal treatment before the law being at stake—she argues that colonial justice trumps imperial justice in the text of the Indian Constitution that comes into force in 1950. For Mukherjee, episodes of nationalisms in the colonial period are akin to political trials, where competing notions of fairness and justice are debated, and the fractures of race, religion, and language mark colonial legal regimes. But here an account of legal practice shifts the emphasis away from the scene of the courtroom, from imagination to imaginary. If instead, we were to view, political imaginaries as shaped by law and legalities, then we confront—alongside our lawyers and civil liberties activists who faithfully documented every instance of the use of the MMPOA—the limits of the law, its double-edged nature, its propensity for violence, and its potential for change.

IV

From the sketch about the legislation and practice of a public order legislation in Madras, it is clear that the debate over civil liberties was not restricted to legal technicalities. It was deeply aware of the economic inequities within which questions of personal freedom arose. What is equally interesting about the use of a civil liberties language in mid-twentieth-century India is that it was not simply a reference to political rights: to vote, assemble, speak or travel. It was not, at least in the context of Madras, a reactionary claim against the ruling Indian National Congress government. The social and political context in which these claims were made by political workers (and the lawyers who defended them/were them) was the growing divide between government and the everyday concerns of citizens, about food production and commodity production and distribution. Recall that the Communist Party was never directly an electoral threat to the Congress in Madras. However, it was perceived as having widespread support among industrial and agricultural workers. In this sketch, I elaborate on sedition cases and conspiracy trials in late colonial Madras, where questions of the limits of the law and its propensity for violence were elaborated.

For students of Indian constitutional law, the Communist leader A. K. Gopalan's litigation at the Supreme Court marks the beginning of judicial engagement with Article 21 and the provisions of the Indian Constitution that engage with the question of personal liberties. Could a properly articulated, clearly delineated "procedure established by law" restrict political practice? The Supreme Court answered in the affirmative, upholding the constitutional validity of preventive detention (this case has since been overruled). Coincidentally, this case had come to the attention of Row and Reddy, although Gopalan was represented at the Supreme Court by leading constitutional lawyer, M. K. Nambyar. (A few years later, Nambyar would be part of a commission along with N. H. Bhagwati and M. P. Amin that indicted the communist government in Kerala of subverting "rule of law)." In this sketch, I examine how A. K. Gopalan and the political landscape of the 1940s Malabar engaged with the question of colonial-era laws and their place in democratic futures. It draws from a handwritten transcript of his courtroom speech during his trial for sedition in Calicut (present-day Kozhikode) in 1947.[20]

First, a brief biography. A. K. Gopalan was, in the interwar years, initially a member of the Congress Socialist Party and later a member of the Communist Party of India in Kerala. His initial political formation was through engagement with working class struggles in Calicut, at the time a part of British Malabar. However, his activities were not confined to Malabar. In 1936, he led a *jatha* (procession) from British Malabar to Travancore to demand accountability from the government. He was arrested both during the civil disobedience movement in the 1930s and later during the Quit India Movement in the 1940s. At the end of the war in 1945, he was arrested and charged with sedition and later subjected to multiple charges under the Madras Maintenance of Public Order, 1947. Following these high-profile legal challenges, he contested Lok Sabha elections and became a member of the parliamentary left, playing the role of a prominent opposition leader. He died shortly after the national emergency was lifted in 1977. In this sketch, I discuss his response to charges of sedition that were leveled against him in 1947 in Calicut. He was shortly thereafter, arrested under the Madras Maintenance of Public Order Act, 1947 and later, the Preventive Detention Act, 1950, both of which authorized extended periods of detention on the "suspicion" of adverse political motives. This sketch precedes these better-known examples.

In his speech before the Additional District Magistrate, Calicut, he noted that the provisions under which he was charged were an artifact of colonial rule, and deserved to have no place in a democratic society. He described himself as a *kaduttha samrajya virodhi* (a staunch anti-imperialist) and refused to apologize. He noted how Malayalis (who were likely among the primary addressees of his speech) were living in Ceylon and Singapore as *dasyas* (slaves) owing to the lack of adequate employment in their home towns. He claimed that Malabar, one of the most prosperous districts in Madras, was made dependent on exports from Burma and Japan. He attributed this lack of prosperity, poverty, and unemployment to British rule.

Gopalan's speech used his own personal history—and more specifically, his own change of heart—to show why communism was not the sole threat to "public order." He noted how he had been a devout Gandhian *satyagrahi* until 1934, and why he had turned to communism when he realized that *satyagraha* was a means for landlords and other powerful groups to cover up their mistakes. His was not a discussion at the theoretical or philosophical level; his argument was rooted in the political and social context of Malabar. He contrasted the violent dispossession of agricultural workers by the Malabar Special Police (a paramilitary organization formed as a special division of the police forces of the Madras province) to those violent acts that the government claimed communists of inciting amongst tenants and landless agricultural workers. Yet, he claimed, it was only the latter that was being classed as a "violent attack" (*akraman*). In contrast to the political trials that marked the earlier part of the twentieth century—such as those by Gandhi, Tilak, or even the high-profile trials for conspiracy in Meerut and Lahore—which had a large public readership/viewership, Gopalan's address to the court is marked by his use of intertwined personal and political histories. His argument for doing away with provisions like sedition in criminal procedure laws was not based in a theoretical understanding of the role of dissent in a democracy, or even communism's opposition to dominant nationalism.

Contrast Gopalan's speech with that of the *habeas corpus* litigation that Row and Reddy engaged in. Where the affidavits that form part of Row and Reddy's petitions contain a recital of facts about the political life of their clients (for instance, that they were never members of a union or that they had merely attended a protest, and not participated in it, a freeze-frame of their political life) Gopalan took it upon himself to narrate his own political formation and why he chose to turn to communism. But in another sense, both Gopalan's speech and the Row and Reddy affidavits both engaged in exposing the ambiguity surrounding the deployment of law against certain forms of the political. Row and Reddy's affidavits stress that the Communist Party was a legal organization (in 1948–9) but however their workers are subjected to preventive detention while the workers of the Congress (also a legal party) are not. Gopalan's speech notes that the acts of agricultural workers in claiming uncultivated land in Malabar was labeled a threat to law and order, while that by the violent tactics of the Malabar Special Police was never condemned as such. In both cases, the law is not outrightly dismissed as violence, but its limits are carefully contextualized, narrated, and exposed.

These explorations were not limited to the political Left. Over the course of its publishing history, well into the 1950s, the *Indian Civil Liberties Bulletin* documented not only the use of repressive provisions of sedition against the Communist Party (most pronounced at the time in southern India) but also that of the Socialist Party, the Akali Dal as well as the Jana Sangh. It noted that socialist leaders like Acharya Kriplani and Ram Manohar Lohia had been charged for inciting violence or "waging war" against the state. The detention of Master Tara Singh under the East Punjab Public Safety Act was keenly followed, and so was fate of the Punjabi Suba movements in the late 1950s. It counted amongst its members, Syama Prasad Mukherjee and Jamnadas Mehta, both of whom were members of the Hindu Mahasabha. This was true of Madras as well. When the Madras Civil Liberties Union held a meeting in August 1952 to protest against the Preventive Detention Act, it was supported by M. V. Ganapathi of the Hindu Mahasabha, R. Ramanathan of the United Socialist Party, P. Ramamurthi and Swami Chidambaranar of the Communist Party, S. B. Adityan of the United Democratic Front; these too cut across the political spectrum of the early 1950s in Madras.[21] This is hardly to suggest that "civil liberties" was a neutral technical terrain, as the editors of the *Bulletin* wrote in their inaugural editorial. Instead, it prompts us to investigate the role of legal procedure as violence, to explore its nature and chart its course, just as the historical actors in these sketches did.

V

This final sketch is about a relative absence in the pages of the *Indian Civil Liberties Bulletin*: the caste question. Unlike the questions of preventive detention or press censorship, these are fleeting references. Like *Gopalan*, one of the earliest constitutional law cases on equality of opportunity and reservation of seats in educational institutions, Champakam Dorairajam and CR Srinivasan, both Brahmin students seeking admission to medical and engineering colleges in Madras, filed suit against the Madras Government, claiming that seats reserved for "Scheduled Caste" and "Scheduled Tribe" students (as well as other communities) was contrary to the "reasonable classification" standard imposed under Article 14 of the 1950 Constitution, providing for the right to equality and equal treatment before the law.[22] Alongside A. K. Gopalan's preventive detention litigation and V. G. Row's test cases on the freedoms of speech and association, *Champakam Dorairajam* is often cited as one of the leading early constitutional challenges that originated in the Madras High Court, but one that properly belongs to the anticanon. Here, I trace how the caste question, which was never extensively discussed in the pages of the *Bulletin*, was indirectly invoked in cases about press freedom emanating from Madras in the early 1950s. These too are glimpses into the extant political imaginaries of the time.

The most immediate context for the *Champakam Dorairajam* litigation is resistance to the non-Brahmin struggles in the Madras Presidency in the 1930s and 1940s. The best known pre-constitutional legal expression was in the form of temple entry authorizations in Travancore (1936) and across Madras (1947). However, this was only a limited removal of social and civil disabilities. Following the introduction of the Indian Constitution, questions of communal representation and reservation were examined in light of new principles, those encoded in Article 17 (abolition of untouchability) and Article 23 (abolition of forced labor).[23] These interpretations went beyond specific provisions as well. For instance, a case was referred to the Madras High Court (in its advisory jurisdiction) to examine whether the temple entry authorization violated the right to equality. The Court's opinion was that rights under Article 25 afforded cultural and educational rights, within which these acts of social reform clearly fell.[24] Legislative interventions to remove "civil disabilities" were in force even during the colonial period in Bombay, Madras, Travancore, and elsewhere.[25] On the eve of independence, schemes for "Harijan welfare" implemented throughout the Madras state in the 1940s and the early 1950s. This included government orders that mandated quotas and communal representation, the likes of which were challenged before the Madras High Court.

Keeping this background in mind, one of the earliest instances recorded in the *Bulletin* is that of restrictions on newspapers that purported to record anticaste agitations. In Madras, this included *Viduthalai* of the Dravidar Kazhagam (DK) led by Periyar E. V. Ramaswami Naicker, the political successor to the Justice Party of the 1920s and 1930s.[26] At the same time, *Dravida Nadu*, edited by C. N. Annadurai of the Dravida Munnetra Kazhagam (DMK) was also charged securities under the same legislation in 1949. The government demanded hefty securities from both newspapers under Emergency Powers (Press) Act, 1931, a colonial-era law that had been extended into postindependence peacetime. This functioned in most cases as press censorship by levying financial burdens on small presses that were usually already struggling but took principled stands critical of the government. This similar treatment meted out to two opposing parties of the Dravidian movement in Madras is particularly worth noting, since it was on the terrain of civil liberties and press freedoms that these two parties were able to agree, given the tumultuous late 1940s for the Dravidian movement. There is another instance of intertwined legal and political imaginaries in this context in Madras. Historian A. R. Venkatachalapathy notes that both the DK and the DMK were united in their opposition to the decision in the *Champakam Dorairajan* case.[27]

This agreement is significant, for the tendencies of the DK and the DMK were divergent at this point. While Annadurai and the leadership of the DMK was interested in contesting elections, that of the DK was not. Compare for instance, the following two responses to restrictions on their political activities. The articles for which the DMK's *Dravida Nadu* was charged under the Emergency Powers (Press) Act, 1931 were critical of the caste system, where the writer noted that a small minority of Brahmins had oppressed the large majority of non-Brahmins for centuries. He traced the long history of social justice movement in Madras, ending with prescriptions for social reform. The judges of the Madras High Court, where the demand for security was successfully challenged, noted that while the wording of certain phrases was unfortunate, it was an attack on the caste system, and not on the community of Brahmins. On the other hand, the DK fashioned itself as a propaganda movement. In 1953, Periyar announced his intention to break idols of the Hindu god Ganesha in a bid to challenge notions of idol worship among Hindus. A meeting was held at the town hall in Tiruchirapalli, speeches delivered and idols broken. A petition was filed before trial courts challenging Periyar's actions for hurting the religious sentiments of Hindus.[28] The Madras High Court, which eventually heard the petition noted that the idols were not consecrated, they were no more than "images of the deities in the drawing rooms of several houses."

(Before the Supreme Court however, this decision was reversed, and the behavior of the DK termed "foolish" and the appeal dismissed.) While scholars have exhaustively written about the Dravidian movement in Madras, these explorations of what counts as "enmity," "hate." and "violence" before the law offer new avenues of what was—and what was not—possible in this mid-twentieth-century political landscape.

It is surprising that the pages of the *Bulletin* did not contain a wider range of anticaste struggles. It is important to note two points, however. First, the *Bulletin* followed the apartheid struggles in South Africa and the school desegregation and busing cases in the United States quite keenly. There were certainly well-known instances of the everyday violence of caste that took place in Bombay, Kerala, and Madras at this time.[29] Second, the membership of the Servants of India Society and those involved in the publication of the *Bulletin* (including S. R. Venkataraman and Dinkar Desai in Bombay) were involved in Harijan Sevak Sanghs in Bombay. So why did these instances not make it into the pages of the *Bulletin*? Following the abolition of untouchability under Article 17 of the Constitution, the Untouchability Offences Act and Protection of Civil Rights Act were enacted in 1955 and amended in 1975 (the Prevention of Atrocities Act would come later in 1989). Under the 1955 Act, "civil rights" were defined as "any right accruing to a person by reason of the abolition of untouchability" under the Constitution. Legislative language seems to have made a distinction between "civil liberties" and "civil rights." But the likely explanation for the omission is that these struggles barely received the same public attention that preventive detention or press censorship cases did. Even as it prepared to evaluate the implementation of the 1955 Act, the Indian government's attempt to get copies of prosecutions by lower courts was futile.[30] The omission is only surprising because in legal practice, civil rights, civil disabilities, and civil liberties were treated as part of the same problematic of the relationship between personal freedom, collective rights, and the state.

Ultimately, none of the early constitutional law cases initially litigated at the Madras High Court were to have lasting effect. In the short term, the Constitution (First Amendment) Act, 1951 undid the rulings in these cases and a flurry of constitutional amendments followed soon after. In the long term, tenets of constitutional interpretation evolved to include many more touchstones, including perhaps most importantly, the idea that Articles 14, 19, and 21 were not to be treated as constitutional silos, but in relation to each other. The Directive Principles of State Policy and the chapter on Fundamental Rights were to be read in light of each other. This effectively overruled the *A. K. Gopalan* and *Champakam Dorairajan* cases and set the stage for personal, economic, and social rights to be interpreted in relation to each other, arguably recognizing what the protagonists in these sketches had much earlier highlighted as political possibilities.

VI

Over the course of its publication history, until its winding up in September 1960 owing to financial difficulties, the editors of the *Indian Civil Liberties Bulletin* collected thousands of instances of civil liberties infringements, gradually expanding the scope of coverage as the bill of rights under the new Indian Constitution was interpreted by courts. Although it began with preventive detention and the rights of organized labor, it ended with extensive references to the decolonization of former British and French colonies on the African continent and the new constitutional arrangements being worked out. Once again, it highlighted the repressive preventive detention legislation being adopted in Kenya and Southern Rhodesia. When the Federation of Malaya granted constitutional sanction for peacetime preventive detention to combat armed insurgencies on the eve of its own independence, the *Bulletin* noted that India could no longer solely claim that inglorious distinction.[31] The repressive policies of the Chinese Communist Party amongst the Bandung countries, particularly in the context of the territorial dispute over Tibet, also occupied print space. Perusing the pages of Bulletin between 1949 and 1960 is therefore akin to exploring the political landscape of the first two decades of Indian independence, never bound solely by the concerns of the emergent nation-state, but also reshaped and reimagined in relation to regional and global political formations.

Yet another dimension is the *Bulletin*'s engagement with comparative legal precedent. From its earliest days, the All India Civil Liberties Council drew comparisons with the work of the American Civil Liberties Union and included snippets of judgments of the US Supreme Court. Comparing the use of preventive detention laws against communists to McCarthyism in the United States, for example, the *Bulletin* noted that even the ACLU did not have to fight against peacetime preventive detention. It also drew upon precedent in South Africa and Ireland; NM Joshi was part of the Royal Commission on Labor in 1930s and Hriday Nath Kunzru was the chairperson of the Indian Council for World Affairs. While many praised the role of Hansa Mehta in the drafting of the Universal Declaration of Human Rights before the United Nations, the editors of the *Bulletin* noted that she had facilitated the inclusion of "procedure established by law" in the text of Declaration thereby justifying preventive detention. In the pages of the *Bulletin*, the revolt of landless laborers against their landlords in Tirunelveli or the smuggling of arms across the border from Madras to Hyderabad were distilled into legal principles that were comparable to the curbs on dissent in democracies elsewhere in the world. Within a single microhistorical frame, the same event—the rebellious lawyering of Row and Reddy, A. K. Gopalan's challenge to sedition laws or the principled challenges to the caste system—was reinterpreted within multiple frameworks. The horizons for political futures was constantly shifting, seamlessly moving between invocations of imperial pasts and democratic futures, molding multiple meanings of citizenship without explicitly adopting the local, regional, provincial, or national as its dominant framework.

It is also useful to look back at these cases from the 1970s. By this time, the *Indian Civil Liberties Bulletin* had ceased publication, but not before thoroughly documenting the misuse of preventive detention laws across the country and instances of "small emergencies" such as the ones imposed through the use of provisions like Section 144 of the Criminal Procedure Code. However, not only had the Preventive Detention Act, 1950 continued to exist on the statute books for a decade after Gopalan challenged it in court, it had been supplemented by the Maintenance of Internal Security Act. For nearly half of the years following independence, wars with China and Pakistan had meant that the Defence of India Rules and Orders were in place. As a member of the Lok Sabha, Gopalan made a fiery speech lambasting the Indira Gandhi government for misusing the Constitution to retaliate against the judgment of the Allahabad High Court invalidating elections. It was to be one of his last speeches. On the eve of the Emergency, there were civil liberties organizations, including Jaya Prakash Narayan's Peoples' Union for Civil Liberties, the Peoples' Union for Democratic Rights and others, that took up the cause of repressive legislation. Looking back on this mid-twentieth-century in India, the exploration of the limits of law, its potential to create violent ruptures as well as open up new paths of being (and becoming) political is necessary to evaluate this later moment—and the salient questions of the twentieth century.

Given these sketches, how might we evaluate the Bulletin's editorial claim that civil liberties were neutral political terrain? Historian Rotem Geva and philosopher Arudra Burra have both shown how the language of civil liberties for example, was invoked not only against, but also by, the political Right.[32] In Geva's work for instance, the East Punjab Public Safety Act was invoked against the right-wing newspaper *Organizer* and the left wing *Daily Pratap* for reportedly inciting communal riots in the days following the India–Pakistan partition.[33] The vibrant scholarship on Indian constitutionalisms is another example. In another iteration of this argument, Rohit De and Sandipto Dasgupta argue that the new Constitution of 1950 proved to be a new field of practice (De) or a historically contingent infrastructure (Dasgupta) within which various sorts of subaltern struggles were played out (De) and governmental schemes for administering the new nation-state formulated (Dasgupta).[34] This essay is a contribution to this growing body of scholarship that is attentive to the question of law and violence, but I hesitate to claim that civil liberties was (or could be) neutral terrain.[35] Instead, what if we were to think of the pages of the *Bulletin*—and the situated stories of struggle that it documented—as revealing an uneven terrain? In other words, "civil liberties" did not already exist as a terrain; it was made by the sedimentations of the struggles recounted in its pages.

In conclusion, this chapter echoes arguments by Mary John and Aditya Nigam in their chapters about the domain of the "political." The historical actors in this essay certainly did not view themselves as radical democrats, and were never advocates of violence or armed struggle. However, they were necessarily interested in the contours of the political, about the structures of law and politics that were necessarily enmeshed with each other. These sketches serve as compelling archival/archived examples of rooted, contextualized, and historicized maps of the relationship between law, state, and violence. The use of political imaginary (in contrast to political *moment, imagination,* or *vocabulary*) to my mind is most useful in dismantling the power of historical "events" or "breaks," to suggest that there are always layers beneath layers, that glimpses of older, deeply rooted social struggles—of pain, violence, and exclusion—are visible behind the shimmering newness of law's attempt at reform and emancipation. The power of the imaginary is not in privileging (as in the case of imagination, perhaps) or recounting a sort of naïve pluralism (as in the case of multiple vocabularies), but in revealing these layers of a silted, sedimented landscape. I would like to highlight two major implications of the argument made in this essay that are worth exploring in greater detail.

First, the shifting boundary markers of what constitutes the "political" must squarely engage matters of state. South Asian histories have masterfully unpacked the question of the political beyond the role of the state (particularly in the work of the Subaltern Studies historians). But the questions of twentieth-century India, especially those beyond the mid-twentieth-century point that await their historians, will have to unpack the role of the state, law, and governmentalities in creating the landscape of political possibilities. This is already evident in histories of the Emergency. Other discussions that are yet to take place include those relating to the extraordinary jurisdictions created in the North East of India, or the occupation of Kashmir by the Indian State (for instance, the detention of Sheikh Abdullah was of deep concern to the editors of the *Bulletin*) Others include the legal regulation of forests and coastlines or the legal-economic geographies created as a result of postliberalization reforms. This is not because the production and circulation of political possibilities beyond the state is not critical, nor is it because the two (within the state, beyond the state, civil society v. political society) are often, as Partha Chatterjee points out, complementary. However, I would argue that matters of the state are critical because many of the initial moves to dismantle or disempower political imaginaries are through law and the state. Further, as the sketches above show, the countermoves are also manifested in legal encounters.

Second, the understanding of the imaginary in terms of a topography intuitively lends itself to the spatial aspects of law, but as the introduction to this volume notes, the "twentieth century" might be threaded together through legal temporalities. Take the question of the extraordinary legal measures discussed in this piece: public safety acts, sedition charges, press censorship. These administrative notations of how law measures out time have also shaped the way in which we have theorized emergencies within legal and constitutional theory: as a sort of on–off switch which freezes and unfreezes the rhythms of political life. In the context of political transitions (from colonial rule to independent rule in South Asia, for example, but also others), these questions become particularly difficult. Some explain the exercise of extraordinary legal authority as a politically expedient, historically contingent move: it was switched "on" for the purposes of navigating a difficult transition, and not prompted by any ideological motives. If extraordinary legal measures undergirded questions of class, caste, and beyond, as the sketches above indicate, this will fundamentally transform our understanding of democracies in the twentieth century.

Notes

1 Studies in the 1960s on the Indian legal profession include Samuel Schmitthener, "A Sketch of the Development of the Legal Profession in India," *Law & Society Review* 3 (1968): 337; Lloyd I. Rudolph and Susanne Hoeber Rudolph, "Barristers and Brahmans in India: Legal Cultures and Social Change," *Comparative Studies in Society and History* 8, no. 1 (1965): 24–49. Specific to southern India, see John Jeya Paul, *The Legal Profession in Colonial South India* (New Delhi: Oxford University Press, 1991) (covering the development of the profession during the nineteenth and early twentieth century). See Mitra Sharafi, "A New History of Colonial Lawyering: Likhovski and

Legal Identities in the British Empire," *Law & Social Inquiry* 32, no. 4 (2007): 1059–94 (for a review of the role of legal elites in the crafting of social, esp. minority identities).

2 See Upendra Baxi, "'Touch It Not, If You Are Not a Historian' Toward a New Historiography of Colonial Indian Law: Recrafting Clio," *Comparative Studies of South Asia, Africa and the Middle East* 38, no. 3 (2018): 375–84 for different modes of writing intertwined legal and political histories using different lenses and at different scales.

3 Kalyani Ramnath, "*ADM Jabalpur's Antecedents*: Political Emergencies, Civil Liberties, and Arguments from Colonial Continuities in India," *American University International Law Review* 31 (2016): 209. Gyan Prakash, *Emergency Chronicles: Indira Gandhi and Democracy's Turning Point* (Princeton: Princeton University Press, 2019).

4 Government Order (GO) No. 2128, July 12, 1947, Proceedings of the Home Department, Tamil Nadu State Archives.

5 The Bihar Maintenance of Public Order Act, the East Punjab Public Safety Act, 1949; the CP & Berar Maintenance of Public Order Act are other examples. For a report of the working of these laws, Indian Civil Liberties Conference and Madras Civil Liberties' Union, eds., *The Indian Civil Liberties Conference (16th and 17th July, St. Mary's Hall, Madras): Report of Proceedings, 16th July, First Day* (Madras: Madras Civil Liberties' Union, 1949).

6 AIR 1950 SC 27.

7 Effect of the expiry of emergency legislation, Under Secretary's Safe (Secret Files) (USSF), No. 170/44, February 2, 1945, TNSA.

8 See Preamble, Madras Maintenance of Public Order Act, 1947. Also G.O. No. 66, June 4, 1947, Proceedings of the Legal Department, TNSA.

9 Christopher Baker, "Colonial Rule and the Internal Economy in Twentieth-Century Madras," *Modern Asian Studies* 15, no. 3 (July 1981): 575–602.

10 Madras Administration Report, 1946, p. 51.

11 Indian Civil Liberties Conference and Madras Civil Liberties' Union, *The Indian Civil Liberties Conference (16th and 17th July, St. Mary's Hall, Madras)*., Part II, p. 6

12 Ramnath, "*ADM Jabalpur's* Antecedents."

13 *Indian Civil Liberties Bulletin* (October 1949), p. 3.

14 Mithi Mukherjee, *India in the Shadows of Empire: A Legal and Political History (1774–1950)* (New York and London: Oxford University Press, 2009).

15 Ivor Jennings, "Politics in Ceylon Since 1952," *Pacific Affairs* 27, no. 4 (December 1, 1954): 338–52.

16 I am grateful to Retired Justice K. Chandru, Madras High Court for alerting me to this aspect during an interview. Before being elevated to the Madras High Court, Chandru worked at the offices of Row and Reddy. Personal interview, Chennai, September 13, 2015.

17 VG Row v. State of Madras AIR 1951 Mad 147; VG Row v. State of Madras W.P. No. 158 of 1953; *Indian Civil Liberties Bulletin* (May–June 1953).

18 Affidavit of the petitioner, July 2, 1949, P. China Somaraju v. *The District Magistrate, West Godavari Crl. M. P. 1699 of 1949* (Madras High Court Record Room).

19 Mithi Mukherjee, "Justice, War, and the Imperium: India and Britain in Edmund Burke's Prosecutorial Speeches in the Impeachment Trial of Warren Hastings," *Law and History Review* 23, no. 3 (2005): 589–630.

20 The transcript in Malayalam is available at the AK Gopalan Center Library, Thiruvananthapuram. Translations are my own.

21 *Indian Civil Liberties Bulletin* (August 1952), p. ii (154).

22 State of Madras v. Champakam Dorairajam AIR 1951 SC 226.
23 Anupama Rao, *The Caste Question: Dalits and the Politics of Modern India* (Berkeley, CA: University of California Press, 2009).
24 V. S. Ramamirtha Ayyar v. M. Narayana Pillai and others Case Referred No. 5 of 1952, Madras High Court.
25 Sri Venkataramana Devaru v. State of Mysore AIR 1958 SC 255.
26 *Indian Civil Liberties Bulletin* (October 1949).
27 A. R. Venkatachalapathy, "DK and DMK: The Double Barreled Gun" 708 *Seminar* (August 2018) (see also the other articles in this special issue on Dravidianism).
28 S. Veerabhadran Chettiar v. E. V. Ramaswami Naicker AIR 1958 SC 1032. The litigation was covered in the *Bulletin* in September 1958.
29 Examples from Bombay were more numerous. For example, the litigation under the Bombay Harijan Temple Entry Act against the display of a notice prohibiting entry to Hindu lower castes (February 1955), and another under Bombay municipal regulations against an employee at a mill who was accused of taking a steel tumbler meant for caste Hindus (January 1956).
30 Elayaperumal, L. Report of the Committee On Untouchability, Economic and Educational Development of the Scheduled Castes and Connected Documents, 1969.
31 *Indian Civil Liberties Bulletin* (May–June 1960).
32 "Free Speech in the Early Constitution: A Study of the Constitution (First Amendment) Bill, 1951," in Udit Bhatia, ed., *Deliberations on Democracy: The Indian Constituent Assembly Debates* (London: Routledge, 2018).
33 Rotem Geva, "The City as a Space of Suspicion: Partition, Belonging and Citizenship in Delhi, 1940–1955" (discussing the prosecution of the *Daily Pratap* under the East Punjab Public Safety Act; also extensively covered in the early issues of the *Bulletin*). See also Rotem Geva, "False Truth: Disillusionment and Hope in the Decade after Independence," in Gyan Prakash, Michael Laffan, eds., *The Postcolonial Moment in South and Southeast Asia* (New York: Bloomsbury Press, 2018) (discussing the broader literary and political landscape of postpartition Delhi).
34 Sandipto Dasgupta, "'A Language Which Is Foreign to Us': Continuities and Anxieties in the Making of the Indian Constitution," *Comparative Studies of South Asia, Africa and the Middle East* 34, no. 2 (2014): 228–42; Rohit De, "Rebellion, Dacoity, and Equality: The Emergence of the Constitutional Field in Postcolonial India," *Comparative Studies of South Asia, Africa and the Middle East* 34, no. 2 (2014): 260–78.
35 For a survey of these developments, see Alastair McClure and Saumya Saxena, "Introduction: Law and Legality in Modern Indian History," *Comparative Studies of South Asia, Africa and the Middle East* 38, no. 3 (2018): 367–74.

Select Bibliography

Baker, Christopher, "Colonial Rule and the Internal Economy in Twentieth-Century Madras," *Modern Asian Studies* 15, no. 3 (July 1981): 575–602.

Baxi, Upendra, "'Touch It Not, If You Are Not a Historian' Toward a New Historiography of Colonial Indian Law: Recrafting Clio," *Comparative Studies of South Asia, Africa and the Middle East* 38, no. 3 (2018): 375–84.

Burra, Arudra, "Free Speech in the Early Constitution: A Study of the Constitution (First Amendment) Bill, 1951," in Udit Bhatia, ed., *Deliberations on Democracy: The Indian Constituent Assembly Debates* (London: Routledge, 2018).

Dasgupta, Sandipto, "'A Language Which Is Foreign to Us': Continuities and Anxieties in the Making of the Indian Constitution," *Comparative Studies of South Asia Africa and the Middle East* 34, no. 2 (2014): 228–42.

De, Rohit, "Rebellion, Dacoity, and Equality: The Emergence of the Constitutional Field in Postcolonial India," *Comparative Studies of South Asia, Africa and the Middle East* 34, no. 2 (2014): 260–78.

Jennings, Ivor, "Politics in Ceylon Since 1952," *Pacific Affairs* 27, no. 4 (December 1, 1954).

McClure, Alastair and Saumya Saxena, "Introduction: Law and Legality in Modern Indian History," *Comparative Studies of South Asia, Africa and the Middle East* 38, no. 3 (2018): 367–74.

Mukherjee, Mithi, *India in the Shadows of Empire: A Legal and Political History (1774–1950)* (New York and London: Oxford University Press, 2009).

Mukherjee, Mithi, "Justice, War, and the Imperium: India and Britain in Edmund Burke's Prosecutorial Speeches in the Impeachment Trial of Warren Hastings," *Law and History Review* 23, no. 3 (2005): 589–630.

Paul, John Jeya, *The Legal Profession in Colonial South India* (Bombay and New York: Oxford University Press, 1991).

Prakash, Gyan, *Emergency Chronicles: Indira Gandhi and Democracy's Turning Point* (Princeton: Princeton University Press, 2019).

Ramnath, Kalyani, "*ADM Jabalpur's Antecedents*: Political Emergencies, Civil Liberties, and Arguments from Colonial Continuities in India," *American University International Law Review* 31 (2016): 1059–94.

Rao, Anupama, *The Caste Question: Dalits and the Politics of Modern India* (Berkeley, CA: University of California Press, 2009).

Rotem, Geva, "False Truth: Disillusionment and Hope in the Decade after Independence," in Gyan Prakash, Michael Laffan, eds., *The Postcolonial Moment in South and Southeast Asia* (New York: Bloomsbury Press, 2018).

Rudolph, Lloyd I. and Susanne Hoeber Rudolph, "Barristers and Brahmans in India: Legal Cultures and Social Change," *Comparative Studies in Society and History* 8, no. 1 (1965): 24–49.

Schmitthener, Samuel, "A Sketch of the Development of the Legal Profession in India," *Law & Society Review* 3 (1968): 337–82.

Sharafi, Mitra. "A New History of Colonial Lawyering: Likhovski and Legal Identities in the British Empire," *Law & Social Inquiry* 32, no. 4 (2007): 1059–94.

Venkatachalapathy, A. R., "DK and DMK: The Double Barreled Gun," 708 *Seminar*, August 2018.

Part Two

Democratic Imaginaries

7

Institutionalizing Democratic Uncertainties: "Election Time(s)" in the Life of Indian Democracy

Anupama Roy and Ujjwal Kumar Singh

In an article published in the middle of the twentieth century, W. B. Gallie presented meticulously crafted arguments to explain what made democracy an "essentially contested concept." Gallie argued that the understanding that specially designed *procedures* would lead to democracy as an outcome limited its meaning. He preferred to see democracy as an *appraisive* concept—indeed "*the* appraisive political concept par excellence"—which provided evaluative frameworks for comprehending a complex phenomenon (1955–6: 184–850). In this chapter, we consider "election time" as a constitutive property of democracy that makes it internally complex. We also invoke it as an analytical category through which temporal conjunctures in the lives of democracies can be prized open for scrutiny. This scrutiny is especially significant for countries like India, which set upon the course of constitutional democracy in the middle of the twentieth century, through emphatic affirmation of popular sovereignty. Such an affirmation required a careful rearticulation of the relationship between the constituent present, a past burdened by the indignity of un-freedom and subjection, and a future that promised liberty, equality, and fraternity. An integral part of transformative constitutionalism (Baxi 2013, Bhatia 2019) was the installation of "universal adult franchise" in a context where the vestiges of deference legitimation (Kaviraj 2003) characteristic of a society marked by deep socioeconomic hierarchies still lingered.

This chapter was first presented in the conference on "Recalling Democracy: Lineages of the Present" held in Ann Arbor Michigan in September 2014. The authors are grateful to the organizers and participants, the volume editors and the referees for their comments. The chapter also draws upon the coauthored book of the authors: *Elections Commission of India: Institutionalising Democratic Uncertainties* (Oxford University Press, 2019).

The first Chief Election Commissioner of India (CEC), Sukumar Sen, who supervised the preparation of the electoral roll based on universal adult franchise, described the process as an "act of faith," reposed by the Constituent Assembly "in the true spirit of democracy," with the "full knowledge of the difficulties involved." He went on to write: "This decision launched a great and fateful experiment unique in the world in its stupendousness and complexities."[1] In her study of the first general election, Ornit Shani argues that "universal" franchise inserted the principle of equality in the electoral roll and a democratic disposition among the people responsible for preparing the roll (Shani 2018: 18). In the process of acquiring a "place on the roll," adult franchise played a role in connecting "the people" to a popular democratic imagination (Shani 2018: 19). Shani suggests that the preparation of the electoral roll on the basis of *universal* adult franchise became part of the "popular narrative," so that electoral rolls manifested "not merely a system of rules that were to be observed but also part of the normative world of people and the stories, individuals make of it themselves" (Shani 2018: 86). Much of this process took place in the absence of an electoral law, without a precise legal-constitutional framework on citizenship, and with provinces beset with specific problems pertaining to registration.

David Gilmartin, in this volume, refers to the deep-seated internal contradiction between law and politics, drawing out the "democratic paradox" (Mouffe 2000: 3–4), i.e., the paradox of putting together the "divergent and irreconcilable logics" and "grammars" of the liberal and the democratic traditions. Gilmartin sees electoral law as both enabling and controlling electoral behavior, as publicly performing the principle of people's sovereignty amidst the interplay of self-interested politics. "Election time," we argue in this chapter, is located in this contradiction. It enables us to trace the exceptional ways in which the electoral process is regulated, and at the same time, helps us process the ways a democratic imaginary may be achieved, which the editors in the introduction to this volume, following Bourdieu, call "a 'particular case of the possible' that is, as an exemplary case in a finite universe of possible configurations."

The paper explores the specificity of election time in India and the polysemous ways in which it has unfolded historically, as constituted juridically in electoral law and through the institutional template of the Constitution. The argument about specificity and polysemy will be made through the study of the first general election in India (1951/52) as the site where electoral laws and institutions for conducting elections acquired form, and subsequently through an examination of the Model Code of Conduct (MCC) as an innovation in supplementary legality, which has become an integral aspect of conducting free and fair elections. Both sections thematically examine the relationship between the legal regulation of elections and its ramifications for popular sovereignty.

Although not a constitutional requirement, the Election Commission of India (ECI) prepared a narrative report after every general election—a practice which continued till 1983. The first Chief Election Commissioner (CEC), Sukumar Sen, considered it "necessary" and "desirable" to prepare "an exhaustive record" of the different aspects of what Sen called a "remarkable *administrative* task."[2] Cumulatively and individually, the reports show how an institution acquires identity through replication of practices associated with the structuration of the state. Simultaneously, the reports are an exercise in reflexivity. Foregrounding its roles as the custodian of citizen's voting rights and an enabler of informed political choice among citizens, the ECI appears to claim an identity which sets it apart from the institutional structures sutured to the state.

Reflecting the context in which the first general election was held, Sukumar Sen's report stressed the importance of appropriate procedures for running an efficient electoral system. Procedural certainty was important for the effective realization of democratic uncertainties. Writing after the mid-term elections of 1968, then CEC S. P. Sen Verma emphasized the importance of dialectics in democracy. For Sen Verma the nature of electoral competition was of primary concern. The objective of electoral governance was to create a "moral order" conducive to an unconstrained space for prior discussion, which gave "the vote" the attribute of intelligent consent.[3] The MCC, which had become relatively institutionalized by 1968, was considered essential for achieving such an order.

"Election Time" and Democracy

While elections are part of the political process, they stand apart because they have separate temporal rhythms, defer the political process till renewed through a collective act of voting, and unleash energies of democratic deliberation which are structured differently from those that obtain in "normal" times. Dennis F. Thompson considers election time as a "discrete" moment characterized by certain "temporal properties"—periodicity, simultaneity and finality—which structure the election process, making it discontinuous with the political process.[4] David Gilmartin describes elections as constituting a "special" time, characterized by the *reversal/suspension* in/of the normal/ordinary working of power and its *replacement* with a different regime of power that provides an unfettered exercise of popular sovereignty (Gilmartin 2009: 248). In his study of the MCC in India in the 1990s (specifically under CEC T. N. Seshan), Gilmartin suggests that the model code constituted special time by putting in place "an electoral morality" which transcended "everyday politics" (Gilmartin 2009: 252–3). A third expression of election time can be drawn from the idea of elections as "electoral trials" used by Nadia Urbinati (2000). While the competitive character of elections is implicit in this formulation, Urbinati foregrounds the ideological content of elections which becomes explicit in public debates. Urbinati sees the electoral trial generating a process of deliberation whereby representation of ideas is achieved democratically.

The normative underpinnings of democracy expressed in these formulations draw from a fundamental concern with the procedural aspects of electoral governance, in particular the "legal doctrine of electoral exceptionalism" which proposes that "the electoral process may be subject to more stringent regulation than ordinary politics" (Thompson 2004: 51). In framing their analyses of electoral exceptionalism, they establish a relationship between the substantive dimensions of democracy and the procedural frameworks of electoral governance, concluding that an extraordinary legal regime for administering elections may be conducive to democracy. The doctrine of electoral legal exceptionalism is distinct from Giorgio Agamben's "state of exception" which is implicated in political crises and expressed as a necessity which becomes an autonomous source of law. The legal exceptionalism of election time is different. Unlike the Agambenian state of exception which reinforces sovereign power, electoral legal exceptionalism aims to reverse the direction of power, to suspend sovereign power and affirm popular sovereignty.

In this chapter, electoral legal exceptionalism is seen as constitutive of election time, paving the way for a distinct mode of enquiry into electoral governance in representative/constitutional democracies. While elections are extraordinary times requiring proficient "rule-making" and efficient "implementation" requiring the deferral of political power through exceptional regulatory control, an electoral trial is not autonomous of social power and class interests, which continue to determine electoral outcomes. Often, elections become surrogates for the resolution of a political crisis, in which case electoral legal exceptionalism may not be able to provide conditions sufficient for the affirmation of popular sovereignty.[5]

It is important to note here that the legal-institutional framework of administering elections, the concern of this chapter, is only one of many aspects of elections. The impact of the political process and the political fields in which institutions are located and function are equally important, and these have been brought into the discussion, albeit, tangentially. While doing so, this chapter is in concurrence with the argument made by Devesh Kapur and Pratap Bhanu Mehta (2005) that institutions are integral to democratic imaginings, but they also give form and structure to the state, and are implicated in the distribution of power between various layers of government, the state and the people, and among people themselves. However, institutionalization of procedures, while enabling the state to act in specific ways, may also be seen as imposing constraints on its powers.

The First General Elections and the Institutionalization of Procedural Certainties

In a story titled "The Election Game" published in *The Hindu* in 1952, R.K. Narayan narrates the excitement among school children enthused by the activities surrounding the first general election of 1951/52. Ramu was one such child who lived close to an election-meetings ground, who spent long hours with his friends in "excited discussion" about the possibility being allowed to vote. While Ramu was convinced that *everyone* could vote, his friends were skeptical: "it was only for grown-ups," they asserted; one child believed that only "tall persons" could vote. But this seemed unlikely. Their geography teacher, who was only as tall as them, was going to vote. Ramu was determined to "slip in somehow" and see what it was like. "They are going to have it after all in our school," he reasoned, but was soon cautioned by a well-meaning friend: "You will be handcuffed if you go there; it is against the law to try and see the vote. Don't you see how many police they have kept there?" Narayan's story described the fever that had gripped the people participating in what he called "a large-scale rehearsal for political life." No one, young or old, was left untouched, "as though a sense of sovereignty [was] aroused even in the most insignificant of us."[6]

This fictional rendition of the first general election reflects the "strangeness" of franchise for the large numbers of hitherto disenfranchised colonial subjects. The transition to a republic and affirmation of popular sovereignty involved expeditious placement of legal frameworks and institutional structures for conducting an election. It involved constituting an electorate by reciphering the national territorial map with that of electoral constituencies, delimited across the country. Making adult franchise *universal* necessitated a governmental activity of identification for a purpose different from other identification regimes, i.e., for the affirmation of democratic citizenship and popular sovereignty. The affirmation regime involved identifying citizens—for the Constitution permitted only citizens to vote—and the delimitation of constituencies within state boundaries on the basis of their population. The constitution provided for territorial constituencies, "one general electoral roll," and a nondiscriminatory constitutional right to vote, where no one would be "ineligible" for inclusion or "claim" the right to be included in a special electoral roll, on grounds of religion, race, caste or sex (Article 325 of the Constitution of India). Representation of the People Acts (RPA) 1950 and 1951 provided the modalities of preparation of the electoral rolls and the delimitation of constituencies. Under the provisions of Section 17 and 18 of RPA 1950, no person can be registered in more than one constituency and no person can be registered more than once in the same constituency and should be "ordinarily" resident in that constituency. Section 19 of RPA 1950 lays down the conditions which determine the registration of a citizen as voter.

An expeditious transition into the terrain of electoral democracy was made possible through an unprecedented exercise of erecting the institutional edifice and the legal framework for the conduct of election, enrolling citizens as voters, and making the electoral space both accessible and intelligible for them through innovations such as separate/multiple ballot boxes and color-coded ballot papers. In a newly independent country attempting to move straight into universal adult franchise instead of incremental enhancement, which had been the practice in other countries, this was a "colossal task" (Guha 2002). The enormity of the process was depicted by Shankar Pillai in a series of cartoons that illustrated through the medium of political satire the "strengths, anxieties and limitations of the new republic" (Devadawson 2014: 4). Quite like R.K. Laxman's iconic "common man," Shankar's protagonist was the Prime Minister himself—Jawaharlal Nehru—who he used as a "critical prism" (Devadawson 2014), to explore the inaugural years of the republic. The three cartoons identified in this chapter take us from R.K. Narayan's popular narratives of the election to the domain of political contestation expressed with the irreverence typical of Shankar. The cartoons are selected from the collection of Shankar's cartoons in a book titled *Don't spare me Shankar*, which is what Nehru reportedly told Shankar while releasing the cartoon magazine, *Shankar's Weekly* (Devadawson 2014: 20). The title indicates Nehru's acceptance of the cartoonist's images as legitimate political speech. The cartoons themselves are an expression of the power of political satire in communicating layered messages in a context where a popular leader wished to make the trust reposed in him democratic by eliciting consent through elections. The humungous nature of the exercise was almost like moving a ponderous elephant by its tail, a difficult task—and clumsy when initiated—but emphatic when set in motion (see Cartoon A).[7]

On February 18, 1950, five "administrators" from the judiciary were shortlisted for the appointment of the CEC, taking the preparations for the first general elections a stage further. The secretariat of the ECI was already functioning under P. S. Subramaniam from the Parliament House. Even though the ECI was not fully functional, the CEC was yet to be appointed, and the legal framework for conducting the election was not fully in place, the ECI's secretariat had already sent circulars to state governments alerting them to the necessity of expediting all the preliminary arrangements for holding elections early in the following year.[8] In March 1950, Sukumar Sen was appointed the first CEC of India. Even as the government hoped to hold an early election to give the Parliament the stamp of popular sovereignty, the firming up of the law governing the conduct of elections took place incrementally, prompting CEC Sen to remark:

> Although such piecemeal legislations were not quite satisfactory and may tend to leave a layman confused in the tangled multiplicity of legislative measures, there was hardly any other alternative.[9]

The task was so great and the political context in which the elections were held so unstable, that political affirmation, which Nehru desired, much to his anguish, could come finally several months later in 1952. Cartoons B and C created by Shankar in November 1950 point to the uncertainties leading to the continual postponement of elections, which were eventually held in February 1952 (Cartoon C), and its ramifications for the legitimacy of decisions being taken by the government and laws being passed by the Parliament, without political/democratic authorization, reducing the Parliament to a "rubber stamp" (Cartoon B).[10]

Cartoon C by Shankar depicts the continual deferral of the elections from its first assigned date of April 1951.[11]

For the ECI, however, the Assam floods or the trouble at the borders or even as Cartoon C seems to suggest, indecisiveness stemming from Congress's own anxieties, were not primary concerns. The immediate concern for the ECI was traversing the challenging course to the Polling Day, evident from the following description given by Ramachandra Guha:

> The size of the electorate at 176 millions, of whom about 85 percent could not read or write, the identification and registration of voters, designing of party symbols, ballot papers and ballot boxes for a mostly unlettered electorate, building of polling stations, recruitment of honest and committed polling officers, as well as providing ample time for political parties to compete and contest the first elections ever, was an exercise of massive proportions .... At stake were about 4,500 seats; two lakh twenty four thousand polling booths had to be constructed and equipped with about two million steel ballot boxes made of 8,200 tonnes of steel. About 380,000 reams of paper were used for printing the electoral rolls; fifty six thousand presiding officers were recruited who were assisted by about 280,000 lesser staff. The election and the electorate was spread over an area of more than a million square miles. The terrain was vast, diverse and in some cases difficult to access. The nature of electorate required some innovations, e.g., the use of large pictorial

symbols drawn from their daily lives by which the illiterate voters could identify their candidates, and the use of multiple ballot boxes.[12]

The enumeration of voters meant setting in motion an enormous bureaucratic activity, in a context where there were no prior electoral rolls based on *universal* adult franchise, and questions of citizenship remained liminal. Instructions were issued for the preparation of electoral rolls for each village as a unit so that when the constituencies were delimited, the village level electoral rolls could be consolidated into the electoral rolls for the constituency. While there was no statutory requirement for the publication of the electoral rolls, the states were directed to publish the preliminary rolls unofficially so that modifications could be made later on the basis of informal information. On the question of enrolling the large number of displaced persons who had migrated to India from territories in Pakistan and were not yet "confirmed" as residents/citizens, the states were advised that the "mere declaration" by such persons of their intention to "reside permanently in a town or village" should be sufficient for their registration irrespective of their actual period of residence in that village/town.[13] The labor of preparing the ballot papers,[14] ordering the ballot boxes in suitable numbers,[15] setting up of polling booths, the security of the polling booths and the ballot boxes,[16] the counting of votes, and declaration of results were the tasks assigned to the ECI. If in later years, the ECI came to see its task as one of providing the conditions for fair competition, exhorting voters to make an informed choice, dominating the newspaper broadsheet as an active participant in the poll process as the electoral rule maker and enforcer, the first narrative report shows none of this zeal for public presence. The newspapers in the months leading to the election, while reporting on the electoral contest remain silent on the ECI. This reticence corresponds to the spirit of the narrative report where the CEC appears to interpret the ECI's constitutional role in conducting election as efficient bureaucratic administration, as a facilitator in a "common task" for a "national purpose."[17]

The Model Code of Conduct and the Special Election Time

Unlike other institutions of the state such as the police, the bureaucracy and the army, which show continuity with the structural logic of "rule and authority" of the colonial state (Kaviraj 2003), the ECI represents the logic of democracy of modern states. There exists no precedent, however, for an election commission of the kind envisaged by the Indian constitution makers (McMillan 2012). Indeed, the ECI has a *pedigree*, which makes for a different set of rules of recognition and validation of its authority.[18] Provided for by the Constitution of India (Article 324), which authorizes the ECI to administer elections, the ECI does not owe its existence to a law of Parliament. It would be fair to assume that the constitution makers set up the ECI as an autonomous body with its source of power in the constitution with the objective to constrain *political* power from influencing the conduct of elections. While making the ECI pre-eminent in the electoral domain, the constitution simultaneously empowered the Parliament to make laws to regulate elections (Article 327). It is significant, however, that the power of the Parliament under Article 327 was made subject to other provisions of the

Constitution including Article 324, which makes the "superintendence, direction and control" of elections, the primary, and primarily, the responsibility of the ECI.[19] In a series of cases beginning with the judgment of a Constitutional Bench of the Supreme Court in 1978, the Supreme Court decided that Article 324(1) does not merely vest all residuary powers in the ECI, but must be envisaged as a "reservoir of powers," in cases "where law [was] silent."[20] This implies that the ECI's repository of powers to administer elections remains unrestrained unless the Parliament explicitly claims them through laws relating to specific aspects of the conduct of elections.

Electoral governance over the years has shown contestation over the relative powers of the Parliament and the ECI over the contours of ECI's powers under Article 324. The intensity of this contest was especially seen over the question of juridical boundaries of "election time," when the powers of the ECI become effective in a way that they override political power. The juridical boundary of election time is integrally related with the incremental enhancement of the ECI's power to regulate the electoral space. The extraordinariness of election time emerges in part from the legal vacuum which exists for the duration of the election. The Constitution (Article 329) puts a bar on judicial "interference" in electoral matters. Under Article 329(b) of the Constitution an election petition calling into question an election of either House of Parliament or the state legislatures can only be made according to the manner provided by an appropriate legislature. While the various high courts and the Supreme Court can hear election petitions, this power accrues from and is dependent on appropriate legislation. Chapter III of the RPA 1951 lays down elaborate provisions for trial of election petitions, their disposal, specification of corrupt practices and election offenses etc. But these provisions do not permit the presentation of a petition before "the date of election of the returned candidate."[21] In the case *N.P. Ponnuswami v. The Returning Officer, Namakkal Constituency* (1952) the Supreme Court affirmed that the word "election" in Article 329(b) was a "compendious expression," which connoted the *entire electoral process* commencing with the notification calling the election and culminating in the declaration of result. The bar on interference of the courts would thus apply to the entire electoral procedure, which once started could not be interfered with.[22]

An uninterrupted "electoral trial" with limits on political and judicial intervention both reinforces the power of the ECI over the superintendence of elections and extends its responsibility to ensure fair and free electoral competition. Over the years, the idea of the electoral space as autonomous and deliberative, appealing to a higher order morality different from everyday politics has got entrenched. Election time is marked out as "special time" to use Gilmartin's category, whereby the bureaucratic electoral apparatus both defers and substitutes the "political" to enable the uncoerced exercise of franchise by the citizen voter. The MCC has played a pivotal role by introducing a *regime of supplementary legality* to regulate the conduct of those aspiring for political power.

The MCC was framed before the state assembly election in Kerala in 1960 by the state government, representatives of major political parties in the state and electoral officials, who drew up a code for *voluntary* observation by political parties. Comprising five sections—"meetings," "processions," "speeches and slogans," "placards" and "general"—the MCC exhorted political parties to "adopt an attitude of mutual tolerance and forbearance" and avoid making remarks likely to "wound the religious susceptibilities of any section of the people." The code invoked collective responsibility through voluntary adherence to mutually agreed principles of orderly conduct during election campaign.[23] In the narrative report of the third general elections, CEC Sen Verma noted the "usefulness" of the MCC in the "hotly contested" election of 1960.[24] As a consequence, the model code was followed again in the 1967 election in Kerala. In 1966–7, conferences of representatives of political parties were convened by Chief Ministers of West Bengal, Tamil Nadu, and Andhra Pradesh to adopt codes similar to the Kerala Code.[25]

In the narrative report of the mid-term elections in 1968–9 for the state assemblies in Punjab, Haryana, Uttar Pradesh, Bihar, West Bengal, Nagaland and Pondicherry, CEC S. P. Sen Verma describes the "winds of change" which had swept the country in the general election of 1967. The diminution of the Congress party precipitated political uncertainty; "defections and re-defections" and President's rule in some states necessitated mid-term elections. In this context of political churning arising out of the dismantling of political consensus, and the fragmentation of the political field, the ECI seized the initiative to propose an "official" MCC for uniform application in the form of an "appeal" to political parties to observe "a minimum standard of conduct and behavior." Successive CECs have interpreted fair and free elections to mean the excision of political interference from the electoral domain. A comprehensive code which would include special provisions to curb the power of the ruling party and the unfair advantage it may enjoy has come to be seen as integral to democratic elections. This has taken the form of rules deferring governmental decision-making and lawmaking during the election, widening thereby the scope of the MCC. It is perhaps this aspect of the MCC, more than any other, which gives election time its unique character as exceptional time.

Most scholars see the 1990s as a turning point in the institutional robustness of the ECI and electoral governance, citing the aggressive implementation of the MCI under CEC T.N. Seshan as evidence (Gilmartin 2009, Rudolf and Rudolf 2008, Katju 2009, McMillan 2010). The emphasis on the 1990s occludes earlier periods of ECI "activism." In the 1977 general election which followed the national emergency, for example, alongside the Janata Party posters of a farmer and plough, and the Congress graffiti of "Support Indira Gandhi—Vote Cow and Calf," were the ECI's posters exhorting the voter to vote without fear. Widely displayed all over India, the ECI posters assured the voter by simply stating: "vote without fear—your vote is secret." In an election coming after twenty-one months of national emergency, suspension of fundamental rights and suppression of civil liberties, the ECI posters had a distinct antigovernment ring. When Prime Minister Indira Gandhi announced on January 18, 1977, that elections would be held in March, detainees—the bulk of whom consisted of political opponents of Indira Gandhi—were released; press censorship and restrictions on public meetings were lifted to facilitate the election. Indira Gandhi made it clear, however, that this was only a temporary reprieve. In her broadcast announcing the election, she declared that for the duration of the election campaign, the "rules" of the "emergency" will (only) be "relaxed," confirming the commonly held belief that elections were being held only to legitimize the changes that she had brought about during the emergency (Weiner 1977).

While Indira Gandhi had been hopeful of electoral victory since the opposition had been enfeebled in the course of the emergency, the outcome of the 1977 election, turned out to be a fearless popular indictment of the Congress. For the first time in the electoral history of India, the Congress party was voted out of power by a unified opposition (the Janata party), which contested the election on the platform of democracy and civil liberties. At a fundamental level, however, the process also manifested people's faith in the electoral system, through which citizen voters could register their protest. This faith expressed through the vote, as Partha Chatterjee appropriately observes, "established in the arena of popular mobilizations in India the capacity of the vote and of representative bodies of government to give voice to popular demands of a kind that had never before been allowed to disturb the order and tranquility of the proverbial corridors of power" (Chatterjee 2006: 49).

In his prefatory note to the narrative report of the ECI, CEC T. Swaminathan described the 1977 election as "historic." The reasons for the decimation of the Congress, Swaminathan wrote, would be the subject of intense academic debates. For the ECI, however, the electoral outcome was important because it had established the ECI as an independent, objective, honest and impartial agency, acclaimed in India and abroad. The courage exhibited by the electorate in bringing regime change was an affirmation of ECI's constitutional role and the vindication of the wisdom of the Constituent Assembly.[26] Significantly, it was during this election that the MCC made its passage from a mutually agreed set of "dos and don'ts" among political parties, to a means of restraining the party in power. James Lyngdoh, the CEC of India from 2001 to 2004, saw this change as one which enabled the ECI to "pitch into the party in power" (2004: 69–70). This put the ECI on a distinct trajectory, marking its transition from being a "referee institution"[27] regulating the conduct of political parties according to rules political parties had framed, to one in which the ECI assumed the role of a rule-making and rule-enforcing body.

Far from being a referee, the ECI became an active player, and quite like the pitcher in a baseball game, the initiator of the electoral game. The transition to a "pitcher's" role in preference to that of a referee came about in the 1970s in a context of political and democratic deficit. The new role was reflected in the revisions that the ECI brought in the MCC in October 1979 to make it more effective. The 1979 MCC was divided into seven parts and an entire part (Part VII) concerned itself with monitoring the conduct of parties in power in the Center and in the states. The 1979 Code was modified in consultation with political parties and reissued in December 1983 titled "Model Code of Conduct for the Guidance of Political Parties and Candidates."

In the 1983 elections to the legislative assemblies in the states of Assam, Tripura, Karnataka, Andhra Pradesh and Jammu and Kashmir, Part VII of the MCC pertaining to the "party in power" and the rules of conduct it must follow was strengthened. In a meeting of political parties convened by CEC R.K. Trivedi the participants agreed that the MCC should also prohibit the following: "financial grants" in any form which may influence a voter, the use of official machinery, vehicles and aircraft, and the entry of ministers in polling stations and counting halls, unless they were themselves candidates, voters, or authorized agents. To further constrain the party in power, the ECI was empowered to set up a monitoring cell to oversee the All India Radio and Doordarshan, to ensure "free and objective presentation of election news."[28] The representatives of political parties also agreed that the ECI should "examine the legal and other implications" of amending the RPA to make any "breach" of the MCC "an electoral offence" (Annual Report, 1983, p.88). Subsequently, the ECI suggested reforms in electoral laws to the government, including the incorporation of provisions of MCC in the RPA, 1951.[29]

By the 1990s, however, the ECI withdrew from the position of pushing for a statutory MCC. Much of its reluctance drew from the fact that a *statutory* MCC would change the source of ECI's authority to execute the code from Article 324 of the Constitution to a parliamentary statute. In other words, it would cede decision-making over which the ECI had exclusive control to a law whose form and content would be controlled by the Parliament. The ECI's powers would then be confined only to the *implementation* of the law. James Lyngdoh shows a clear preference for the powers of "superintendence and control" emerging from Article 324 of the Constitution, and a quick preventive action and remedial measure in the immediate context of an election, rather than deferral to a prolonged judicial procedure that would follow statutory provisions. Lyngdoh argued that while conducting elections occasionally involved quasi-judicial functions, it was intrinsically an executive task. Expressing conformity with the legal exceptionalism of "election time," he declared that there was "no point in prosecuting a person after he had committed the offence" (Lyngdoh 2004: 9–80).

The ECI has taken recourse to a combination of measures to ensure adherence to the MCC. In most cases, however, action against specific candidates has been taken in the form of a public "show of displeasure" and "condemnation." In the Gujarat state legislative assembly election in 2007, the war of words between Narendra Modi, then Chief Minister of the state, and Sonia Gandhi, President of the Indian National Congress, prompted the ECI to issue letters expressing displeasure to both leaders for violating "issue based" election campaigns.[30] Immediately before the 2009 general election, Varun Gandhi, a member of the Bharatiya Janata Party (BJP) and its "likely candidate" in the Lok Sabha election from Pilibhit Parliamentary Constituency in Uttar Pradesh, delivered communally charged speeches at two public meetings. The ECI issued notices to Varun Gandhi and the BJP and directed the Chief Electoral Officer (CEO) of Uttar Pradesh to file criminal cases against Varun Gandhi under the Indian Penal Code (IPC). These included Section 153A (promoting enmity between different groups on grounds of religion), Section 295A (deliberate and malicious acts intended to outrage religious feelings of any class of Indian citizens by insulting its religion or religious beliefs), Section 505(2) (statements creating or promoting enmity, hatred or ill will between classes) and Section 125 of the RPA 1951 (promoting enmity between classes in connection with elections). In January 2019, campaigning in the state assembly election in Delhi, BJP candidate Kapil Mishra referred to the election as an India–Pakistan match, and to the anti-Citizenship Amendment Act protests in Shaheen Bagh and other parts of Delhi as "mini Pakistan." The ECI banned Mishra from campaigning in Delhi for two days for violating the MCC and asked the Delhi police to file an FIR against him under the IPC for disturbing communal harmony.[31] While Mishra lost to the Aam Aadmi Party (AAP) candidate in the election, he continued his incendiary tirade against Muslims. The Delhi police was unable to check the violence against Muslims that ensued in February 2020 and the ECI was implicated in the imbroglio for allegedly providing the voter list with pictures to the Delhi police, a charge that it vehemently denied.

In 2014 the ECI asserted its powers by directing the Cabinet Secretary and the Chief Secretaries of state governments and Union Territories, and the CEOs of all states that with the announcement of Lok Sabha election, all governmental decisions would henceforth be subject to the ECI's scrutiny. Among the instructions issued by the ECI was the "total ban" on the transfer of officers who were involved in administering elections.[32] Significantly, these officers, including the Commissioner of Police and the District Collector, are under the administrative control of the ECI for the duration of the election. The ban on transfer did not, however, prevent the ECI from transferring officers to enable the conduct of "fair and free" election. On March 26, 2014, the Election Commission ordered the transfer of forty-four top officials in Uttar Pradesh, including district magistrates and police chiefs, who it said were likely to be influenced by the Samajwadi Party (SP), the ruling party in the state.[33] A similar order for transfer of seven officers in West Bengal was met with stiff resistance by the state government. Chief Minister Mamata Banerjee refused to implement the order of transfer and the replacements suggested by the ECI. A compromise was reached with the state government agreeing to transfer the officers named by the ECI and replacing them from a panel approved by the commission.[34]

The deferral of decision-making when the MCC is in operation during election time has often been criticized in some quarters for putting the government in "pause mode." In the 2014 election, for example, movement of files in government departments and ministries slowed down and important decisions were held up for the approval of the ECI. The ECI denied permission to Manish Tiwari, Minister of Information and Broadcasting, to participate in a National Community Radio programme.[35] While denial of permission to fill up vacancies in public institutions till the elections is routine, in 2014, the Defence Ministry referred its decision to appoint the next Army Chief to the ECI, seeking approval to make the appointment.[36]

On the other hand, election time produces an extraordinary convergence of the local bureaucratic apparatus with electoral machinery generating efficient government during election time. The District Collector/Deputy Commissioner is District Election Officer responsible for monitoring election related work i.e. addition/deletion/modification in voter lists during annual revision of electoral rolls starts from September each year. Special summary revision of electoral rolls is carried out in the election year. The Assistant Commissioner Revenue/SDM is the Electoral Registration Officer (ERO) who accepts or rejects the enrolment form. Tehsildars are Assistant Electoral Registration Officers who monitor the Booth Level Officers (BLOs) and are responsible for getting the enrolment forms filled up and recommending them to the ERO for approval. BLOs are mostly teachers drawn from education department, but may also include Junior Engineers, officials of departments like agriculture, patwaris of Revenue Department etc. This routine election work is an ongoing process and the following chart reflects how the Revenue Administration is also part of electoral administration.[37] In Lok Sabha elections DCs are designated as Returning Officers and

ACs/SDMs as Assistant Returning Officers. In State Assembly Elections ACs/SDMs are designated as Returning Officers and Tehsildars as Assistant Returning Officers. Officers heading state electoral administration do not agree that election time is one of government paralysis and disagree with the association made, often by parties in power that the MCC impedes development processes. The officials prefer to see governance during election time as "a pristine form of government," in which the ECs "writ runs."[38] Ironically, however, when performed effectively, the ECI's job during election time constrains the party in power.

Conclusions

The ECI's responsibility to produce conditions conducive for uncoerced expression of popular sovereignty has been seen as an "Orwellian drama" (Sarkar 2011) and also as "pure governance unsullied by politics" (Gilmartin 2009). The legal structuring of the first general election was aligned with installation of the collective political subject—"we the people"—as the source of constitutional authority. The MCC reflects the sustained importance of unsullied politics and the importance of legal-institutional measures to achieve this condition. More than the early years of the Republic, the protection of the electoral domain as a space of fair competition has become the function of firm and efficient electoral laws. The regime of electoral laws extends from the right of the voter to be informed affirmed, by the Judiciary in 2002, to the disqualification of those convicted of crimes from contesting elections in 2013. The electoral space is replete with purgatory laws. Yet, it is the MCC, which makes "special election time," transforming the modalities of superintending elections, the substitution of political with bureaucratic authority, and the securitization of political space. The voluntariness of the MCC at its inception has given way to supplementary legal force. The continual enhancement of the repertoire of the ECI's powers to ensure compliance has been affirmed by the judiciary as falling within the purview of the ECI's constitutional responsibility. The ECI has been wary of substituting the MCC with statutory law, which would take it from the domain of supplementary legality to explicit legality, but would also constrain the ECI's ability to take immediate action against violators. The supplementary legality of the MCC draws from the notion of necessity as a source of the regulatory powers of the ECI, outside the regime of electoral law. The extent to which these conditions are conducive to choice, and do not create conditions in which free speech and expression is thwarted in a burgeoning regime of surveillance, is open to a debate. This is especially important given a curious paradox that has played out since the close of the twentieth century. The first concerns what Aditya Nigam, in this volume, calls the "rage against representative systems"—witnessed in mass movements against corruption in public places and in the various "occupy" movements, demanding "real democracy" and "rejecting" politics. In the "conduct" of elections, this is made manifest in what Yogendra Yadav has called "the simultaneity of involvement and alienation which has characterized the Indian electorate" (2010: 187), reflecting the tensions between two fundamentally conflicting tendencies in Indian politics—the process of democratization, which has led to higher mobilization and greater politicization, particularly of the marginal sections, and simultaneously, the weakening of people's trust in institutionalized politics. The increasing voter turnouts in successive elections points to the democratic paradox alluded to earlier in the paper, in the persisting contradiction between the exercise of choice by the voter and the conditions in which choice is exercised. Viewed from the appraisive lens, till the time the "political" remains sutured to the power to rule even when constituted through the electoral domain, democracy will remain an unfinished project. The second concerns the manner in which the institutional apparatus of electoral governance remains inside the state apparatus. In the ultimate analysis, the first CEC Sukumar Sen's assertion of ECI's distinctive identity and its role in serving a national purpose at the launch of democracy in India continues to be relevant for recalling democracy.

Notes

1 ECI, Report of the First General Election 1951–52: 10.
2 Narrative Report of the First General Election 1951–52, p. i. [emphasis added].
3 Narrative Report 1968–69, p. 9–11.
4 The different "rhythm" of electoral time is constituted by the convergence of three temporal properties—periodicity, simultaneity, and finality. Thompson elaborates these as follows: "Because elections take place periodically, current majorities can overcome the dead hand of past majorities. To the extent that voting takes place simultaneously, elections express the will of a determinate majority rather than the preferences of a series of different majorities. Because elections produce final results, they legitimate the authority of a current majority until the next election … other democratic values, such as fairness and civic engagement, are also strengthened to the extent that the electoral process realizes these temporal properties" (Thompson 2004, p. 51).
5 In such a context, the ECI may actually be perceived as promoting the interests of the State, against the democratic aspirations of the people. The legislative assembly elections in Jammu and Kashmir (September 2002), for example, opened up debates on the credibility of elections in conditions that were not conducive to free, fair, and fearless exercise of franchise. On the other hand, in Gujarat the same year, the ECI managed to defer assembly elections for a few months, to ensure that elections were held when the moment of crisis following the communal violence, had alleviated.
6 R. K. Narayan, "The Election Game," *The Hindu*, February 3, 1952. The story can be read in the anthology, R. K. Narayan (2000).
7 Cartoon titled "Adult suffrage was a mighty experiment under the new constitution" dated October 21, 1951, in *Don't Spare me Shankar,' Cartoons from Shankar's Weekly*, CBT, New Delhi, 1983, p. 74. The cartoons are available at www.Indianpoliticalimaginaries20thcentury.com.
8 "Preparation for India's General Election: Election Commissioner May Be Appointed Soon," *Times of India*, February 18, 1950, p. 1.
9 Narrative Report of the First General Election, 1951–52, p. 6.
10 Cartoon by Shankar in the context of the postponement of the first general elections under the new constitution which were subsequently held in 1952, "General elections

have been postponed," dated November 19, 1951 in "*Don't Spare me Shankar,*" *Cartoons from Shankar's Weekly*, CBT, New Delhi, 1983, p. 56. The cartoons are available at www.Indianpoliticalimaginaries20thcentury.com.

11 A cartoon by Shankar in the context of the postponement of the first general elections, dated November 26, 1951 in "*Don't Spare me Shankar,*" *Cartoons from Shankar's Weekly*, CBT, New Delhi, 1983, p. 57. The cartoons are available at www.Indianpoliticalimaginaries20thcentury.com.

12 Ramachandra Guha, "The Biggest Gamble in History," *The Hindu Magazine*, January 27, 2002.

13 Report (1951–52: 20–1).

14 A 180 tons of paper was used for 600 million ballot papers, at the cost of Rupees 1,077,401, Report (1951–52: 103).

15 The ballot boxes were prepared by Godrej and Boyce Manufacturing Co. Ltd. Bombay, Hyderabad Allwyn Metal Works, Oriental Metal Pressing Works, Bombay, paper seals for securing boxes against tampering, prepared by the India Security press, Nasik. About 2,600,000 ballot boxes were manufactured. Ibid.: 209.

16 A total of 338, 854 policemen were deployed for polling duties all over the country. Ibid.: 33.

17 Narrative Report, First General Election (1951–52), pp. 209–10.

18 Ronald Dworkin refers to the pedigree of rules, that is the manner in which they were adopted or developed (as distinct from their content). See Ronald Dworkin, *The Model of Rules*, 2004, p. 17.

19 Sadiq vs. Election Commission, A 1972 S.C.187.

20 These judgments are Mohinder Singh Gill v. The Chief Election Commissioner, New Delhi, 1978 (SCC 405), Vineet Narain and Others v. Union of India and Another (1998 SCC 226), and Union of India v. Association for Democratic Reforms & Anr (SC 249/2002).

21 The Representation of the People Act, 1951, Section 81 (Presentation of Petitions).

22 N.P. Ponnuswami v. The Returning Officer, Namakkal Constituency, Namakkal, Salem District and four Others (The Union of India The State of Madhya Bharat Interveners), Supreme Court of India, (Civil Appellate Jurisdiction), Case No. 351 of 1951, (decision dated January 21, 1952). Landmark Judgements on Election Law, Election Commission of India, New Delhi, 1999.

23 Narrative Report of the Third General Elections in India, Election Commission of India, Delhi, 1962: 58–61.

24 Ibid.: 61.

25 Ibid.: 61–5.

26 Preface, Report, Sixth General Election (1977: 81–2).

27 Devesh Kapur and Pratap Bhanu Mehta categorize the Election Commission and the Supreme Court as order maintaining, referee institutions, exercising primarily the task of restraining other public institutions within a given framework of rules (Kapur and Mehta 2005: 4).

28 Annual Report of the ECI (1984: 88).

29 Ibid.: 42.

30 See "EC Displeasure over Modi, Sonia Speeches," *The Hindu*, Delhi, December 23, 2007, p. 1; "Ensure adherence to model code in future," ibid.: 10.

31 "Election Body asks Police to file FIR against BJP's Kapil Mishra," January 25, 2020, *NDTV.com*, accessed on December 21, 2020.

32 Election Commission circular no. 437/6/1/2014-CC & BE, available on eci.nic.in, accessed on March 14, 2014.
33 Election Commission transfers 44 senior officers in UP', Press Trust of India, March 26, 2014.
34 "Poll Panel Transfers Eight Officers, Mamata Refused to Obey," *Business Standard*, April 7, 2014.
35 "UPA-II Ministries Hit Pause Button, Keep Files Pending for New Government," *The Indian Express*, April 7, 2014.
36 "Election Commission to Consider Army Chief Appointment Issue," *The Hindu*, May 3, 2014.
37 the chart is available at www.Indianpoliticalimaginaries20thcentury.com
38 CEO of the state of Bihar in conversation with the authors on June 28, 2016.

Select Bibliography

Baxi, Upendra, "Preliminary Notes on Transformative Constitutionalism," in O. Vilhena, Upendra Baxi and F. Viljoen, eds., *Transformative Constitutionalism: Comparing the Apex Courts of Brazil, India and South Africa* (Johannesburg: Pretoria University Law Press, 2013), pp. 19–47.

Bhatia, Gautam, *The Transformative Constitution: A Radical Biography in Nine Acts* (Noida: HarperCollins, 2019).

Chatterjee, Partha, *The Politics of the Governed* (New York: Columbia University Press, 2006).

Devadawson, Christel R., *Out of Line: Cartoons, Caricature and Contemporary India* (Delhi: Orient Blackswan, 2014).

Gallie, W. B., "Essentially Contested Concepts," *Proceedings of the Aristotelian Society*, New Series 56 (1955–1956): 167–98.

Gilmartin, David, "One Day's Sultan: T. N. Seshan and Indian Democracy," *Contributions to Indian Sociology* (n.s.) 43, no. 2 (2009): 247–84.

Kapur, Devesh and Pratap Bhanu Mehta, eds., *Political Institutions in India: Performance and Design* (New Delhi: Oxford University Press, 2005).

Katju, Manjari, "Election Commission and Changing Contours of Politics," *Economic and Political Weekly* XLIV, no. 16 (2009): 8–12.

Kaviraj, Sudipta, "A State of Contradictions: The Post-Colonial State in India," in Quentin Skinner and Bo Strath, eds., *State and Citizens: History, Theory, Prospects* (Cambridge: Cambridge University Press, 2003), pp. 144–63.

Lyngdoh, James Michael, *Chronicle of an Impossible Election* (Delhi: Viking, 2004).

McMillan, Alistair, "The Election Commission," in Niraja Gopal Jayal and Pratap Bhanu Mehta, eds., *The Oxford Companion to Politics in India* (New Delhi: Oxford University Press, 2010).

McMillan, Alistair, "The Election Commission of India and the Regulation and Administration of Electoral Politics," *Election Law Journal* 11, no. 2 (2012).

Mouffe, Chantal, *The Democratic Paradox* (London, New York: Verso, 2000).

Report on the First General Election Of India 1951–52, vol. 1 Election Commission of India, Delhi, 1955.

Rudolph, Lloyd I. and Susanne Hoeber Rudolph, "Redoing the Constitutional Design: From an Interventionist to a Regulatory State," in Lloyd I. Rudolph and Susanne Hoeber Rudolph, eds., *Explaining Indian Democracy: A Fifty-Year Perspective,*

1956–2006, Vol. II: The Realm of Institutions: State Formation and Institutional Change, Oxford Collected Essays (New Delhi: Oxford University Press, 2008).

Sarkar, Shyamal, "Orwellian Drama in Marxist Domain," *The Editstreet*, March 21, 2011.

Shani, Ornit, *How India Became Democratic: Citizenship and the Making of the Universal Franchise* (Cambridge: Cambridge University Press, 2018).

Thompson, Dennis F., "Election Time: Normative Implications of Temporal Properties of the Electoral Process in the United States," *American Political Science Review* 98, no. 1 (February 2004): 51–64.

Urbinati, Nadia, "Representation as Advocacy: A Study of Democratic Deliberation," *Political Theory* 28, no. 6 (December 2000): 758–86.

Weiner, Myron, "The Indian Election—A Diary," *Centre for International Studies*, (Cambridge, MA: MIT, 1977).

8

Voting and the Visual: Electoral Symbols, Legal Discourse, and the Sovereign People

David Gilmartin

The idea of "free and fair" elections is one central to virtually all modern conceptions of democracy, and yet the meaning of this term, which has been subjected to relatively little comparative cultural analysis, is one that continues to spark debate. It is in some sense a commonsense phrase, suggesting the embedding of the conduct of elections in an administrative regime independent of the immediate political control of the parties contesting the elections. But in actual fact, the meaning of "free and fair" is extraordinarily complex. The remit of election administration, and, indeed, the meaning of the phrase "free and fair," has varied widely across societies. Its emphasis has in some countries and contexts focused on the "impartial" administrative tasks of preparing voter rolls, protecting the process of casting ballots, and ensuring the accurate counting of votes. But in other contexts, it has focused also on the oversight of election campaigns more broadly, including the administrative protection of "free" voter choice from both statist and societal pressures. At stake in such oversight has often been a vision of individual voter choice as threatened not only by government power, but also by multiple forms of social coercion, ranging from the manipulation of information (and the press), the unequal (or "unfair") use of money to influence votes, and the manipulative use of "undue influence" by powerful leaders in society, whether religious or secular. "Fair" elections have required, in some formulations, the establishment of what is sometimes called a "level playing field."

Tracking the conceptual meanings of "free and fair" in such contexts, in fact takes us toward one of the great conundrums of modern democracy. For at stake in such questions is precisely the question of what constitutes the realm of "politics" itself. Though elections are imagined everywhere as embedded in the realm of political competition, without which they could not possibly be seen as legitimate, their legitimacy hinges also on their framing within a structure imagined to stand apart

I would like to thank those who responded to earlier drafts of this paper at a panel of the American Anthropological Association, Washington, December 2014, at a Yale South Asia Center Seminar, April 2015, and at a lecture hosted by the History department, University of Colorado, Boulder, in April 2016. I also thank, especially, Sandria Freitag, Pamela Price, and Sumathi Ramaswamy for their comments.

from "politics." For elections to be "free and fair," they must, somehow, transcend the ultimately political nature of the men and women who contest and participate in them.

But from where, then, if not from the "people" who vote and contest them, does the authority to provide an external framework for "free and fair" elections derive? Here we encounter the central question about politics and democracy raised by Manu Goswami and Mrinalini Sinha in the introduction to this volume. To fully understand the scope of politics in the context of democracy, it is necessary, as they suggest, to move beyond a definition of "politics" as simply the "competition for political power," in order to understand a larger vision of "the political" that encompasses frameworks of collective authority, even when cast in opposition to the realm of popular "politics" more narrowly defined.

In twentieth-century India we can see this in the particular ways that the mid-century projection of the concept of the "people's sovereignty" served as a foundation for democracy. But the vision of the people lying behind this imagining of sovereignty was one that brought together—and put into tension—two very different concepts of who the "people" were. The concept projected the "people," on the one hand, as an abstract and unitary collective of "free" and "equal" individuals, an imagined collective self as it were, whose intrinsic autonomy and freedom defined a touchstone for the ultimate authority of the state. But this concept of the "people" was balanced by another vision, of the "people" as a congeries of fragmented and conflicted individuals and groups, whose very divisions, conflicts, and competing interests and identities—whose "politics" in other words—defined the necessary power of the state as a source of authority and order standing apart from the people. These two visions found their most powerful reflection in the conception of "law" embedded in the Indian constitution, as simultaneously an emanation from the people, and as a construct standing "above" (or apart from) the people's politics.

This image of law was one with deep roots in the old British colonial language of legitimation.[1] The proceduralism of law was for the British a central trope for juxtaposing the colonial state as a manifestation of modern reason, against a "traditional" Indian society deeply shaped by religion, patronage, and custom. At independence, many of India's early leaders rejected sharply the racialized and self-serving character of this British colonial approach to law, which occluded the Indian people from any share in sovereignty.[2] Nevertheless, the vision of law as a critical legitimizing prop for state authority retained its power. In fact, a key imperative of India's constitution-making was the redefinition of the law, not simply as a bulwark of order, but as an emanation from the Indian "people" as a "national" collective, an image standing in counterpoint to the image of Indian "society" as "traditional," fragmented, and divided by caste, religion, language, interest, and social class. This was reflected in the very language of the Indian constitution itself, which in its preamble rhetorically cast the constitution (and the "rule of law" it embodied) as a gift from the "people of India" *to themselves*—thus defining the "people" both as the autonomous *source* of the legal order that the Constitution embodied, and as the targets of the disciplinary "rule of law" that it contained.[3]

While the distinctive form taken by the Indian constitution was complex, this dual vision of the "sovereign people" provides a critical backdrop for understanding the distinctive meanings that the concept of "free and fair" elections subsequently came to carry in Indian democracy. For if the law was in one sense an emanation from the collective national unity of the Indian "people" (a symbolic concern that drove the adoption of a uniform standard for universal adult suffrage for India's elections), it also took form in a context in which most of India's early leaders remained, in actual practice, strongly invested in a vision of India's "masses" as still far away politically from the ideal of "enlightened" citizenship that this image of national unity projected. Elections were thus a time when voters were widely viewed as easily swayed in practice by local social pressures, and it was common in elite discourse to stress the centrality of appeals to what came to be called "vote banks," with most rural voters in particular seen to be casting ballots largely under the influence of patrons, according to caste, village, and local community pressures.[4] Though this was often lamented, it also provided—critically—a ready justification for the continuing elite domination of Indian politics, which many of India's early high caste leaders saw as important to political stability. Given this perspective, the emphasis on procedural regularities in voting can be seen in critical ways less as a model for *actually* transforming local politics (though it contained, as we will see, an important pedagogical agenda), than as a powerful tool for underscoring the idealized *image* of the free, self-contained citizen voter as a necessary icon underlying the very structure of the constitution, and for giving meaning to the concept of "popular sovereignty."[5]

It would be wrong, of course, to suggest that the emphasis on "free and fair" elections was completely unconnected to real administrative efforts to limit open intimidation and coercion in elections, a concern that runs through early Election Commission reports. Indeed, the successful completion by the EC of the first general election in 1951–2 was widely celebrated as a triumph of disinterested administration.[6] But the *symbolic* significance of the image of the free, agentive voter was also deeply embedded in the law of voting practice. This was reflected, for example, in the centrality of the secret ballot. Whatever the actual social pressures shaping voting alignments, the image of the free autonomous individual was powerfully dramatized by this procedural technology, which confined the voter at the very moment of choice to a space set apart from society and politics, the voter standing alone with his/her own conscience.[7] And it was this same idealized image of the voter—juxtaposed against the realities of "politics"—that defined the critical, dynamic role of law, including the old English legal concept of "undue influence," in electoral structure. In actual practice, of course, the meaning of free individual agency in the midst of a society defined by dependence, influence, hierarchy, and politics remained extremely difficult—if not impossible—to concretely define. But its projection—even as an almost mystical concept—was no less important for that, for it remained central to the structure of oppositions that shaped a good part of electoral adjudication.

Difficulties in defining the meaning of individual "agency" (or "choice") as a central principle of voting were, of course, in no way peculiar to India. Indeed, the relation between law and politics in the face of these difficulties has long represented a critical, and much debated, question in the theory of democracy—and of "free and fair" elections as a concept. As Jurgen Habermas has written, liberal democratic theory has long harbored a deep-seated and perhaps irresolvable contradiction relating to how politics and law intersect in constituting democratic order. At the heart of this contradiction is precisely the question of law's role in the constitution of the free, sovereign individual—imagined to exist, somehow, as anterior to politics. "According to the liberal view," Habermas has written, "the democratic self-determination of citizens can be realized only through the medium of [modern positive, compulsory, individualistic] law, the structural properties of which ensure liberty." Without law, in other words, true individual freedom would always be subject to compromise by mankind's *inherently* social and political nature. But if the autonomous, self-determining individual could only find full realization through law, then from where could the authority of the law itself emanate? Modern liberal democratic theory in such a reading could only rest, in the end, on a fundamental contradiction, with the law both necessary to the realization of the "democratic self-determination of citizens," and yet, at the very same time a structure inevitably setting "limits," as Habermas puts it, "on the people's sovereign self-determination."[8]

This contradiction played itself out in India in very distinctive ways. In many countries—most notably the United States—the greatest threat to the "self-determination of the individual," as Habermas put it, was widely perceived to emanate primarily (though certainly not exclusively) from the coercive power of the *state*. It had thus long been the association of law with the power of the state that made it deeply suspect as a key to freedom. But in India, the threat to the sovereign individual was perceived at the time of independence to lie far less in the power of the state (though that was undoubtedly a concern to many) than in the coercive, parochial pressures embedded in *society* itself. The roots of this view were many, but critically important, as we have seen, were the intersecting legacies of India's colonial past and elite fears deriving from India's move to universal adult suffrage after 1947 with an overwhelmingly illiterate population.[9]

Party Symbols, Visual Culture, and the Law

I would like to take one central technology of voting, the mobilization and regulation of pictorial party symbols, as a critical window on this process, and one that allows us to link this story to the critical role of sight in the constitution of the modern, agentive self. Visual symbols in fact came to be central to the technology of Indian voting from a very early time, as a response—in part—to India's low levels of literacy. Before 1947, voting methods, under a limited franchise, had varied. A common method was that voting slips were put in different colored boxes associated with different parties or candidates. After independence, separate boxes for different candidates and parties were still used, but marked by symbols rather than different colors, and these symbols soon became key elements in popular political identifications. The system evolved eventually toward a common paper ballot with names, parties, and symbols, and ultimately to the Electronic Voting Machines used today. The original importance of visual symbols as a practical adjunct to the secret ballot in a largely illiterate electorate is beyond doubt. But the nature of these symbols—and their relationship to the image of the autonomous voter and to the modern politics of the visual—is a subject only just beginning to be studied.

As Simona Vittorini has argued, the introduction of pictorial symbols can in some ways be read as part of the pedagogical, "nation-building" agenda that marked the Nehruvian era; it was part and parcel in this reading of the state concern to educate the people in their new sovereign role as free, rational agents, at the same time disciplining their parochial politics. Election symbols were thus deliberately chosen, in her argument, for their *lack* of any emotive, religious, or ethnic implications (Figure 1). They were projected instead as wholly indexical, designed specifically as line drawings, without color, and without intended emotive connotations, intended preeminently to subsume emotive individual desires within the framework of rationalized party identifications. "Aiming at discouraging the domination of parochial, caste, religious and factional politics, they were vehicles of indoctrination and constitutive elements," she argues, in the construction of "disciplined citizenship."[10] Their association with institutionalized parties was thus critical. Though separate schedules of symbols were used for state and independent candidates as well, the association of symbols with political parties—as rationalizing entities—lay at the heart of an elite, assimilative national political vision.

In practice, of course, the meanings attached by voters to these symbols were hardly so simple and their interpretation needs to be grounded in larger debates about the role of the visual in twentieth-century Indian politics. As scholars such as Christopher Pinney, Sumathi Ramaswamy, and Sandria Freitag have all, in different ways, shown, circulating images in twentieth-century India often lay at the interface between what might be heuristically termed "individual rationality" and "emotive self-assertion."[11] Following some European theorists, some scholars of India have looked to the visual realm in India as an arena for tracking the modern projection of the seeing, rational individual as the foundation for modern sovereign authority. The conceptual foundations of this framing were perhaps most famously explored in Martin Heidigger's essay on the "World Picture,"[12] emphasizing the centrality of "objective" observation of the world (aided by technology) in conjuring the image of the reasoning individual, standing apart from the "world" (with all its parochial identities), as the ultimate source of modern sovereign power. But such an image, if perhaps easily linked to India's technology of voting symbols as interpreted by Vittorini, hardly exhausted the ways that visual symbols had shaped images of individual autonomy and freedom in twentieth-century politics.

Indeed, visions of the "people" during the Indian independence movement were more commonly projected in highly emotive ways, drawing on deep histories of devotionalism and religious attachment. As Ajay Sinha puts it, the increasing market-based circulation of printed visual material in the twentieth century—posters, calendars etc.—played a key role in shaping "the desires and expectations of common people in relation to the dominant politics of India,"[13] sometimes linking projections of national identity to images of goddesses and gods that seemed to call forth collective sacrifice and selfless (sometimes even violent) individual devotion. In such a framing individual agency was linked less to vision's rationalizing and objectifying powers than it was to sight's capacity to produce affective bonding: whether tied to the power of *darshan*, as Pinney argues; to the deep devotionalisms associated with the envisioning of the nation as a mother goddess, as Ramaswamy argues in her study of the iconography of Bharat Mata; or to the new visions of local identities constructed as viewers turned circulating images to their own distinctive local uses, as is developed in the work of Freitag. The

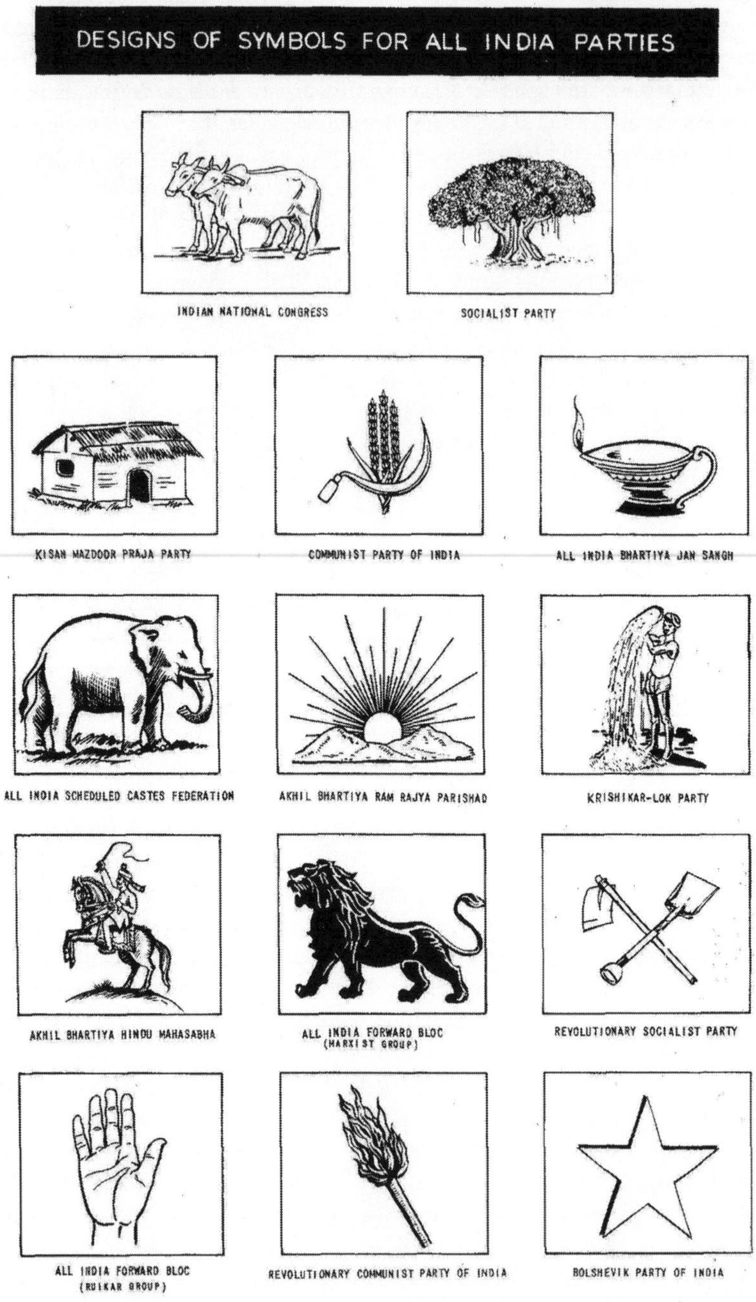

Figure 1 Election Commission of India. Report on the First General Election in India 1951–1952. vol. I (New Delhi: Government of India Press, 1955), between pp. 84–85.

affective power of these images defined a story of the nation, as Pinney has written, "quite distinct from the familiar stories of a non-visual history,"[14] a story shaped less by the rationalities of formal Congress party organization (or even Gandhian forms of self-control) than by the forms of individual autonomy and attachment activated by emotive images of devotional sacrifice and attachment.

However much party symbols may have been designed and projected as rationalizing images, therefore, they operated in a complex world of visual projections, and it was against this backdrop that the law relating to electoral symbols operated. To provide a rough outline of these legal processes, I focus on representative cases coming from three different eras in the evolution of Indian democracy and its legal structuring, first from the 1950s, then from the 1970s and 80s in the aftermath of Indira Gandhi's Emergency, and finally from 2012. All of these cases provide a window on the conflicted ways that the law (and electoral administration) operated to conjure the image of the "free," autonomous voter amidst the complexities of the pressures and influences of the Indian electoral system.

The Nehruvian Era

Cases during the 1950s, the first decade of India's democracy and the heyday of Jawaharlal Nehru's influence, provide clear evidence of the complex balancing between the "disciplining" power of party symbols, and the broader, emotive mobilization of such visual images in everyday democratic practice that marked evolving Indian electioneering. The legal framework for these cases was provided by the dual structure of legal oversight created by India's constitution and the Representation of the People Act of 1951. While the Election Commission was given constitutional authority to run the administration of elections, the courts heard election petitions after the fact alleging violations of law in the conduct of elections.[15] A number of court cases on the "misuse" of electoral symbols (i.e., on their manipulation to produce what the law called "undue influence" challenging free individual choice) stand out from these years, cases that also prompted commentary from the Election Commission as it first developed its strategies for electoral administration in the 1950s. The RPA, which provided the statutory framework for the courts to hear election petitions challenging elections, specifically prohibited election candidates not only from improperly using state or bureaucratic machinery or coercion for winning votes, but also from appealing for votes "on grounds of caste, race, community or religion." Yet appeals to a variety of loyalties, including caste, community, and religion, were ubiquitous in Indian elections during these years. Given their centrality to politics, the courts thus tended generally to use their authority as adjudicators of "free and fair" not to directly challenge the operations of these loyalties but to project the law's rationalizing oversight as a principle of the larger political order in which everyday "politics" was embedded. Though a number of election results were overturned by these cases, they nevertheless operated less to actually transform "politics," than to mobilize an image of the free, individual, sovereign voter—imagined as a vessel of free choice—as a bedrock principle defining the ultimate "sovereignty of the people."

Two linked cases from Karnataka in the 1950s (then known as Mysore state), dealing with the use of the yoked bullocks symbol of the ruling Congress Party itself, can be taken as exemplary of the way such claims often played out.[16] After the 1957 elections, two election petitions were filed specifically charging that the Congress symbol had been illegally deployed in electioneering to link the party with the image of Nandi, Shiva's bullock, an image that was said to have particular religious significance for the Lingayat community, a caste community historically defined by adherence to the teachings of the medieval Hindu reformer, Basava—and a large voting bloc in the state. This was a classic charge of "undue influence," or the attempted intrusion of potentially coercive forms of authority into the realm of voter freedom. For the Lingayats, as the Mysore High Court put it, it was an undisputed article of faith "that Kalyana Basava [the founder of the Veerashaiva tradition] was the incarnation of Nandi, the mount of Siva." The Congress, these election petitions charged, had thus sought to compromise the freedom of choice of individual Lingayat voters by linking the Congress symbol to the *spiritual* authority of Basava, while seemingly linking this authority to the imperatives of Lingayat caste. "The charge," as the court put it, citing the language, of the statute, "was that not only were the Lingayat voters in the Parliamentary Constituency subjected to some form of undue influence but were also subjected to a systematic appeal on the ground of religion or Caste ... "[17] Here the party symbol of the Congress, the yoked bullocks, paraded through the streets in many Congress election rallies, had seemingly morphed from a simple indexical marker of the party appearing on ballot boxes, to a visual image intended specifically to impute a collective emotive bond between the Congress and the religion (and caste identity) of the Lingayats. It had become, in other words, at least as the petition charged, a devotional image capable of undercutting free, sovereign individual voter choice.

Nevertheless, the court balked at using the law to suppress the operation of what seemed so integral to local politics, for in this case the "misuse" of the party symbol could not be easily separated in their view from the larger Congress political appeal to Lingayat interests and values. Key here was the court's interpretation of a Congress election pamphlet, presented in evidence, that focused precisely on the meanings to be attached to "The Congress Symbol" (Figure 2: I have extracted the text of the pamphlet from the judgment here and added an image of the official Congress symbol). Evidence of the Congress's allegedly "corrupt" attempt to associate their party symbol with religious devotion to Shiva's Nandi, "the mount of God" was, the court admitted, readily apparent in the pamphlet's text, and it was on this ground that the petitioners argued that the pamphlet's language violated the law. But the attribution of religious meaning to the visual symbol, the court determined, could not be read apart here from the discursive world in which the symbol figured, as a full reading of the pamphlet made clear. The party symbol seemed instead to crystallize a whole range of Congress associations—from the religious to the economic to the deeply personal, from the economics of farming, to the importance of local cooperation, to an appeal to selfless, desireless individual action. The court in fact made note of the problematic, and potentially actionable, nature of the association of the Congress symbol with Shiva's Nandi (and with Basava as an incarnation). But at the same time, they balanced this with a recognition that the visual meanings of the party symbol were in cases such as this part of a multivalent, discursive world, shaped not only by the specificities of

"Congress Election Symbol"

This is the picture of two yoked bullocks. Bullocks remind (us) of villages. The charm displayed by them when moving on fields, in forests and on meadows and on green pastures pleases the minds of ryots and is a feast to their eyes.

Bullock is Shiva's Nandi—Basavanna. Just as it is the mount of God it is also the servant of the Country's economic system and the foundation and the transcendent power of the farmer.

The sight of the bullocks reminds (us) of the ideal of universal love, the welfare of the entire creation and Dharma. Gandhiji, the father of our Nation, once said that the cow is the poem of compassion.

Bullocks which are the off-spring of the Gomatha (mother cow) are the very life and the secure wealth of agriculture.

The election symbol of the Congress is a symbol of service—Agriculture is the foundation of India's progress and industrial advance.

In agriculture lies village life. Bullocks constitute the entire fortune of the ryots. The pair of bullocks stands for co-operation. The picture of the two bullocks standing together ready to serve invites the co-operation of the farmer. It is only when the farmer pitches and plies the plough, paddy and cotton are grown and there is an abundance of jola and wheat.

Thus it is that the election symbol of the Congress is the symbol of service through mutual help and co-operation, through self help and sacrifice. This represents the harmonious blend and mingling of the power of the living beings with the power of the machine and it is also an exposition in practice of the principle of desireless action.

Voters should therefore cast their valuable votes into the box bearing such a symbol and uphold the plans, policies and programmes of the Congress.

--Text from 1957 Congress Election Pamphlet, *translated from Kannada, in Sangappa* v. *Shivamurthiswamy, 23 ELR 51 (1968), pp. 59-60.*

Figure 2 Image I created from text of 1957 Congress election pamphlet included in Sangappa *v.* Shivamurthiswamy (In the High Court of Mysore at Bangalore), 23 ELR 51 (1968), with the image of Congress election symbol (from Figure 1) added.

language, but also by those of local cultural context. In the result, the court refused to overturn the recorded verdict of the people's votes and rejected the petition. If the case itself underscored the law's claim to protect the sovereign voter from "undue influence," and to police the misuse of party symbols in the name of "free and fair" elections, it also reflected the ongoing difficulties for the courts in defining a clear relationship between legal authority and individual agency, not to mention the complex relationship between the emotive power of visual images and the discursive power of language. But on another level, the very structure of the adjudication also suggested the important ways in which the law's framing of "undue influence" mobilized an image of the "free" voter as a critical conceit for the operation of the "people's" sovereign imagining, standing apart in some ways from the realities that constituted "politics."

Indira Gandhi and Beyond

More contentious and problematic were cases focusing on the later Congress symbol, the Open Hand, which came into usage after the Emergency of 1975–7, during the time when the Congress, now led by Indira Gandhi, had itself begun to call into question some of the principles of Nehruvian rule, in the name of radical social change and populist mobilization.[18] This was a time when the nature of the law and the courts was brought into direct discussion and contestation, particularly in the wake of the declaration of Emergency, whose justifications were cast, at least in part, in terms of the sovereignty of Parliament trumping the sovereignty of the "people" themselves. Moreover, the relationship of politics to electoral law also took on heightened meaning during these years as a result of the controversy surrounding Indira Gandhi's own conviction in 1975 for violations of the RPA, specifically for misuse of government machinery to win her election—the event that led directly to her Emergency declaration. All of this gave new urgency to questions relating to the legal boundaries of electioneering and influence—and to the ways that appeals to visual symbols were framed and assessed by the courts and the EC.[19] Once again, the nature of the "people's sovereignty" was caught up in the juxtaposition of two very different visions of the "people."

Though controversies about the Open Hand as a visual symbol took many forms, some of the most pointed challenges in these years related to its meanings for Muslims, and to the association of the Open Hand (particularly, but hardly exclusively, for Shias) with the family of the Prophet (the *ahl-i bayt*).[20] But the backdrop to these cases lay in earlier legal cases challenging more broadly the use of religion in appeals for Muslim votes. The classic judgment in this genre was that of the Supreme Court in Ziyauddin Bukhari *v.* Brijmohan Mehra, which in 1975 had overturned a Bombay city election on the grounds that a candidate had used threats of anathema against voters supporting another candidate who advocated the reform of Muslim personal law, thus preying, as the court put it, "upon the minds and feelings of the ordinary, average voters," and thereby generating "powerful emotions" that had the power to "deprive people of their powers of rational thought and action." If voting was to be meaningful, the court implied, candidates had to show self-control and self-discipline, terms powerfully linked to the old, Nehruvian pedagogical agenda, which sought to discipline emotive religious appeals in the name of national unity (and of the people's sovereignty as an idea). If self-control was in question, in other words, the law had to step in to protect the freedom of the individual from "undue influence," and from the "blind and disruptive passions" that threatened to undermine the meaning of democracy, thus necessitating in this case the overturning of the election result and the ordering of a revote.[21] The case did not hinge specifically on visual influence. But as the court's reference to "blind" passions suggested, beneath the decision lay a normative association of sight with the realm of free, reasoned choice—a frame much like that which had underlain a view of election symbols as simply indexical, rationalizing visual markers.

Such language provided an important backdrop for later cases, including a key case involving the Open Hand, from the Andhra Pradesh Legislative Assembly elections of 1978, immediately after the end of the Emergency. In this election, the victorious Congress (I) candidate in Chittoor district was charged in a Janata Party election petition with having corruptly manipulated the outcome by appealing to the religious passions of Muslim voters, in this instance by conflating the Congress electoral symbol, the open hand, with the "Ali ka Panja," a visual religious symbol with the five fingers of an open hand representing the Prophet's family. This was a symbol long associated with some Muslim religious observances (notably Muharram), and it was one carried in public religious processions much as the hand symbol was carried in public Congress election rallies.

This conflation represented, the petition charged, a fundamental misuse of the symbol, for it threatened the underlying freedom of individual choice central to the election. As the losing Janata candidate testified before the court, there was at that time a vibrant, ongoing public debate about the treatment of Muslims in India that had been galvanized by Muslim resistance to slum clearance in Delhi during Indira Gandhi's Emergency. But despite "the publicity given by the Radio, news papers and other journals regarding enquiry by the Shah Commission," as one witness testified, the parading of the open hand through Muslim villages in the constituency during the Andhra elections had completely overwhelmed rational debate—and thus, by implication, the voters' free choice. The Janata candidate's attempts to appeal to "Muslim elders," as he put it, were repeatedly interrupted by children chanting "Ali ka hath Zindabad" ("Long live the hand of Ali!"), as they paraded the open hand symbol through the village.[22] The evidence in the case thus echoed the earlier warnings of the Bukhari judgment. But here it was specifically the emotive power of the visual, seemingly reducing discursive debate to the chanting of immature children (a key marker of what the sovereign, rational individual was not), which threatened democracy's most basic meanings.[23]

Yet here too the court, while underscoring the responsibility of the law to protect "the purity and sobriety of the elections by ensuring that the candidates do not secure the valuable votes of the people by undue influence, fraud, communal propaganda, bribery or other corrupt practices," was wary of actually overturning the election, particularly in a context where conflicting oral testimony seemed, as they noted, to carry the politics of the election itself into subsequent court proceedings. The court found its own legal "sight" in danger of being blinkered by the claims and counterclaims of witnesses, mobilized by opposing political parties, who seemed to be trying to refight the election in the courts. The court's uncertainty about how to deal with such testimony made clear the tension between the law's seemingly disinterested procedure, and the actual application of legal judgment in a "political" world where even court testimony could be suffused with politics. "We must emphasize the danger of believing at its face value oral evidence in an election case without the backing of sure circumstances or indubitable documents," the court thus declared. " ... There is no X-ray whereby the dishonesty of the story can be established and, if the court were gullible enough to gulp such oral versions and invalidate elections a new menace to our electoral [system] would have been invented though the judicial apparatus." The court thus decided, in the end, to let the election stand.[24] Even the courts lacked sufficiently powerful rational sight ("X-ray" vision, in this formulation) to fully subordinate the worlds of everyday "politics" to a "rule of law" that could guarantee voter freedom. But the tension between the law as a potential enabler of the freedom of the voter, and as a form of external authority that could represent a threat to the voter's autonomy—the key democratic tension identified by Habermas—was here on prominent display.

The tensions surrounding the multiple meanings that could be attached to the Congress symbol in fact remained evident in the subsequent career of the Open Hand over the next decade. The potentially emotive power of the symbol took on yet more powerful meanings after the assassination of Indira Gandhi in 1984. As Ramaswamy has argued, images of Indira Gandhi as a slain "martyr" that appeared at this time are easily placed in a longer genealogy of devotional images of "mother India," dating back to the preindependence period.[25] Yet the mobilization of such visual images in the 1984 Congress election raised questions about the echoes of martyrdom that could now be read into the Congress symbol itself. The association of the symbol with martyrdom had been evident in testimony relating to the earlier Andhra case just discussed. The open hand, as we have seen, signified not only the *ahl-i bayt*, but also the martyrdom of the Prophet's grandson, Husain, particularly when carried atop Husain's riderless horse in Muharram processions, and in that context known, as witnesses in the Andhra case noted, as "DulDul Panja."[26] With the hand prominently displayed during the 1984 elections on posters that also featured Indira Gandhi's assassination, as was the case, for example, on some 1984 election hoardings in Hyderabad, the presence of the Congress symbol, combined with the image of Indira as martyred "mother India," served potentially to generalize the evocation of martyrdom to multiple audiences (and to multiple visions of community).[27] This use of the Open Hand with images of Indira's assassination was not (as far as I am aware) made the subject of formal petitioning after, or EC complaint during, the 1984 election campaign (though it is worth noting that election rhetoric equating Indira Gandhi with "Durga Mata" *was* the subject of earlier petitioning arising out of 1980 elections).[28] Nevertheless, this juxtaposition suggested the visual mechanisms by which multiple readings of the symbol were conflated—with "Ali ka hath" and "Amma ka hath" ("the hand of Ali" and "the hand of Mother," as one witness had specifically characterized the hand's overlapping meanings in court evidence in the 1978 case) seemingly joined as emotive icons giving distinctive meaning to devotion and martyrdom—and perhaps to the appeal for votes.[29] It suggested how easy it was to mobilize party symbols along multiple trajectories.

The Post-1990s Era: From Hath ("Hand") *to Hathi* ("Elephant")

Critical changes marked the operation of the Election Commission after the early 1990s. This was the era of rising Hindu nationalism in India, of the increasing importance in

Indian electoral politics of new, lower caste-based political parties, and of the rise of new media. But most important for us here, it was a time of new assertiveness by the EC in efforts to use its administrative and legal authority to discipline election campaigns in the name of the free choice of the individual voter. It was in this context that the EC began to give increasing importance to what was called the "Model Code of Conduct for the Guidance of Political Parties and Candidates" as a frame for its actions.[30]

The code itself was not new. Its origins dated back to the early 1960s, when it emerged as a compendium of nonjusticiable rules accepted by the parties, which was issued by the EC theoretically as simply a mutually agreeable guide for the conduct of elections. It embodied key elements that lay at the heart of EC policy, including prohibitions on the exercise of undue influence (including government influence) and appeals to religion, caste and community in ways that would compromise the ideal of the free, independent voter. Many of its provisions were drawn in substance from the 1951 RPA. But the very form of the Model Code also suggested the distinctive ways that EC policy-making had evolved, for although the code seemingly empowered the discipline of law and procedure as keys to the protection of "free and fair" elections, it downplayed the role of positive law in EC electoral administration and emphasized instead the EC's role as the upholder of a distinctive electoral morality. This was reflected in the conceit that the Model Code emanated ultimately not from positive law but from the free agreement of the political parties—and thus from the higher aspirations of the "people" themselves. It could thus be represented, perhaps, as a new form for addressing the dilemmas between law and freedom that election oversight entailed.

Most relevant for us here, this approach also entailed a new relationship to the realm of the visual as well. Not only did the EC increasingly try (particularly under Chief Election Commissioner, T. N. Seshan in the early 1990s) to *publicize* violations of the code in the expanding media as a new form of public pressure on politicians, thus making the EC itself much more visible, but it also gave increasing attention to the public "look" of elections, using the Model Code aggressively to limit, for example, the placement of posters, hoardings etc. and the timings of public meetings. Critically, this was associated with a new public *visibility* for the EC itself, a sharp contrast, as Anupama Roy and Ujjwal Kumar Singh note in their chapter in this volume, with the relative invisibility of the EC's role in the elections of the 1950s. This visibility was associated also, with the increasing assertion by the EC of a distinctive legal position, deriving directly from the Constitution, which transformed them from simply a "referee" to an active participant in the electoral process, constraining the power of the government.[31] Increasingly, the EC sought to expand its authority by conflating law with a higher morality that stood above political interest or particularistic identity.

It was within this context that the EC's approach to the "misuse" of party symbols evolved in new directions after the 1990s. Perhaps the best known recent illustration of this was the ECs decision during the Uttar Pradesh Legislative Assembly elections of 2012 to order, on the grounds of Model Code provisions, the wrapping of large numbers of monumental elephants, the election symbol of the Bahujan Samaj Party, a predominantly dalit party led by then Chief Minister, Mayawati, during the BSP's campaign to retain control of the Assembly of which it had won control in 2007. Mayawati's UP ministry represented a critical moment of self-assertion by long-oppressed dalits, and the elephants were no doubt part of a "landscape of empowerment," as Amita Sinha and Rajat Kant have put it, deliberately intended to call to mind the sovereign eclat of kingship, a particularly powerful association for Mayawati's BSP given its dalit background.[32] In this sense their meanings had long been open to strikingly opposing constructions, as markers of new dalit claims to dignity and power for Mayawati's dalit supporters on the one hand, and as signs of overreach, tastelessness, corruption, and immaturity for many higher-caste opponents on the other. Mayawati's elephants (and other statues) had in fact been the subject of earlier litigation in 2010, when their original construction had been challenged as a corrupt use of the "the public exchequer" for party advancement. The EC had been asked in connection with this litigation to revoke the party's elephant symbol on these grounds. But when the Supreme Court ruled the original construction of the statues was legal (as the prerogative of an elected government), the EC had refused to take any action on the elephants, only pointing toward the potential problems with these monuments that might ensue in future elections. Then, the EC declared, it would "no doubt" have to take "appropriate steps and measures to see that the statues of Ms. Mayawati and BSP's symbol 'elephant' [which had been built with government funds] do not disturb the level playing field and give undue advantage to BSP vis-à-vis other political parties."[33] This was the logic that led to the ECs order that the elephants had to be wrapped once the 2012 election campaign officially opened. The order reflected not only an attempt to enforce the Model Code's strictures against undue government influence during an election campaign, but also the EC's particular sensitivity to the "power of images in swaying the masses," as Sinha and Kant put it.

The BSP's own reaction to the wrapping order was swift and furious. Far from projecting a procedural authority that stood above political competition, the EC had shown by its actions, as Mayawati herself put it, a deep-seated "anti-dalit," and "casteist" mindset. Why hadn't they mandated the covering of other parties' election symbols, the General Secretary of the BSP asked in a formal complaint to the commission. What about the BJP's ubiquitous lotus symbol, found in a multitude of north Indian ponds, or the Congress's open hand, which was not only of special meaning to Muslims, but was also, he contended, common on statues of Hindu deities? After all, he noted, "it is through the hand that people seek ashirwad [blessing] from gods through their deities/statues."[34] Beyond this, he wrote, the wrapped elephants in fact differed from the BSP party symbol in critical ways (Figure 3). "The elephant statues were in welcome posture with trunks raised and were different from the party's symbol wherein the elephant was seen with its trunk down."[35] Here, ironically, it was the BSP itself that appealed to the limited, simple, indexical form of the party symbol, in order to argue that its own monumental elephants represented something completely different and thus should not be taken as a party symbol subject to EC regulation and control during electoral time.

The BSP was not alone, however, in critiquing the EC's order. Few other parties were willing to buy into Mayawati's complaint that the EC's action showed anti-dalit bias (indeed, many took satisfaction in the comeuppance to Mayawati's queenly pretensions reflected in the EC's action, which reflected in many cases their own

Figure 3 Photograph of EC Workers Covering Elephants in UP, by REUTERS/Parivartan Sharma (Alamy Stock Photo), January 10, 2012, Noida. The added image of the BSP Election Symbol is from Wikimedia Commons: Furfur, CC BY-SA 3.0 <https://creativecommons.org/licenses/by-sa/3.0>, via Wikimedia Commons.

significant anti-dalit biases).[36] But many were nevertheless critical also of the seeming legal paternalism—and the seeming suspicion of popular politics—that underlay the EC's attempts to discipline the use of party symbols and to enforce the Model Code. For some, this was a clear case of the law being used to suppress the free political competition among the people. A critique of EC paternalism—and electoral interference—was thus evident in the comments of a range of politicians, even beyond the leaders of the BSP. As Lalu Prasad Yadav declared, referring to the Rashtriya Janata Dal electoral symbol in Bihar: Is the EC "going to break my lantern too?"[37] And as a BJP spokesman put it, "If elephants have to be wrapped up because [the] elephant is also the BSP symbol and the Election Commission thinks the statues can influence voters, then why don't they cover every lotus growing in ponds and not allow any individual on the street to raise his hand," thus tracking the BSP's own objections in order to underscore EC high-handedness.[38] The wrapping order was in fact widely viewed by politicians as a sign of legal overreach, an example of using dynamite, as one commentator put it, "to get rid of a measly mosquito."[39] Reflecting a fundamental lack of trust in the people, the EC had seemingly used its constitutional authority to attack the very conception of voter autonomy that it was entrusted to protect.

Perhaps more importantly the covering of the elephants was also the target of criticism (and ridicule) from another perspective relating more specifically to the operation of the visual in politics, one that focused not so much on the EC's paternalism as on its misunderstanding of the relation between knowledge, sight, affect and political "influence." As many critics pointed out, the covering of the elephants hardly hid from public knowledge the existence of the monumental BSP pachyderms that still lurked beneath the coverings. The wrapping of the elephants was thus widely mocked in the press for the implication that hiding something from direct sight somehow negated knowledge of its existence, or its political influence—thus the absurdity of Election Commission leaders, as shown in a cartoon by Keshav in *The*

Hindu, contemplating wrapped elephants marked with the notation: "this is not the BSP symbol."[40] The notion that the EC's action somehow freed voters to imagine that other party symbols might equally be lurking beneath the wrapping was lampooned in another published newspaper cartoon showing a group of blind party leaders each now imagining through touch (in an evocation of an old parable) that somehow their own party symbol might lie beneath the elephant's wrapping.[41] The implication, of course, was that it was the Election Commission that by ordering the elephants' wrapping had shown its own blindness to the actual operation of visual perception.

Yet this was hardly the first time that the EC had shown itself sensitive to the potential visual influence of symbols of the government in power in "unfairly" swaying voters, whether party symbols or not. This EC concern was reflected in earlier policy directives dictating that during election campaigns "even pictures of elected political leaders in government offices had to be taken down."[42] These were removed completely for the term of election campaigns and put up again only after elections were finished. Still, they were not left, like the wrapped elephants, "hiding" during the election campaign, as it were, in plain sight.

How, then, might we explain, apart from the size and immovability of the elephants, the logic behind the EC's decision? Clearly, the notion that the EC actually *intended* to obliterate consciousness of Mayawati's elephants as a visual presence in the world of the 2012 UP Assembly elections is implausible on its face. The image and meanings attached to the elephants, even as they lay under wraps, were of course known to all, and, indeed, were widely discussed by the EC itself. Most likely, therefore, the EC's intent was not a visual erasure of the elephants, but the deliberate injection by the EC of a powerful *new* image of its own into the sea of visual images defining the election campaign. The *wrapped* party symbol could be read in this context as a symbol of the ultimate authority of the EC itself—and the *ideal* of the autonomous free voter embodied in the Model Code—cast as an overlay on the controversies surrounding the political meanings of Mayawati's elephants, which continued unabated. The fact that everyone *knew* the elephants were still underneath—and still evoked highly emotive political loyalties—was in fact central to this new image's power. The procedural (and moral) ideal of the free voter citizen as the bedrock of the people's sovereignty "covered" the operation of "political" competition, much as the cloth wrapping covered the monumental pachyderms.

To put forth such an interpretation is in no way to suggest, of course, that this is how everyone saw it. But it points, critically, toward both the power—and the ambiguities—associated with the concept of "free and fair" elections in India. Local electoral "politics" in India remain widely saturated with caste-based mobilizations, patronage, payoffs, and influence ("undue" and otherwise), *in spite of* the EC's concomitant success in making the Model Code a living force in India's popular consciousness. As many analysts have noted, forms of caste-based political mobilization have proved central to what some have called the significant "deepening" of India's democracy in the decades since the 1990s, associated in particular with the rise of lower caste parties, like Mayawati's BSP.[43] At the same time, the politics of patronage and payoffs have prompted increasing calls for greater legal oversight over electoral "corruption," as illustrated, for example in the rise of the Aam Aadmi party.

In these circumstances, the meaning of "free and fair" elections in India has come to relate less to the successful imposition of a legal regime to *control* (or even to contain) "politics," than to the successful juxtaposition of an electoral code defined by its vital association with an image of the "free voter," against the continuing and messy operation of a politics deeply embedded in India's social, cultural, economic and religious realities. This is not to say that the structure of the law as a form of legal *discipline* over politics has been unimportant; to the contrary, the EC's reputation for disinterested electoral administration and the ability of the courts to overturn elections in the face of procedural violations and "undue influence" (and of the EC to delay them in the face of Model Code violations), has been central to the meanings that the phrase "free and fair" elections has carried in India—even if the EC's "disinterest" has sometimes been open to critique. But as the law's intersection with visual party symbols illustrates, the disciplinary, pedagogical projection of the law has vastly exceeded its actual control over a realm of popular politics in India that is saturated with public performance and competing visual images. Electoral law has operated, far more powerfully, as an instrument for balancing the two, conflicting (and in some ways never fully reconcilable) images of the "people," on which the sovereignty of the people rests—and it is this that has given a distinctive meaning to "free and fair" elections in India, marked simultaneously by its vitality and ambiguity.[44] Like the EC's elephants, both present and absent beneath their wrapping, the constitutional "elephant in the room" has remained the impossible contradiction between law and politics at the heart of democracy. To focus on the intersection of the visual and the law—and the long history of litigation about the "misuse" of electoral symbols in India's courts and their regulation by the EC in real time—thus provides us a window not only on the distinctive meaning of "free and fair" elections in India, but also, in comparative perspective, on democracy itself, and on the nature and meaning of the "people's" sovereign power.

Notes

1 See, for example, Mithi Mukherjee, *India in the Shadow of Empire: A Legal and Political History*, 1774–1950 (Delhi: Oxford University Press, 2010). Mukherjee argues that British claims to sovereign legitimacy were rooted in the concept of "justice as equity," that is, in the ability of the rulers to deliver justice and order precisely by their ability to stand apart from the divisions and conflicts of society and deliver justice equitably. This was a form of authority cast by them as a fundamental attribute of the "rule of law." One should stress, of course, that this legitimizing projection often in sharp counterpoint to the wide range of authoritarian policies the British mobilized.

2 A good example lay in Gandhi's characterization of the operation of the colonial legal system in India as virtually a form of slavery. Lawyers, he said, had "enslaved" India.

M. K. Gandhi, *Hind Swaraj and Other Writings*, ed. Anthony Parel (Cambridge: Cambridge University Press, 1997), Chapter 11.

3 This language was adapted from the Irish constitution. The text of the Preamble (before later amendment) is at: https://en.wikisource.org/wiki/The_Constitution_of_India_(Original_Calligraphed_and_Illuminated_Version)/Preamble

4 The concept of "vote banks," which was first coined in the 1950s by the anthropologist, M. N. Srinivas, has been the subject of considerable analysis and argument, though it has remained central to most elite analysis of India's popular electoral politics. A history of this concept and its meanings is developed in Satish Deshpande's article in this volume.

5 A similar argument is made by Ornit Shani with respect to the earlier preparation of the first voter rolls based on universal adult suffrage. Ornit Shani, *How India Became Democratic: Citizenship and the Making of the Universal Franchise* (Cambridge: Cambridge University Press, 2018).

6 See, for example, Ramachandra Guha, *India after Gandhi: The History of the World's Largest Democracy* (New York: Harper Perennial, 2008), pp. 137–59.

7 For a larger historical framing of the secret ballot, see Romain Bertrand, Jean-Louis Briquet and Peter Pels, eds., *The Hidden History of the Secret Ballot* (Bloomington: Indiana University Press, 2006). For some thoughts on its relationship to Indian election law, see David Gilmartin, "Towards a Global History of Voting: Sovereignty, the Diffusion of Ideas, and the Enchanted Individual," *Religions* 3, no. 2 (May 2012): 407–23.

8 Jurgen Habermas and William Rehg, "Constitutional Democracy: A Paradoxical Union of Contradictory Principles?" *Political Theory* 29, no. 6 (December 2001): 766. Habermas attempted to traverse this paradox in part through a vision of popular sovereignty as procedure, manifest not only in the operation of the law, but also in the generation of a form of popular will through the discursive—and thus procedurally constrained—public sphere. See Jurgen Habermas, "Popular Sovereignty as Procedure," in James Bohman and William Rehg, eds., *Deliberative Democracy: Essays on Reason and Politics* (Cambridge: MIT Press, 1997), pp. 54–60.

9 The rate of India's illiteracy (however ambiguous the technical meaning of this term) at that time was over 80 percent; for comparative purposes, it was closer to 25 percent in the last (2011) census.

10 Simona Vittorini, "Two Bullocks, a Ladder and a Lamp: Electoral Symbols in Nehruvian India," *Nations and Nationalism* 20, no. 2 (2014): 304. The chart comes from Election Commission of India, *Report on the First General Election in India, 1951–1952* (New Delhi: Govt. of India, 1955), between pages 84 and 85.

11 See, among other works, Christopher Pinney, "*Photos of the Gods*": *The Printed Image and Political Struggle in India* (New York: Oxford University Press, 2004); Sumathi Ramaswamy, *The Goddess and the Nation: Mapping Mother India* (Durham: Duke University Press, 2010); and Sandria B. Freitag, ed., *The Visual Turn: South Asia Across the Disciplines* (New York: Routledge, 2015).

12 Martin Heidegger, "The Age of the World Picture," in *The Question Concerning Technology and Other Essays*. Translated by William Lovitt (New York: Harper & Row, 1977).

13 Ajay Sinha, "Visual Culture and the Politics of Locality in Modern India: A Review Essay," *Modern Asian Studies* 41, no. 1 (2007): 190.

14 Pinney, p. 8.

15 Up through the end of the 1950s, election petitions were heard first by special Election Tribunals, and then on appeal by the High Courts. Subsequently they were heard by High Courts directly. The outlines of the structure of election law and administration in India, central to the operation of "free and fair" elections, is discussed in the article of Anupama Roy and Ujjwal Singh in this volume. A key to this system, as they note, was a structure of special "electoral time," the special time of election campaigns, which were subjected to different structures of law from what might be called "normal, political time." The courts oversaw elections through the hearing of petitions filed after election results were announced. But during the actual time of election campaigns (the dates of which were—and are—explicitly delineated), the courts were barred from hearing election cases, with oversight during that time left to India's national Election Commission. See also, David Gilmartin and Robert Moog, "Introduction to 'Election Law in India,'" *Election Law Journal: Rules, Politics, and Policy* 11, no. 2 (June 2012): pp. 136–48.

16 Shankaragauda v. Sirur Veerabharappa (In the High Court of Mysore at Bangalore), 23 ELR 1 (1968), and Sangappa v. Shivamurthiswamy (In the High Court of Mysore at Bangalore), 23 ELR 51 (1968).

17 Ibid., p. 59.

18 After the split of the Congress in the late 1960s, Indira Gandhi's Congress symbol became the Cow and Calf. After the Emergency, Congress (I) adopted the Open Hand. The evolving history of the EC's authority to allocate symbols is covered in B. Venkatesh Kumar, "Power to Allot Symbols," *Economic and Political Weekly* 35, no. 38 (September 16–22, 2000): 3387–91. See also the Election Symbols (Reservation and Allotment) Order, 1968 (http://eci.nic.in/eci_main/ElectoralLaws/OrdersNotifications/Election_Symbol_2011_order_1968.pdf)

19 For an overview of the shifts of this period within the larger framework of electoral law/administration, see the article of Rao and Singh in this volume.

20 This is not to suggest that religious controversy about the open hand symbol involved only Muslims. There were allegations in a case from Madhya Pradesh that the hand symbol was used to evoke a vision of Indira Gandhi as a goddess, though the court in that case rejected any reading of the hand as a Hindu religious symbol. Vidya Bhushan Thakur v. Hiraram Verma and Others (High Court of Madhya Pradesh) 72 ELR 40 (1987), p. 70.

21 The decision was written by Justice M. H. Beg and the case was Ziyauddin Burhanuddin Bukhari v. Brijmohan Ramdass Mehra and Others, AIR 1975 SC 1788. See also, for a discussion of the case, Ronojoy Sen, "In the Name of God: Regulating Religion in Indian Elections," *South Asia* 33, no. 1 (2010): 157–8.

22 P. Mal Reddy v. A. Mohan Reddy and Others (In the High Court of Andhra Pradesh at Hyderabad), 65 ELR 1 (1986), pp. 8–9. The Shah Commission was appointed in 1977 to inquire into the excesses of the Emergency and issued its report in late 1978. Among the many controversial (and politically charged) issues dealt was the "demolition" of Muslim neighborhoods in old Delhi.

23 Children, of course, play a major role in delineating the parameters of the people's sovereignty, for they represent by far the largest category of people excluded from the vote in India (as in most democracies) precisely as a marker of their *lack* of the rational maturity symbolically central to "people's" sovereign definition.

24 Ibid., p. 27.

25 Ramaswamy, *The Goddess and the Nation*, pp. 275–81.

26 P. Mal Reddy v. A. Mohan Reddy and Others (In the High Court of Andhra Pradesh at Hyderabad), p. 4.

27 For a picture of one of these election hoardings, showing a map of India carrying the martyred Indira Gandhi, with the Congress hand symbol also prominent displayed, see Sumathi Ramaswamy, "Maps, Mother/Goddesses, and Martyrdom in Modern India," *Journal of Asian Studies* 67, no. 3 (August 2008): 823.

28 See Vidya Bhushan Thakur v. Hiraram Verma and Others. 72 ELR 40 (1987).

29 Ibid., p. 29.

30 For a good overview of the Model Code's history, see Ujjwal Kumar Singh, "Between Moral Force and Supplementary Legality: A Model Code of Conduct and the Election Commission of India," *Election Law Journal: Rules, Politics, and Policy* 11, no. 2 (June 2012): 149–69.

31 Though the era of T. N. Seshan's leadership of the EC marks the major shift in this regard, Roy and Singh place the beginnings of this shift in the period just after the Emergency. For a fuller discussion of T. N. Seshan's role in transforming and publicizing the Code in the first half of the 1990s, see David Gilmartin, "One Day's Sultan: T. N. Seshan and Indian Democracy," *Contributions to Indian Sociology* 43, no. 2 (March–August 2009): 247–84.

32 Amita Sinha and Rajat Kant, "Mayawati and Memorial Parks in Lucknow, India: Landscapes of Empowerment," *Studies in the History of Gardens & Designed Landscapes* (2014): 1–16. http://www.tandfonline.com/doi/full/10.1080/14601176.2014.928490#.VGyqp8mJcSY

33 EC order, October 11, 2010. http://eci.nic.in/eci_main/ElectoralLaws/Final_BSP_Order.pdf

34 Letter, Satish Chandra Mishra, Nat'l Gen. Sec., BSP to R. K. Srivastava, Principal Sec., EC, Nirvachan Sadan, January 15, 2012. http://eci.nic.in/eci_main1/current/eci19012012_2.pdf

35 *The Hindu*, January 16, 2012.

36 As one journalist wrote, "I would not be surprised if Mayawati tries and twists this to gain sympathy by raising her usual 'Dalit ki beti' bogey to impress upon her voters that she was being targeted simply because she was a Dalit." See *IBNlive*, January 9, 2012. http://ibnlive.in.com/news/up-polls-parties-join-ec-in-playing-statues/219265-37-64.html

37 *The Hindu*, January 17, 2012. http://www.thehindu.com/news/national/other-states/are-you-going-to-break-lanterns-next-asks-lalu/article2801626.ece

38 *NDTV*, January 9, 2012. http://www.ndtv.com/india-news/election-s-operation-cover-up-of-mayawatis-statues-keeps-officials-busy-567893

39 Sidharth Mishra, "Reporter's Notebook," *The Pioneer*, January 16, 2012. http://eci.nic.in/eci_main/recent/16-1-12editorial.pdf

40 Keshav's cartoon was originally published in *The Hindu*, January 10, 2012. It is available online at https://www.thehindu.com/opinion/cartoon/article2788542.ece

41 This was a cartoon by R. Prasad in *Mail Today*. The two cartoons were featured together in Krishna Prasad's online blog, *Churumuri*, January 10, 2012. https://churumuri.wordpress.com/tag/bahujan-samaj-party/

42 S. Y. Quraishi, *An Undocumented Wonder: The Making of the Great Indian Election* (Delhi: Rupa Publications, 2014), p. 317.

43 See Yogendra Yadav, "Understanding the Second Democratic Upsurge: Trends of Bahujan Participation in Electoral Politics in the 1990s," in Francine R. Frankel et al., eds., *Transforming India: Social and Political Dynamics of Democracy* (New

Delhi, India: Oxford University Press, 2000), pp. 120–45. There is a large, and growing literature, on the nature of India's popular politics in this era; for just two good examples, see Lucia Michelutti, *The Vernacularisation of Democracy* (Delhi: Routledge, 2008), and Jeffrey Witsoe, *Democracy against Development: Lower-caste Politics and Political Modernity in Postcolonial India* (Chicago: The University of Chicago Press, 2013).

44 This has been reflected also in simultaneous praise and critique of the management of elections of India that has marked politics across the spectrum (and indeed, in the world at large, where the EC has gained a reputation in many countries as a model for election management). The ambiguous image of the EC in India has at no time been clearer than in reactions to its role in the 2019 Lok Sabha elections resoundingly won by Narendra Modi.

Select Bibliography

Bertrand, Romain, Jean-Louis Briquet and Peter Pels, eds., *The Hidden History of the Secret Ballot* (Bloomington: Indiana University Press, 2006).

Freitag, Sandria B., ed., *The Visual Turn: South asia Across the Disciplines* (New York: Routledge, 2015).

Gilmartin, David, "One Day's Sultan: T. N. Seshan and Indian Democracy," *Contributions to Indian Sociology* 43, no. 2 (March–August 2009): 247–84.

Gilmartin, David "Towards a Global History of Voting: Sovereignty, the Diffusion of Ideas, and the Enchanted Individual," *Religions* 3, no. 2 (May 2012): 407–23.

Gilmartin, David and Robert Moog, "Introduction to 'Election Law in India,'" *Election Law Journal: Rules, Politics, and Policy* 11, no. 2 (June 2012): 136–48.

Guha, Ramachandra, *India after Gandhi: The History of the World's Largest Democracy* (New York: Harper Perennial, 2008).

Habermas, Jurgen and William Rehg, "Constitutional Democracy: A Paradoxical Union of Contradictory Principles?" *Political Theory* 29, no. 6 (December 2001): 766–781.

Habermas, Jurgen and William Rehg, "Popular Sovereignty as Procedure," in James Bohman and William Rehg, eds., *Deliberative Democracy: Essays on Reason and Politics* (Cambridge: MIT Press, 1997), pp. 54–60.

Heidegger, Martin, "The Age of the World Picture," in *The Question Concerning Technology and Other Essays*. Translated by William Lovitt (New York: Harper & Row, 1977).

Kumar, B. Venkatesh, "Power to Allot Symbols," *Economic and Political Weekly* 35, no. 38 (September 16–22, 2000): 3387–91.

Michelutti, Lucia, *The Vernacularisation of Democracy* (Delhi: Routledge, 2008).

Mukherjee, Mithi, *India in the Shadow of Empire: A Legal and Political History*, 1774–1950 (Delhi: Oxford University Press, 2010).

Pinney, Christopher, "*Photos of the Gods*": *The Printed Image and Political Struggle in India* (New York: Oxford University Press, 2004).

Quraishi, S. Y. *An Undocumented Wonder: The Making of the Great Indian Election* (Delhi: Rupa Publications, 2014).

Ramaswamy, Sumathi, *The Goddess and the Nation: Mapping Mother India* (Durham: Duke University Press, 2010).

Ramaswamy, Sumathi, "Maps, Mother/Goddesses, and Martyrdom in Modern India," *Journal of Asian Studies* 67, no. 3 (August 2008): 819–53.

Sen, Ronojoy, "In the Name of God: Regulating Religion in Indian Elections," *South Asia* 33, no. 1 (2010): 157–8.

Shani, Ornit, *How India Became Democratic: Citizenship and the Making of the Universal Franchise* (Cambridge: Cambridge University Press, 2018).

Singh, Ujjwal Kumar, "Between Moral Force and Supplementary Legality: A Model Code of Conduct and the Election Commission of India," *Election Law Journal: Rules, Politics, and Policy* 11, no. 2 (June 2012): 149–69.

Sinha, Ajay, "Visual Culture and the Politics of Locality in Modern India: A Review Essay," *Modern Asian Studies* 41, no. 1 (2007): 187–220.

Sinha, Amita and Rajat Kant, "Mayawati and Memorial Parks in Lucknow, India: Landscapes of Empowerment," *Studies in the History of Gardens & Designed Landscapes* (2014): 1–16. http://www.tandfonline.com/doi/full/10.1080/14601176.2014.928490#.VGyqp8mJcSY

Vittorini, Simona, "Two Bullocks, a Ladder and a Lamp: Electoral Symbols in Nehruvian India," *Nations and Nationalism* 20, no. 2 (2014): 297–316.

Witsoe, Jeffrey, *Democracy against Development: Lower-caste Politics and Political Modernity in Postcolonial India* (Chicago: The University of Chicago Press, 2013).

Yadav, Yogendra, "Understanding the Second Democratic Upsurge: Trends of Bahujan Participation in Electoral Politics in the 1990s," in Francine R. Frankel et al., eds., *Transforming India: Social and Political Dynamics of Democracy* (New Delhi, India: Oxford University Press, 2000), pp. 120–45.

9

Representations of Electoral Politics: Notes on the Conceptual Career of the "Vote Bank"

Satish Deshpande

आजकल की राजनीति में पोलिटकस *घुस आयी है।*[1]
Aajkal ki rajneeti mein *poltix* ghus aayi hai.

Apocryphal politician

Indians speak English in many languages, and the word "politics" is among dozens of English words now commonly used in all our languages. And although its pronunciation may differ, its meaning is roughly the same in every language. In the everyday idiom of a dozen major languages across India, the term borrowed from English is always used in a pejorative sense. While words like *rajneeti* (Hindi) or *rajkeeya* (Kannada) or *siyasat* (Urdu) do not have exclusively positive connotations, "politics" is always only bad politics.

The negative meaning of quotidian uses of "politics" may be read as a symptom of the larger complex that Achille Mbembe refers to, in the context of Africa, as "the fuss over transitions to democracy and multi-partyism."[2] In most parts of the colonial world the transition to postcolonial independence took on one of the various forms of the "passive revolution," involving the more or less orderly transfer of power from a foreign imperialist to a local nationalist elite, leaving subaltern masses on the fringes. However, the emancipatory rhetoric of nationalism had to speak in an egalitarian idiom, and this usually meant that old forms of dominance had to clothe themselves afresh, in accordance with new fashions of local and global legitimacy. Though they fell short of being revolutionary in the conventional sense, the upheavals of decolonization—especially when they introduced universal franchise and open elections—inevitably led to the fracturing of older constituencies and the emergence of new ones. This in turn meant that "politics" would acquire different meanings and different publics, and

This paper was first presented at the "Recalling Democracy: Lineages of the Present" conference at the University of Michigan in September 2014, and later at seminars at the Center for Studies in Social Sciences, Kolkata and the National Institute of Advanced Studies, Bengaluru. I am grateful to Mrinalini Sinha and Manu Goswami, the organizers of the Michigan conference, for the opportunity to branch out into this field, especially for their patience in the face of missed deadlines. Thanks for comments and suggestions are owed to William Glover, Juan Cole, Sankaran Krishna, David Gilmartin, Dwaipayan Bhattacharya, Manas Ray, and Manabi Majumdar.

that the evolution of postcolonial politics would shift the shape of these publics, calling for newer modes of representation.

The South Asian term "vote bank" offers a useful vantage point from where the relationship between publics and modes of representation may be mapped. In Indian usage, "vote bank" is a strongly pejorative term invoking "bad" politics. Its entry into media and popular usage dates from the late 1960s, a time when the meaning of politics itself changed. Earlier notions of politics were dominated by the form given to it in the anticolonial struggle, especially from the 1920s onward. In this period of high nationalism, political activity was actually imagined as something other than "mere" politics, since it invoked the hegemonic ideals of the patriotic struggle for freeing the nation, and later, for "nation building." Against this, "vote bank politics" is basically interest group politics that appeals to caste or community solidarities that can be described as "sectarian" or "narrow" in comparison to nation. Because of its pejorative connotations, vote bank is never claimed as a description for one's own supporters—it is always used to denigrate rival parties or politicians for practicing "vote bank politics."[3]

Vote bank was originally invented by social anthropologists to highlight the salience of rural patron–client networks for electoral politics in the 1950s and 1960s. Today, the term thrives in popular culture and the media, and within academia. Its meanings have broadened beyond its early, almost exclusive, association with caste to include vote banks defined by religious community (especially Muslims), and sometimes also by occupation or class, though this is relatively unusual.

How has a single term managed to lead a double life in two very different environments, even as it flourishes in one and merely survives in the other? The rest of this paper tries to answer this question by exploring the meanings of vote bank and the work that it is doing in each context. It is organized in three parts: part one outlines the role of vote bank in dominant ideology as revealed by the manner of its deployment in the popular media; part two follows the career of the concept in academic contexts; finally, a brief conclusion reiterates the main argument.

The Vote Bank in Dominant Common Sense

Common sense in the interpretation made famous by Antonio Gramsci refers to the taken-for-granted beliefs and values produced and reproduced through the personal experiences of everyday life. The social location of the dominant social group—in this context, upper-caste Hindus—is treated as the "normal" and universal standpoint and values and beliefs implicit in everyday interactions are calibrated to cater to it. The dominance of this common sense derives from its power to influence everyone, including those who do not in fact occupy this standpoint. Terms like vote bank play an important part in maintaining the hold of dominant common sense. Two specifics sites within dominant common sense are taken up here, namely Wikipedia, and English language newspapers in India.

Wikipedia, the online databank that describes itself as "the free encyclopedia that anyone can edit," has more than 5.5 million entries in English.[4] One of these entries is on "votebank," and this is what it has to offer[5]:

> A votebank (also spelled vote-bank or vote bank) is a loyal bloc of voters from a single community, who consistently back a certain candidate or political formation in democratic elections. Such behaviour is often the result of an expectation of real or imagined benefits from the political formations, [sic] often at the cost of other communities.
>
> Votebank politics is the practice of creating and maintaining votebanks through divisive policies. As this brand of politics encourages voters to vote on the basis of narrow communal considerations, often against their better judgement, it is considered harmful to representative democracy.

The most interesting aspect of this entry is the tension between its simultaneous attempts at moral characterization and factual description. The first sentence, for instance, seems to describe politics at large in a mostly unexceptionable way. Why would one object to "a loyal bloc of voters" who "consistently back a certain candidate or political formation in democratic elections"? Possible reasons are provided by the additional information that these voters "are from a single community," and that their actions are motivated by the "expectation of real or imagined benefits," which might be "at the cost of other communities." The tension is reduced considerably in the second paragraph where judgment and description are more closely matched. To point us in the right direction we have phrases like "divisive politics," "narrow communal considerations," "against their better judgment" and finally, "harmful to representative democracy."[6]

The empirical claim being made here is that vote banks actually exist and function as described—i.e., there are groups of voters so steeped in their community identity and so innocent of proper politics that they simply vote blindly for their community interests. The moral claim is that when people vote for the interests of their own caste or religious community, they are doing something wrong or at least politically incorrect. However, the crucial point is that these claims are not actually put forward as claims—they are presented as factual assertions, with the confident expectation that they will be not be questioned. This expectation, in turn, indicates that the Wikipedia entry has in mind a specific kind of reader who occupies a particular subject position and social location, that of a nonpoor, upper-caste Hindu. This determination is arrived at through a process of elimination. Since members of all lower castes and minority religions are liable to be labeled as vote banks, the residual group that cannot be so named is non-lower-caste, nonminorities, i.e. upper-caste Hindus. While this is how the term vote bank politics originated, the rise of right-wing Hindutva political formations is now beginning to bring changes.

This point can be further clarified if we move from the context of Wikipedia to the media-centric site of political cartoons. Even a casual reader of English newspapers in India is certain to come across the term "vote bank," especially around election time, when the term is ubiquitous. A popular subject for cartoons it has been worked on by every major Indian cartoonist. What is the standpoint from which this image acquires intelligibility and/or offers affirmation?

The first of the three cartoons is probably the most famous vote bank cartoon.[7] It is by the legendary cartoonist Abu Abraham, and was published in the *Indian Express* newspaper in 1974, in the context of the elections to the Uttar Pradesh assembly, where caste was widely recognized to be a major factor influencing the strategy of all major parties.[8] It plays on the phrase "caste your vote" to produce the memorable critique of caste-based politics in its caption: "vote your caste here." The second cartoon is by Mumbai cartoonist Manjul, and dates from around the time of the 2008 global banking crisis.[9] It shows the then Prime Minister and Finance Minister of India, Manmohan Singh and P. Chidambaram, against a backdrop of several caste-, religion-, and region-based "vote banks," with Chidambaram saying "Our banks are completely safe." The notable feature of this cartoon is that a "Hindu vote bank" also features. The last cartoon is one of the relatively few featuring Narendra Modi in this context. It is by the Mangalore cartoonist Satish Acharya, and exploits the news reports at the time of the 2007 Gujarat assembly elections (when, as required by all candidates, Modi had declared personal assets of Rupees 40 lakhs) to have him say "Thank God, they didn't ask for my vote bank details."

The interesting thing about these cartoons is that they leave a lot of work to be done by the viewer/reader. They also presume that the reader *will* do this work, and in this sense they follow a classic strategy of interpellation. Despite individual variations, these cartoons presuppose a particular standpoint for which, and from which, they are created. They hail readers from this location, and when readers acknowledge the hail, they also implicitly accept the responsibility of actually building and rendering that location livable. The pleasure of the image—the self-affirmation it offers—is available from one particular standpoint, that of a "pure" citizen, unmarked by any caste, community or regional affinities. However, it is only recently, with the undeniable emergence of a sizeable "Hindu vote bank" that this unmarked position has appeared to also exclude upper-caste Hindus. Earlier, that is, before the 2010s, generally speaking, the standpoint from where such cartoons spoke was that of the only group for whom vote banks were not practical, which was that of upper-caste Hindus. Given that the "middle class" is disproportionately upper-caste Hindu, this dominant position was treated as the natural position that applied to, or ought to apply to everyone.

In view of the fact that lower castes and minorities (even if we limit the latter to Muslims) would together account for over 80 percent of the Indian population, they cannot be the natural addressee of popular culture versions of the term "vote bank." How would such cartoons address, for example, a Yadav youth from small town UP, a practicing and devout Muslim, a Jat, a Dalit, a Thevar, a Vokkaliga, or a Patidar—in short, any member of the many castes and communities commonly accused of being implicated in "vote bank politics"? The short answer is that they wouldn't. But a longer answer would have to speak of the conditions of upper-caste Hindu hegemony that led the media to produce and treat such representations as normative.

The moral-political reach of dominant modes of representing the "vote bank" in Indian public culture always exceeds their empirical-descriptive grasp. The evidence to support the harsh judgment that dominant common sense passes on the "vote bank" is always inadequate. Both the empirical claim—that there exist groups of voters who always vote blindly on caste/community grounds—and the moral claim—that to do so is ethically wrong—are subject to serious qualifications. Indeed, these qualifications are serious enough to render these claims untenable. But to say only this is to miss the central point that the persuasiveness of ideologies is not based on logic or factual accuracy. This may be the moment to turn to an arena like academics, where persuasion is supposed to depend on precisely such considerations.

Academic Contexts: From the 1950s to the Present

If, as claimed above, the notion of the vote bank deployed in the media and popular culture is marked by misrecognition and excess, does the same hold for academia? How do we account for the fact that the term continues in academic usage despite early recognition of its unviability? The following account is divided into two rough periods, the first from the 1950s, when the term was invented, until the 1970s, and the second for the period from the 1990s until the present day.

Early Encounters: 1950s–1970s

The current consensus on the origin of the term "vote bank" places it in a 1955 article by M. N. Srinivas, "The social system of a Mysore village."[10] At the end of a section on "Patrons and Clients," in which Srinivas has been describing the changes following independence and the advent of elections, is the following:

> The coming of elections gives fresh opportunities for the crystallization of parties around patrons. Each patron may be said to have a 'vote bank' which he can place at the disposal of a provincial or national party for a consideration which is not mentioned but implied. The secret ballot helps to preserve the marginal affiliations of the marginal clients.[11]

From the context—a discussion of how patronage relationships work in what is now southern Karnataka—it is clear that Srinivas is using "vote bank" to refer to *a kind of person*. More specifically, the "vote bank" is a powerful rural landlord-patron who controls a significant bloc of votes because large numbers of villagers, especially those from the lower castes, depend on him for their livelihoods.

This interpretation is confirmed by Srinivas in an article published seven years later:

> The Constitutional decision to give franchise to all adults has had far-reaching effects on our social and political life. For the first time in their history, the traditionally underprivileged sections of our society have a say in the choice of their rulers. People who used to get ordered about by the upper castes have now to be approached for their votes. This has given them a new sense of importance though, even now in the rural areas, traditional patron-client relations are somewhat effective in the matter of voting. That is to say a rural patron, who is usually a big landlord has in his power a number of people who are obliged to him in a variety of ways—they may be his servants, tenants, debtors, and followers. The patron expects his clients to vote the way he wants them to, and many of his clients obey him. *This is why I have called rural patrons vote-banks and urban politicians have to cultivate these 'vote banks' if they wish to stay in power.* But the institution of

> the secret ballot ensures that voting does not entirely go along the lines of patron-client ties, and it would be safe to predict that voting will be increasingly free. When I revisited my field village of Rampura in the summer of 1952 I found that the candidate who had the powerful support of the village headman had been defeated and the latter suspected that his Harijan clients had 'double-crossed' him and voted for the rival.[12]
>
> (italics added)

Srinivas clearly reiterates the term "vote bank" as a reference to the person who controls votes in a rural setting. But what is most striking about it is the strong sense that the rural patriarchs who are the "vote banks" are already losing their hold on their clientele, and that the secrecy of the ballot protects the otherwise powerless subaltern voter. It is worth remembering that the first recorded instance of the breakdown of a powerful "vote bank" dates from the first general election of 1952. It is also noteworthy that this is not an exceptional instance: Srinivas is already sure by 1962 that vote banks in general (rather than just the ones he knows from his fieldwork) have no future.

The next significant use of the term follows in the very next year—1963—and is found in a work on Orissa by the English anthropologist F. G. Bailey who posed the question: "What is the relationship between parliamentary democracy in Orissa and the older traditional forms of social and political organisation?"[13] Specifically concerned with old and new political institutions, Bailey adopts a wider view than Srinivas and broadens the notion of the vote bank.[14] A short chapter on "The politician's problem" asserts:

> There is—with rare exceptions—no group in the traditional society which regularly corresponds to the modern constituency. But some traditional groups, recruited on principles which have nothing to do with representative democracy, nevertheless influence its working. Candidates may try to capture traditional groups and use them as vote-banks. The traditional group itself may take an active part in representative politics. It may, for example, become a pressure group. Thirdly, the structure of traditional society may become the mould within which representative politics operate at constituency level. Old loyalties and allegiances may continue within the new framework of representative politics.[15]

It is immediately obvious that, with Bailey, the concept of vote bank moves from being a type of person to *a kind of social group*. Also important is the open-ended status of such groups, which may be active or passive, those who exert pressure or those subjected to it. And in anticipation of a later discussion, it is worth emphasizing that throughout the works cited, both Srinivas and Bailey insist that vote banks cannot guarantee electoral outcomes.

The next major discussion happens toward the end of the 1960s, by which time the vote bank idea migrated from social anthropology to political science. Based on a long term project on voter behavior in the 1962, 1967, and 1969 general elections led by Rajni Kothari, Dhirubhai Sheth directly addresses the issue of vote banks and the alleged "herd behaviour" of Indian voters:

> Despite the steady increase in voter turnout and despite frequent shifts in electoral support for the parties, especially at the constituency level, the notion of herd behaviour of the Indian electorate still persists. It is an image of a voter for whom voting is a ritual or at best an act of fulfilling extra-political obligations. While voting, he is not only unaware of the political implications of his act but is supposed to be unconcerned and innocent of the fact that he is involved in an act of choice. Political reality is something quite external to his universe of perceptions and evaluations. If he changes his party support from one election to another, he is not guided by any political or civic considerations, but is only responding to a change in factional arrangement within political parties at the local level or to the exhortations of 'middle men' who are in command of 'vote banks'.[16]

Sheth goes on to acknowledge the role of "primordial sentiments" in politics:

> To be sure, a thoroughly rational and discriminating voter is as mythical an entity as an irrational member of a herd. The voters do respond to the pulls of the system and they do get drawn into politics through their primordial sentiments activated during election campaign (sic) and such other political stimuli. These, however, may well be treated as predispositions formed during one's political socialisation rather than as strait jacketed determinants of political behaviour. The fact that an individual seeks membership of a variety of groups itself suggests complexity and heterogeneity of his needs which may change and greatly vary in one and the same individual. Consequently, his interests are also flexible and negotiable. It is, therefore, unrealistic to assume group bonds in such manner that all his choices can be explained in terms of his membership of these groups.[17]

Writing a year later, Rajni Kothari speaks of a new phase in postindependence Indian politics that begins with the 1967 general elections. This involves the transition from traditional modes of mobilization (such as vote banks) to more modern forms:

> In the past, the Congress has had an edge over the Opposition largely through its much greater ability than the opposition parties to draw continuous support from committed voters. As old loyalties erode, the power of party organisations and "vote banks" to deliver assured support declines, and voting decisions are based more on the basis of direct political choices and the appeal of the campaign, the earlier style of reaching out to the people must give place to a new style.[18]

It would seem, therefore, that by the beginning of the 1970s, social scientists had a fairly firm grasp on the vote bank phenomenon. The basic problem with the concept is revealed when we compare its academic and popular versions. The popular notion of vote bank tends to take the politics out of elections by suggesting that bloc voting by social groups is evidence of "herd mentality" rather than a rational decision. The pejorative intent behind the term is to equate "vote bank politics" with an unthinking loyalty to "primordial" group identities, which either does not qualify as politics at all or is indelibly marked as bad politics. It is not as though the social science of the

1960s has all the explanations; in fact, it is possible to argue that it harbors its own biases, particularly about caste politics. But unlike its popular culture counterpart, the academic version of vote bank is not marked by descriptive errors or excess.

In fact, one could say that it is precisely their descriptive detail that saves accounts like those of Srinivas and Bailey from explanatory excess. For Srinivas it is clearly the material dependence on the rural "big-man" that compels his clients to cast their votes as desired by him. Indeed Srinivas is already witness to acts of silent defiance as early as the first general election of 1952—so there is no question of any mysterious force or essence-like quality that makes a bloc of voters vote in unison. So too with Bailey, who recognizes that traditional groups have sufficient agency to actively choose to vote in particular ways. And although he does refer to the role of traditional values and loyalties in his more nebulous third path, there is no sense that there is anything other than a known and rational social institution at work here, even if its rationality is not that of modern liberal democracy. Moreover, with both Srinivas and Bailey the many concrete examples detailed for the term vote bank are subordinated to a larger descriptive project. In such accounts the vote bank cannot—it is not allowed to—float free of its quotidian sociopolitical context and acquire projected meanings that exceed its observed modalities.

However, beyond empirical description, the contributions of the social sciences are more ambiguous. On the larger question of the interpretation and analysis of caste politics—which is the main kind of "vote bank politics" emerging in this period—mainstream academia is still largely under the influence of modernization and Marxist perspectives, neither of which is hospitable to caste, regarding it purely as an impediment. Nevertheless, some beginnings are being made in adapting global-western theories to address the specificities of Indian society and politics. Among the most influential of such attempts are those by Rajni Kothari, who reorients the orthodox view that sees politics as being corrupted by caste to insist that it is caste that is being politicized, and that (in itself) this is a normal rather than a pathological process. Also important is the early work of Susanne and Lloyd Rudolph, who sought to show that emergent institutions based on caste (such as caste associations) were actually undermining the traditional caste system. In the Nehruvian era, which extended until the end of the 1960s, the urge to suppress public discussion of caste and to maintain a "caste-blind" public sphere was so strong that it took a long time for these efforts to be appreciated.[19]

Even allowing for the hegemonic sway of Nehruvian caste-blindness, it remains a puzzle as to why well-documented descriptions doubting the efficacy of the vote bank idea failed to ensure its early demise. One possible reason could be shifts in the forms of political representation. The model of clientalism underlying Srinivas's notion of the vote bank implied that the patron would be from the dominant caste while the clients would be from the lower castes. However, there was also emerging a more direct form of representation, described today as "identity politics," where voters of a particular caste or caste cluster would vote for a candidate of their own caste. It is conceivable that evidence for the failure of the dominant caste landlord as "vote bank" was seen as not applicable to the vote bank understood as a caste group asserting itself politically. A further consideration is that the content of "regional" and "national" politics as well as the relationship between these domains were rapidly changing.

Whatever the reasons, critics of the vote bank idea failed to knock it out and it continued to be used in academic analysis in the 1970s and 1980s.[20] In the 1990s decisive changes in the political scene gave a new lease of life to the vote bank idea and boosted its fortunes in both popular culture and academic analysis, though its gains in the former far outstripped its advances in the latter.

Decisive Transformations: The 1990s and After

The 1990s were a transformative phase in almost every aspect of Indian society, economy and polity. Two sets of changes were most crucial for the vote bank concept. The first was the arrival of caste politics on the national stage, and the establishment of coalitional formations with a strong role for regional parties, processes that had been gathering momentum in the 1980s. The second was the opening up of the media sphere to global conglomerates, and the morphing of India into a media-saturated society, with electronic media leading the way. The strong synergy between these two factors could almost count as a third factor in its own right.

During the 1990s globalized television and pop psephology were added to an already overheated post-Mandal political environment. As a media-magnified avatar of its earlier self, vote bank in the 1990s became the preferred means for replacing the complexities of the political with essentialist notions. Community and particularly caste identities were assumed to automatically result in the fusing of blocs that perform as one cohesive unit in the electoral arena. Even if these purported blocs do not actually behave in the predicted ways, or even when they provide ample justification to question whether they are in fact homogenous blocs, they continue to be called vote banks. While the enthusiasm of the media and its pundits for terms like vote bank is understandable, the spreading of this contagion to academia is not so easily explained. The curious fact is that in academic circles, the idea of the vote bank appears to develop an inexplicable resilience that allows it to survive in defiance of the constantly reiterated reports of its imminent demise.

Thus we find arguments made in the 1960s repeated almost verbatim three decades later. Here, for example, are the political scientists Sarah Joseph and Gurpreet Mahajan expressing their dismay—in 1991—at the fact that social scientists have not given up the term:

> The notion of vote banks is crucial to the strategy of most parties as also of election analyses but it is difficult to gauge how successful these strategies have been. The recent elections, for instance, challenged many assumptions about vote banks. Neither OBC vote, nor the Muslim or Hindu vote fulfilled the expectations of different parties. However, the notion of caste/community vote banks is apparently so deeply entrenched that no falsification is possible by counter-instances. Reluctant to give up this notion, analysts have explained counter-instances as 'splits' in the vote banks.[21]

They reiterate Sheth's 1970 argument "questioning the notion of vote banks which assumes a determinate relationship between an identity and voting preferences" (ibid.) and go on to emphasize, yet again, that people have multiple identities and the core content of politics—the competition for mobilizing existing and newly invented group solidarities for a political cause—gets erased by notions like vote bank which rob voters of agency.

But the immunity against falsification shows no signs of waning. A decade and a half after Joseph and Mahajan, Yogendra Yadav still finds it necessary to point out, in an Epilogue written for a collection of sociological and social anthropological studies of the 1967 and 1971 elections,[22] that even though caste was clearly important, it did not function in the form of vote banks, and that none of the eighteen studies in the volume reports finding a successful vote bank in action.[23] And so we find obituaries still being written in the 2000s for the resilient myth:

> The operation of caste cleavages was and continues to be one of the determinants of electoral politics. Yet this operation never took the form that is suggested by the metaphor of vote banks. In that sense, vote banks were always something of a myth. What we should be debating is the change in different forms and levels of caste-based voting.[24]

Since the 1990s, evidence questioning the actual efficacy of alleged vote banks has accumulated with every election. If we recall the definition offered in the Wikipedia entry quoted in the previous section, then there is ample evidence to establish that caste and community groups accused of behaving like vote banks have often done precisely the opposite. For example vote banks often exasperate pundits by changing their loyalties, sometimes quite suddenly and counter-intuitively, from one party or candidate to another. More often than not, the expected "benefits" for vote banks are so indirect and nebulous that they are not worth the name. A good example of this is the frequently cited case of Muslims bloc voting for the "strongest non-BJP or non-Shiv Sena etc. candidate"; the "benefit" from this is surely too indirect to be considered venal.[25] There are also periodic instances where vote banks abandon their expected loyalties to support regimes perceived as "delivering development," which should count as the "good" politics implicit in the idea of the vote bank.[26]

But empirical arguments against the vote bank concept were available from the 1960s onwards—they only proliferated and gathered momentum in the 1990s. What is really new for this decade is the fundamental rethinking on the question of caste, and more generally, of what could (or ought to) count as "good" politics. This began to explicitly address the moral claim contained in the vote bank idea, namely that voting guided by caste or community considerations was inherently wrong or politically regressive. The Mandal upheaval rendered visible the "public secret" at the heart of the Indian polity—upper-caste Hindus were a small minority numerically, but they monopolized leadership positions in every field, including commerce, the bureaucracy and politics. The high-minded Nehruvian refusal to see, hear or speak caste had helped to frame recognition of caste (in reservation policy or other antidiscrimination laws) as the exception and castelessness as the rule. The Mandal moment revealed that, in practice, caste was ubiquitous and most potent in the areas where it was most denied. The long delayed assertion of the intermediate castes, at the national level, forced the reframing and recalibration of politics itself.

The academic world was caught off balance by Mandal and took time to respond. But by the end of the decade, Javeed Alam posed the question: "Is caste appeal casteism?,"[27] to make a convincing case for answering it in the negative, albeit with qualifications. When all classes are invested in their caste identities (even if expressed differently), efforts by the dispossessed to unite in order to struggle against their "collective unfreedom" cannot be considered regressive merely because it invokes caste rather than class. Alam argues for the need to adapt and modify both Marxist and liberal political theory to accommodate a social situation where neither the individual nor the class is the primary vehicle for political mobilization. This is but one example of the many ways in which social scientists began to question their earlier willingness to brand all invocation of caste or community as politically regressive. More important was the belated recognition that caste was not necessarily absent where it was not explicitly invoked, or even denied.[28] By the 1990s massive evidence accumulated to establish that half a century of caste-blind development had done little to change the caste composition of either the haves or the have-nots. As more attention began to be paid to social inequalities, the reality of "opportunity hoarding" by the social elite—in the face of the state's professed attempts to eradicate poverty and reduce inequalities—was exposed.

As a result in subsequent decades we saw more careful attempts to understand the politics of so-called vote banks. For example, Christophe Jaffrelot tries to take seriously the question: Why should all collectively decided voting be considered irrational or "harmful to representative democracy"? Examining acts of strategic decision making and "tactical voting" by different caste groups in elections, he suggests that the caste vote "is subject to deliberation," and this makes it a more considered act:

> Voting appears here to be both a collective and a rational act. Though external influence is still at play, it no longer comes from traditional power sources; it makes itself felt through the advice that the group in question has sought in order to vote in its own best interests. The array of measures implemented by the Election Commission to guarantee a secret and reasoned vote has promoted the development not of an individual rational voter but of a collective and rational voter. … Indeed, the procedures implemented so strictly by the Election Commission for creating an *individual voter* exerting his free will are largely responsible for the political emancipation of the lower castes and their capacity to exert *collective voting*. (emphasis original)[29]

Since the 2000s, academic usage of the term vote bank has transitioned toward the more standard forms of reference to blocs of voters defined, among other attributes, by their caste or community. For example, analyses of voting behavior, especially pre-election surveys, often speak of Dalit, Yadav, Muslim, or lately also the "Hindu" vote. This usage does not presume that the bloc will necessarily vote in the same way in every election, or even vote as a single homogenous bloc, while also recognizing stable long-term interests. In short, the excesses associated with the vote bank concept are now being avoided, and when employed, it is almost invariably qualified toward its original intent to capture the influence of clientelistic networks on electoral politics.[30]

And yet the vote bank endures in academic writing. At this stage, its survival owes to its continued currency in popular culture, though that too may be changing. Vote bank proves irresistible in times when labeling, branding, and instant dissemination are the major methodological devices of a media-fed and media-led market for "news" and "expert analysis" of electoral politics.

Conclusion: The (Ideological) Representation of (Political) Representation

The point of this chapter has been neither to defend the vote bank idea nor the caste-community based politics that it is usually taken to stand for. My intention has been to treat vote bank as a symptom or an indexical reference that points to something else, namely a specific standpoint from where politics and the world at large are (or can be) seen. Taken in this way, vote bank can be an entry point into the larger question of how the effort to render politics intelligible itself already presupposes—and yet also produces afresh—a certain relational stance or standpoint.

It seems clear that the vote bank concept has been more influential in popular culture than academic discourse. Looking at its career in popular culture, there seem to be three important moments. The first is its emergence into popular usage in the 1970s; the second is the marked acceleration in its circulation in the 1990s; and the third, dating from the 2010s is the period of what looks like a slow decline. If vote bank is indeed an index or a symptom, then each of these points ought to correspond, at least roughly, to significant shifts in modes of representing politics.

As indicated earlier, the emergence of the vote bank idea was associated with the decline of the "Congress system"[31] in the latter half of the 1960s. This "system" basically had the Congress Party operating as a loose coalition of precisely the sort of interest groups that would later be labeled as vote banks. The inability of the Congress to contain these forces led to their emerging as separate groupings, thus giving rise to the term.[32] The second moment of the Mandal upsurge is when caste-based politics established itself at the national level, breaking out of the regional confines within which it was kept by the Congress system. This upsurge forced into the open the upper-caste monopoly over power (at the national level) and lead to an irreversible shift in how politics was viewed. If on the one hand the 1990s seemed to announce that caste has arrived and was here to stay, on the other hand, it was the decade that the process of political disaggregation and reaggregation (as part of new coalitions) began. At this stage, vote bank was mainly an othering gesture that, from an implicit upper-caste standpoint, sought to denigrate the politics of the lower castes. However this relatively simple juxtaposition was destined to be short-lived as more complex relations emerged by the turn of the century.

In the 2000s, there were at least three new factors that made it increasingly difficult for the simplistic us/them form of the vote bank idea to survive. Interestingly, all three factors arguably point to the deepening and intensification of democracy, albiet in different ways.

First there is the recent emergence—demonstrated decisively in the 2014 general election—of the affluent middle class voter. It had been a truism in Indian electoral analysis that the middle classes did not vote, while the poor always did. One interpretation of the vote bank idea was that it was floated by and for the nonvoting class to disparage the politics of the poor and the underprivileged who were active in electoral politics. However, in recent times, middle class people have been taking an active part in popular campaigns of different kinds—for the urban environment, against rape and sexual violence, against corruption, or even for newly emergent parties like the Aam Aadmi Party in Delhi. The 2014 election was the first election in which the voter turnout of the nonpoor was comparable to that of the poor, registering a big jump from previous levels. Indeed, analysts see this rise in the middle class vote as one of the significant contributors to the phenomenal performance of the Modi-led BJP in the 2014 election.[33] When the middle classes participate actively in elections, they are no longer able to easily identify with the implicit standpoint of the vote bank idea that appears to occupy a position outside or above politics.

The second factor is of course the rise of right-wing Hindutva politics in the Modi era. With "Hindus" now liable to be cast as a vote bank—as in the Satish Acharya cartoon discussed in the previous section—the term can no longer function as a gesture of othering or disparagement. The third factor is the political inevitability of the disaggregation of large disparate groupings like the Other Backward Classes. Having emerged as a residual neither/nor category—not as "high" as the upper castes and not as "low" as the Dalits and Adivasis—the OBCs are not really held together internally. As seen in most Indian states, this administrative category is being rapidly differentiated as the substantial inequalities within it gain political expression. Since one of the requirements of the vote bank concept is homogeneity, the processes of fission and fusion in the identities labeled as vote banks are likely to weaken the hold of the term.

While it remains to be seen whether the trend toward its waning influence continues, there is little doubt that it would need to reinvent and reposition itself if it is to survive. Whatever its fate, the vote bank idea retains its historical relevance for directing attention toward the shifting relationships between politics and publics in the postcolonial phase of India's long twentieth century.

Notes

1 "Politics" (*poltix*) is barging into politics (*rajneeti*) these days.

2 Achille Mbembe, *On the postcolony* (Berkeley, CA: University of California Press, 2001),p. 66.

3 However, this may be a peculiarly Indian, rather than a South Asian, practice. In Pakistan, for example, "vote bank" seems to be a neutral term that may be used to describe one's own core supporters. Thanks are due to Juan Cole for pointing this out. See also Guha's citing of the Pakistani cricketer-politician, Imran Khan; Ramachandra Guha, "The Career of a Concept," *The Hindu*, January 20, 2008.

4 According to the main page of the portal, accessed on November 10, 2017, at: https://en.wikipedia.org/wiki/Main_Page. I am not well informed on the ongoing debates on Wikipedia, and hence hesitate to offer a precise characterization. Wikipedia is invoked here because it is a public and popular forum created mainly by nonexperts that is influential in shaping opinion in un-self-reflexive ways—exactly the kind of habitat where notions like vote bank live and flourish.

5 I first accessed the votebank entry in August 2014, but made of a copy of the content only on July 27, 2015; when I checked on it again while finalizing this paper (on October 28, 2017), I found that it had been revised and expanded; these changes have been noted below wherever they are relevant to the current context.

6 In the current (2017) version, the text quoted above forms the entire introductory part of the entry. The earlier (2015) version of the entry also contained the following two paragraphs, which have been deleted:

> The term was coined in India, where the practice of votebank politics is rampant. Since then, it has gained currency in other Asian countries with a significant English-speaking population.
>
> Vote bank is a derogatory term used to describe plurality in politics.

7 The cartoons are available at www.Indianpoliticalimaginaries20thcentury.com

8 For Abraham's career see R. Krishnakumar,“ A Saga of Courage,” obituary notice on Abu Abraham, in *Frontline* 19, no. 26 (December 22, 2002). http://www.frontline.in/static/html/fl1926/stories/20030103003110100.htm

9 Manjul has worked for several different papers, but this particular cartoon appeared in the *Daily News and Analysis* newspaper.

10 M. N. Srinivas, "The Social System of a Mysore Village," in Mckim Marriott, ed., *Village India* (Chicago: University of Chicago Press, 1955). Reproduced in M. N. Srinivas, *Collected Essays* (New Delhi: Oxford University Press, 2002).

11 Srinivas, "The Social System of a Mysore Village," p. 70.

12 Srinivas, "Changing Institutions and Values" [1962] in in Srinivas, *Collected Essays*, 447–8.

13 F. G. Bailey, *Politics and Social Change: Orissa in 1959* (Berkeley, CA: University of California Press, 1963), p. vii.

14 Curiously, there seems to be no mention of Srinivas in this work, though the term vote bank appears suddenly and without preamble, first as a subheading ("The size of vote-banks") in the same chapter, but earlier in the text than the passage quoted below. However Prof. A.M. Shah has informed me (personal conversation) that Srinivas and Bailey were friends and that the latter certainly would have heard about "vote bank" from Srinivas himself.

15 Bailey, *Politics and Social Change,* p. 113.

16 Dhirubhai L. Sheth, "Political Development of Indian Electorate," *Economic and Political Weekly*, Annual Number, (January 1970): 137.

17 Ibid., p. 138.

18 Interestingly, Kothari's language suggests that vote banks had indeed been powerful in the past, a claim that both Srinivas and Bailey were skeptical of, as seen above. Rajni Kothari, "The Political Change of 1967," *Economic and Political Weekly*, Annual Number, (January 1971): 243.

19 As the Rudolphs note in a retrospective work:

"[C]aste was anathema to the modernists of the Nehruvian nationalist generation. ... Nehruvians imagined a nation of equal citizens. ... For Nehruvian nationalists [this] ... meant eradicating ascribed differences, pre-eminently caste and the caste system. Absent eradication of caste and the caste system, denial stepped in. Our early writing about caste was treated as a non-subject, an illegitimate subject, or a reactionary subject." Lloyd I. Rudolph and Susanne Hoeber Rudolph, *Explaining Indian Democracy: A Fifty Year Perspective, 1956—2006, vol. 3: The Realm of the Public Sphere: Identity and Policy* (New Delhi: Oxford University Press, 2008), p. 1.

20 See Arun Sinha, "Vote Banks Break Down," *Economic and Political Weekly*, (March 26, 1977): 529–31; and and B. B. Jena and J. K. Baral, "A Fresh Look at Vote Banks: Some Case Studies from Orissa," *Indian Journal of Political Science* 40, no. 3 (September 1979): 395–417. for examples of work where vote bank is the primary or only focus. The more common instances, however, are those where vote bank is used en route to addressing a broader subject.

21 Sara Joseph and Gurpreet Mahajan, "Elections and Democratic Process in India," *Economic and Political Weekly*, (August 24, 1991): 1954.

22 A. M. Shah, ed., *The Grassroots of Democracy: Field studies of Indian Elections* (New Delhi: Permanent Black, 2007).

23 Most studies in the Rajni Kothari-led project on the 1967 elections also report similar findings—"primordial" loyalties are far too pragmatic and flexible to fit the mechanical conception of the vote bank.

24 Yogendra Yadav, "Epilogue," in Shah, ed., *The Grassroots of Democracy*, pp. 353–4.

25 For a more detailed 1990s discussion of the Muslim vote bank, see Asghar Ali Engineer, "Politics of Muslim Vote Bank," *Economic and Political Weekly*, (January 28, 1995): 197–200.

26 Examples include Nitish Kumar's re-election as chief minister of Bihar in 2010, and (though it is more complex), the Modi-led triumph of the BJP in the 2014 general elections.

27 Javeed Alam, "Is Caste Appeal Casteism? Oppressed Castes in Politics," *Economic and Political Weekly*, (March 27, 1999): 757–61.

28 Satish Deshpande, "Caste and Castelessness: Towards a Biography of the 'General Category'," *Economic and Political Weekly* 48, no. 15 (April 13, 2013): 32–9.

29 Christophe Jaffrelot, *Religion, Caste and Politics in India* (London: Hurst & Company, 2011), p. 595.

30 See, for example, Christophe Jaffrelot's reference to "Congress co-opted vote bank 'owners'" who are usually upper-caste landlords Jaffrelot, "The Rise of the Other Backward Classes in the Hindi Belt," *The Journal of Asian Studies* 59 no. 1 (2000): 86, 108; Patrick Heller's mention of Srinivas's use of the term for rural "notables," Heller, "Degrees of Democracy: Some Comparative Lessons from India," *World Politics* 52, no. 4 (July 2000): 504; or Dipankar Gupta's assessment that vote banks have declined because the former rural patrons are no longer as powerful as they once were, Gupta, "Caste and Politics: Identity Over System," *Annual Review of Anthropology* 34 (2005): 416.

31 Kothari, "The Congress 'System' in India," *Asian Survey* 4, no. 12 (1964): 1161–73.

32 For details, see Kothari, *Politics in India* (New Delhi and Hyderabad: Orient and Blackswan, 1970), which is the original source of this general line of argument. See also Lord Meghnad Desai, "Development and Nationhood: An India Perspective,"

Indian Journal of Industrial Relations 42, no. 3 (2007): 319–31, where a direct link is posited between the decline of the Congress and the rise of vote bank politics.

33 Eswaran Sridharan, "Behind Modi's Victory," *Journal of Democracy* 25, no. 4 (2014): 20–33; Jaffrelot, "The Class Element in the 2014 Indian Election and the BJP's Success, with Special Reference to the Hindi Belt," *Studies in Indian Politics* 3, no. 1 (2015): 19–38.

Select Bibliography

Alam, Javeed, "Is Caste Appeal Casteism? Oppressed Castes in Politics," *Economic and Political Weekly*, (March 27, 1999): 757–61.

Bailey, F. G., *Politics and Social Change: Orissa in 1959* (Berkeley, CA: University of California Press, 1963).

Desai, Lord Meghnad, "Development and Nationhood: An India Perspective," *Indian Journal of Industrial Relations* 42, no. 3 (2007): 319–31.

Deshpande, Satish, "Caste and Castelessness: Towards a Biography of the 'General Category'," *Economic and Political Weekly* 48, no. 15 (April 13, 2013): 32–9.

Engineer, Asghar Ali, "Politics of Muslim Vote Bank," *Economic and Political Weekly*, (January 28, 1995): 197–200.

Guha, Ramachandra, "The Career of a Concept," *The Hindu*, January 20, 2008.

Gupta, Dipankar, "Caste and Politics: Identity Over System," *Annual Review of Anthropology* 34 (2005): 409–27.

Heller, Patrick, "Degrees of Democracy: Some Comparative Lessons from India," *World Politics* 52, no. 4 (July 2000): 484–519.

Jaffrelot, Christophe, "The Class Element in the 2014 Indian Election and the BJP's Success, with Special Reference to the Hindi Belt," *Studies in Indian Politics* 3, no. 1 (2015): 19–38.

Jaffrelot, Christophe, *Religion, Caste and Politics in India* (London: Hurst & Company, 2011).

Jaffrelot, Christophe, "The Rise of the Other Backward Classes in the Hindi Belt," *The Journal of Asian Studies* 59, no. 1 (2000): 86–108.

Jena, B. B. and J. K. Baral, "A Fresh Look at Vote Banks: Some Case Studies from Orissa," *Indian Journal of Political Science* 40, no. 3 (September 1979): 395–417.

Joseph, Sara and Gurpreet Mahajan, "Elections and Democratic Process in India," *Economic and Political Weekly*, (August 24, 1991): 1953–5.

Krishnakumar, R. " A Saga of Courage," Obituary Notice on Abu Abraham, *Frontline* 19, no. 26 (December 22, 2002). http://www.frontline.in/static/html/fl1926/stories/20030103003110100.htm

Kothari, Rajni, "The Congress 'System' in India," *Asian Survey* 4, no. 12 (1964): 1161–73.

Kothari, Rajni, *Politics in India* (New Delhi and Hyderabad: Orient Blackswan, 1970).

Kothari, Rajni, "The Political Change of 1967," *Economic and Political Weekly*, Annual Number, (January 1971): 231–3.

Mbembe, Achille, *On the Postcolony* (Berkeley, CA: University of California Press, 2001).

Rudolph, Lloyd I. and Susanne Hoeber Rudolph, *Explaining Indian Democracy: A Fifty Year Perspective, 1956—2006, vol. 3: The Realm of the Public Sphere: Identity and Policy* (New Delhi: Oxford University Press, 2008).

Sheth, Dhirubhai L., "Political Development of Indian Electorate," *Economic and Political Weekly*, Annual Number, (January 1970), 137–48.

Sinha, Arun, "Vote Banks Break Down," *Economic and Political Weekly*, (March 26, 1977): 529–31.

Sridharan, Eswaran, "Behind Modi's Victory," *Journal of Democracy* 25, no. 4 (2014): 20–33.

Srinivas, M. N., "Changing Institutions and Values in Modern India," *Economic and Political Weekly*, Annual Number, (February 1962): 131–7.

Srinivas, M. N. "The Social System of a Mysore Village," first published in Mckim Marriott, ed., *Village India* (Chicago: University of Chicago Press, 1955). Reproduced in M. N. Srinivas, *Collected Essays* (New Delhi: Oxford University Press, 2002).

Wikipedia, "Votebank," Accessed on November 10, 2017, https://en.wikipedia.org/wiki/Votebank; also accessed on July 27, 2015 at the same address.

Yadav, Yogendra, "Epilogue," in A. M. Shah, ed., *The Grassroots of Democracy: Field Studies of Indian Elections* (New Delhi: Permanent Black, 2007).

10

Dispossession and Democracy: The Land Acquisition Act and the Future of India's Land Wars

Michael Levien

Introduction

This chapter analyzes the contradiction between the land requirements of neoliberal capitalism and the political weight of farmers in India's electoral democracy. While this contradiction has deep roots in the political economy of twentieth-century India, it manifested with the explosive farmer protests of the mid-to-late oughts and reached a momentary resolution with the passage of The Right to Fair Compensation and Transparency in Land Acquisition, Resettlement and Rehabilitation Act of 2013 (LARRA). This legislation, which was over six years in the making before finally being passed in the final year of the second Congress-led United Progressive Alliance (UPA II), replaced the British vintage Land Acquisition Act (LAA) of 1894 that—quite notoriously—had been the principal instrument of forcibly dispossessing land for the previous 120 years. The bill was advertised as an attempt to rectify the historic abuse of the LAA, and to strike a compromise between industry and farmers by giving the latter a "fair deal." The latter was ultimately even framed as a "right," in line with the rights-based legislations (to information, education, food, work, and forests) of the previous decade. But altering the legal framework by which the state could redistribute the country's land surface from farmers to both private capital and its own agencies was more contentious than most legislation: the bill had clear and conflicting material implications for different social classes, impinged on the organizational interests of different arms of the state, and had the potential to seriously affect India's economic growth. The long process of drafting, debating, and amending this bill under UPA II—and its subsequent dilution by the BJP government—provides a window not only on the new centrality of land dispossession to postliberalization capitalism in India, but also on the character of the Indian state as it seeks to facilitate rapid growth via private investment while managing the political conflict this generates in the context of an electoral democracy.

The premise of this chapter is that the contemporary politics of land acquisition, as manifested in the contestation around LARRA, must be understood in relation to a *dramatic transformation* in the political economy of dispossession in postliberalization India. This transformation is, in different ways, missed by commentators who see today's land grabs as part of a continuous process of "development" or "primitive accumulation." Together, these accounts make it appear as if the privatized and speculative forms of dispossession in the neoliberal era—private SEZs, real estate colonies for the wealthy, Formula 1 race tracks—represent a generic and necessary "development"[1] or an inevitable stage in the development of capitalism.[2] Such rigid conceptualizations do little justice to the postcolonial specificity of capitalism in India and its transformations in the late twentieth and early twenty-first century.

My argument, in contrast, is that the proliferating land wars that LARRA sought to diffuse should be seen as a product of a dramatic postliberalization shift in what I call *regimes of dispossession*.[3] The land grabs driving today's "land wars" are not simply more of the same "development-induced displacement" (which assumes the constancy of development), nor are they part of India's transition to capitalism (which has already occurred); rather they reflect a significant shift in the economic purposes and class interests driving the Indian state's practice of land dispossession in the neoliberal period. From dispossessing land for public sector infrastructure, mining, and heavy industry in the Nehruvian period, since the early 1990s Indian states have become land brokers for private capital for increasingly rent-driven, speculative, and nonlabor absorbing purposes. This transformation began in the 1990s, but reached maturity with special economic zones (SEZ) and other forms of PPP infrastructure and real estate development in the mid-2000s. With this shift, the capacity of the Indian state to illicit compliance to dispossession has greatly attenuated. While the developmentalist imaginary of the Nehruvian state was quite effective at diffusing and marginalizing protest against land acquisition for many decades, this new regime has proven far more tenuous, generating widespread "land wars" that have proven unprecedentedly successful at obstructing dispossession and thus accumulation. LARRA was a response to this new regime's relative lack of legitimacy compared to its Nehruvian predecessor, and a consequent need to find a stronger material basis for making farmers comply with dispossession. It was, in essence, an attempt to absorb a Polanyian[4] countermovement into a compromise on the terrain of commodification. But orchestrating such a compromise remains elusive.

This paper analyzes the politics of amending LARRA in light of this transformation. Drawing on interviews with key agents in the latter process, it examines how the interests of farmers and capital refracted through different arms of the political system and bureaucracy to shape the final legislation. It shows, first, that farmers were able to find some allies within the "soft" arms of the central government as well as among the national political parties who advocated for significant pro-farmer concessions—a testament to the political force of their countermovement, the questionable legitimacy of dispossessing land for private capital, and the weight of farmers in India's electorate. However, it also shows how an offensive by capital, supported by the growth-facilitating arms of the central government and, crucially, state governments intent on maintaining their land brokering powers, succeeded in significantly diluting the bill.

While capital—and some academics[5]—considered the final bill so pro-farmer that it would impede economic growth, I suggest conversely that it was unlikely to placate even those farmers who are willing to negotiate over compensation.

Land acquisition, then, is now a major contradiction between democratic politics and capitalist growth in contemporary India, and is almost certainly insoluble with the context of a neoliberal growth model. The question, then, is whether this impasse leads to the consolidation of a more authoritarian capitalist state or whether antidispossession movements can contribute to a more democratic political imaginary and egalitarian political economy.

Genesis of the Land Broker State

In the early 1990s, India's model of state-led development began to definitively give way to a new one, and this led to a significant change in the state's role in acquiring land. There was nothing automatic about the restructuring of state governments into land brokers for private capital, but the turn toward neoliberalism greatly militated toward this outcome.

First, economic liberalization in the early 1990s unleashed increasing private demand for land for industry, infrastructure, and real estate. With the decision to liberalize private investment and to diminish the public sector's role in the economy,[6] the share of private capital in the economy steadily increased and became dominant by the end of the decade.[7] This radical reversal from an economy dominated by public sector capital to one dominated by private capital logically implied a reversal in their relative demand for land. But liberalization also changed the nature of that demand.

The process of economic liberalization that began in the 1990s created "a voracious appetite for space to meet the demands of industrialization, infrastructure building, urban expansion and resource extraction."[8] This demand grew steadily over the 1990s, receded somewhat during the East Asian financial crisis-triggered slowdown between 1997 and the early 2000s, and ascended new heights in the mid-2000s as India's growth rate reached 9 percent and a liberalized real estate market entered a dramatic boom.

Why couldn't this demand for land be met by the ordinary operation of real estate markets? Most of the land available for such projects lay in the hands of India's large small-holding farmers and there are well-known obstacles to consolidating large chunks of rural land. First, very small holdings make negotiations difficult and holdouts likely. Second, legal problems are almost guaranteed for large projects given the prevalence of unclear or disputed titles. Third, many farmers remain reluctant to sell land for multiple reasons, including the lack of attractive exit options from agriculture generated by the present development model. The growing demand for land initiated by liberalization in India thus confronted the supply barrier of rural land markets that do not provide "an open field" for the circulation of capital.[9] If large land consuming private investments—say over a few hundred acres—were to go forward, the state would have to dispossess land for them.

There were two main incentives for states to help capital overcome this obstacle. First, liberalization also unleashed fierce interstate competition for investment.[10] Land dispossession quickly assumed a critical role in this competition.[11] The flight of Tata

Motors from West Bengal to Gujarat after meeting stiff opposition in Singur powerfully illustrated the centrality of land to the interstate competition for footloose capital.

The second incentive for states to move into the land brokering business was the enormous licit and illicit rents this would make possible. Acquiring land and selling it to private investors became a significant source of revenue for industrial development corporations, urban development authorities, and other parastatals. Moreover, this increasing state role in land acquisition and allocation expanded the opportunities for illicit rent, which takes the form of government officials and politicians buying land in advance of projects being announced (or selling that information to others) or demanding bribes for land allocation, land conversion or shifting project boundaries. This postliberalization nexus of government officials, politicians, brokers and developers has generated "corruption" and black money on a scale that makes the "license raj" look quaint.[12]

The upshot is that state governments restructured themselves into land broker states. No longer confining themselves to the dispossession of land for state-led projects of productive material expansion, states turned to dispossessing peasants for any private economic purpose that constituted "growth," including real estate speculation. Indeed, states began dispossessing land merely so that private companies (and the government itself) could capture the differential between the price paid to farmers and its ultimate market value—what I term the "rate of accumulation by dispossession." Under India's neoliberal regime maximizing this rate has itself become the purpose of dispossession.

As this new regime of dispossession came to scale during the mid-2000s boom, it triggered escalating land wars across the country. It was this unprecedented countermovement that drove the reformation of India's Land Acquisition Act after 120 years of reliable use.

The Right to Be Dispossessed Fairly

Countermovement

Social movements, NGOs, and intellectuals had been challenging the LAA and demanding a national resettlement and rehabilitation law since the 1980s (cf. Fernandes and Thukral 1989). While these efforts finally achieved a national resettlement and rehabilitation policy in 2004 and laid the intellectual foundation for LARRA, it was the political momentum generated by the land wars of the late 2000s that moved the ship of state toward a substantial overhaul of India's eminent domain framework. Although the well-publicized land struggles represented only the tip of the iceberg, the Nandigram violence of March 2007 arguably constituted a transformative event that restructured the political field.[13] The massacre by CPM cadre and police of fourteen farmers protesting forcible land acquisition for a private (and foreign) SEZ was widely condemned in the media, and brought the issue of SEZs and land acquisition squarely into the national limelight. In contrast to the older struggles against dams, the fact that the issue now clearly pitted farmers against large private corporations (including foreign ones) gave critics much greater ammunition, and almost all of the major parties soon expressed misgivings about acquiring land for SEZs, which were easily portrayed as "real estate grabs" (Levien 2013a). The consequent gains of the TMC in West Bengal further proved that land acquisition had become, for the first time in India's history, an electorally salient issue. The Nandigram and Singur struggles also importantly elevated Mamata Banerjee onto the national stage as a vocal critic of land acquisition within mainstream politics—and initially within the UPA. Other political parties picked up on her formula and, in states where they were in opposition (regardless of their practice when and where in power), began seizing on local land struggles as opportunities to attack the ruling government as "pro-corporate" and "anti-farmer."

This new contentiousness of land acquisition was felt by most states, but unevenly. While dispossession was also accelerating in the hills and possibly adding fuel to the Maoist insurgency (Sundar 2016), the shift toward dispossessing land for real estate and urban-industrial infrastructure brought land struggles into the plains where it encountered not marginalized *adivasis* but more politically influential middle and large farmers. States with powerful farmer movements, such as Haryana and Uttar Pradesh, were forced to adopt significantly more generous compensation and R&R packages on their own. Rajasthan and Maharashtra already had more generous than average compensation policies on the books. While other states such as Gujarat, Andhra Pradesh, and Tamil Nadu continued to acquire land relatively cheaply, they were also experiencing significant—if less publicized—opposition that was delaying projects and prompting them to introduce more limited reforms. In its waning days, the chastened Left Front adopted a new land acquisition policy in West Bengal; once taking power, the TMC largely brought land acquisition to a halt. By the end of the 2000s, almost no state's land acquisition policies remained unchanged.[14]

The central government, for its part, began the process of amending the LAA in 2007 in the aftermath of the Nandigram carnage and amidst widespread opposition to SEZs and other projects. As SEZs dropped like flies, and other megaprojects became bogged down in costly delays, it became clear that changing the law might be necessary economically as well as politically. After discussions within Sonia Gandhi's National Advisory Council (NAC), the Ministry of Rural Development introduced a revised national resettlement and rehabilitation policy that was passed by the cabinet in October 2007. In the winter of 2008, the government introduced two bills into the Lok Sabha, one to amend the LAA and another to turn resettlement and rehabilitation requirements into law. The bills were passed by the Lok Sabha in 2009 and referred to the Rajya Sabha but lapsed. New and slightly amended versions were passed by the cabinet in 2009 but ultimately not introduced into parliament. The process languished for several years as UPA 1 transitioned to UPA 2, and a new electoral mandate possibly made the matter less urgent.

In May of 2011, a violent uprising erupted in villages of western UP that proved consequential for giving the amendments new momentum. Farmers in the villages of Bhatta and Parsaul, on the outskirts of Greater Noida, were angry at having their land acquired at below-market prices for the 165-km Yamuna Expressway, a project that was being built on a PPP basis by the Jaypee Group. In addition to acquiring land for the six-lane highway, the project also involved transferring large tracts of adjacent land—25 million square meters in five locations—for real estate development.

Farmers were enraged that their land was being acquired—through the urgency clause of the LAA, which allows for expedited acquisition in fifteen days with no hearing of objections—at very low prices and handed over to private builders at many times that rate. In May, farmers kidnapped three officials of the Uttar Pradesh State Transport Corporation who were conducting a survey for the project. When police tried to rescue the officials, a bloody gunfight ensued in which two farmers and two policemen died and more were injured. Rahul Gandhi snuck into the villages on a motorbike and embarked on a *padyatra* (foot march) with farmers, castigating Chief Minister Mayawati's BSP government for its callousness.[15] While Gandhi had taken up the land acquisition issue once before, supporting the Dongria Kondh in their fight against a Vedanta bauxite mine in the Niyamgiri Hills of Orissa,[16] Congress sources claim that Bhatta-Parsaul agitation was a key turning point in Gandhi's involvement with the land acquisition amendments.[17] The uprising presented the Congress with a wedge issue against the ruling BSP in the run-up to the critical 2012 state assembly elections.[18] In the verbal duel that ensued, Gandhi and Mayawati each promised to introduce new land acquisition acts/policies—at the center and state levels, respectively—that would be more "pro-farmer" than the other.

Shortly thereafter Jairam Ramesh was given the portfolio of rural development and tasked with pushing through the land acquisition amendments. Within a few months, the Ministry of Rural Development had combined the two bills into one—a critical move, recommended by the NAC, that would procedurally tie the acquisition of land to the provision of resettlement and rehabilitation—and published a new draft for comments. A Parliamentary Standing Committee was convened and issued recommendations by 2012. The MoRD held several consultations; the bill was debated in parliament and in the media, substantially amended, and finally passed in September 2013. It was during this two-year window that the contending political forces began to seriously articulate their views in public, lobby government, and attempt to shape the outcome of the bill.

While almost all of the bill's 100 plus clauses were intensely fought over during this process, the main sources of disagreement can be divided into three categories: 1) the scope of "public purpose," and specifically whether the government should acquire land for private companies; 2) the level of compensation and other R&R benefits that should be given to farmers; and 3) the procedural requirements for acquiring land and whether they should prioritize rapid completion of projects or safeguarding farmers' interests. Other issues included whether the act should be applied retroactively, whether it should apply to over a dozen other legislations that covered land acquisition for specific sectors (like railways, highways, mines, nuclear power, etc.), and whether the bill should limit acquisition of irrigated farmland to protect food security. Understanding the political conflict around the bill and the implications of its final form requires delving into some of these intricacies.

Legislating the Countermovement: The Original Bill

The bill introduced by Jairam Ramesh in 2011 significantly broadened the definition of "public purpose" to cover most types of private investment,[19] but with the proviso that land acquisition for private companies and for PPP projects would require the consent of 80 percent and 70 percent respectively of the "affected families" (not just land owners). In Scheduled Areas,[20] acquisition of land required prior consultation with *gram sabhas* (village-level assemblies). The bill also put limits on the ability of states to change the purpose of land use after acquisition (a notorious abuse), created a time limit within which the land must be used (initially ten years), and required that if the land was resold, 40 percent of the appreciation would go back to the original landholder.

The bill also increased the compensation due to farmers, pegging it initially at six times the assessed market value including what is called "solatium"—an increment meant to compensate for the involuntary nature of the transaction. Crucially, however, this assessed market value—what is called the "circle rate"—would continue to be based on registered property sales of farmland, which are under-reported to avoid Stamp Duty, do not reflect potential nonagricultural uses, and are consequently much lower than actual market values. The bill's most progressive feature was that it mandated a number of resettlement and rehabilitation measures, including for landless laborers, tenants, artisans, and other groups who do not own land but whose livelihoods are affected by acquisition.[21] It also specified the various infrastructural facilities that would have to be provided at resettlement sites (which have historically been dismal).

Procedurally, the bill's most significant innovation was to unite land acquisition and resettlement and rehabilitation into one law, thus tying the transfer of land to the provision of these benefits. The bill further called for the creation of state- and project-level committees to monitor compliance and a national resettlement and rehabilitation authority to adjudicate disputes in a timely manner (thus attempting to take challenges out of court). The bill also restricted the much-abused urgency clause to cases of national defense and natural calamities; placed restrictions on the acquisition of irrigated land as a proportion of a district's cultivable area; and contained heavy penalties for government officials who knowingly violated any of the law's provisions. It would have been applicable to all yet-to-be-completed cases of land acquisition that had been dragging on for five or more years. But it significantly excluded fifteen central legislations that covered land acquisition for specific sectors (including highways, mines, power plants, defense installations, railways, and initially SEZs).

Debate and Dilution

Neither of the two main social interests arrayed around the bill were pacified. Farmer organizations and movements did not want any land acquisition for private companies, objected to the broad definition of public purpose, and wanted 100 percent consent. They further worried that the process of gaining consent would be rushed and manipulated, pointed out that the recommendations of the Expert Group would not be binding, and argued that land acquisition should be subject to Gram Sabha consent not consultation. Most thought the compensation provisions were inadequate as the price multiplier would still not compensate for the undervaluation of registered land prices and many of the R&R provisions beyond cash compensation were optional. These objections crossed ideological divides of left and right-leaning groups. From different ideological perspectives, these groups wanted to roll back the neoliberal regime of dispossessing land for private capital and to substantially increase compensation and R&R benefits when acquisition did occur.

Capital, on the other hand, thought that the bill was so pro-farmer that it would bring economic growth to a grinding halt. All of the major industry associations—the Confederation of Indian Industries (CII), the Associated Chambers of Commerce and Industry (ASSOCHAM), and the Federation of Indian Chambers of Commerce and Industry (FICCI)—along with regional associations, the builder's lobby, and individual corporate executives were united in opposing it.[22] They argued that private projects should be treated on par with government projects, and pushed to expand the public purpose provision to clearly include any activity they were engaged in—whether factories, real estate development, or PPP infrastructure. They argued that the consent clause and other provisions would be a nightmare to implement and would delay projects. There were some shades of difference within industry on the extent to which they were willing to compromise on compensation levels. Ramesh tried to convince them that by removing the cause of farmer protests, the bill would actually reduce costs and uncertainties. Some segments of industry recognized this and were willing to increase compensation in exchange for greater political certainty. Others were less willing to offer concessions, and considered the proposed compensation levels extreme. Ultimately, industry groups lobbied to reduce the price multiplier. The dip in India's growth between 2011 and 2013 worked in their favor, as they—and notably Prime Minister Manmohan Singh—identified delayed infrastructure projects as a major factor hampering India's growth. They advanced their views in the PSC, in consultations with the Ministry of Rural Development, and very vocally in the press. Their media barrage escalated in the weeks leading up to the parliamentary vote in August 2013.[23]

These two basic positions—"pro-farmer" and "pro-industry"—refracted through the political system, different arms of the bureaucracy, and different levels of government. As Ramesh explained, "*within* government we had both these points of view" (Interview, 7.5.14). Even before Ramesh's draft, disagreement had surfaced within Sonia Gandhi's National Advisory Council, which included several prominent social activists. Aruna Roy and Harsh Mander came out against acquiring land for private companies, while former bureaucrat N.C. Saxena defended it as necessary for economic growth (NAC n.d.; Interviews, various dates). With opinion divided in her council of advisors, Sonia Gandhi appeared initially hesitant about how to proceed. When Ramesh took up the bill, he rejected the more radical recommendations of the NAC and sidelined Mander in favor of Saxena.[24] Ramesh made it clear that their draft was too radical.

In their submissions to the Parliamentary Standing Committee, different government ministries divided along sectoral lines. Commerce and Industry, Urban Development, Power, Road Transport and Highways, Mines, Railways, Petroleum and Natural Gas, and Atomic Energy all pushed to exempt their agencies' projects from consent, to relax procedural hurdles, and to keep the cost of acquisition down. On the other side, Tribal Affairs, Panchayati Raj, and Social Justice and Empowerment pushed for a more radical bill than the one proposed by Ramesh's Rural Development.

Within the UPA's council of ministers, opinion was so sharply divided between the "progressive" and "neoliberal" camps that the Prime Minister convened a "Group of Ministers"[25] to sort out their disagreements. Ultimately, Ramesh was forced to offer several concessions to the pro-industry group, such as loosening the retroactive clause and exempting thirteen central legislations. On the latter, Ramesh remarked that including them "would not only have been politically suicidal but even the Cabinet would not have cleared it."[26] But when the Group of Ministers appeared to reach a compromise position of 67 percent consent for PPP projects (which Ramesh accepted), Sonia Gandhi vetoed the idea with an eye toward the elections.[27] And it was Rahul Gandhi who came up with the idea of changing the bill's name from one that suggested that government wanted to take people's land to one that sounded like a new right (Interview, Congress politician, 7.9.14).

Some of the sharpest conflict was between the central and state governments. The states—including those ruled by Congress—were almost uniformly opposed to the bill. They resented this intrusion on their prerogatives (land is a state subject though land acquisition is on the concurrent list), and argued for flexibility in adopting their own procedures and compensation levels. As Ramesh put it, "state governments wanted to be in a position basically to acquire land overnight ... Political parties wanted a national policy .... State governments said, you let us be, we have our own policy" (Interview, 7.5.14). States were keen, in other words, to maintain their land brokering functions even while their political parties recognized the need for a more pro-farmer central bill.

There were important disagreements across political parties at the national level, but all were concerned with appearing pro-farmer and most of their (public) critique came from that direction. The Parliamentary Standing Committee, chaired by the BJP's Sumitra Mahajan, remarkably issued recommendations that were in almost all respects more progressive than Ramesh's bill, including no acquisition for private companies. This was the position of the TMC, which argued that there should be 100 percent rather than 80 percent consent, and refused to support the bill. The Left also argued that the bill was a sell-out to private companies and abstained from voting, even as it was repeatedly jeered and bated by TMC parliamentarians for their atrocities in Nandigram and Singur.[28] The BJP ultimately supported most aspects of the bill, and publicly called for higher compensation to farmers. The party was, however, concerned with impeding growth and demanded several last minute amendments before the bill could clear the Rajya Sabha.[29]

By the time the bill emerged from the political gauntlet of corporate lobbying, intra-bureaucratic conflicts, fierce opposition from the states, and parliamentary debate, numerous concessions had been made. These consisted mostly of dilutions in favor of industry. At the behest of industry and its advocates within the government, the effective compensation price multiplier had been reduced from 6 to either 2 or 4 depending on the distance from the city—a criteria it was left to the states to establish. Irrigation projects became entirely exempted from consent and SIA, and "land for land" compensation—a key demand of anti-dam movements—became optional. The states were given flexibility on many issues—such as regulating the amount of irrigated land that could be acquired and determining what size of private purchase would require Social Impact Assessment (SIA) and R&R benefits—which ensured their nonimplementation or dilution. One significant pro-farmer evolution from the original bill was requiring *gram sabha* consent rather than consultation in Scheduled Areas. The maximum time limit for holding unutilized land before it reverted back to either the original owners or state land bank was reduced from 10 to 5 years (though pro-farmer advocates insisted it should only go back to the original owner). The SEZ Act was also removed from the list of exempted legislations.[30]

In the end, no one was happy. Farmer groups, the Left, and the TMC deemed the final bill too pro-industry. Industry was convinced it was the opposite and threatened that the bill would drastically increase project costs, delay their implementation, and slow growth. Ramesh proclaimed that this mutual unhappiness was the sign of a successful compromise.[31] While the bill had something for everyone to dislike, whether it would be successful in its aims—orchestrating a compromise between farmers and capital that will discourage protests and meet the land demands of neoliberal capitalism—is a different question.

Land Wars Forever? Democracy and Neoliberalism

LARRA was a political response to the unprecedented "countermovement" generated by a qualitative change—as well as quantitative increase—in the role of land dispossession in Indian capitalism. While the Nehruvian state proved adept at legitimizing dispossession and suppressing resistance to the large public sector projects of the postindependence years, the postliberalization regime of dispossessing land for private—and especially real estate driven—accumulation quickly proved tenuous. Escalating land wars against SEZs and other forms of private investment quickly put the state on the defensive, as the issue became politically explosive and even electorally salient. As these struggles actually started to significantly obstruct large private investments, changing the Land Acquisition Act was no longer simply good politics but arguably necessary to the continuance of the prevailing economic model. As the ruling UPA government contemplated how to alter the legal framework for dispossessing land, they essentially had two options: they could retreat from the neoliberal regime of dispossession into something more like its Nehruvian predecessor, restricting the state's role to acquiring land for the public sector; or they try to put the neoliberal regime on a firmer base of material compliance.

They chose the latter. The former would have been tantamount to forsaking significant components of the neoliberal growth model that each government had been assiduously building over the past two decades. This has principally involved reducing the role of the public sector and attracting private investment into every sector of the economy, whose growth (and thus the private profits of which it consists) has become the principal aim of statecraft. But when confronted with the barrier of a land surface controlled in very small parcels by the world's largest rural population, the "free market" has shown itself to be dependent on the widespread expropriation of private property. The neoliberal growth model, while not "necessary" itself, necessitated a dramatic expansion in the land brokering role of state governments, turning self-professed liberals—as Gramsci put it—into ardent interventionists. But legitimizing the state's role in dispossessing farmers for large private capital in a democracy dominated by a relatively poor rural electorate turned out to be no easy matter. It was much harder to persuade farmers—and even a broader public—that private and rent-heavy projects like SEZs served the national interest and constituted a "public purpose" in the same way as large dams. There was a contradiction between the land requirements of neoliberal capitalism and the exigencies of electoral democracy in a still predominantly rural country.

At the same time, the land boom generated by the neoliberal growth model offered a possible way out: land prices. One of the factors animating discontent—especially in the peri-urban plains—was the vast differentials between the prices paid to farmers and the market value of land once handed over to capital and zoned for residential-commercial purposes. What I have called the rate of accumulation by dispossession—the ratio between the compensation given to farmers and the land's post-acquisition market value—was dramatically increasing, and this theoretically made possible greater concessions to farmers. Concerned economists began to advance formulas for finding the "reserve price" of farmers. Where forced by farmer protests, states started experimenting in practice. But interstate competition militated toward keeping compensation low or driving investment away from states where it was high; a floor price to substantially reduce agrarian unrest in the country as a whole would have to come from the central government.

LARRA was an attempt to substitute land prices for legitimacy. To invoke Polanyian terms, it sought to channel a countermovement against the forcible commodification of land into a class compromise on the terrain of commodification itself. Ramesh's bill sought to retain—and legally enshrine—state power to dispossess land for private profit, but tried to introduce legal mechanisms to give farmers a greater share of the profits in the form of land prices and other R&R benefits. It also sought to introduce a procedure for acquiring land that would appear more transparent and *feel* less coercive. Rahul Gandhi's renaming of the bill to make fair land acquisition a new right was an attempt to put a friendly face on what has usually been a brutal and coercive process of redistributing land upwards.

What was surprising, however, about the process of debating and amending the bill was the degree of support even within government for restricting the scope of the neoliberal regime of dispossession and more substantially democratizing control over land. While it had many loopholes, Ramesh's bill did ultimately establish consent thresholds for private and PPP projects. It is remarkable that significant sections within the central government—albeit from less powerful ministries—and across parties advocated for the complete restriction on acquisition of land for private capital. This demonstrates, first, the very real difficulty of legitimizing the dispossession of land for private profit, and the continuing salience of Nehruvian norms as a basis for critiquing neoliberalism's worse excesses.[32] The fact that irrigation projects were ultimately exempted from the legislation and SEZs were not attested to the greater difficulty in politically justifying the private land acquisitions of the neoliberal era.[33] The stance of political parties reflected this difficulty in the context of a historically unprecedented antidispossession backlash, and the realpolitik of electoral competition in which, as a Tehelka (2014) editorial put it, "no party can afford to sound non-socialist when it comes to the peasantry."[34] The fact that elections were around the corner by the time of the 2013 parliamentary debate was very significant.

If the debate around the bill demonstrated some degree of relative state autonomy from the short-term interests of capital, Ramesh personified what Marxists have called Bonaparteism[35]: with capitalists unable to see beyond their noses, he tried to orchestrate a class compromise that he believed would be in the long-term interests of capital itself. He argued that the bill would remove the source of farmer protests and litigation that delayed projects, and would "defeat Naxalism." As one of his deputies put it in an editorial, the bill would be good for business as it would "reduce uncertainty, steamline the process, lower acquisition costs, and create a win-win model of land acquisition .... It is far better for both parties to compensate fairly and get the process right upfront, rather than run into trouble downstream."[36] Some enlightened fractions of the business intellegenstia agreed. An *Economic Times* editorial sought to reassure their readers that the bill might increase costs but "it also has a benefit: freedom from Singur-type reversals and the reduced likelihood of social dissent climbing to levels that add to the ranks of the Maoists .... Avoiding social conflict has a price, worst paid as a policing expenditure."[37]

But the attempt to save capitalism from capitalists by humanizing dispossession was a hard sell, and the short-term interests of capital ultimately came to the fore. Ramesh's bill, itself falling far short of what most farmers' movements wanted, was met with a capitalist class offensive supported by the growth-promoting arms of the central state and state governments keen on maintaining their land brokerage functions. The dilutions and resulting loopholes were substantial. The thirteen legislations exempted from the bill left a huge domain of land acquisition—including many sectors that increasingly operate on a PPP basis—out of the consent, SIA, and other procedural requirements of the bill (though they must bring their compensation levels up to par within a year). The exemption of irrigation projects will leave millions of people displaced by large dams with the same abusive system. There is ambiguity as to whether states can simply acquire land for their "land banks," which makes it government property, and later allot it to private industry without consent (if so, it renders the consent provisions meaningless). How to implement the consent provisions was left to states, which fails to inspire confidence given how they have manipulated *gram sabha* approvals in the past (as in the POSCO case). The result was a bill that did put some hurdles in the way of acquisition for private capital, but by no means roadblocks. Driving down compensation levels from 6 times to 2 or 4 times the circle rate—and leaving state's ample room to manipulate which it will be—demonstrated a remarkable short-sightedness that will probably be detrimental to the long-term interests of capitalists themselves.

Which leads to the question: will the bill succeed in its aims of preventing land wars while not impeding growth? Capitalists made no secret in their opinion that the bill erred on the side of farmers, and several economists—such as Arvind Panagariya (2014)—concurred.[38] Chakravorty worried that it has "raised the price of land acquisition to unsustainable levels" (2015), and predicted that the "The political problem of resistance to land acquisition will go away ... but an even bigger economic problem will be created" (2014: 184).[39] I would argue precisely the opposite: while the bill will increase costs (that is the point) it will not constitute a significant obstacle to capital. Rather, the price of acquired land will remain below actual market prices, and it is precisely the political problem of unhappy farmers that will not go away. I put forward three reasons for why LARRA was unlikely to substantially increase the probability of farmer compliance.

First, the rent-driven and nonlabor absorbing forms of development driving land acquisition in India today—exemplified by SEZs, high-tech cities, and real estate projects in the guise of infrastructure—have little to offer the two-thirds of the population that live in rural areas. If the Nehruvian state dispossessed land for economic purposes that farmers could at least be *theoretically* included in—irrigated agriculture and public sector industrialization—the neoliberal regime of dispossession does not even offer this possibility. For India's vast semi-proletariat, this makes holding on to even small pieces of land to supplement wage-labor far preferable to pure landlessness—even in the context of relatively stagnant agricultural growth. While economists justify forcible land acquisition by the macro-level efficiency of transferring land from agriculture to "higher value" land uses,[40] what they fail to fully appreciate is the micro-level rationality that is often behind farmer's opposition to this transfer. The vast chasm between India's neoliberal growth trajectory and the majority of India's rural population—a compounding of historical development failures[41]—constitutes a huge structural factor behind the contentiousness of land acquisition in India today. Not being able to offer farmers a significant place in the development generated by dispossession puts all the weight on land prices as an incentive for compliance.

Finally, and perhaps more fundamentally, the idea of utilizing the exchange value of land to build a class compromise between capital and farmers assumes what needs to be explained, which is how farmers come to value their land at its exchange value. The land wars of the last ten years have shown that not all farmers can be bought, or at least that their "reservation price" is not anywhere near what is being offered by state and capital. While many farmers' struggles, especially on the peri-urban plains, are struggles over prices, it is a mistake to collapse, as Partha Chatterjee does, all of dispossession politics into ad hoc negotiation over its terms.[42] There remains a second category of antidispossession movement that have shown absolutely no interest in compensation. From Nandigram to Niyamgiri, Raigad, Singur, and Jagatsinghpur, we find numerous examples of farmers unwilling to even consider compensation. One should notice that not all of these are in *adivasi* dominated hill areas, where such attitudes are considered to be more prevalent. By refusing to value their land at its exchange value, these farmers cannot be brought into a class compromise on the terrain of commodification. They will continue to constitute a huge obstacle to the land brokering of state governments, and the new law is unlikely to change that.

The passage of LARRA in the waning days of UPA II thus revealed the following: a state struggling to legitimize dispossession for private and increasingly real estate driven private investments in the context of an exclusionary development model; a capitalist class unwilling to offer substantial material concessions and a state that is not sufficiently autonomous to impose them. The result was a law that was in most ways better than the notoriously brutal LAA, but that is still unlikely to make many—if not most—farmers surrender their land willingly. This leaves, of course, the time-honored route of coercion and violence—but that itself is becoming increasingly difficult as the issue gains electoral salience. At bottom of LARRA's insufficiency is a contradiction between the land demands of neoliberal capitalism and the weight of farmers in India's electoral democracy.

While it is impossible to bring this story fully up to date, the major approach of the central government since then has been to keep LARRA on the books but allow state governments to undercut it with their own more pro-industry amendments and rules, which include sidestepping consent and SIA provisions by exempting many types of projects, reducing compensation and allowing state governments to bank unutilized acquired land instead of returning it to previous owners.[43] This devolution has effectively undermined the national level floor that LARRA intended to establish and reinvigorated the race to the bottom. Social movements decry these dilutions while industry insists that LARRA remains an obstacle to development. Land wars continue to emerge against all manner of projects—Land Conflict Watch (n.d.) reports almost 800 ongoing conflicts as this volume goes to press—even if the issue has momentarily receded from the spotlight due to a slowing economy, pulled down by overindebted infrastructure and real estate sectors even before the Covid-19 pandemic, and the Modi government's full throttled push toward a Hindu nation, with all the resistance and authoritarian crackdown that has followed.

If momentarily on a low simmmer, India's "land question" will most certainly boil over again. It is, in fact, irresolvable under the conditions of neoliberal growth in India's electoral democracy. While unable to compel farmers to "sacrifice for the nation," as in the days of Nehruvian developmentalism, the government's only hope of stabilizing India's neoliberal regime of dispossession is brokering a class compromise with land prices. I have suggested that there are several obstacles to accomplishing this, including an exclusionary growth model and the continued existence of noncommodified orientations to land in rural India. But the third obstacle is the state's own unwillingness and ability to make the concessions that could even come close to pacifying farmers. While the UPA's 2013 law was itself so diluted as to likely be incapable of diffusing farmer protest, there is no doubt that subsequent dilutions drastically increase the probability of farmer opposition. If and when high growth returns to the Indian economy and, with it, intensified pressure on land, this leaves coercion as the only remaining method of producing farmer compliance. The Modi government has, as in so many other domains, appeared prepared to resort to authoritarian tactics to acquire land only to be reminded of the issue's political sensitivity among the rural electorate.[44] It seems likely that the Modi government will continue to try to dilute consent and procedural hurdles for business while going easier on compensation. It may pursue a geographically bifurcated model in which it offers material concessions to politically influential farmers in the plains while increasing repression against marginalized or electorally insignificant rural populations that refuse to bargain. But the former are not easily avoided in siting large capital projects and there is no shortage of opposition parties willing to use the issue as a cudgel. The conundrum shows no sign of disappearing; land acquisition is likely to remain the sharpest point of contradiction between capitalist imperatives and democratic politics in India for the foreseeable future.

Notes

1 Sanjoy Chakravorty, *The Price of Land: Acquisition, Conflict, Consequence* (New Delhi: Oxford University Press, 2013).
2 Partha Chatterjee, "Democracy and Economic Transformation in India," *Economic and Political Weekly* 43, no. 16 (2008): 53–62.
3 Michael Levien, "Regimes of Dispossession: From Steel Towns to Special Economic Zones," *Development and Change* 44, no. 2 (2013): 381–407.
4 Karl Polanyi, *The Great Transformation: The Political and Economic Origins of our Time* (Boston: Beacon Press, 2001).
5 Arvind Panagariya, "UPA Hurts India as It Exists," *The Times of India*. March 11, 2014; and Sanjoy Chakravorty, "Improving an Unworkable Law," *The Hindu*, January 7, 2015.
6 C. P., Chandrasekhar and Jayati Gosh, *The Market That Failed: Neoliberal Economic Reforms in India* (New Delhi: LeftWord Books, 2002).
7 Kohli, Atul, *Poverty Amid Plenty in the New India* (Cambridge: Cambridge University Press, 2012), p. 45.
8 Maitreesh Ghatak and Parakshit Ghosh, "The Land Acquisition Bill: A Critique and a Proposal," *Economic and Political Weekly* 46, no. 41 (2011): 65.
9 David Harvey, *The Limits to Capital* (London: Verso, 2006), p. 271.
10 Rob Jenkins, *Democratic Politics and Economic Reform in India* (Cambridge: Cambridge University Press, 1999); and Lloyd I. Rudolph and Susanne Hoeber Rudolph, "Iconisation of Chandrababu: Sharing Sovereignty in India's Federal Market Economy," *Economic and Political Weekly* 36, no. 18 (2001): 1541–52.
11 On the broader trend of land liberalization and new forms of urban governance, see Nikita Sud, *Liberalization, Hindu Nationalism and the State: A Biography of Gujarat* (New Delhi: Oxford University Press, 2012); and Michael Goldman, "Speculative Urbanism and the Making of the Next World City," *International Journal of Urban and Regional Research* 35, no. 3 (2011): 555–81.
12 Kanchan Chandra, "The New Indian State," *Economic & Political Weekly* 50, no. 41 (2015): 46–58.
13 I borrow loosely here from William Sewell's theory of structure-transforming events. William H. Sewell, *Logics of History: Social Theory and Social Transformation* (Chicago: University of Chicago Press, 2005).
14 Then there are states like Bihar that were simply not acquiring much land to begin with. According to one high-level official, this was due to a combination of factors such as very poor land records that greatly complicate the process, and the fact that it was simply "too politically hot potato" in such a contentiousness and electorally competitive state. He explained, "You'll have *dharnas*. Then the political opposition will pick up on it .... It's explosive politically." For want of land, even the enterprising Chief Minister Nitish Kumar was unable to attract companies that wanted to locate in the state (Interview, 7.4.14).
15 BJP President Rajnath Singh also tried to enter the village, but was turned away. He held a twenty-four-hour fast in Ghaziabad to protest "the atrocities of the

UP government and growing lawlessness in the state" NDTV, "Prime Minister Announces Compensation for Bhatta-Parsaul Victims," *NDTV*, May 22, 2011.

16 On a March 2008 visit to Niyamgiri, Gandhi claimed, "Kalahandi [the district of Orissa] and the tribals have one soldier in Delhi, and his name is Rahul Gandhi" (quoted in Rajdeep Sardesai, *2014: The Election that Changed India* (Gurgaon: Penguin, 2014), p. 62). In August of 2010, the environment ministry refused to grant the project environmental clearance. The Minister of Forest and Environment at the time was Jairam Ramesh, a Congressman with close ties to Rahul and Sonia Gandhi, and who subsequently spearheaded the formulation of LARRA as Minister of Rural Development.

17 In interviews, several high-level Congress officials who were deeply involved with LARRA emphasized the importance of the Bhatta-Parsaul agitation, and particularly the role of Rahul Gandhi, in pushing the new bill forward.

18 The BSP ultimately lost, but the Congress failed to capitalize and even lost the Bhatta-Parsaul seat. This appears to have been partly because of overriding caste politics in the region, but may also have been due to Rahul Gandhi's failure to follow through in helping farmers and perhaps Mayawati's change in compensation policies.

19 This included land acquisition for "private companies for the production of goods for public" (which could be presumably be anything), mining activities, highways, ports, power, irrigation, airports, educational, sports, health care, tourism, agro-processing, housing "for such income groups, as may be specified from time to time by the appropriate government," and any other purpose notified by the government. What is significant is that many projects in these sectors are built by private companies on a PPP or purely privatized basis, and have a significant real estate component.

20 Under the Fifth Schedule of the Indian constitution, Scheduled Areas are those designated as having large "tribal" populations.

21 This included the provision of housing units; "land for land" for those displaced by irrigation projects; either mandatory employment for one family member or a Rupees 2,000 per month annuity for twenty years or a one-time payment of Rupees 5 lakh per family; a one year subsistence grant of Rupees 3,000 per month plus an additional Rupees 50,000 for SC and ST families living in scheduled areas; transportation costs for shifting houses; compensation for cattle sheds and small shops; a one-time grant to artisans and small traders; the granting of reservoir fishing rights to those displaced for irrigation projects; a one-time resettlement allowance of Rupees 50,000; and a number of other provisions specifically for SC and ST families.

22 The exception was the position briefly taken by FICCI that the government should not have a role in acquiring land for private companies. This anomolous difference of opinion with CII was explained when FICCI's Secretary General, Amit Mitra, ran for the West Bengal State assembly in 2011 on the TMC ticket, and upon victory became Mamata Banerjee's Finance, Commerce and Industries Minister. FICCI's position on the issue promptly took a 180-degree turn and aligned with that of the other industry associations.

23 Ramesh summarized the contrasting positions thus: "you see, the one set of stakeholders wanted to make the bill more progressive, you know, and they felt that compensation was inadequate, the definition of public purpose was very broad, and they didn't want any acquisition for private companies or for PPP projects. This is what I would call the progressive view. Then you had the industry view, and the builder view … which said that, look, just increase compensation, you know, make

it eight times or ten times, and be done with it, don't tamper with the structure of the law, and don't introduce any provisions that would make acquisition time-consuming, or subject to public approval .... They were against the idea of social impact assessment. They were against the idea that the Gram Sabha should give its approval for land acquisition" (Interview, 7.5.14).

24 According to Mander, Ramesh found the NAC draft to "fundamentalist" and "anti-industry."

25 A Group of Ministers, or GoM, was a widely used device in the UPA government to sort out disagreements between coalition partners over its Minimum Common Program.

26 Anita Joshua, "New Land Acquisition Law Rolled Out," *The Hindu*, January 1, 2014.

27 Subodh Ghildiyal, "Sonia Gandhi Vetoes Dilution of Land Acquisition Bill," *The Times of India*, October 20, 2012.

28 In one of several spirited exchanges, TMC Rajya Sabha member—and game show personality—Derek O'Brien referred in his speech to the May 2007 Nandigram violence as the "Ides of March," and the best evidence that the land acquisitions system "Needed to be rescued from self-serving brokers and agents such as those who live in the headquarters of Alimuddin Street in Kolkata" (Parliament of India 2013).

29 After which it had be reintroduced to the Lok Sabha and passed a second time with amendments.

30 It is unclear why it was there in the first place, as the SEZ Act does itself contain provisions for land acquisition. State governments had been acquiring land for SEZs using the LAA.

31 "Land Acquisition Act Will Help Tribals and Farmers: Jairam Ramesh," *The Hindu*, September 29, 2013.

32 Ray and Katzenstein 2005.

33 Ramesh rationalized this concession by claiming, "In any case, I feel irrigation is a public good, done by governments, and is essential for agricultural prosperity." T. K. Rajalakshmi, "'This is Not the Best but It Is Progressive,'" *Frontline*, September 18, 2013.

34 Tehelka, "Land Ahoy!" *Tehelka*, July 26, 2014.

35 Marx 1978[1952]; Nicos Poulantzaz, "The Problem of the Capitalist State," *New Left Review* 58 (1969): 238–62.

36 Varad Pande, "A Business Case for the New Land Acquisition Law." *Mint*. September 9, 2013.

37 "Land Acquisition Bill: Policy Can Create Conditions to Soften the Blow," *The Economic Times*, August 21, 2013.

38 Arvind Panagariya, "UPA Hurts India as It Exists," *The Times of India*, March 11, 2014.

39 Sanjoy Chakravorty, *The Price of Land: Acquisition, Conflict, Consequence* (New Delhi: Oxford University Press, 2013). And Sanjoy, Chakravorty, "Improving an Unworkable Law," *The Hindu*, January 7, 2015.

40 Abhijit Vinayak Banerjee, et al., "Beyond Nandigram: Industrialisation in West Bengal," *Economic and Political Weekly* 42, no. 17 (2007): 1487–9; Pranab Bardhan, "Industrialization and the Land Acquisition Conundrum," *Development Outreach* (April 2011): 54–7. Sanjoy Chakravorty, *The Price of Land: Acquisition, Conflict, Consequence* (New Delhi: Oxford University Press, 2013).

41 Atul Kohli, *Poverty amid Plenty in the New India* (Cambridge: Cambridge University Press, 2012); Jean Dreze and Amartya Sen, *An Uncertain Glory: India and Its Contradictions* (Princeton: Princeton University Press, 2013).

42 Partha Chatterjee, "Democracy and Economic Transformation in India," *Economic and Political Weekly* 43, no. 16 (2008): 53–62. In addition to providing no analytical leverage, the term"political society" is a misleading lens for these land struggles, as Baviskar and Sundar observe. What could be more "civil society" than organizing protests, pressuring political parties, filing legal cases, and participating in parliamentary debates around a new "rights-based legislation"? A. Baviskar and N. Sundar, "Democracy versus Economic Transformation?" *Economic and Political Weekly* (November 15, 2008): 87–9.

43 Manu Menon, Kanchi Kohli and Debayan Gupta, "In State-Level Changes to Land Laws, a Return to Land Grabbing in Development's Name," *The Wire*, September 28, 2017. Bhasker Tripathi, "Conflicts across India as States Create Land Banks for Private Investors," *IndiaSpend*, September 18, 2017.

44 The June 2014 leaking of an IB report accusing NGOs involved in supporting land acquisition and antinuclear protests as development-obstructing agents of foreign interests appeared to be preparing the ground a crackdown.

Select Bibliography

Ahluwalia, Isher Judge, "The Contribution of Planning to Indian Industrialisation," in Terence J. Byres, ed., *The State, Development Planning and Liberalisation in India* (New Delhi: Oxford University Press, 1998), pp. 254–97.

Banerjee, Abhijit Vinayak, et al., "Beyond Nandigram: Industrialisation in West Bengal," *Economic and Political Weekly* 42, no. 17 (2007): 1487–9.

Bardhan, Pranab, *Awakening Giants, Feet of Clay: Assessing the Economic Rise of China and India* (Princeton: Princeton University Press, 2010).

Bardhan, Pranab, "Industrialization and the Land Acquisition Conundrum," *Development Outreach* (April 2011): 54–7.

Bardhan, Pranab, *The Political Economy of Development in India* (Delhi: Oxford University Press, 1984).

Baviskar, A. and N. Sundar, "Democracy versus Economic Transformation?" *Economic and Political Weekly* (November 15, 2008): 87–9.

Bhanot, Renu and Mridula Singh, "The Oustees of Pong Dam: Their Search for a Home," in Enakshi Ganguly Thukral, ed., *Big Dams, Displaced People* (New Delhi: Sage Publications, 1992), pp. 101–42.

Burman, Roy, "Social Processes in the Industrialisation of Rourkela (with Reference to Displacement and Rehabilitation of Tribal and Other Backward People)" (1968).

Cernea, Michael, *The Economics of Involuntary Resettlement: Questions and Challenges* (Washington, DC: World Bank, 1999).

CMIE (Center for Monitoring Indian Economy), "Sharp Increase in Projects Getting Shelved," Retrieved August 15, 2012. (http://www.cmie.com/kommon/bin/sr.php?kall=wclrdhtm.php&cmienvdt=20120704101759176&pc=099000000000&type=INSIGHTS).

Chakravorty, Sanjoy, "Improving an Unworkable Law," *The Hindu*, January 7, 2015.

Chakravorty, Sanjoy, *The Price of Land: Acquisition, Conflict, Consequence* (New Delhi: Oxford University Press, 2013).

Chandra, Kanchan, "The New Indian State," *Economic & Political Weekly* 50, no. 41 (2015): 46–58.

Chandrasekhar, C. P. and Jayati Gosh, *The Market That Failed: Neoliberal Economic Reforms in India* (New Delhi: Left Word Books, 2002).

Chatterjee, Partha, "Democracy and Economic Transformation in India," *Economic and Political Weekly* 43, no. 16 (2008): 53–62.

Chaturvedi, Rakesh Mohan and C. L. Manoj, "NCP Chief Sharad Pawar Brings Anti-Land Bill Parties Together," *The Economic Times*, July 29, 2015.

Duflo, Esther and Rohini Pande, "Dams," *The Quarterly Journal of Economics* 122, no. 2 (2007): 601–46.

Dreze, Jean and Amartya Sen, *An Uncertain Glory: India and Its Contradictions* (Princeton: Princeton University Press, 2013).

Dwivedi, Ranjit, *Conflict and Collective Action: The Sardar Sarovar Project in India* (London: Routledge, 2006).

Fernandes, Walter, "Sixty Years of Development-induced Displacement in India," in Hari Mohan Mathur, ed., *India Social Development Report 2008: Development and Displacement* (New Delhi: Oxford University Press, 2008), pp. 89–102.

Fernandes, Walter and Enakshi Ganguly Thukral, eds., *Development, Displacement, and Rehabilitation: Issues for a National Debate* (New Delhi: Indian Social Institute, 1989).

Ghatak, Maitreesh and Parakshit Ghosh, "The Land Acquisition Bill: A Critique and a Proposal," *Economic and Political Weekly* 46, no. 41 (2011): 65–72.

Goldman, Michael, "Speculative Urbanism and the Making of the Next World City," *International Journal of Urban and Regional Research* 35, no. 3 (2011): 555–81.

Government of India, *The Land Acquisition, Rehabilitation and Resettlement Bill, 2011: Report of the Standing Committee on Rural Development* (New Delhi: Lok Sabha Secretariat, 2012).

Guha, Ramachandra, *India after Gandhi: The History of the World's Largest Democracy* (London: Macmillan, 2007).

Gulati, Manisha, "The Infrastructure Sector in India 2010–2011," in *India Infrastructure Report 2011: Water: Policy and Performance for Sustainable Development* (New Delhi: Oxford University Press, 2011), pp. 379–96.

Hart, Henry C., *New India's Rivers* (Bombay: Orient Longman, 1956).

Harvey, David, *The Limits to Capital* (London: Verso, 2006).

IDFC (Infrastructure Development Finance Corporation), *India Infrastructure Report 2008: Business Models of the Future* (New Delhi: Oxford University Press, 2008).

IDFC (Infrastructure Development Finance Corporation), *India Infrastructure Report 2009: Land—A Critical Resource for Infrastructure* (New Delhi: Oxford University Press).

Jenkins, Rob, *Democratic Politics and Economic Reform in India* (Cambridge: Cambridge University Press, 1999).

Kale, Sunila S., "Democracy and the State in Globalizing India: A Case Study of Odisha," *India Review* 12, no. 4 (2013): 245–59.

Kale, Sunila S. and Nimah Mazaheri, "Natural Resources, Development Strategies, and Lower Caste Empowerment in India's Mineral Belt: Bihar and Odisha during the 1990s," *Studies in Comparative International Development* 49 (2014): 343–69.

Kalia, Ravi, *Chandigarh: The Making of an Indian City* (New Delhi: Oxford University Press, 1999).

Khagram, Sanjeev, *Dams and Development: Transnational Struggles for Water and Power* (Ithaca: Cornell University Press, 2004).
Klingensmith, Daniel, *"One Valley and a Thousand": Dams, Nationalism, and Development* (New Delhi: Oxford University Press, 2007).
Kohli, Atul, *Poverty amid Plenty in the New India* (Cambridge: Cambridge University Press, 2012).
Kothari, Rajni, "The Non-Party Political Process," *Economic and Political Weekly* 19, no. 5 (1984): 216–24.
Krishnan, Eesvan, "Land Acquisition in British India, c. 1894–1927," Doctor of Philosophy, University of Oxford, 2014.
Levien, Michael, "Special Economic Zones and Accumulation by Dispossession in India," *Journal of Agrarian Change* 11, no. 4 (2011): 454–83.
Levien, Michael, "The Land Question: Special Economic Zones and the Political Economy of Dispossession in India," *Journal of Peasant Studies* 39, nos. 3–4 (2012): 933–69.
Levien, Michael, "The Politics of Dispossession: Theorizing India's 'Land Wars,'" *Politics & Society* 41, no. 3 (2013): 351–94.
Levien, Michael, "Regimes of Dispossession: From Steel Towns to Special Economic Zones," *Development and Change* 44, no. 2 (2013a): 381–407.
Mankodi, K. "Resettlement and Rehabilitation of Dam Oustees: A Case Study of Ukai Dam," in E. G. Thukral, ed., *Big Dams, Displaced People* (New Delhi: Sage Publications, 1992), pp. 77–100.
Nilsen, Alf Gunvald, *Dispossession and Resistance in India: The River and the Rage* (London: Routledge, 2010).
Pande, Varad, "A Business Case for the New Land Acquisition Law," *Mint*, September 9, 2013.
Parasuraman, S., *The Development Dilemma: Displacement in India* (New York: St. Martin's Press, 1999).
Parry, Jonathan P. and Christian Struempell, "On the Desecration of Nehru's 'Temples': Bhilai and Rourkela Compared," *Economic and Political Weekly* 43, no. 19 (2008): 47–57.
Polanyi, Karl, *The Great Transformation: The Political and Economic Origins of Our Time* (Boston: Beacon Press, 2001).
Poulantzaz, Nicos, "The Problem of the Capitalist State," *New Left Review* 58 (1969): 238–62.
Rudolph, Lloyd I. and Susanne Hoeber Rudolph, "Iconisation of Chandrababu: Sharing Sovereignty in India's Federal Market Economy," *Economic and Political Weekly* 36, no. 18 (2001): 1541–52.
Sangvai, Sanjay, *The River and Life: People's Struggle in the Narmada Valley* (Mumbai: Earthcare Books, 2002).
Sanyal, Kalyan, *Rethinking Capitalist Development: Primitive Accumulation, Governmentality, and Post-colonial Capitalism* (New Delhi: Routledge, 2007).
Scott, James C., *Weapons of the Weak: Everyday Forms of Peasant Resistance* (New Haven: Yale University Press, 1985).
Searle, Rena, "Making Space for Capital: The Production of Global Landscapes in Contemporary India," Unpublished PhD dissertation, University of Pennsylvania, 2010.
Sharma, S., "The Vanquished Tribal World of Shifting Cultivation," in A. Bhalla, ed., *Images of Rural India in the 20th Century* (New Delhi: Sterling Publishers, 1992), pp. 69–85.

Struempell, Christian, “The Politics of Dispossession in an Odisha Steel Town,” *Contributions to Indian Sociology* 48, no. 1 (2014): 45–72.

Sud, Nikita, *Liberalization, Hindu Nationalism and the State: A Biography of Gujarat* (New Delhi: Oxford University Press, 2012).

Sundar, Nandini, *The Burning Forest: India's War in Bastar* (New Delhi: Juggernaut Press, 2016).

Thukral, Enakshi Ganguly, ed., *Big Dams, Displaced People* (New Delhi: Sage Publications, 1992).

Tripathi, Bhasker, “Conflicts across India as States Create Land Banks for Private Investors,” *IndiaSpend*, September 18, 2017.

Part Three

Political Commentaries

11

Remembering the Emergency and the Question of Politics

Mary E. John

Introduction

It is a truism that all histories, one way or another, are histories of the present. This essay was conceived and drafted in the months following the fatal gang rape of Jyoti Singh in the city of Delhi. Everyone is no doubt aware of the gang rape that took place on December 16, 2012, in a bus plying at night on a major arterial road that circles the city, and, more especially, of its aftermath. India Gate—since many years a depoliticized place for family and tourist outings, surrounded by looming sandstone structures housing major government ministries, with the President's Estate on the horizon—was taken over for several days on by thousands of protestors demanding justice for the victim and freedom for women. Women's organizations and student groups had taken out their own processions prior to this outpouring, well covered in the press and media, but no one was prepared for the kind of groundswell that was to follow. Most surprising of all, however, was the response of the state to these protests, which took the form of imposing Section 144 of the Criminal Procedure Code. Put in place in 1860 after the Indian "Mutiny" of 1857 when India came directly under the British Crown and new governance structures were created, Section 144 prohibits the "unlawful assembly" of not more than ten persons, and is usually associated with riots and mob violence. The language of the text of the law, which can be imposed by a magistrate in what is called "an emergent situation" to prevent "public nuisance and damage to public tranquillity" is suitably Victorian. By law, Section 144 is a temporary measure. But, in the intervening months, it took on a permanent quality in Delhi itself, one usually associated with "distant" regions of militarization and conflict such as Kashmir, the North Eastern states, or Chhattisgarh. In the years after "the Emergency" of 1975 these areas had become the not-so-little emergencies constitutive of present-day India. But Delhi too was no longer immune. When a night protest at India Gate was planned in June 2013 by students opposing the Delhi University's decision to summarily introduce a four-year undergraduate programme in place of its existing three-year degree structure—any student who turned up at the venue was immediately arrested and jailed. Therefore, even the urban middle classes, India's quintessential citizens, now lived in times when any protest in the capital city, it would appear, could be deemed to be a potential emergency.

This experience stoked the sense of disquiet I had come to feel about certain default notions of the political held by those like myself with explicit affiliations to movements (in my case the women's movement). Put baldly, being political amounts more or less to taking an oppositional stance to power, along with the corollary that such opposition makes common cause with democracy. This has the effect of making the political only too legible, leaving too many issues and problems untouched. My fear was that our taken-for-granted alignments with politics could be in some danger of turning into an alibi, especially in times increasingly dominated by right-wing regimes. It is not accidental that recent years have witnessed the rising hegemony of a certain version of democratic politics, one however, that narrows down the problem of politics and severely compresses histories of political engagement, visions of alternate social orders, the nature of the state, and so on. Precisely because we live out the political as active members of movements, moreover, these very movements have suffered from a lack of political reflection.

These probings into default notions of the political took me, perhaps not so surprisingly, to "the Emergency," as the internal Emergency years in India between 1975–7 have simply been called. In his contribution to this volume, Aditya Nigam has also asked for a reexamination of contemporary notions of politics. His focus is on mass movements within actually functioning democracies, rather than, say, third-world dictatorships or periods of authoritarian rule. While he wonders whether the "anti-political" stand of some of these movements in relation to political parties could be inaugurating a new kind of politics altogether, my questions took me backwards in time. In my view, the National Emergency of 1975–7 has not just been the site of the birth of many contemporary movements such as the women's movement, it has gone on to shape dominant conceptions of the political itself, while effectively submerging a host of problems that in fact came to a head during this very period. Born of the Emergency as these movements are, they have been coloured by a certain experience of power as primarily repressive, and the imperative for a resistance that is largely oppositional. I began my search with the received wisdom that the Emergency has been given scant attention, granting it at most "exceptional" status. In the popular academic imagination, the Emergency is all but forgotten, or so the story goes. But this could not be more mistaken—activists and scholars have certainly not left the Emergency untouched. Even more interesting is how remarkably divergent existing views turn out to be, both in their modes of analysis and in terms of the significance placed upon it. Indeed it is this very divergence, the kinds of questions that analyses of the Emergency have left in their wake, and what some of these views nonetheless share that has helped open up the challenging and at times intractable dimensions of the political that a narrow conception hides from view.

The next sections of this chapter attempt brief summaries of major perspectives on the Emergency: For some it is indeed debatable as to what place this particular period should occupy in India's post independence history, others have explored it through the lens of a "critical event," yet others believe it to be no less than a watershed for grasping the changing nature of contemporary politics. I will further suggest another reading of the Emergency, one that makes room for how the Emergency was even seen to have been enabling of progressive political agendas. Taken together these interpretations provide important insights into the dissatisfaction with the political I have tried to articulate, its taken-for-granted legibility. They also reveal significant gaps in analyses, namely the nature and scope of social movements.

Though drafted in the wake of the gang rape of 2012,[1] the final revisions to this essay took place after Narendra Modi's unprecedented reelection in 2019. My concluding question can therefore only be, what can one make of the repeated invocation that we now live in the times of an undeclared Emergency, whose end is nowhere in sight?

The Indian Emergency in Contemporary History

> Throughout the sixty years since India became independent,
> there has been speculation about how long it would stay united,
> or maintain the institutions and processes of democracy.
> Ramachandra Guha,
>
> *India after Gandhi: The History of the World's Largest Democracy*, 2007

A certain commonsense circulates widely in India about the National Emergency that was imposed by Prime Minister Indira Gandhi in 1975, to be lifted less than two years later when elections were called and she and her Congress Party were swept out of power. The anthropologist Emma Tarlo has summed it up as an attitude of "collective silence which often clings to violent and disturbing events."[2] The historian Ramachandra Guha believes that Indians suffer from a deeper malaise, namely that of having failed to appreciate the very history of the nation that is India. The problem, according to him, is strictly speaking academic—history, as the study of the past, ended on August 15, 1947, the minute India became an independent nation. In the decades that followed we have had to rest content with political scientists studying general elections once in five years and social anthropologists visiting Indian villages every decade or so.[3]

Obviously, such remarks are meant to provoke rather than stand as statements of fact. A number of scholars, political scientists, and legal theorists being rather prominent among them, have offered extensive reflections on various aspects related to the Emergency—Bipan Chandra, Ayesha Jalal, Rajni Kothari, Lloyd and Suzanne Rudolph, Partha Chatterjee, Granville Austin, Anil Kalhan, Vasuki Nesiah, Arvind Rajagopal among others, apart from numerous commentaries by politicians, government officials, activists, and observers. P. N. Lekhi, among those arrested in 1975 and who then served on the Shah Commission (set up to investigate the constitutionality of the Emergency after it was lifted), has pointed out that strictly speaking between the ratification of the Constitution on January 26, 1950, and the lifting of the internal Emergency on March 22, 1977, the nation was under a state of emergency for almost half of those years. The difference was that whereas the others were fully "consensual," being in response to a state of external threat and war (the war with China in 1962, the war with Pakistan in 1964, and the war over the "liberation" of Bangladesh from Pakistan in 1971), the declaration of the internal Emergency came as a "thief at midnight," with estimates of 150,000 people forcibly detained, among other fundamental violations.[4] And what of the growing militarization of significant regions—not just the frontier states of Kashmir and the North-East, but India's so-called "Red corridor"?

But Guha's voluminous record of India after independence clearly seeks to attest that this is a history of a more rather than less triumphant democracy. So yes, its blood-soaked beginnings, which included the assassination of Mahatma Gandhi, could be equally described as "Independence" or "Partition." The subsequent decades of Jawaharlal Nehru's rule involved wars with Pakistan and China as well as vain efforts to steer India's economy through the unchartered waters of a "mixed economy," in which Soviet-style Five Year Plans coexisted uneasily with a growing capitalist class. The reign of his daughter Indira Gandhi, despite being the one who imposed the Emergency and suspended parliamentary democracy, included her triumphant return to power in 1980 via free and fair elections, only to be gunned down in 1984 by her Sikh bodyguards. Finally, it is Nehru's grandson and Indira's son—Rajiv Gandhi—who authored the next installment of this dynastic history by setting the stage for a new mode of governance that would eventually transmute into "neo-liberalism." According to Guha, despite all of these and much more, Indian democracy is protected by the very features—size and extreme diversity—that colonialists and Western observers were fond of citing as reasons why India was (and certainly would be) an impossible and ungovernable nation. Indeed, Guha goes even further to suggest that India's deep inequalities, however problematic, also turn out to be a strength, making dictatorial rule an exception.

According to this reading, then, India has so indigenized the notion of democracy, including a form of nationalism without the cultural, ethnic or linguistic "glue" that the Western world set up as the mandatory model, that those two years some decades ago when India's first and only woman Prime Minister suspended fundamental democratic rights, arrested tens of thousands of political opponents, and subjected the urban poor to evictions and sterilizations, could be comfortably cast as a small chapter headed "The Autumn of the Matriarch."[5] The problem, according to Guha, was individual not institutional. Whatever its virtues, this mode of writing a third world nation's history does not lend itself to raising any further questions about the nature of the political, since it has the effect rather of rendering such inquiry superfluous.

Let me turn to the views of another historian of our present, Partha Chatterjee. Guha fails to acknowledge that the fiftieth anniversary of Indian Independence in 1997 was an obvious occasion for gauging the state of the nation, and resulted in a spate of volumes on the subject.[6] The particular text that interests me here is Chatterjee's *A Possible India*, which is a compendium of pieces of varying length, many of which first appeared as weekly commentaries in the journal *Frontier*, and which he offered in 1997 in place of "the book on Indian politics that he will never write."[7] Chatterjee writes about issues occasionally with the benefit of hindsight, but more often just as or even before they unfolded. The earliest two articles in this collection in fact book-end the Emergency: The first was written a few months before the Emergency was actually imposed in June 1975, while the second essay was published soon after it was lifted when general elections were held.

Chatterjee sets the tone with his perspective on the unprecedented task before the Indian nation state, one that was unique in modern world history. " … [T]he Indian bourgeoisie was faced with a challenge which no bourgeoisie in the world has ever tackled successfully: to make an industrial revolution under capitalism within a political structure of electoral democracy and universal adult suffrage."[8] Taking his examples from European history, he identifies the two paths unavailable to India—the "classical" English form where political democracy is only achieved well after capitalism has been established, including the conquest of social hegemony by the bourgeoisie; and secondly, the German Prussian path where an absolutist, centralized and undemocratic state initiated the necessary capital accumulation, thus demanding a union of state and civil society, which culminated in fascism. (Interestingly, for someone who, as he says in the Preface, was at this stage in his intellectual formation drawing quite "unabashedly" from the conceptual apparatus of Marx, Lenin and Mao Zedong, the trajectories of China or Russia are never brought into the discussion.) As Chatterjee emphasizes, India inherited a national movement with a complex and deep structure of support across classes both urban and rural, and had to chart a path of development with a weak bourgeoisie in a land-scarce labor-surplus economy. Beginning already with Nehru, this led, in his view, to a form of "Caesarism," a concept taken straight from Antonio Gramsci's *Prison Notebooks*.[9] Caesarism refers to a kind of political brinkmanship, whereby first Nehru and then Indira Gandhi, managed to appear as a neutral party above the various contending ruling forces while offering a populist "socialist" ideology, but without the structural reforms that would make socialism more genuine.

Most accounts of the imposition of the Emergency have emphasized its repressive effects, unleashed to contain a growing economic crisis and consequent unrest by groups and movements, ranging from political opponents, Maoist inspired insurgencies, workers, peasants, tribals, students, and even housewives. Chatterjee argues instead that the Emergency was necessitated by the very logic of Caesarism itself. When Indira Gandhi's election was in danger of being challenged by the Allahabad High Court order (on technical grounds), this required a new level of centralization through emergency powers, for which there was considerable consent, at least initially. Two consequences led to its subsequent collapse. On the one hand, the very loss of the mechanisms that had earlier ensured the balance of forces—between the centre and the states, the business classes and the landed gentry. On the other, popular opposition to those government schemes wreaked especially on the poor in north India, the urban resettlement and more widespread family planning programmes (about which more shortly).

Chatterjee's formulations raise some very important questions. Firstly, there are no signs that the Emergency was an area of silence, indeed it appears to have been a definitive if not formative experience. But there is more. Reading Chatterjee with the benefit of hindsight makes palpable the significant shifts in his frames of analysis, so that it is not just the importance of a particular historical moment—here the Emergency—that is at issue but the very language deployed to explain it.

There is the initial confidence with which a certain Marxist vocabulary was made to work so seamlessly to illuminate the event and the processes that led to it. This language is not always as visible in the subsequent commentaries in the book that deal with the tumultuous years that followed. Writing some years later in the crisis ridden year of 1984 Chatterjee re-emphasizes the Caesarist thesis, seeing in the rule of Indira Gandhi the shift from the earlier more diffuse representational function of the Congress Party across levels and regions, to its concentration "in the fountainhead of all representation—the person of the Prime Minister who, beyond all political divides, loyalties, interest groups, supposedly stood in a direct relationship with the nation."[10] Chatterjee struggles to name the crisis brought about by the Emergency as fundamentally a crisis of the state itself, in its developmental if not socialist form. Its centralizing tendency, resort to state violence and the wielding of arbitrary power made the system inherently unstable, while no other viable political organization of class rule seemed to be in the offing. The Left, in his view, ought to have stepped in at this point to provide an alternative, but instead was caught within the very same language of national unity, secularism, divisive tendencies and so on. Writing a decade later in 1996, the shift in analysis is more discernable: a decaying centre, growing antidemocratic attitudes among the elites and well-educated and a pushing downwards of what Chatterjee calls democracy's centre of gravity. This morphs into the "politics of the governed" where the older conflicts between capitalist growth and democratic transformation continue, but in a world in which Chatterjee has given up the possibility that "the masses will be anything other than the objects of government."[11] He now sees a triumphant bourgeoisie supported by civil society in the form of the urban middle classes as having successfully brought India to its neoliberal present. Has, then, the unprecedented happened that he earlier thought was simply impossible, namely the achievement of capitalist hegemony under conditions of liberal democracy by a third world nation?[12] Or to put this differently, has the crisis of the developmental state, earlier articulated in the Marxist vocabulary of Caesarism and made visible by the Emergency, been resolved by the Foucauldian turn to governmentality under neoliberalism?

To me, therefore, the importance of revisiting the Emergency lies in the need to reflect more explicitly and critically on such shifting conceptualizations of the realm of the political itself, the state and its citizens, from Caesarism and the possibilities of socialism, to the battles of civil and political society, democracy and corporate capitalism. In some of Chatterjee's more recent writing the Emergency and the populist power of Indira Gandhi continue to be significant points of reference. This is evident in his reflections on three contemporary political imaginaries in this volume. In response to critics who find his conception of political society to be too bound up in local community negotiations for government benefits and without a larger politics of resistance to state oppression, Chatterjee sees political society as marking a new democratic moment precisely in the wake of the acknowledged failures of the Emergency in its repressive dealings with the urban poor. He even suggests that political society can evolve further into larger mobilizations through caste blocs or at the regional level. It is only a new federalism that could offer a challenge to heightened centralization and Modi's nationalism.[13]

Before I take these questions further, let me introduce a rather different optic onto the significance of the Emergency, namely that of an anthropologically constructed "critical event."

The Emergency as Critical Event

> It is impossible to draw an ethnography of the fear that spread amongst the capital's poor, fed by a combination of rumour, reality, imagination and experience.
> Emma Tarlo,
> *Unsettling memories, Narratives of India's "Emergency,"* 2003.

The anthropologist Emma Tarlo accidentally discovered the Emergency, she says, when the three wheeler she was traveling in lost its way while in search of a poor Delhi neighbourhood for another study. Landing up inside the municipal office of what turned out to be a resettlement colony, its dusty untouched files yielded up accounts of the history of its inhabitants that took her to the Emergency years because that was when most of them were brought to this locality after their slum dwellings were demolished elsewhere. Her book *Unsettling Memories: Narratives of India's "Emergency"* seeks to ethnographically establish the meaning of the Emergency as it is now remembered by the men and women whom she encountered and interviewed in the course of this new research. She explicitly tries to figure her study as a "critical event." This term comes from the work of Veena Das, who in her much acclaimed book *Critical Events* published in 1995 brought the discipline of social anthropology, more known for its descriptions of traditional villages and cultural practices, into a rather different relationship with contemporary India and its recent history as a nation. Interestingly for our purposes here, the Emergency does not figure anywhere in Das' chosen catalogue of such events, which begins with the Partition experience of British India between 1947 and 1950 and ends with the *sati* (widow immolation) of Roop Kanwar in the state of Rajasthan in 1987.

Emma Tarlo sharply juxtaposes the voices of the people she interviews to two master narratives, as she calls them. The first is the official version of the Emergency as it was extolled by Indira Gandhi and the Congress Party, only to be subsequently expunged through the state's reshaping of public memory after it was lifted. The second is the counter narrative of political opposition, barely audible during the regime of state censorship but which then rose to a crescendo when the Emergency ended. Tarlo's account of the latter is the weakest aspect of the book, in spite of her awareness of the range of experiences and political perspectives of those thrown into jail or forced to go underground, of others who later "confessed" to their complicity, the many revelations and claims of a "second independence." She reduces this heterogeneous opposition to a simple "tragi-comedy"[14] based on texts written in the mode of hyperbolic excess, which, after all, belongs to all such political moments. These counter narratives are written off for being elite, for falsely claiming to represent "the people," and for being unable to sustain themselves for long.

Be that as it may, the "people" are at the heart of Tarlo's ethnography, rendered real through the anthropologist's face-to-face encounters in a space of proximity. We hear the voices of men and women, Hindu and Muslim, the Scheduled Caste municipal employee, upper caste school teacher, demolition worker, government clerk. All of them are asked to recall those times when the bull dozers came unannounced, when they found themselves with nothing but a tiny patch of land in a wilderness, or were able to buy off the government by offering others in their place in the sterilization campaigns. The Emergency is approached as a "puzzle," with many pieces missing, difficult to figure out. Tarlo is at her best when she questions her own assumptions about what it means to have suffered that time, discovering that "forced deals" and the capacity of some to play the system at another's expense even from a position of vulnerability gives more interpretive scope to this critical event, however traumatic. In place of the helpless suffering and noble resistance held aloft in post-Emergency oppositional narratives, she sees her task as one of establishing what it meant to survive when the sterilization certificate functioned as an identity card, a passport for life itself under conditions of state control. The most frightening aspect of an oppressive regime, in her view, is its ability to induce participation—this was a critical event that, above all, produced active victims.

But what flummoxes Tarlo even further is that her respondents, without exception, eulogize Indira Gandhi. She fully expected to discover that Indira Gandhi and especially her son Sanjay Gandhi (infamous for his proactive role in the demolition drives in Delhi) would be cast as villains, no less. But even those who had changed their allegiance from the Congress in the intervening years of growing religious communalization among both Hindus and Muslims, confined their criticisms and disappointments to the present time and its rulers. Tarlo asks herself how different these people's views were from the official discourse of the Emergency propounded by Indira Gandhi herself and her supporters. When it came to laying blame for what people had undergone, it was not the leadership that Tarlo's respondents faulted but the various middlemen and low level state functionaries they had encountered in their everyday lives—doctors and nurses, clerks and petty bureaucrats, local political leaders and their henchmen. But wasn't this precisely what Indira Gandhi had claimed in the last days of Emergency rule, that there was nothing wrong with her policies, only with their abuse by some overzealous officials?

Tarlo feels her way somewhat tentatively here. She accepts the people of the resettlement neighbourhood as the ultimate pragmatists—all they wanted was an end to the demolitions and sterilizations. The Emergency by no means occasioned a transformation of political consciousness, indeed, it brought out the ways in which, depending on one's location in a hierarchy of social relationships, people act in order to survive. At another level she wonders what changes or improvements subsequent regimes brought to their lives, if any. And finally, she tries to bring together the counternarrative of opposition—characterized by shock, guilt, and fear, as well as resistance—with these people's memories, as stoked by her desire to create an ethnography out of them. The final words in her book are "complexity" and "contradiction," frequently deployed phrases among academics when closure is required, in this case about the puzzle of what it means to be political.

But if Tarlo is unclear about what made this critical event a transformative one, another commentator writing somewhat later is quite unambiguous—the Emergency was nothing less than a watershed in India's postindependence history.

The Emergency as a Watershed in Indian Politics

> [During the Emergency] 'middle class' became a proxy for state reason, ventriloquizing arguments and designs of those at the helm of government and a force for criticism when government views were ignored or overlooked in the political process.
>
> Arvind Rajagopal, "The Emergency as Prehistory of the New Indian Middle Class" 2011.

In an article positioning itself against the existing scholarship, Arvind Rajagopal has argued that the profound role of the Emergency in bringing the nation from a phase of state led development to the present era of neoliberalism has been quite decisively missed out.[15] His explicit focus is on what he calls the New Indian Middle Class. This is the class that becomes, according to Rajagopal, the "humble hero" of national development after the Emergency, not the state itself and least of all the state's professed interest in the welfare of the poor. If we to go back to Partha Chatterjee's arguments about the nature of Caesarist rule and its role in maintaining a balance of forces between contending ruling classes (the capitalists and the rural landlords), Rajagopal is making a claim about the significance of a different class fraction. This is a class that is wooed for its financial savings by a new generation of corporate entrepreneurs, that must be addressed through a governmental apparatus of consent, and for whom, therefore, new communication strategies must be devised. Finally, this is a class that defines its identity in terms of culture and consumption, in sharp opposition to the labour led ethos of the preceding era.

The Emergency in this account is thus understood to have been a crucible of extraordinary proportions. It was required to bridge a massive divide in economic regimes, by a combination of a system of coercion and a freeing up of new forces that would gain hegemony in the decades that followed. In its broadest strokes such shifts have been witnessed across the globe, both East and West, as welfarist or more socialist oriented modes of development yielded to market led and consumer oriented economies. More specific to India, perhaps, is Rajagopal's parallel claim that prior left politics shaped by labour struggles gave way to struggles over community and culture, as religious communalism and anticaste movements filled the vacuum left by workers' strikes and lockouts in the 1980s and thereafter. Rajagopal's specific argument in the context of India's parliamentary system was that Indira Gandhi believed fully in her Caesarist relationship to the people. This included her capacity to use ideologically populist policies for the benefit of the poor even if it cost her some opposition from the business classes, because they were nonetheless dependent on state support. What she misjudged was the role that coercion and censorship would play among the middle classes, through the subsequent campaigns of the opposition and the role of the Press.

> Thus, the Emergency itself may be said to have brought to a crisis the era of the developmental state, with its assurance that planners and policy-makers could assess what the people wanted and dictate accordingly. It showed the limits of the state's capacity to govern without actively and continuously seeking and winning popular consent .... The complementary era of market liberalization, involving new arguments pertaining to the economy.., highlighted the relatively autonomous domain of public opinion as an emergent second layer of the state that was, however, not distinguishable *as* the state.[16]

There is much in Rajagopal's ambitiously formulated claims that need more careful attention. He is certainly not as alone as he might think he is in making them. Many of his arguments have been prefigured by no other than P.N. Dhar, Indira Gandhi's Secretary during those very years, though with interesting differences. Dhar (echoing Chatterjee's discussions mentioned earlier) sees the justification of the Emergency for a generation of "soft" national leaders who had been shaped by opposition to the state and its laws under colonialism, but who now needed to manage the process of capital accumulation necessary for economic transformation under universal adult suffrage. Political unrest, *pace* Rajagopal, was not only prominently created through left led labour struggles and militancy, but by movements like the Nav Nirman movement with Rightwing Hindu cadre of the Rashtriya Swayam Sevak Sangh (RSS) at their core, by the leadership of Jayaprakash Narayan who defied any of the labels "Marxist, socialist, Gandhian, anarchist and populist"[17] that might be thrown at him, but also globally by an economic crisis engendered by the OPEC oil prices hike. Therefore, according to Dhar, the Congress needed the Emergency to undo the power of state led economic policies and so allow the capitalist classes to expand and gain greater control. Thus while both Dhar and Rajagopal figure the Emergency as a clear historical divide, Dhar is more triumphant where Rajagopal is critical. I find myself closer to Dhar when it comes to considering the range of movements of the 1960s and early 70s which can hardly be simply reduced to labour and Trade Union activism—to add to Dhar's list, there was student unrest of an unprecedented scale backed by a range of political parties in several regions, the birth of the militant Shiv Sena in Bombay with its language of Maratha pride, new political actors like housewives who took to the streets to protest spiraling prices, along with violent opposition to caste based reservations, especially in the state of Gujarat. Rajagopal has, however, put his finger on the significance of "the middle class," and even suggests that it may be less real than imagined. Others have also emphasized the changing ideological role of the middle class in relation to the state, development, production and consumption in the history of independent India.[18]

In having opened up the vexed questions of coercion and consent, Rajagopal invites comparison with Emma Tarlo's narratives of "active victims" for whom Indira Gandhi continues to be the greatest leader India has ever known. Questions of consent and the repressive functions of the State apparatus however do not exhaust the meanings of the Emergency, as my final examples hope to suggest. For what is missing is the productive dimension of the Emergency, including its initiative in promoting the aesthetic and political values of the very middle classes that Rajagopal believes made transformation into neoliberalism possible.

The Emergency State as a Productive Space

> Women's Studies was made possible by the Emergency.
>
> Vina Mazumdar, "Women's Studies in India," 1990 (p. 6)

If there is any form of cinema that intellectuals of my generation would hark back to in the era of Bollywood it would be the New Cinema of the 1970s that gave us rural India and its feudal struggles in the mode of realism. Ashish Rajadyaksha, in his volume of essays *Indian Cinema in the Time of Celluloid: From Bollywood to the Emergency*, has laid bare a remarkable intervention by the state under Indira Gandhi aimed at the reform of the film industry overall. His account (which does not lend itself to quick summary) uncovers the financial structure whereby this very state funded a cinema that was "independent, indeed politically vocal, and experimental,"[19] a cinema in fact fully opposed to the Emergency in 1975, in order to advance the state's larger agenda of undercutting the financial and social bases of popular Hindi cinema. Even more telling is Rajadhyaksha's discussion of how this moved beyond economic and political considerations to a new battle over the very aesthetics of film—the confrontation between the avant garde and social realism (personified by such film directors as Mani Kaul versus Satyajit Ray), conducted against the backdrop of mainstream cinematic melodrama.

Another site for thinking otherwise about the Emergency emerged out of my explorations into the field of women's studies and feminism in India. The rise of the contemporary women's movement goes back to the Emergency years when women within left political groups—including especially the more militant left such as the Communist Party of India (Marxist-Leninist) (CPI (ML))—suffered the repression of that period along with their male comrades.[20] Many reconstituted themselves afresh in 1978 and '79 as women's organizations with a new language of "autonomy," which meant (as is often forgotten today) autonomy from direct affiliation with left political formations, not a rejection of party politics.[21] At the same time, other processes were also set in motion in the early 1970s, that are even less well known, but equally significant for understanding the "women's question" in postindependence India. In 1971, the Government of India put together a Committee on the Status of Women in India (CSWI). Quite unbeknownst to the Committee members, this took place at the behest of the United Nations as a preparatory step for producing country level reports for the upcoming International Year of Women in 1975. Tellingly, Indira Gandhi initially sought to suppress the UN communique and had no interest whatsoever in setting the necessary process in motion.

However, to cut a long story short, the India Report named *Towards Equality* was indeed produced in time thanks especially to the efforts of the crusading Minister Phulrenu Guha of the Department of Social Welfare, the role of the Minister for

Education, Nurul Hassan, external assistance for undertaking various studies from the ICSSR, and Mazumdar's own tasks as a newly inducted Member Secretary, among others.[22] This was a report that shocked its own authors for all the evidence it brought to bear regarding the worsening of women's status on a host of fronts—economic, social and political—not just during the period of colonialism but, often at a more aggravated pace, in the first decades of Indian independence. Barely had the CSWI Report been published in December 1974 and a tiny research centre—the Research Centre for Women's Studies—set up in SNDT Women's University in Bombay, when the Emergency was declared. Even as state repression was doing its work, *Towards Equality* was allowed to make its way to the UN meet in Mexico with all its negative findings intact (John 2008).

This is a good place to probe the complex relationship between women's studies and the state, visible in Vina Mazumdar's frequent retelling of the first institutional response by a government body to the many unexpected findings in the Report, which demanded the full attention of social scientists—sociologists, political scientists, economists and demographers. The Indian Council of Social Science Research (ICSSR) funded by the government began the first sponsored programme of women's studies in 1975 right after the Emergency was declared, and was the only programme to be promoted at the time. It is this situation that led Vina Mazumdar to say wryly that women's studies owed its origins to the Emergency. Just to make myself clear here, we are not talking about a movement born through resistance but in the mode of state support. "Let us concentrate on women" said the head of the ICSSR J.P. Naik. "I do not think that the political implications of such research will be immediately understood by the powers that be."[23] Women's studies was mooted in the mode of an alibi, in order "to provide a cover for social scientists to demonstrate the need for restoring democracy in India."[24] Clearly the long genealogy of perceiving women's issues as "social" was being redeployed in this moment to imply that they could masquerade as *merely* social and therefore not pose a political challenge to the state.

I do not think we have been able to get a grip on what this tells us about state power, one that can be at once repressive and progressive, capable of both destruction and support. Mazumdar's brush with power was as fundamental to her orientation and special relationship to the world of state policy, as was the experience of repression for future leaders of the women's movement. In particular, the experience of a bureaucratic apparatus that was able to both use and evade the state in the build up to the Emergency appears to have been a frequent source of inspiration. The point is not in the least that one should regard the Emergency in a more positive light. The suggestion is to recognize how a more obviously institutional field like women's studies and even a movement such as the women's movement, develops in a complex relation to politics, and is more implicated with the state and structures of power than it might like to acknowledge. Vina Mazumdar alerts us (without any Foucauldian overtones of governmentality whatsoever) to a productive notion of power that could be harnessed during the darkest times, in order to slyly make political moves possible, in this case make the state accountable to its most marginalized citizens.[25]

It is time to try and recapitulate the extraordinary array of views of the Emergency that I have so cursorily drawn upon so far, in relation to the problems of an oppositional politics that I started out with. Ramachandra Guha rightly points out how little historical work has been done on any aspect of India after independence (though we might differ considerably with his own interpretations and emphases); for Partha Chatterjee the Emergency was a point of departure in his own writing, one that enabled the interpretive frame of Caesarism along with the call for a left alternative, a frame that was subsequently dropped in favour of the "politics of the governed"; Emma Tarlo struggles with the discovery that her chosen critical event has no place in the lives of those who suffered its policies most directly, and who do not have the right political consciousness in their worship of Indira Gandhi; Arvind Rajagopal believes that the Emergency incubated an enormous transformation in both economic regimes and political struggle; and finally Vina Mazumdar opens a window onto a bureaucratic apparatus that managed to both circumvent as well as use the Emergency to give birth to the field of women's studies in India.

There is much more that should be said about the Emergency. Omitted here have been the views of those who see commonalities in all South Asian nations due to the carry over effect of the emergency powers of the very colonial governments that were their legacy.[26] I have also not referred to the extremely significant work by legal scholars who have shown from a Constitutional point of view that there is never a simple abuse of Constitutional rights which is then rectified through a return to "normalcy" when emergency powers are lifted, least of all in third world postcolonial nations. Emergencies, rather, do the critical work of changing the very contours of the normal, so much so that they produce what Vasuki Nesiah has described as "continuities" between the times and approaches that are categorized as "ordinary" and those … that are perceived as "pathological."[27]

But where the views I have been discussing can help rethink the scope of emergency power, they are not as insightful when it comes to considering the other side of the story. There is a near absence of discussion about social movements among most of the scholars considered. Guha has little to say, given his focus on the figure of Indira Gandhi herself; Tarlo is more or less dismissive of those who opposed the Emergency; and Rajagopal is too partial and selective. It is disappointing when the multitude of ways that activists and movements have chosen to make common cause with, speak on behalf of, the people and their wrongs are not adequately addressed, whatever the levels of their failure.

In Lieu of a Conclusion

This chapter began by invoking the aftermath of the Delhi gangrape in 2012. A palpable sensibility of the emergency of normal times was evident already then, though no one was prepared for what has followed. At the time of revising this chapter, commentators are still trying to analyze the national elections of 2019, and what this tells us about the kind of power a figure like Narendra Modi wields. It should not be cause for surprise that Modi has been frequently compared to Indira Gandhi, nor that references to living in an undeclared Emergency have gained in momentum since 2014, when he was first elected. It is in this context that a new study,

Gyan Prakash's *Emergency Chronicles: Indira Gandhi and Democracy's Turning Point*[28] looks at convulsions worldwide—from the Occupy movement to Tahrir square to Anna Hazare—to ask what happened in 1975 that was different. Prakash is among those to argue that there was nothing sudden or exceptional about the Emergency, indeed, that the Constitution itself contained emergency provisions, thus making the suspension of fundamental rights a lawful exercise. Cold war institutions such as the Ford Foundation are also chronicled for their critical role in the changing fortunes of the Congress Party prior to the Emergency.

There is an air of nostalgia in some of the book's accounts of the acts of repression toward left-wing students who were whisked away in the dead of night. Given my disappointment in the relative lack of existing scholarship on movements, Prakash's interest in a figure like Jayaprakash Narayan was particularly welcome. Against the backdrop of enormous and diverse unrest in the years leading up to the Emergency, JP (once a close family friend of the Nehru family) became the oppositional face to Indira Gandhi, dropping his demand of a morally charged antipolitical call for total revolution to maneuver Gandhians, socialists and the Hindu right-wing Jana Sangh into deposing her. Prakash is keen to make JP's politics more intelligible, to show that he was not a populist even when he ended up narrowing his aims into a fight "with bare knuckles."

This would indicate that there is much more to be understood about the groundswell from below of those years. It is one thing to try and make sense of a leader like Jayaprakash Narayan who could be a Naxal sympathizer and yet have the RSS in his ranks. Prakash opens his book by comparing JP to Anna Hazare, a contemporary figure who has invited a host of divergent evaluations, including that his followers may well have found their future in the BJP. But it is not enough to repeat—this is done over and over again throughout the book—that India is characterized by so much inequality, with so little democracy, as though this could be a sufficient framework of analysis.

It is also not clear whether the book enables us to grapple with the implications of what happened then in relation to the present. We are now facing a new danger of writing histories overwhelmed by the present, where the "before" and "after" of the Emergency becomes one "long undeclared Emergency," as in Pankaj Mishra's review of Prakash's book.[29] I do not think such descriptions are either accurate or helpful. Of course, comparisons are inevitable, and in too many instances the present appears even bleaker. Compare the pragmatic machinations of the respondents described by Tarlo with the long patient queues of people during demonetization who were prepared to suffer fundamental losses for the cause of Indian nationalism. The state has now brought into play the innocuous sounding Unlawful Activities Prevention Act (UAPA), (created by the Congress in 1967), whose powers of detention are greater than those of the dreaded Maintenance of Internal Security Act (MISA) under the Emergency, since no evidence is even required when raids and arrests are made. Prakash mentions in passing that Modi has the kind of power Indira Gandhi occupied during the Emergency, but without repressing the courts, the press or political parties—which only means that too much has changed in the interim.

This makes explicating changes and shifts in movements even more challenging. If a figure like Jayaprakash Narayan was able to lead identifiably "left" and "right" wing political formations under the Emergency, today many movements and their leaders defy ideological categorization. Taking the women's movement as my example, I have been trying to argue for a more careful understanding of how social movements are born, ebb and flow, take on representational tasks, all the while produced within, while also contesting, institutions of power. They are never simply oppositional, the constitutional outside. In fact, it is perhaps only now that we can appreciate the kinds of maneuvers and complicities that were historically part and parcel of movements like the women's movement. Movements today are experiencing a profound crippling through being *reduced to an oppositional stance, a voice of dissent*—sometimes through open right-wing attacks but more often through losing those vital connections to power (including to the apparatus of the state) that were central to politics. Democratic politics has been possible by a range of actions and initiatives, including productive interventions within institutions, ranging from bureaucracies and courts to universities. During the Emergency some of these spaces were used to both circumvent and take advantage of relations of power. Today, we cannot rest content with ideas of politics as only oppositional—such a conception would do an injustice to the multiple legacies of the Emergency. Nor would they take us very far in the battles that await.

Notes

1 An earlier version of this essay appeared as "the Emergency in India": Some Reflections on the Legibility of the Political in *Inter Asia Cultural Studies*, 2014.

2 Emma Tarlo, *Unsettling Memories: Narratives of India's "Emergency"* (Delhi: Oxford University Press, 2003), p. 2.

3 Ramachandra Guha, *India after Gandhi: The History of the World's Largest Democracy* (New Delhi: Picador, 2007), pp. xxii–xxiii.

4 P. N. Lekhi, *Witness for Prosecution: Sedition Unmasked* (Delhi: Allied Publishers, 1979), p. 18.

5 Guha, *India after Gandhi*, pp. 493–521.

6 Sunil Khilnani, *The Idea of India* (London: Penguin Books, 1997); Partha Chatterjee, ed., *Wages of Freedom: Fifty Years of the Indian Nation State* (Delhi: Oxford University Press, 1997); Romila Thapar, *India: Another Millenium?* (New Delhi: Penguin Books, 1997).

7 Partha Chatterjee, *A Possible India: Essays in Political Criticism* (Delhi: Oxford University Press, 1997), p. viii.

8 Ibid., p. 144.

9 Antonio Gramsci, *Prison Notebooks*, vols. 1, 2 & 3. Ed. Antonio Callari Translator Joseph A. Buttigieg (New York: Colmbia University Press, 2011 [1948]).

10 Chatterjee, *A Possible India*, p. 102.

11 Ibid., p. ix.

12 Partha Chatterjee, *The Politics of the Governed* (New York, NY: Columbia University Press, 2004); and Partha Chatterjee, "Democracy and Economic Transformation," *Economic and Political Weekly*, (April 19, 2008): 53–62.

13 Partha Chatterjee, "Populism Plus," *The India Forum* (June 7, 2019).

14 Tarlo, *Unsettling Memories*, p. 36.
15 Arvind Rajagopal, "The Emergency as Prehistory of the New Indian Middle Class," *Modern Asian Studies* 45, no. 5 (2011): 1003–49.
16 Ibid., p. 1012.
17 P. N. Dhar, *Indira Gandhi, the "Emergency" and Indian Democracy* (New Delhi: Oxford University Press, 2001), p. 246.
18 Satish Deshpande, "Imagined Economies," *Journal of Arts and Ideas, Special issue "Careers of Modernity,"* edited by Tejaswini Niranjana, nos. 25–26 (December 1993): 5–35. Satish Deshpande, *Contemporary India: A Sociological View* (New Delhi: Penguin Books, 2004).
19 Ashish Rajadyaksha, *Indian Cinema in the Time of Celluloid: From Bollywood to the Emergency* (New Delhi: Tulika Books, 2009), p. 240.
20 K. Lalita, "The Progressive Organisation of Women in Andhra Pradesh," in Mary E. John, ed., *Women's Studies in India: A Reader* (New Delhi: Penguin Books, 2008), pp. 32–42.
21 Ilina Sen, *The Space within the Struggle* (New Delhi: Kali for Women, 1990); and Nandita Gandhi and Nandita Shah, *Issues at Stake: Theory and Practice in the Women's Movement in India* (New Delhi: Kali for Women, 1992).
22 Vina Mazumdar, *Memories of a Rolling Stone* (New Delhi: Zubaan, 2010).
23 Mary E. John, ed., *Women's Studies in India: A Reader* (New Delhi: Penguin Books, 2008), p. 5.
24 Mazumdar, *Memories of a Rolling Stone*, p. 85.
25 For an extended discussion of Vina Mazumdar's ideas about politics see my essay "Thinking about Politics and Power with Vina Mazumdar," *Indian Journal of Gender Studies* 2017, from which this discussion is taken.
26 Ayesha Jalal, *Democracy and Authoritarianism in South Asia: A Comparative and Historical Perspective* (Cambridge: Cambridge University Press, 1995).
27 Vasuki Nesiah, "The Princely Impostor: Stories of Law and Pathology in the Exercise of Emergency Powers," in Victor V. Ramraj and Arun K. Thiruvengadam, eds., *Emergency Powers in Asia: Exploring the Limits of Legality* (Cambridge: Cambridge University Press, 2010), p. 122.
28 Gyan Prakash, *Emergency Chronicles: Indira Gandhi and Democracy's Turning Point* (New Delhi: Penguin Books, 2018).
29 Pankaj Mishra, "A Long and Undeclared Emergency," *New York Review of Books*, July 18, 2019.

Select Bibliography

Chandra, Bipan, *In the Name of Democracy: J.P. Movement and the Emergency* (New Delhi: Penguin Books, 2003).

Chatterjee, Partha, "Democracy and Economic Transformation," *Economic and Political Weekly*, (April 19, 2008): 53–62.

Chatterjee, Partha, *The Politics of the Governed* (New York, NY: Columbia University Press, 2004).

Chatterjee, Partha, "Populism Plus," *The India Forum*. (June 7, 2019).

Chatterjee, Partha, *A Possible India: Essays in Political Criticism* (Delhi: Oxford University Press, 1997).

Chatterjee, Partha, ed., *Wages of Freedom: Fifty Years of the Indian Nation State* (Delhi: Oxford University Press, 1997).

Das, Veena, *Critical Events: An Anthropological Perspective on Contemporary India* (Delhi: Oxford University Press, 1995).

Deshpande, Satish, *Contemporary India: A Sociological View* (New Delhi: Penguin Books, 2004).

Deshpande, Satish, "Imagined Economies," *Journal of Arts and Ideas, Special issue "Careers of Modernity,"* edited by Tejaswini Niranjana, nos. 25–26 (December 1993): 5–35.

Dhar, P. N. *Indira Gandhi, the "Emergency" and Indian Democracy* (New Delhi: Oxford University Press, 2001).

Gandhi, Nandita and Nandita Shah, *Issues at Stake: Theory and Practice in the Women's Movement in India* (New Delhi: Kali for Women, 1992).

Guha, Ramachandra, *India after Gandhi: The History of the World's Largest Democracy* (New Delhi: Picador, 2007).

John, Mary E., "The Emergency in India: Some Reflections on the Legibility of the Political," *Inter Asia Cultural Studies* 25, no. 4 (2014): 625–37.

John, Mary E., "Thinking about Politics and State Power with Vina Mazumdar," *Indian Journal of Gender Studies* 25, no. 1 (2017): 111–25.

John, Mary E., ed., *Women's Studies in India: A Reader* (New Delhi: Penguin Books, 2008).

Kalhan, Anil, "Constitution and 'Extraconstitution': Colonial Emergency Regimes in Postcolonial India and Pakistan," in Victor V. Ramraj and Arun K. Thiruvengadam, eds., *Emergency Powers in Asia: Exploring the Limits of Legality* (Cambridge: Cambridge University Press, 2010), pp. 89–120.

Khilnani, Sunil, *The Idea of India* (London: Penguin Books, 1997).

Kothari, Rajni, *State against Democracy: In Search of Humane Governance* (Delhi: New Horizons Press, 1989).

Lalita, K., "The Progressive Organisation of Women in Andhra Pradesh," in Mary E. John, ed., *Women's Studies in India: A Reader* (New Delhi: Penguin Books, 2008), pp. 32–42.

Lekhi, P. N., *Witness for Prosecution: Sedition Unmasked* (Delhi: Allied Publishers, 1979).

Mazumdar, Vina, *Memories of a Rolling Stone* (New Delhi: Zubaan, 2010).

Mazumdar, Vina, "Women's Studies in India," in Bharati Ray, ed., *Women's Studies in the Emergent Indian Scenario* (Calcutta: Calcutta University Press, 1990), pp. 4–9.

Prakash, Gyan, *Emergency Chronicles: Indira Gandhi and Democracy's Turning Point* (New Delhi: Penguin Books, 2018).

Rajadyaksha, Ashish, *Indian Cinema in the Time of Celluloid: From Bollywood to the Emergency* (New Delhi: Tulika Books, 2009).

Rajagopal, Arvind, "The Emergency as Prehistory of the New Indian Middle Class," *Modern Asian Studies* 45, no. 5 (2011): 1003–49.

Rudolph, Lloyd I. and Suzanne Rudolph, *In Pursuit of Lakshmi: The Political Economy of the Indian State* (Chicago: University of Chicago Press, 1987).

Sen, Ilina, *The Space within the Struggle* (New Delhi: Kali for Women, 1990).

Tarlo, Emma, *Unsettling Memories: Narratives of India's "Emergency"* (Delhi: Oxford University Press, 2003).

Thapar, Romila, *India: Another Millenium?* (New Delhi: Penguin Books, 1997).

12

Radicalizing Democracy in India: Three Political Imaginaries

Partha Chatterjee

Looking at the recent experience of democracy in India, I see three distinct roads that have sought to move it in a more radical direction. Each of them is informed by a distinct political imaginary with a long genealogy. Although each road is characterized by internal debates and organizational rifts, and thus includes several variants, they all proceed from a critique of the liberal constitutional form of representative democracy as practiced in India through competing political parties, a permanent bureaucracy, and an independent judiciary. Thus, the political imaginaries I will talk about envision, in line with Susan Buck-Morss (2000) rather than Jacques Lacan or Cornelius Castoriadis, a topographical landscape peopled by political actors engaged in real political practices.[1] The three imaginaries are, first, that of armed struggle, second, the assertion of the civic over the political, and third, the dominance of the political over the legal.

Armed Struggle

Maoism in India is usually dated to a peasant uprising in 1967 in a place called Naxalbari in the state of West Bengal where a coalition government including the Communist Party of India (Marxist) (CPI(M)) had just come to power. A local unit of the party started an uprising among landless peasants and sharecroppers in Naxalbari seeking forcible seizure of land held by landlords. The leaders of the CPI(M), unwilling to jeopardize the future of their government, sent in the police to crush the uprising. This led to a split and, in 1969, the CPI (Marxist-Leninist) was formed,

I first presented this paper at the AIIS conference on "Indian Political Imaginaries" in New Delhi in January 2014. I have since discussed it at Jawaharlal Nehru University, University of California at Los Angeles, University of York, and the Centre for Studies in Social Sciences, Calcutta. I am grateful to all who made valuable comments on earlier drafts of the paper.

explicitly aligning itself with the Chinese Communist Party and advocating armed struggle against class enemies. Popularly known as Naxalites, the new party activists came under severe repression from the Congress government of Indira Gandhi in the early 1970s. Several hundreds were killed by the police and thousands imprisoned.[2] Despite being split into several factions, the Naxalites survived in the 1980s and 1990s, under the flag of the People's War in the forest regions of Andhra Pradesh largely populated by people classified as tribal. In 2004–5, however, this long insurgency was crushed by police violence and many surviving cadres moved to the forest regions of Chhattisgarh. In the meantime, various splinter groups came together in 2005 to form the CPI (Maoist) which now led a new insurgency among the tribal peoples of Chhattisgarh and Jharkhand in central India. That is currently the principal base of the Maoist movement, even though it also exists in Maharashtra, Bihar, Odisha, and West Bengal and among students and professionals in the cities.

Genealogically, the political imaginary that constitutes the field of practice of Maoist politics can be traced to histories of anticolonial armed struggles from the late eighteenth century as well as the histories of peasant insurgency. This imaginary visualizes power structures as essentially founded on the superior ability to mobilize violence. Dominant classes are able to wield power in society because they have superior means of violence. When the power of dominant classes takes the structured form of state power, it acquires the legally sanctioned means to exercise violence. Any successful resistance to such power must, therefore, challenge the structures of state and class violence by armed struggle. This political imaginary extols the history of repeated revolts by peasants and tribal peoples in colonial India against state agencies, landlords, and moneylenders, even though it recognizes the historical limits of peasant insurgency in transforming the structures of state power. It also valorizes the armed actions of revolutionary nationalists against British rule for their uncompromising militancy, even as it considers individual assassinations and keeping away from mass politics as signs of political immaturity. Further, of all the three imaginaries, this one is the most explicitly internationalist, because it aligns itself with the history of the international communist movement, especially of the Bolshevik strand led by Lenin and Stalin, and accepts the Chinese revolution under the leadership of Mao Zedong as the model that the Indian revolution must follow.[3]

In laying out the landscape of its political practice, the Maoist movement has sharply differentiated itself from the politics of the parliamentary Left. Bernard D'Mello, a sympathetic commentator, has identified some of the characteristics of a distinctly Maoist politics that are derived from the historical experience of the Chinese revolution.[4] First, Maoists insist that the poor peasantry rather than the urban proletariat must constitute the mass support base of the movement. Second, they believe in an uninterrupted process of revolution proceeding in stages. Third, they place great emphasis on a national democratic revolution that makes capitalism more compatible with democracy, thus allowing a smoother transition to socialism. Fourth, their strategy is that of protracted people's war in which rural bases are built and run like miniature self-reliant democratic states where land is given to the tiller; these bases are expected to multiply and finally encircle the cities. Fifth, they seek to win support in the cities by championing a genuinely anti-imperialist nationalism.

Sixth, they claim to supplement the democratic centralism of the party with a mass line in order to preclude the emergence of a new political-bureaucratic elite. These characteristics, D'Mello insists, separate the politics of Indian Maoists from all other parties and movements within an electoral democracy.

The Maoist political imaginary, deeply invested as it is in a military contest with the Indian state, is clearly etched over territorial space. There are areas that are firmly under its control, others where its control is unsure, and still others where it has little presence. The areas of greatest control are in the forested regions of Chhattisgarh, peopled largely by tribal populations engaged in a mix of subsistence agriculture and forest-related laboring occupations. Attempts to expand these zones of control are dependent upon military strategy where armed Maoists must confront the military and political responses of the central and state governments. The horizon of this strategic imaginary is sometimes said to extend to a corridor connecting central India with Nepal where a prolonged Maoist insurgency led to the overthrow of the monarchy and the inclusion of Maoists within the electorally constituted government. Further, the political actors involved within the spaces of Maoist control are not merely poor local inhabitants but, crucially, organized party cadres from other regions.

In its recent phase, Maoists have engaged in spurts of armed conflict with the security forces of both central and state governments. In particular, they have ambushed paramilitary and police convoys and launched raids on police camps in order to secure arms, inflicting large casualties. More controversially, they have attacked civilian targets such as moving trains and buses, killing dozens of innocent people. In May 2013, they ambushed a motorcade with key Congress leaders of Chhattisgarh, killing most of them. Faced with the criticism that these are little more than acts of terrorism, the Maoist leadership has occasionally admitted such mistakes but also justified these acts as retaliation against politicians who had attacked them.[5]

At the same time, within the zones of insurgency, the Maoists have attempted to establish forms of self-government, even though their hold over these areas is neither permanent nor total. Sympathetic accounts of how the Maoists run daily life in their "base area" have been provided by Arundhati Roy, Gautam Navlakha, Nandini Sundar, and Bernard D'Mello.[6] The guerrilla zone in the Bastar district of Chhattisgarh is run by the Jantanam Sarkar (people's government), operating through elected Revolutionary People's Committees organized in three tiers, the lowest governing three to five villages. Alongside, there is a military structure consisting of about 10,000 fighters of the People's Liberation Guerrilla Army and nearly 50,000 armed villagers organized into militias. Life in the guerrilla army is hard, disciplined and egalitarian. Apart from military training, there is an emphasis on the continued education of the fighters, most of whom are young tribal men and women. More significantly, there is an effort to cleanse them of what the Maoist leadership considers retrograde aspects of tribal culture such as alcohol and premarital sex. A separate women's organization has been set up to fight patriarchy and some 40 percent of members of the guerrilla army as well as the people's committees are women.

Within these villages, Maoists claim to have set up a "people's economy." Much of economic life revolves around the forest. A large source of employment is wage work involving the cutting of bamboos for the manufacture of paper and the collection of *kendu* leaves used to wrap the *bidi* (cheap cigarettes) that poor people smoke. Over the last decade, Maoists have successfully put pressure on paper mills and contractors to increase the hugely exploitative wage rates, so that the local people now earn the legal minimum wage. Further, the movement has virtually expelled the government's forest department from the area and reclaimed considerable cultivable land located within the forests. Even more importantly, the Maoists have appropriated the land earlier held by tribal chiefs. Consequently, there is almost no landlessness in the Bastar villages controlled by Maoists and, even though nutrition levels are low, there is no absolute poverty or hunger. To improve agriculture, irrigation tanks are being dug, and Maoist leaders are not averse to seeking the help of government agencies for improved varieties of seeds and information on better techniques of cultivation. Maoists claim to have trained "barefoot" doctors to treat common diseases such as malaria, cholera and elephantiasis. They have also set up mobile primary schools for their fighters for which they have prepared their own textbooks.

Many of these claims have been contested by critics of the Maoist movement.[7] Most crucial is the question whether the armed struggle against the Indian state has taken precedence over the needs of the people. First, the armed militias and a major part of the guerrilla army consist of tribal recruits, whereas the military and political leadership is drawn from middle-class party activists from Andhra Pradesh, Bihar and West Bengal. There is, consequently, a predictable charge that tribal soldiers are being used as cannon fodder by a middle-class party leadership. Second, recruits are inducted into the guerrilla army from a young age, depriving them of a normal education and throwing them into a life of great hardship. Third, even though the Maoists collect "taxes" from companies and contractors operating in the area and "royalties" on forest products such as bamboo and *kendu* leaves, it is unclear how much of this revenue is spent on the region and how much goes to fund military operations. The allegation is that the continued dependence of the Maoists on money extracted from companies and contractors perpetuates the existing exploitation of forest resources without improvement in the lives of the people. In other words, the Maoists have allowed their local power to become locked into the larger grid of extraction of wealth from the area. Finally, their military tactics have frequently prompted the Maoists to mete out severe punishment, including execution, on local people suspected of supplying intelligence to the police or being active on behalf of other political parties. The trials held by "people's courts" deliver summary punishment in public.

The Maoists have responded by pointing out the harsh conditions of state repression under which they are defending their zones of control. It was their inability, they say, to resist the penetration of the police intelligence network that caused their collapse in Andhra Pradesh in 2004–5; they are determined not to repeat the mistake in Chhattisgarh and other areas where they have now established a foothold. "It is not paranoia but sheer necessity that is driving us to smash the enemy network that is dangerously spreading into the areas of struggle."[8] They add that the Indian government is waging a war of annihilation against the tribal people of central India, and their defenders, the Maoists, because it has come to a long-term agreement with multinational corporations and collaborating Indian business houses to exploit the mineral resources of the region; their development projects of building roads and supplying electricity are merely a part of that plan.[9]

In their public statements, the Maoist leaders sometimes acknowledge that what they have achieved "in a few pockets of the backward areas does not provide a wide-ranging viable alternative model by itself." In particular, they have not been able to offer an alternative politics in more developed rural regions of the country or in the cities.[10] Their sympathizers insist that "Maoism should commit to radical democracy" in which there will be equality because without it the rich will be more free than others, but also liberty without which some will have more power than others.[11] They have no doubt that the liberal democracy that exists in practice in India is thoroughly rotten.[12]

For the people of Bastar, as Nandini Sundar points out, the Maoists represent a countervailing power to the state which, even as it promises schools, health services, roads and electricity, has a proven record of being on the side of exploitative forest contractors and mining companies.[13] The people accept that the tentacles of the state have reached into their lives. But instead of the messy negotiations of political society, they look upon the armed resistance of the Maoists as their principal resource in negotiating with the state. In the meantime, prolonged armed conflict deepens military–political leadership and defers the promised building of a more radically democratic society.

The Revolt of Civil Society

For the last two decades, the urban middle classes of India have expressed in various forms their frustration at the opaque machinery of government which, they feel, has failed in delivering benefits and services to the people. They attribute the failure, first, to the government's succumbing to sectional demands of electorally powerful groups at the cost of the public interest and second, to the pervasive corruption at all levels of government. Having built up slowly, this anger and frustration came out in organized fashion in a massive mobilization in Delhi's Ramlila Maidan in August 2011. The issue was the introduction in the Indian Parliament of the Lokpal Bill, a legislation to create an ombudsman institution with powers to investigate and punish corruption among government officials. The movement led by Anna Hazare demanded that the Lokpal have independent powers to investigate allegations against all ministers of central and state governments, all government officials and all members of the judiciary and to punish them without having to go through the normal judicial system. These demands the government was unwilling to concede on the ground that they would create an immensely powerful executive and judicial authority outside the constitutional framework and threaten the balance between Parliament, the Prime Minister and the Supreme Court.

When at its peak, the Anna Hazare movement became the subject of much controversy. For its supporters, it broke out of conventional patterns of mobilization by political parties and interest groups and drew active support from wide sections of the people, especially urban middle classes and youth who had shown nothing but distaste for political rallies, slogans and voting in elections. The demonstrations demanding an end to corruption in government brought tens of thousands of people from different cities and towns of northern India. The electronic and print media and social network sites were fully engaged in the movement, showing the extraordinary interest generated among the otherwise politically unenthusiastic people reached by these networks. There were pronouncements of revolution along the lines of Tahrir Square. Some critics of the movement, on the other hand, saw—quite predictably—signs of a conspiracy by opposition parties to destabilize the government. Other critics saw more ominous signs of a fascist mobilization aimed at stifling, by threats and blackmail, the normal institutions of parliamentary democracy.

What is the political imaginary laid out here? Despite the personal image of Anna Hazare as a nonviolent resister, the use of the fast as a political technique, and the surfeit of moral rhetoric, there was little in the movement's demands to suggest an espousal of the Gandhian view of the good society rooted in a harmoniously organized rural world. In fact, the greatest support for the movement came from different urban sections seeking greater social mobility. The imaginary here must be sought in an unresolved tension in the very conception of modern representative democracy. There is, on the one hand, a theoretical assumption of sovereignty residing in the will of the people. But in practice, this can exist only as an abstract idea, with the actual work of government being carried out by legislators and officials who act as representatives of the people. Two contradictory forces are allowed to contend here. While representatives are supposed to follow the mandate of their constituents, they must also play the role of robust leaders and educators of society, acting on the basis of information, experience and foresight. All representative democracies today check the popular mandate only once every four or five years, carrying out the business of government according to the established knowledge and practices prevailing within a political class. In most cases, the choice offered to the electorate is between alternatives located entirely within established political practices.

There has been a reaction to these entrenched practices of representative democracy in many countries of the world, producing widespread distrust of those who govern. Several forms of opposition have emerged such as the exercise of vigilance by citizen's groups, the public denunciation of officials, the expression of negative politics by saying "no" to policies without affirming an alternative, and the increasing resort to courts and media trials. Pierre Rosanvallon (2008) has called these practices "counter-democracy," suggesting that they are carried out as radical correctives to existing democratic practices rather than as a rejection of democracy itself.[14] Some of these counterdemocratic practices have been pushed further to take the form of populism.

The Anna Hazare movement was populist, but unlike most others of its kind, it was explicitly antipolitical and in this respect was quite novel. It was populist in Ernesto Laclau's sense in which groups with a variety of complaints and demands came together by asserting that their demands were equivalent since they were all demands of the "people" directed against a common "enemy."[15] In this case, the enemy was designated as the class of politicians and government officials, all of whom were said to be corrupt. Existing methods of dealing with corruption were unacceptable since they were all internal to the structures of government—whether administrative or judicial—and so were already wrapped within the web of political corruption. What was needed was a moral authority standing outside the political establishment which would adjudicate and punish all complaints of corruption in government.

It is remarkable how strongly the argument was made by Anna Hazare himself, and repeated by his associates, that the answer to corruption was not the law, because the law was already tainted, but morality. Who would qualify to fill the offices of the Lokpal? They would be persons of unimpeachable integrity held in high esteem by the public. This echoes the deep suspicion in the popular mind that the law and the judicial procedures are easily manipulated by corrupt persons in power. The only remedy to corruption in government, claimed Anna supporters, is a nonpolitical institution of persons with acknowledged moral probity who would have powers of investigation and punishment over all government officials.

The moral critique highlighted the antipolitical tenor of the movement. Since the campaign focused on corruption in government, it opened up a wide-ranging debate over its extent and causes. It was pointed out, for instance, that government was not the only place where there was corruption; the private sector was no less corrupt. The response to this was that the pervasive climate of government regulation of property, land, economic production, trade and the environment made it impossible for the private sector to do business except by lubricating the wheels of government with bribes. Ordinary people with honest intentions could not get even routine work done in government offices without bribing some minor functionary. Of course, this meant that even honest persons were implicated in the web of corruption. After all, corrupt officials in the municipality or the police station were also members of the urban middle class that was most vociferous in its complaints against government corruption.[16] If one cast the net wider, one could say that the millions of people in India who were involved, either as students or teachers, in the vast business of private coaching for public examinations were part of an immense network of corruption that subverts the school and university system in which teachers are paid out of government funds to do the teaching for an extra fee in private coaching centers. One could say the same thing about government doctors. And outside the middle class, there are millions of urban poor who find a place to live and earn their subsistence by squatting on land that does not belong to them or setting up shops on the street without authorization. Are they all to be punished for corruption?

The answer to this objection was that in most cases people could tell those who were forced to participate in a corrupt practice because they had little choice from those who engaged in it out of greed. The former were essentially good people who, if the social climate were free of corruption, would never stoop to it. The latter were the source of corruption because for them it was the means to become rich quickly. The criterion for distinguishing between the two groups was a moral one and the quibbles of the law only served to muddle things. The innate moral sense of the people could separate the good persons from the corrupt ones. In the present context, the political class had become the enemy of the people.

It was this moral message that underlay the populism of the Anna movement. Virtually everyone in government, whether career functionaries or elected politicians, are corrupt because they use every instrument of governmental power to enrich themselves. In this situation, the formal distinction between government and politics itself becomes irrelevant, since career appointments and promotions in government are settled by political patronage. It is the political, in short, that has come to stand as the enemy of the people.

This moral message of Anna Hazare's movement had a powerful impact on the expanding middle classes of northern India in 2011. These are people who do not generally have to approach local politicians or officials for help with the routine business of life. Their network of social connections is usually sufficient to tide over most problems in dealing with government institutions, without having to resort to corruption. When they do find that a routine procedure cannot be performed without a supposedly customary bribe, they are understandably enraged. Even more galling are stories of politicians or officials making millions in kickbacks from government contracts and being let off by the courts. Supporters of Anna Hazare told one another a thousand such stories.

Outside their circles, there were, of course, millions of others whose daily lives are deeply entangled in politics. Their marginal livelihoods are often dependent on political protection. If they had to put a child into a better school or get a relative admitted free into hospital, they would have to approach a political leader for help. It is a politician who might arrange for a bank loan or assistance from the *panchayat* or local government. For such people, there is no life free of politics. Even though they might curse every politician under the sun, they would still go out and vote because for them it is vitally important. Corruption for them is not usually a moral question. As far as they are concerned, the rich and the powerful are not properly moral subjects at all, because they are products of a system that is fundamentally unfair. The only relevant question is which politician will be of help and which won't. And that is a political, not moral, question.

It is striking that the Anna Hazare movement had little purchase in rural areas, even in the northern states. And southern and eastern India was left virtually untouched by it. But it is interesting that unconventional populist movements of this type have emerged in several countries in the last few years. It shows widespread disillusionment with routinized forms of politics. The Tea Party movement in the United States is an interesting parallel because that too targeted the political establishment as its enemy. However, the remedy it suggested—cutting the size of government and lowering taxes—is far more recognizable as a conservative political ideology than the antipolitical moral rhetoric of the Anna movement. The Tea Party method of electing its own representatives to Congress and influencing government policy is also quite different from the proclaimed vow of the Anna Hazare team, before Arvind Kejriwal, a leading member of the movement, broke away to launch the Aam Aadmi Party. The Occupy Wall Street movement also had some resemblance to the Anna movement in that it too targeted "the one per cent" as the self-seeking culprits responsible for the misery of "the ninety-nine per cent." However, the leaderless nature of the movement and the presence of the anarchist and liberal left made it unlike the Anna movement. Comparisons with the upsurges in the Arab world are interesting but far more problematic, since the latter emerged in the context of long histories of authoritarian military rule. The most striking parallel, however, is with the massive urban movements in Thailand against the popularly elected governments of Thaksin and Yingluck Shinawatra. Those movements allege that the corrupt political machine of the Shinawatra family is able to win parliamentary majorities by buying votes from the poor rural masses, effectively disenfranchising urban voters.

The distinction between the antipolitical moral stance of the Anna movement and the strategic view of corruption adopted by other nonelite movements in India such as the Bahujan Samaj or Dalit movements raises an interesting issue. Poor people in India have shown a marked tendency to participate in large numbers in electoral democracy, while the urban middle classes have become apathetic. But there is a contrary political imaginary to that of mass democracy that is still powerful in India, especially among the educated classes. That is based on the principle of enlightened despotism. Faced with the corrupt inefficiency of democratic governance, many yearn for authoritarian leadership—bold, decisive, moral, and untainted by the pollution of politics. As a political imaginary, it is not opposed to the idea of representation, but it insists that the ruler must represent the true and enduring as opposed to the contingent and transient interests of the people. Anna Hazare's movement attracted a great deal of this sentiment deriving from an older elitist imaginary now redeployed on the terrain of counterdemocratic politics. And it is arguable that at least a section of the middle classes moved by the moral rhetoric of the Anna movement later veered to Narendra Modi as a bold, decisive and incorruptible national leader in the parliamentary elections of April–May 2014. The connection between the antipolitical moral populism of the Anna movement and the authoritarian populist leadership of Modi, standing above the entire gamut of Indian politicians, requires close ethnographic study.

The electoral successes of the Aam Aadmi Party (AAP) in Delhi in 2013 and 2015 only partly reflects the political imaginary of the Anna Hazare movement. To the extent that it tapped the counterdemocratic sentiments of the metropolitan middle class and youth by nominating as candidates people entirely outside the known political class, the new party followed the Anna movement. However, its appeal to the poorer sections of the electorate required entirely new methods of mobilization of electoral support. The moral rhetoric against corruption had to be expanded into credible campaign promises of tangible results. Thus, AAP promised to lower the electricity charges of poorer consumers and deliver a certain volume of free water to every poor family in Delhi. Entry into electoral politics has now forced AAP to fashion itself as a populist electoral force in political society without losing its counterdemocratic edge. It is a task that has never been attempted before in India and, judging by the recent turmoil within its own organization, it appears to be an uphill struggle. By 2019, the electoral career of the Aam Aadmi Party in Delhi is on a downswing; it appears to have been fully normalized as yet another regional populist party.

Politics over Civics

The state of Emergency declared by Indira Gandhi in 1975–7 was the last sustained attempt to push through a developmental agenda by authoritarian bureaucratic methods of the kind that had been used, with varying effectiveness, in many other Third World countries. For India's governing classes, the failure of the Emergency drove home the lesson that biopolitical projects that have to do with the physical conditions of the life of the people could not be successfully pursued without passing them through the sieve of voluntary consent (especially in view of the catastrophic results of the sterilization drive). Further, it also became clear that welfare measures could not be effectively administered except by negotiation with the affected population groups. The difficulty was that the ordinary conditions of citizenship and representation on which the constitutionally ordained structure of rights and duties was founded could not uniformly be made to apply to all population groups, especially not to the urban poor making a living in the informal economy. What were the terms on which they might be recognized as parties to governmental negotiation?

The idea of political society[17] recognizes something *new* in the way governmental authorities began to negotiate with population groups. This no longer fitted the old form of patron–client relations between local notables and their protégées, nor was it quite the same as a political fixer getting things done at a government office on behalf of a local community. In older models, the form of the local community was already given by the history of social structures, and the function of the patron too was usually made possible by prevailing hierarchies of class and status. Political society, on the other hand, often *creates* a community where none existed before, or else it *gives new form* to older community structures. That is to say, population groups by engaging with political society acquire the moral character of community.

But the period following the end of the Emergency was also the time when postcolonial democracy gained wider and deeper foundations in rural India. Could it be that this merely meant the multiplication of the old patron–client relations on a much wider scale? Or was it in fact the realization at last of the dream that many of the founders of the Indian republic had nourished—the consciousness and exercise of full rights of republican citizenship by millions of Indian peasants? It was neither. Rather, it was the emergence of political society around new forms of negotiation between rural population groups and governmental agencies. Rapidly expanded governmental activities in rural India were providing the grid for population groups to be mobilized into the moral form of communities with voice and identity. Consequently, the idea of political society marked a *new moment* in the democratization of Indian politics and society.

This is not to insist, of course, that the older forms were suddenly obliterated. For many people, especially in rural India but also in the cities, the connection to the political world continued to be mediated through powerful patrons such as landlords, or caste leaders, or religious authorities. But in the first decade of the new millennium the forms of political society became more common everywhere, in cities as well as in the countryside. They seemed to respond more appropriately to better calibrated and flexible governmental policies on the one hand and the growing desire on the other among the populations for greater voice in deciding how they are governed.

Take the familiar example of squatter settlements of the poor in numerous cities of India. These urban populations occupy land that does not belong to them and often use water, electricity, public transport and other services without paying for them. But governmental authorities do not necessarily try to punish or put a stop to such illegalities, because of the political recognition that these populations serve certain necessary functions in the urban economy and that to forcibly remove them would involve huge political costs. On the other hand, they cannot also be treated as legitimate members of civil society who abide by the law. As a result, municipal authorities or the police deal with these people not as rights-bearing citizens but as urban populations who have specific characteristics and who must be appropriately governed. On their side, these groups of urban poor negotiate with the authorities through political mobilization and alliances with other groups.

On the plane of governmentality, populations do not carry the ethical significance of citizenship. They are heterogeneous groups, each defined by empirically observed characteristics and constituted as a manipulatable target population for governmental policies. Consequently, if, despite their illegal occupation of land, they are given electricity connections or allowed to use municipal services, it is not because they have a right to them but because the authorities make a calculation of costs and benefits and agree, for the time being, to give them those benefits. However, this can only be done in a way that does not jeopardize the legal order of property and the rights of proper citizens. The usual method is to construct a case such that the particular illegality associated with a specific population group may be treated as an exception that does not disturb the fundamental rule of law. Governmental decisions aimed at regulating the vast populations of the urban poor usually add up to a series of exceptions to the normal application of the law.

Populations respond to the regime of governmentality by seeking to constitute themselves as groups that deserve the attention of government. If as squatters they have violated the law, they do not necessarily deny that fact, nor do they claim that their illegal occupation of land is right. But they insist that they have a right to housing and livelihood in the city, and, if they are required to move elsewhere, they must be provided with rehabilitation. They form associations to negotiate with governmental authorities and seek public support. This becomes a major form of political participation, of invoking their status as formal citizens but acting in ways that often contravene the approved practices of civic life. Their political mobilization involves an effort to turn an empirically formed population group into a virtuous community. The force of this appeal hinges on the generally recognized obligation of government to provide for the poor and the underprivileged.

If we consider the example of elections in India, for instance, we will find that the overwhelming bulk of political rhetoric concerns what governments have or have not done for which population groups. The function of rhetoric here is to turn the heterogeneous demands of populations into morally coherent and emotionally persuasive form of popular demands. In this sense, populism is the only morally legitimate form of democratic politics. It is important to emphasize that unlike traditional theories of modernization that regard such populism as a perversion of democratic politics, attention to the underlying political imaginary requires us to treat it with seriousness as a new and potentially richer development of democracy. It is also worth pointing out that one of the persistent findings of election studies in India is the relatively high electoral participation of poor and underprivileged sections (Yadav 2000).

The field of negotiation between governmental authorities and population groups is necessarily uncertain, laying down no firm principles, recognizing no definite rights, but leaving everything to temporary negotiation of claims. Groups in political society have to pick their way through this uncertain terrain by making a large array of connections outside the group—with other groups in similar situations, with more privileged and influential groups, with government functionaries, with political parties and leaders. They often make instrumental use of the fact that they can vote in elections. But the instrumental use of the vote is possible only within a field of strategic politics. This is the stuff of democratic politics as it takes place on the ground in India. It involves what appears to be a constantly shifting compromise between the normative values of constitutional propriety and the righteous assertion of popular demands.

Governmental authorities, on the other hand, when conceding a demand by making an exception to the law in a particular case, have to be careful that the interests of proper law-abiding citizens are not thereby threatened. Thus, squatters may be allowed water and electricity connections at specific negotiated rates as an exception to the usual structure of rates paid by regular customers, or vendors may be allowed to set up temporary stalls on the pavement without threatening the regular shops that have licenses and pay taxes, or small industries and services in the informal sector may be allowed to ignore labor laws and pollution regulations that apply to the formal sector. Declaring exceptions of this kind is a balancing act and creates unstable arrangements that may be disturbed either because the courts decide that the exception is unjustified or the political balance shifts against the population group concerned.

Given the huge number of demands that arise in a heterogeneous society where the vast majority of the population lives and works in the informal sector outside the properly regulated zones of civil society, administrative responses end up in an array of temporary and often inconsistent exceptions. Population groups too do not seek to fundamentally change the existing structure of rules and regulations but claim that an exception be made in their case. As a result, the working of political society ends up in the piling up of exceptions.

The daily politics of disparate localized groups does not constitute a revolutionary challenge to the structure of state authority. As a political imaginary, it seems to have little potential for radical social change. Many commentators think that the idea of political society empties the political actions of poor people of any concerted resistance. Instead, it seems to focus exclusively on the negotiated transactions between government agencies and target population groups over the distribution of governmental benefits. It involves limited struggles and prevents a long-term strategy or vision of radical transformation.[18]

The charge is not entirely untrue. The form of politics spawned by political society has a horizon limited to the demands of particular groups and does not seek to generalize its claims to all citizens. But the techniques of struggle frequently go beyond the limits of the law and sometimes even use violence (or show of violence) in order to demonstrate extraordinary outrage or draw the attention of the wider public. Some commentators have rather optimistically viewed these struggles as an example of "deep democracy" involving learning and a "politics of patience."[19] But it seems more appropriate to evaluate the radical potential of transformation in political society more cautiously. There is resistance in political society, sometimes even of a spectacular kind. But more often than not, it is resistance that tests rather than violates the limits of conventional political practice. In so doing, it sometimes manages to induce responses from governmental agencies that change the familiar forms of the conventional.

Some of these changes happen cumulatively. Thus, repeated local struggles against eviction have led to a conventional view in most Indian cities that long-standing slums cannot be cleared. The recognition by the authorities of the claims of one group of pavement vendors becomes a precedent that can be used by other groups. Urban groups of this kind have managed to build national coalitions to coordinate their struggles, learn from one another and present to the authorities more coherent sets of demands. The struggles of street vendors in cities across the country finally led in 2013 to a federal law seeking to recognize and regulate the occupation. The long struggles against slum demolition have brought forth national policy statements from the government laying down a framework for the rehabilitation of evicted populations. But there are moments when uncoordinated local struggles could, simply by their simultaneity, force the issue into the limelight and bring forth a policy response. Thus, agitations in different parts of the country against the acquisition by government of land for industry led to new legislation in 2013 offering better terms of compensation to those who lose their land. Examples of such coordinated resistance in political society are clearly growing. Possibly, the process is an early stage of the developments one saw in Brazil under the Workers' Party led by Lula da Silva where there was far greater success in winning specific rights and entitlements for poor populations as a result of sustained local struggles. This road to a more radical democracy in India still remains largely uncharted.

However, there is another aspect to the evolving history of political society in India that must also be noted. Most negotiations in political society are local. But because of their entanglement with electoral democracy, they have in recent times become consolidated into larger populist mobilizations. The building of large caste coalitions has been one such method. The politics of the two main Dravida parties in Tamil Nadu is an example, as are those of the Yadav-led coalition of Other Backward Classes (including Muslims) and the Dalit Bahujan mobilization in Uttar Pradesh. But a more recent development is the articulation of local political society into the demands of a regional formation. Much of this is prompted by the readiness of political parties to respond to political society through populist promises. The examples of the Trinamul Congress led by Mamata Banerjee in West Bengal, the Biju Janata Dal led by Naveen Patnaik in Odisha, the Aam Aadmi Party led by Arvind Kejriwal in Delhi, the YSR Congress led by Y. S. Jaganmohan Reddy in Andhra Pradesh and the Telangana Rashtra Samithi led by K. Chandrasekhar Rao in Telangana come readily to mind. The multiplicity of these examples makes it necessary to examine more closely the connection between political society and populism in the Indian states.

Populism: A Distinct Imaginary?

All state governments in India, as well as the central government, now seek to deal with demands from political society through governmental policies that selectively benefit sections of the electorate. This technique has replaced earlier gestures toward providing universal benefits to all citizens along the lines of the welfare state. As a result, policies to benefit specific electoral constituencies do not in themselves constitute a marker of populism. To be meaningfully understood as populist, a movement must represent itself in such a way as to define a border between the people and their enemy. This border may run along existing linguistic, ethnic, or religious divisions, or new fault lines may be rhetorically created between the wealthy and the poor, or the powerful elite and the deprived masses, or a despotic ruling party that benefits only its own supporters. When such a movement comes to power, it faces the problem of maintaining the border between the people and their enemy because its bases of electoral support are liable to change over time. This problem is often resolved by rhetorically identifying the people with the person of the leader; the leader's enemies then become the enemies of the people. The populist leader is a sovereign chosen by the people who can deliver justice and welfare for the people and score victories over its enemies. He or she is authoritarian in style, runs a centralized machinery of power in which no challenger is allowed to emerge and is not averse to using force to repress the opposition. However, the populist leader must periodically renew their mandate by defeating competing parties in a popular election; populist rule is not dictatorial. It is noteworthy that several of India's populist leaders, especially women leaders such as Jayalalithaa, Mayawati and Mamata Banerjee, have been assigned familial positions of authority in relation to the people.

Electoral conditions in the Indian states are much more favorable to the rise of populist movements than at the Centre. Research in the last two decades on the print literatures and visual material in the different language regions of India have produced a rich picture of the political imaginary of the nation constructed since the late nineteenth century. It is clear now that the idea of India, not so much as a nation-state but as the identity of the nation with a people, was conceived differently in each language region, depending on its particular history and social structures.[20] Given the fact that the overwhelming medium of political communication in India is in the regional languages, it must be the case that effective national imaginaries are expressed in the vernaculars rather than in the English writings of canonical Indian thinkers and academics. Consequently, it is not surprising that the emotional power of the imagined community of a people, represented by a popularly chosen leader, united against an oppressive enemy is evoked much more effectively in the states.

Do populist movements represent a distinct political imaginary? Laclau insists that while populism has its own political rationality, it does not come with any particular content. Indeed, the signifier called the people can be filled by any ideological content.[21] Thus, populist movements or regimes can be left-wing or right-wing, and even allow for an unpredictable mix of leftist and rightist policies. Hence, simply because a movement is populist does not endow it with a specific political imaginary. A vision of a transformed society has to be superimposed on the populist movement.

However, the conditions under which a populist party must operate in an electoral democracy make it difficult, if not impossible, for it to carry out a project of social transformation. As we have seen, populist consolidations are built by stringing together a variety of heterogeneous demands in political society into an emotionally significant collective called the people who are faced with an oppressive enemy. But such demands are fulfilled by the tactical extension of benefits to specific groups. Political society is not a space for changing the beliefs and practices of people, nor can a populist leadership adopt the position of a cultural vanguard to launch such a project of cultural pedagogy.[22] Hence, even if such a transformative political imaginary comes to be attached to a populist movement, it would either have to transcend populism or succumb to the tactical immediacy of electoral calculations. A good example is the story of the Dravida Kazhagam which began with the rationalist Self-Respect Movement of E. V. Ramasamy but had to shed its cultural project as it joined the electoral mainstream to embrace every element of conventional religiosity under the AIADMK party of Jayalalithaa.

This argument begs the legitimate question: is the rule of the Bharatiya Janata Party (BJP) under Narendra Modi populist? If one looks at it purely in terms of the selective extension of benefits by a regime personified by a single all-powerful leader who claims to stand for the nation, then the current BJP government will certainly qualify as the first populist government at the centre since Indira Gandhi's rule. What complicates the picture is the fact that the BJP also has a transformative social agenda of Hindutva. This involves a political imaginary in which India is a homogeneous nation-state where the majority Hindu community must have precedence and others must be assimilated into the majority culture. The principal political task is to turn India into a world power of the first rank. Pakistan is the principal enemy of the nation. Hence, Muslims, and those who question the Hindutva project of strengthening the Indian state, are disloyal and must be treated as potential enemies. This imaginary drives forward a transformative social project of propagating Hindutva through every medium of communication including print, visual and electronic media and institutions such as schools, universities and cultural organizations. The Hindutva project may use governmental power when available, but does not depend on it; it can continue even when the BJP is not in power. Hence, even if the present moment is one in which the imaginary of a Hindu nation-state overlaps with a populist regime in power, it is merely conjunctural. The former project seeks to establish a social hegemony that transcends electoral populism.

I have described three different trajectories of radicalizing democracy in India. They appear to be mutually exclusive. Activists in middle-class civil society organizations would feel that they have nothing to do with the messy compromises of political society. And the armed struggle of the Maoists would seem to be entirely beyond the pale of the constitutional and electoral politics of both civil and political society. Nonetheless, at a deeper structural level, the three roads and imaginaries are not unconnected. What happens in one can influence what happens in the other two. And if one looks for the point of view of specific marginalized populations, one would find that they sometimes use more than one road. Thus, Dalit and Adivasi groups taken as a whole are invested in the armed struggles in central India at the same time as they carry out negotiations in political society and, quite often, use constitutional avenues to pursue democratic equality. Hence, even though their significance and potential may vary, all three imaginaries remain relevant for the future of Indian democracy.

Notes

1 Susan Buck-Morss, *Dreamworld and Catastrophe: The Passing of Mass Utopia in East and West* (Cambridge, MA: MIT Press, 2000).
2 Sumanta Banerjee, *In the Wake of Naxalbari* (Calcutta: Subarnarekha, 1980).
3 Pradip Basu, *Towards Naxalbari (1953–1967): An Account of Inner-party Ideological Struggle* (Calcutta: Progressive Publishers, 2000).
4 Bernard D'Mello, "What Is Maoism?" *Economic and Political Weekly* 44, no. 47 (November 21, 2009): 39–48.
5 Ganapathi, Interview of General Secretary, CPI (Maoist), by Jan Myrdal and Gautam Navlakha, February 14, 2010, sanhati.com.
6 Arundhati Roy, *Walking with the Comrades* (New Delhi: Penguin, 2011); Gautam Navlakha, *Days and Nights in the Heartland of Rebellion* (New Delhi: Penguin, 2012); Nandini Sundar, *The Burning Forest: India's War in Bastar* (New York: Verso, 2017); and Bernard D'Mello, *India after Naxalbari: Unfinished History* (New York: Monthly Review Press, 2019).
7 Nirmalangshu Mukherji, *The Maoists in India: Tribals Under Siege* (London: Pluto Press, 2012).
8 Spokesperson, CPI(Maoist) 2009.
9 Arundhati Roy, *Walking with the Comrades* (New Delhi: Penguin, 2011).
10 Spokesperson, CPI(Maoist) 2009.
11 Bernard D'Mello, "What Is Maoism?" *Economic and Political Weekly* 44, no. 47 (November 21, 2009): 39–48.
12 Bernard D'Mello, "The Near and the Far: Why Is India's Liberal-Political Democracy Rotten?" *Economic and Political Weekly* 48, no. 22 (June 1, 2013): 36–46; and *India after Naxalbari: Unfinished History* (New York: Monthly Review Press, 2019).
13 Nandini Sundar, *The Burning Forest: India's War in Bastar* (New York: Verso, 2017).
14 Pierre Rosanvallon, *Counter-democracy: Politics in an Age of Distrust*. Transalated by Arthur Goldhammer (Cambridge: Cambridge University Press, 2008).
15 Ernesto Laclau, *On Populist Reason* (London: Verso, 2005).
16 Akhil Gupta, *Red Tape: Bureaucracy, Structural Violence, and Poverty in India* (Durham, NC: Duke University Press, 2012).
17 Partha Chatterjee, *The Politics of the Governed: Reflections on Popular Politics in Most of the World* (New York: Columbia University Press, 2004); and *Lineages of Political Society: Studies in Postcolonial Democracy* (New York: Columbia University Press, 2011).
18 Ajay Gudavarthy, ed., *Re-framing Democracy and Agency in India: Interrogating Political Society* (London: Anthem Press, 2012).
19 Arjun Appadurai, "Deep Democracy," *Public Culture* 14, no. 1 (Winter 2002): 21–47.
20 Partha Chatterjee, "A Relativist View of the Indian Nation," in S. Anandhi, Karthick Ram Manoharan, M. Vijayabaskar and A. Kalaiyarasan, eds., *Rethinking Social Justice: Essays in Honour of M. S. S. Pandian* (New Delhi: Orient Blackswan, 2019).

21 Ernesto Laclau, *On Populist Reason* (London: Verso, 2005).
22 Partha Chatterjee, *In the Name of the People: Reflections on Popular Sovereignty Today* (New York: Columbia University Press, 2019).

Select Bibliography

Appadurai, Arjun, "Deep Democracy," *Public Culture* 14, no. 1 (Winter 2002): 21–47.

Banerjee, Sumanta, *In the Wake of Naxalbari* (Calcutta: Subarnarekha, 1980).

Basu, Pradip, *Towards Naxalbari (1953–1967): An Account of Inner-party Ideological Struggle* (Calcutta: Progressive Publishers, 2000).

Buck-Morss, Susan, *Dreamworld and Catastrophe: The Passing of Mass Utopia in East and West* (Cambridge, MA: MIT Press, 2000).

Chatterjee, Partha, *In the Name of the People: Reflections on Popular Sovereignty Today* (New York: Columbia University Press, 2019a).

Chatterjee, Partha, *Lineages of Political Society: Studies in Postcolonial Democracy* (New York: Columbia University Press, 2011).

Chatterjee, Partha, *The Politics of the Governed: Reflections on Popular Politics in Most of the World* (New York: Columbia University Press, 2004).

Chatterjee, Partha, "A Relativist View of the Indian Nation," in S. Anandhi, Karthick Ram Manoharan, M. Vijayabaskar and A. Kalaiyarasan, eds., *Rethinking Social Justice: Essays in Honour of M. S. S. Pandian* (New Delhi: Orient Blackswan, 2019b).

D'Mello, Bernard, *India after Naxalbari: Unfinished History* (New York: Monthly Review Press, 2019).

D'Mello, Bernard, "The Near and the Far: Why Is India's Liberal-Political Democracy Rotten?" *Economic and Political Weekly* 48, no. 22 (June 1, 2013): 36–46.

D'Mello, Bernard, "What Is Maoism?" *Economic and Political Weekly* 44, no. 47 (November 21, 2009): 39–48.

Gudavarthy, Ajay, ed., *Re-framing Democracy and Agency in India: Interrogating Political Society* (London: Anthem Press, 2012).

Gupta, Akhil, *Red Tape: Bureaucracy, Structural Violence, and Poverty in India* (Durham, NC: Duke University Press, 2012).

Laclau, Ernesto, *On Populist Reason* (London: Verso, 2005).

Mukherji, Nirmalangshu, *The Maoists in India: Tribals Under Siege* (London: Pluto Press, 2012).

Navlakha, Gautam, *Days and Nights in the Heartland of Rebellion* (New Delhi: Penguin, 2012).

Rosanvallon, Pierre, *Counter-democracy: Politics in an Age of Distrust*. Translated by Arthur Goldhammer (Cambridge: Cambridge University Press, 2008).

Roy, Arundhati, *Walking with the Comrades* (New Delhi: Penguin, 2011).

Sundar, Nandini, *The Burning Forest: India's War in Bastar* (New York: Verso, 2017).

Yadav, Yogendra, "Understanding the Second Democratic Upsurge: Trends of Bahujan Participation in the Electoral Politics of the 1990s," in Francine Frankel, Zoya Hasan, Rajeev Bhargava and Balveer Arora, eds., *Transforming India: Social and Political Dynamics of Democracy* (Delhi: Oxford University Press, 2000).

13

Democracy and the Moment of Politics

Aditya Nigam

Democracy Today

Recent movements across the world have raised unsettling questions about the very meaning of democracy. From the Occupy Wall Street movement to the *Indignados* in Spain and Greece (*Aganaktismenoi* in Greek), and the anticorruption movement in India, we have witnessed a rage against the representative system alongside demands for "real democracy." Often, the rage against the representative system has manifested itself in the form of a rejection of politics as such.

This new situation in many parts of the world points not merely to a new chapter of the history of "democracy," apparently already known in all its fullness, but equally significantly, calls for *a redefinition of what we know as "politics" itself.*

The past decade had seen the eruption of a desire for democracy in many Asian countries as well—Nepal, Pakistan, Burma, Thailand, followed by the Arab Spring in 2010–11, in turn followed by the mass movements in the Hong Kong part of China. However, most of these movements were directed against autocratic regimes and read as raising the issue of a "democratic deficit."

Democracy, in these movements, became a sign that collected around it all sorts of desires, ranging from the desire to be free to the desire to consume. At one level, these were not very different from the way the idea of democracy functioned in the mass uprisings against state socialism toward the end of the twentieth century. The movements and rebellions on the "Asian and Arab street" (to modify an expression from Asef Bayat) were directed against the oppressive and corrupt dictatorial regimes that presided over these countries.[1] However, these movements did not seem to pose a challenge to the idea of democracy as embodiment of "popular will" through electoral representation, primarily because they were taking place in polities that were either dictatorships or monarchies.[2]

But when "Tahrir Square" becomes the signifier of a global desire for democracy and when its call reverberates in the Occupy Wall Street movement or other protests across Europe, there seems to be a different notion at work. When mass movements erupt in the heart of celebrated democracies of Europe or the United States—calling for Real Democracy Now![3] they have a different story to tell. The mass demonstrations against the proposed multimillion Euro bailout for banks in Spain and against harsh austerity measures in Greece told the story of a democracy hijacked by corporations and powerful banks. In both the United States and Europe the question of proposed "economic" measures, were seen as unequivocally political while, at the same time, formal politics was repudiated. Indeed, what is significant is the way the question of democracy is raised alongside a rejection of extant politics

The recent round of mass struggles in India falls within this latter category of movements taking place within a largely functioning democracy. The anticorruption movement that emerged under the banner of India Against Corruption (IAC) in 2011, with Anna Hazare as its figurehead, spoke in the name of democracy and yet, rejected "politics" altogether.[4] And once again, the term "corruption" here served as a hinge, connecting the two supposedly distinct domains of "politics" and "economics."

Both motifs appear with considerable regularity in all movements across the world: First, their "anti-political" stance, which manifests itself not only in terms of their rhetoric against political parties but also in a disdain for what we can call "the political" itself.[5] Second, there is the *recurrent theme of corruption, thievery and fraud* that appears in many of them. Between them, I will suggest, they demand a reappraisal of our understanding of the relationship between "the political" and "the economic," of the mythical separateness of the two domains as if they are governed by discrete logics and principles. The economic state of joblessness or poverty or of a simultaneous bailout of powerful banks is not a matter of the immanent logic of something called "the economy" alone but a profoundly political question. However, our response cannot be the standard Marxist one, which sees the political and the economic as mutually imbricated, but tends to reduce the political to a mere effect of the economic—at least in some "last instance." I have argued elsewhere that there is no permanent separation of the two domains and that the boundaries between them are unstable, giving us different constellations of the political and the economic.[6] Understood thus, we can see neoliberalism, for instance, as one way of redrawing the boundaries between the two domains. Contemporary movements, on the other hand, demand their redrawing in a very different way. For the purposes of this paper, I will focus instead, on the first question—namely that of politics as such.

"Populism" and the Postideological Moment

A brief comment on the rejection of the political is in order before we proceed. One thing seems evident in the recent uprisings in Asia and the Arab world as well as movements in the United States and Europe: They possibly signal the passing of that particular form—the party form—that has structured all modern politics in the last two centuries. To this form belongs the history of twentieth-century totalitarianisms but also actually existing twentieth-century democracies held hostage to the interests of the powerful, as Jacques Derrida has suggested (Derrida 1994: 102). It is this form, I argue, that has revealed itself as the instrument for the destruction of politics in the political.[7] This is as true of societies where parties have become instruments of naked power as it is of those where they function within a formal democracy but increasingly look like one another.

It is this form that is now suspect for mass movements all over the world. Yet no new modes of rule have emerged to replace this form—and so every revolution or mass upsurge ends up overthrowing dictatorial regimes only to be replaced by new parties all wanting to head in the same direction. However, today, we are no longer innocent about parties and their professed claims of ideology. Even in India, where elections routinely register large turnouts, people seldom vote because they believe in the ideological platform of the party they choose; most people vote "tactically," because they must keep certain channels of access to power open for themselves.

The "anti-political" stance of contemporary movements points toward a rejection of the party form and the attendant conflation of the representative system with democracy. Some of these characteristics have long been associated with the phenomenon of "populism" but many contemporary movements go beyond populism insofar as they are not articulated around charismatic figures but mediated through new media technologies that make direct horizontal communication possible. Such mobilizations are ephemeral; they come into being and disappear with equal rapidity.

These movements make no attempt at "capturing power" and changing things by taking hold of the state. They have no ideals to realize, no blueprints to which the world must conform—to borrow from what Marx said of the Paris Commune. Indeed, these are precisely the aspects that have made them targets of attacks on the Left, namely their "lack of ideology" and their "post-political" character. Nonetheless, this disavowal of "power politics" speaks of a deeper problem with the understanding of politics and democracy as theatres of the "will to power." The discipline/s of political science and political theory have long happily worked with the assumption that it is popular will that constitutes political power and that parties and leaders merely "represent" the "people." Contemporary movements and struggles no longer seem inclined to innocently buy this fiction, given their larger critique of power and representation—even though some like the Aam Aadmi Party in India or Syriza in Greece have entered the business of formal politics and government.

We can begin to understand the question/s posed by these movements if we recognize that their *simultaneous* rejection of the political, *alongside* espousal of democracy, is not a contradiction but a pointer toward a crying need to reconceptualize "democracy" and "politics" afresh.

Critiques of representation are nothing new. However, earlier critiques of representation were premised on a notion of popular sovereignty and what Pierre Rosanvallon calls the "exaltation of the will" (Rosanvallon 2006: 190). They led back either to notions of direct democracy or civic republicanism. The idea of direct democracy never acquired wider purchase because it seemed unsuitable to large modern societies. The republican idea fared better but insofar as it was based on the heroic notion of a permanently active citizenry it was destined to lose to the idea of representation. Liberalism's power in this respect came from the fact that it recognized that people do not always want to "be political" in the Arendtian sense. Hannah Arendt's idea that freedom resides in the capacity to act politically and that freedom exists as long as one acts demanded too much of an ordinary citizen. In this sense, liberalism alone recognized the space for the nonheroic and the ordinary.

In the discussion that follows, I wish to move beyond notions of politics and democracy grounded in assumptions of will, power, representation, and so on, that structure our understandings of everyday political practice. As a consequence, we tend to misrecognize, for instance, the simple act of voting as an exercise of will; of choosing representatives. As against this, I want to suggest, popular practices of voting, engaging with party politics and participating in mass movements are better understood in terms of what ordinary people do—a game that they play with the political class, in order to make everyday lives more meaningful. In other words, I recognize with Jacques Ranciere, that democracy as such does not exist and that power is always exercised by oligarchies, but is redirected under pressure from democratic struggles toward an orientation to the popular. (Ranciere 2006: 52) Such "redirection" does not happen in any ongoing fashion; rather, it occurs in moments when popular struggles force transformations. Characteristically, power returns to oligarchies in "normal" times. Moments of "spectacular" eruption need to be seen in their close connection to the everyday and how they rewrite the everyday.

In what follows, I explore issues regarding politics and democracy through an investigation of two specific instances from recent Indian politics. Both instances can actually be read as a part of the same moment, which constitutes a backdrop to the current phase of mass struggles. At stake in both is the place of "the economic" in the political. It was through the virtual destruction of politics in the political domain and the staging of a neoliberal consensus that the formal business of party politics continued. Recent mass movements disrupted that happy consensus. To that extent, they should be seen as political in the profoundest sense, irrespective of their explicit rhetoric. This is the question I have elsewhere termed the "implosion of the political" (Nigam 2008) or more simply the "destruction of politics in the political."

The particular moment of the erasure of politics in the 1990s typifies the emergence of a neoliberal consensus. My critical engagement with Partha Chatterjee's work prepares the context for entering the issue of "politics" and "the political" beyond this moment of neoliberalism.

The Erasure of Politics: "Democratic Upsurge" of the 1990s

The 1990s saw the electoral rise to power of a whole range of Dalit and backward caste parties across North India. This unleashed what has been called the "second democratic upsurge" which deepened the processes in motion since the "first democratic upsurge" of the 1960s when the ruling Congress lost power in nine states (Yadav 2000). The first upsurge had been a manifestation of the "widening" of the "participatory base" of the electoral system with the lower castes entering it in a big way. The second upsurge was seen as a robust continuation of that "downward thrust." (Yadav 2000: 121) This "silent revolution" has transformed the political composition of state legislatures and the parliament, displacing the hegemony of the English speaking upper caste secular elite (Jaffrelot 2003). The new electoral upsurge represented the rise of forces, which were underprivileged in terms of caste background and culturally speaking were vernacular at once regional and rustic. Their arrival on the scene marginalized an older, English-educated elite and the elitist nature of Indian politics since Independence.[8]

This 1990s democratic upsurge has been widely recognized. Yet, the question of what it might possibly mean has actually never really been posed. Are we to understand that representatives of the subaltern always act in the interests of their own community/ class? Do they necessarily act in ways that are democratic? Are subaltern representatives immune to the logic of representation that operates in the context of other social groups? Do subaltern representatives simply "represent" the will of their people, or do they, like all representatives also determine/ constitute that will? Can we say that there is something about the formal political domain—the logic of rule[9]—that works on parties themselves, such that, diverse though they be, they come to acquire some common features and interests? If our answer to the last question is in the affirmative, then representation is seldom about the represented, but rather the logic of rule. Consequently, there can be no straight line that runs one way, from "the people" to "the representative." Precisely for this reason the question of the democratic upsurge calls for greater scrutiny.

The idea of a democratic upsurge has led to the recognition that we now have nonelite representatives from lower caste and vernacular backgrounds dominating state legislatures and parties—and that is something *intrinsically* democratic, perhaps even sacrosanct. This understanding has become common sense such that most political and social scientists and media commentators take the electoral rise of the subaltern castes as coterminous with the expansion of democracy.

Thus, for instance, at the height of the anticorruption movement in 2011 and later in 2012–13, after the formation of the Aam Aadmi Party (AAP), the main attack against the movement and AAP from within the "political system" was mounted in the name of the subaltern. The movement's strident attack on the "political system" as such, made it easier for its critics to conflate the "system" with "lower castes and dalits." Apart from epithets like "fascist" and "populist" being hurled at the movement, there was also the question that was routinely thrown at its leaders: whom do you represent? Why don't you contest elections and prove your strength? Sections of the radical intelligentsia rose up in defense of the parliament—sections who, one would have thought, had no investment whatsoever, in the parliamentary system. And behind their strident defense of a largely ineffective parliament was a now-sacrosanct belief that the parliament, following the Mandalite democratic revolution, was dominated by lower caste and dalit members and *that was why* "elitist" "middle class" activists were out to destroy it. The fact that it was the two main parties—the Congress and the BJP—that were the main targets of the anticorruption movement, made no difference to the general thrust of the radical attack. One section of the radical intelligentsia perhaps harbored the idea that neoliberal elites actually wanted to dispense with parliamentary institutions. It was argued that the movement was, for this reason, in sync with the position of the antireservation elites. The radical intelligentsia, therefore, felt called upon to stand in defense of "politics" against the antipolitical rhetoric of the movement. (Arundhati Roy (2011), Partha Chatterjee (2011b), Arjun Appadorai (2011)

I argue instead that this democratic upsurge was simultaneously accompanied by an implosion of the political. First, virtually coeval with the rise of lower caste parties was the advent of neoliberal orthodoxy across the bureaucracy, judiciary, media, and the highly vocal globally circulating Indian elite. This was the conjuncture of the collapse of the Soviet Union and other East European state socialisms, which deprived Left-wing critics of neoliberalism of any credible argument. As a consequence, not only did neoliberal arguments for privatization and deregulation gain unprecedented currency; it no longer had any credible critics left. The reified idea of the "economy" as a domain that only specialists understand and neoliberalism as some sort of a *zeitgeist* apparently uniting the whole world, added to its power. All parties concurred that whatever else they might fight each other on, the economy would not be one of them. The code ensured that the fundamental "rules of the economy" would be protected by them—via the appeasement of private corporate capital. Issues central to the neoliberal project, including easing of labor laws for capital, easing environmental clearances, acquisition of land and providing other incentives like tax waivers etc. became part of a new governing consensus.

Political opposition to the neoliberal project evaporated overnight; politics vacated the streets. The 1990s led to a drastic redrawing of the boundaries between the economic and the political—which more than anything else, amounted to a destruction of politics in the political.[10]

Second, this was also the period of a media explosion—as satellite television gradually started spreading to different corners of the country and twenty-four-hour news channels grew at an exponential rate. Issues relating to communal violence and secularism remained for the large part the major points of contention in the political domain. Caste issues also became framed within the larger secular–communal binary that prevailed during this period.

Third, the unraveling of the Congress and the rise of backward caste and Dalit politics also meant the rise of region-based parties, all of whom became players at the national level. As single party majorities gave way to coalitions, all parties either went into government or waited to be in one. The logic of rule pressed on them with equal vigor.

There were political mobilizations on the streets. Mobilizations of the Hindu Right organizations continued, though even here, it was more the nonparliamentary wings like the VHP and Bajrang Dal who appeared most active. Far away from the urban centers, in forest areas and adivasi villages, struggles against land acquisition, against forced evictions for the sake of mining companies, struggles against mass displacement continued, with loose coalitions of social movements and smaller left-wing groups taking the lead. In some areas, the resistance took the shape of armed Maoist insurgency. In my reading these instances confirm rather than refute the hypothesis of the implosion of the political, for they demonstrate how the logic of rule pushed *politics and political contestation* out of the *formal political process*. The logic of rule operated to redraw the contours of the political such that it lays down what can be said and what cannot; what can be done and what cannot. In a way that recalls Jacques Ranciere's idea of the two logics of "police" and of "politics," there seems to be a permanent war between the logic of rule that operates through the "statifying" logic of order and politics (Ranciere 2006). Though Ranciere does not use the category of "the political," one can read in his work a clear distinction between politics as a specific activity or practice that *need not* always happen in the domain we identify as "the political." Politics is that which disrupts the police logic, or what I am referring to as the logic of rule. Politics happens when it disrupts the drive to order characteristic of the logic of rule. Politics need not always be self-consciously "political": insofar as it redraws the boundaries of the sayable and the doable, politics does its work, whether or not it claims to be political.

This is the sense in which one can read the recent anticorruption movement as political, despite its antipolitical positioning, which it shares with many other contemporary movements. The movement instituted a break in the logic of rule that has operated at least since the 1980s and became entrenched in the 1990s, whereby it ceased to matter which party was in government.

Let us now take a closer look at another instantiation of this destruction of politics—in the Left ruled state of West Bengal in the last quarter of the twentieth century.

Marxists in Power: The Logic of Rule

In May 2006, the Left Front (LF) government in West Bengal returned to power for the ninth time, under the leadership of Buddhadeb Bhattacharjee, the incumbent chief minister who had taken over from Jyoti Basu when the latter retired from active politics in 2000. The victory was spectacular.[11]

There is consensus that this unprecedented performance of the LF was primarily due to the "reinvention" of the CPI(M) and the generation of "Brand Buddha" (i.e. Buddhadeb Bhattacharjee) as the new face of Marxist politics (Basu 2007: 289). The key element of this "reinvention" was its total immersion in the logic of rule that has already been evident in the LF's policies and practice from 1977.

It may not be out of place here to recall that the United Front (UF) governments of 1967 and 1969 which were led by the CPI(M) were far more heterogeneous in character. The participation of the CPI(M) in these governments had been justified in terms of their imagined role as "instruments of struggle" (Basavapunnaiah 1985).[12]

It was within this perspective that the two UF governments functioned. During their tenure, militant struggles of the industrial working class and peasants (for the take over of *benami* land) were "unleashed." New coercive forms of struggle like the *gherao* were an invention of this phase of UF rule, leading to massive flight of capital from the state to other parts of the country. The fall of these governments was accompanied by massive repression alongside significant progressive agrarian legislations (Dasgupta 1984). Some of the surplus land that had been taken over by the peasants soon reverted back to the *jotedars* (Ibid).[13]

By the time the Left Front came to power in 1977, it had learnt its lessons. It knew it had to deal with massive unemployment in the state, apart from other crises including anarchy in higher education and massive electricity shortages. With university examinations and results being delayed by years and unprecedented unemployment life in the state and its capital Kolkata had become unbearable. The CPI(M) and LF decided to address these problems by reining in worker militancy and providing a "healthy investment climate." On the agrarian front, it was acutely aware that militant land struggles of the 1960s were no longer possible. Out of this realization came "Operation Barga"—the ambitious programme for the registration of sharecroppers that would enable permanency of tenure and protect them from landowners.

From the very outset the LF government prioritized the business of running the government, addressing the unemployment issue through industrialization, and tackling the crisis in the power sector. Its innovative programme of decentralization through panchayats along with Operation Barga accomplished a significant change in the rural power structure that provided it a strong base among the rural poor. This became the backbone of LF's political support in the state even as it lost support among the middle classes.[14]

As the CPI(M) and the LF settled into the routine work of government, that became the party's raison d'être and the appeasement of capital as its centerpiece. Thus the decade of the 1980s when industry after industry closed down and managements resorted to frequent lockouts and large-scale defrauding of workers of the provident fund and ESI dues, Ranabir Samaddar wrote of "a decade of strike by capital" (2013: 3–7). To cap it all, stagnation had set in despite impressive performance in the power sector and improvement in agricultural growth (Dasgupta 1984).

Largely because of its belief in the virtues of industrialization in ridding the state of unemployment, the LF committed to a programme of West Bengal's industrial development. However, there were obstacles in the way, as the state government could not move an inch in the direction of setting up industrial projects without the central government's approval. In the mid-1980s, attempts were made to set up industries in what was termed the "joint sector" with limited success.[15]

Ironically, the CPI(M) and the LF found themselves suddenly liberated in the early 1990s, as neoliberal economic reforms dismantled controls and opened up the possibility of state governments directly inviting industrialists to set up industries. This is the period then, when major urban restructuring was undertaken, in keeping with the trend of urban transformations in other parts of India. The city was reimagined with a globally oriented, consuming middle class at its center. This transformation is best exemplified in the development of Rajarhat New Township on the suburbs of Kolkata. It is one of the cases of resettlement discussed by Partha Chatterjee as an instance of negotiations in political society (2004: 72–3). In other less benign accounts, however, Rajarhat embodies the "savage commodification of land and the resurgence of private property—private roads, private power generation equipment, private pleasure houses, private sources of drinking water, private schools, private villas, private housing estates with private guards, and, the most private of all, private production units in special economic zones (SEZs)" (Samaddar 2013: 86). This transformation of the city was effected through another, that of the CPI(M) and LF rule. The transformation of the CPI(M) is not merely from a party of movement to a party of government; it was now a party with deeply entrenched economic interests, especially in real estate—a transformation poignantly captured in Moinak Biswas's film *sthaniyo shongbad*.

Buddhadeb Bhattacharjee was the icon of what the corporate media referred to as the "New Left." It was with his ascent to chief ministership and the fashioning of a new capital-friendly CPI(M) that the middle class returned to the Left Front fold in a big way. Buddhadeb made no bones about the fact that he considered previous LF rule as lost decades. The corporate media was effusive in its support. And until then, the CPI(M) retained its firm base in the peasantry. Electorally, this was a formidable combination and that was what won Bhattacharjee and his LF the election in 2006.

Singur-Nandigram Moment: Return of Politics

However, this combination was highly unstable. For as soon as the industrialization program was put into action, it brought the peasantry into direct conflict with the government.

Within days of the government's swearing in, the first explosive encounter occurred in Singur, a highly fertile area where large tracts of agricultural land had been forcibly acquired by the government to be handed over to the Tatas for their Nano car factory. People watched in horror as TV screens showed armed police personnel landing up in Singur to cordon off the land, in the face of fierce resistance by the peasantry.

Singur was followed, within a few months, by another explosion, this time in the Nandigram area in East Midnapore district. Nandigram erupted in early 2007 when information leaked out that the Haldia Development Board was at the point of acquiring 14,500 acres of land for the setting up of a Special Economic Zone by the Indonesia-based Salim group of Industries. As the news spread, angry villagers set up roadblocks, set fire to the local CPI(M) office, and clashed with the police leading to two violent counterattacks by the CPI(M). The second of these attacks, in November 2007, was aimed at the "liberation" of Nandigram, i.e., its recovery for the CPI(M) to which it had become inaccessible from the initial days of the revolt (Nigam 2010: 175–6).

The Singur-Nandigram moment inaugurated a rapid unraveling of the Left Front's political support base. This base was not a coalition but the result of a series of investments in the figure of Buddhadeb and the political machine called the CPI(M). Buddhadeb Bhattacharjee as the embodiment of a Left that had steadfastly stood with the rural poor coexisted with the Buddhadeb in whom the hopes of a new corporate-friendly, consumption-oriented West Bengal were vested. If Singur inaugurated a break with the CPI(M)'s three decade tenure, Nandigram took it to new insurrectionary heights. The combined effect was visible in the dissipation of the CPI(M)'s most stable support base, namely the peasantry, within a year of its spectacular electoral victory. The rapidity with which the CPI(M)'s organization and social support unraveled was breathtaking. It led to the electoral defeat of the CPI(M) in the panchayat elections, followed by its stunning defeat in the 2009 parliamentary elections and finally in the state assembly in 2011. The process of unraveling continues even now.

Nandigram burst forth on the political horizon at an all-India level. Not only did it become a symbol that galvanized ongoing struggles against land acquisition, it also instituted a partial break in the *logic of rule as it came to operate after the second democratic upsurge*. Its impact put the central government on the back foot on the issue of land acquisition. Indeed, the new land acquisition legislation (Land Acquisition and

Rehabilitation and Resettlement Act, 2013) enacted by the UPA government of that time continued to dog the NDA government (Chakravorty 2015: 35).[16]

The story of LF and CPI(M) rule instantiates a more general condition whereby *the logic of rule establishes itself only by displacing politics from the formal domain of politics.* What this drive accomplishes is the opening up of all other domains of life as potential sites of politics: what can no longer be articulated in the political domain can now, in principle, be articulated at any point, from any location. Any site can be the site of politics, insofar as politics is about challenging and redrawing the boundaries of what can be said and made visible and insofar as it interrupts the "normal" rhythm.

Partha Chatterjee's appropriation of Foucault's idea of governmentality brings it into a relationship with the question of "democracy." Chatterjee's claim is that in "most of the world," it is the domain he calls "political society" that becomes the actual domain of politics, for that is where the governed make their claims. Interestingly, this domain is distinct from both, *the formal domain of politics* as well as from what I have identified as the *activity called politics*. Chatterjee's idea of politics, however, seems quite restrictive for it is always about negotiations leading to resolutions, however unstable. Chatterjee's framework does not allow us to read the Singur/Nandigram moments, for instance, as anything other than aberrations. Mass politics, which neither relies on the sanitized logic of civil society nor remains within the confines of "negotiation" and "forming associations" in order to represent their interests to the rulers, seems destined to lie outside political society in Chatterjee's reckoning.[17] In his framework, eruptions like Singur and Nandigram remain ungraspable. Essentially, he considers "insurgency" (of the Nandigram type) as but "a crucial and revealing moment in subaltern history" that can at best throw light on the daily life of ordinary existence but *"cannot ever fully explain it"* (Chatterjee 2011a: 150, emphasis added). In other words, the function of such insurgencies, to him, is to illuminate everyday life at best. He does not see them as transformative in our sense of politics as producing effects.

Chatterjee rightly cautions his readers not to look for "imposing a singular conception of the political subject derived from older traditions of revolutionary politics":

> Yesterday, the political subject was on hunger strike in Manipur, protesting against the atrocities of the army. Today, he is digging up roads in Nandigram to prevent the police from coming in. Tomorrow, when Nandigram calms down, she will be throwing stones at the police in Kashmir. But in any one of those places, after the extraordinary act of resistance ceases either because it is repressed by force or runs out of stream or, as sometimes happens, wins its immediate demands, does the political subject vacate the scene when everyday politics is resumed? Or, does she pursue a different mode of political action? *It is the latter activity that I find interesting, because it generally receives little attention.*
>
> (Ibid: 148–9, emphasis added)

While I agree that one should not read revolutionary subjectivity in these acts of rebellion, my disagreement with Chatterjee's reading of such moments concerns the very idea of politics itself.

Against his reading, I propose that we see such moments of eruption as *the return of politics which force a reopening of the "resolution" that the logic of rule institutes in order to conduct the work of government.*

It is a great merit of Chatterjee's intervention that he takes the question of politics and democracy away from the problematic of the will, especially through his reformulation of democracy as the "politics of the governed." Drawing on Foucault's idea of governmentality vis-à-vis the standard paradigm of sovereignty and right, Chatterjee elaborates a notion of popular politics that is certainly free of many of the difficulties that attend what Rosanvallon has called the "exaltation of the will." Chatterjee's move has the advantage of shifting our gaze on to the level of the popular, in contradistinction to Foucault's preoccupation with disciplinary power and governmentality.

However, by hitching the idea of popular politics, conducted in the domain of political society, exclusively to governmentality and welfare, he impoverishes the idea of popular politics itself. Everyday politics, beyond the moment of spectacular eruption, becomes for him just another way of finding a place under the shadow of governmentality. To cite Chatterjee himself:

> The destitute woman in a West Bengal village in the 1960s [who] would have probably sat outside the landlord's house or begged in the bazaar; today she goes to the panchayat or party office. I think that difference deserves not to be brushed aside.
>
> (Chatterjee 2011b: 149)

The reference here is to a woman in a West Bengal village who went from the panchayat office to the ruling party office to that of the block development officer, "making her plea for some help." She would in the process manage to get something—food ration, a sari, or a blanket, or perhaps even some cash … after forms were filled and she had put her thumb impression on them. Says Chatterjee: "This woman survived by daily manipulating the local levers of an utterly *banal political machine*, but *I find it unconscionable to exclude her from the domain of political subjectivity*" (Chatterjee 2011b: 148, emphasis added).

Power, "Politics" and the Everyday

What really is politics? What is the specificity of the activity that we call "politics"? Is every connection that people make with the official machinery political—including filling forms and accessing governmental welfare? Can we distinguish such connections from the daily war of attrition that goes on between the municipal and police authorities and ordinary folk, as the former step up their drive against, say, cycle rickshaws and hawkers? Is that an important facet of what Chatterjee calls the everyday? What is the relationship of this kind of "politics" with the formal domain of politics where elections are held, governments formed, policies formulated and executed?

Starting with the slogan "personal is political" once raised by feminists, which sought to include the domain of family and intimate relations within it, a whole range of fields are designated as being political—for instance, culture, knowledge, school, asylum, and so on. Foucault's intervention that talked of the "microphysics of power" constituted another critical moment in this designation of everything marked by power relations as political—though that may not have been Foucault's own concern. While there may be an element of truth in each of these assertions, it is necessary to specify what exactly is it that is *political* in each instance? Take the sphere of intimate relations or the institution called the school. Is it possible to label every activity in these spheres as "politics" without reducing the term to a meaningless expression?

Instead, we might recognize that politics can, in principle take place in any site or location, but that it does not turn that site into an endlessly proliferating "political" domain. This means that we need to see politics as a specific kind of activity that can occur anywhere. For the present, *we can make a preliminary distinction between power and politics, in order to isolate the specific* moment of politics *from the operations of power in general.*

Power does not always produce antagonisms since its success is predicated upon the willing consent of the dominated. That power is the most sophisticated that produces willing subjects in the course of its operations.[18] There are moments however, when the dominated refuse to be dominated. This does not mean that they will immediately rise in revolt but they produce a dissonance in the "normal" rhythms of power. The modality of production of this dissonance could be a mere utterance, a refusal to comply or the enunciation of a claim. But things do not remain the same thereafter. In other words, I am suggesting that that while politics always operates in a field of power, it is not reducible to it. It is the activity that produces dissonance in the normal rhythms of power.[19] In that sense, politics occurs in the caesura when power faces its own dissipation to produce the willing subject.

Everything that involves a brush with the government is not politics. Politics can neither be seen, from this point of view, as an activity defined solely with reference to its relationship to state and government, just as it cannot be understood as an infinitely capacious term that absorbs all relations of power within itself. Everyday life is not politics. It is not all about politics. But politics occurs not in routinely accessing governmental welfare benefit but when normal rhythms are disturbed.

Such interruptions are not always democratic or radical; they can manifest as reactionary mass movements. But often, in an electoral-representative polity, matters appear to be more complicated than the above outline sketch might suggest. Thus, in order to conclude, it is worthwhile recalling another aspect of our recent history. The implementation of the recommendations of the Mandal Commission by VP Singh's government in 1990 was a governmental act, at least on the face of it, and it drew unprecedented mass protests. It will be a mistake however to read the government/mass movement relation here in simple Rancierean terms. Although the moment of interruption came via the government there was actually the playing out of a much more complicated dynamic where governmental power became a momentary instrument in the breaking of the code, so to speak. What we saw in the mass movements of privileged upper caste youth, on the other hand, was a defense of age-long privileges. I do not have the space here to trace the details of how the Mandal Commission recommendations came to fructify in this moment of 1990, but its history reaches back four decades to the constitution of the Kaka Kalelkar Commission in the 1950s.[20] What is worth underlining is the fact that between the 1950s and the late 1970s, especially in the post-Emergency situation, the Janata Party became the vehicle of many backward castes. That was what enabled the re-emergence of the agenda of reservations for backward castes, leading to the 1978 Mandal Commission. The Commission tabled its report in 1980 and it was once again put in cold storage by the Congress government till the new formation of the National Front led by VP Singh, and backed by most backward caste parties, came to power. This complicated story reveals that the brief moments in which the backwards caste representatives were in government, prior to the democratic upsurge, were deeply unsettling for the traditional structures of caste-class power (Menon and Nigam 2007: Chapter 1). The neat Rancierean divide between the police/state logic on the one hand, and politics on the other, breaks down here. What we have instead is the way politics—or *political practice*—traverses at once the popular and the "governmental," producing effects that would forever change Indian society and politics.

The discussion above invites us, on the one hand, to isolate the moment of politics as something that can happen in any site; on the other, it enables us to see that the site that is formally designated as the site of politics is often evacuated of political practices. The logic of rule represents the erasure of politics but it is also threatened by the possibility of politics.

This reformulation of politics is directly connected to the question posed at the beginning, namely that of the everyday, that is disavowed by the problematic of will on which the entire edifice of the political rests. By taking the question away from any notion of a heroic, permanently active citizenry and seeing politics as an activity that occurs only in specific moments, it allows us to understand moments of spectacular mass struggles in continuity with the everyday.

Notes

1 I use this expression in Asef Bayat's sense where the "political street" refers to a space of "collective sensibilities, shared feelings and public judgement of ordinary people in their day-to-day utterances and practices" (Bayat 2010: 212).

2 Jacques Ranciere reminds us that even though "representation" is a way of aggregating "popular will," the two were actually opposing terms. As he puts it: "Originally representation was the exact contrary of democracy … The Founding Fathers and a number of their French emulators saw in it precisely the means for the elite to exercise power *de facto*, and in the name of the people … " (Ranciere 2006: 53).

3 This was the name of one of the key platforms and also a slogan at the recent mass demonstrations at Madrid's Puerto del Sol (May–June 2011).

4 Subsequent movements like the one against the gang rape of a paramedic Delhi student in 2012 and by students of Jadavpur University protesting against sexual harassment can be read as emerging within a similar space of possibilities. For a detailed discussion of the Jadavpur movement, see Panjabi (2015).

5 My understanding of the distinction between "politics" and "the political" comes closer to Nicos Poultantzas's differentiation between the "juridico-political structure of the state," or "the political" and "political class practices (political class struggle)" which he calls "politics" (Poulantzas 1968: 37). Poulantzas uses the expression "the juridico-political *super*structure of the state" but we need not take the idea of the superstructure seriously. Indeed, we can drop the idea of a structure. In my opinion, this distinction can still work, even if we think of the state as an assemblage of multiple practices that function *as if* they constitute a structure—what Timothy Mitchell has called the production of the state as a structural effect (Mitchell 1991: 94). As opposed to this, we have the idea of politics as political practices. Political practice refers, says Poulantzas, to the transformation of a definite object (Mitchell 1991: 41). In other words, if the state effect is manifested in the elimination of conflict, the function of the state "as a cohesive factor in a formation's unity" (Mitchell 1991: 47), it is politics that constitutes the transformative moment. This usage is different from the one current in much of contemporary philosophy that follows Claude Leforts. For Lefort: "The political is thus revealed, not in what we call political activity, but in the double movement whereby the mode of institution of society appears and is obscured. It appears in the sense that *the process whereby a society is ordered and unified across its divisions* becomes visible. It is obscured in the sense that the locus of politics … becomes defined as particular, while the principle which generates the overall configuration is concealed." (Lefort 1988: 11, emphasis added).

6 In an unpublished paper, "Political Econographies and 'Capital': Revisiting the 'Passive Revolution Argument,'" presented on the occasion of the Silver Jubilee of the Forum for Contemporary Theory, Baroda, February 10–11, 2014.

7 The need for making a distinction between the formal domain of politics and the activity that we may call politics arises from my explorations of contemporary Indian politics. Here I have come up against a paradox: that of the evacuation of politics within the formal domain of politics even as politics and claim-making keeps making its appearance in other domains.

8 Paradoxically, the only exception to this change has been Left Front governed West Bengal. Under CPI(M) and LF rule, the state legislature remained a bastion of the upper caste, *bhadralok* elite.

9 The Hindi term "rajniti" is a close approximation. See Nigam (2013) (in Hindi).

10 With the restructuring of the city and the increasing contest over urban space with the ubiquitous presence of the automobile, the map of the Indian city—and of the democratic process—was redrawn. The automobile rewrote the city and demands of smooth traffic flows delegitimized the political street.

11 The LF bagged 235 out of 294 seats and a vote share of over 50 percent—36 seats and 2 percent votes more than it had won in 2001. There are enough indications that by 2001, the first election to be contested by the CPI (M)-led LF in the post-Jyoti Basu era, the magic of the Left had started wearing thin.

12 In 1967, the party produced a document titled *New Situation and the Party's Tasks* in order to clarify its role in participating in state governments. Following the split in the CPI in 1964, the section that formed the CPI(M), took an ambivalent position with respect to parliamentary transformation and thus, had to justify what its participation in government would mean. Additionally, the presence, by 1967, of a powerful radical Left movement in the shape of "Naxalism" that had emerged from within the CPI(M) and which rejected parliamentary participation

necessitated a clearer enunciation. It should be remembered that "Naxalism," in its heyday in 1967–71, had a powerful appeal among the youth of West Bengal and within large sections of the party. The path laid out by the 1967 document was two-fold which saw governments as instruments furthering the cause of mass struggles, *alongside* administration with a view to providing some "immediate relief" to the people.

13 Internal party briefings sought to convey that all lands were reverted to their *benami* owners—and this became justification for abandoning militant land struggles.

14 In retrospect, however, it seems that even this programme was deeply flawed insofar as it entrenched the practice of sharecropping rather than instituting tenancy abolition (Bandyopadhyay 2001).

15 Industrialization was turned into an emotive one by the Left Front, by pointing to "continued discrimination" by the Central government and the CPI(M) (the leading party of the Front) organizing blood donation camps to raise money for the Bakreshwar Thermal Power plant and the Haldia Petrochemical complex.

16 Chakravorty observes that the issue of land acquisition "reached a breaking point around 2007 … partly as a result of several high profile, violent cases" (Chakravorty 2015: 37).

17 Thus as he wryly puts it: "Insurgent Nandigram in West Bengal, after rebelling against a governmental regime dominated by one political party in 2007, has now *settled back into the same governmental regime*, but now dominated by another political party." See Chatterjee (2011a: 93, emphasis added).

18 This is where the question of what many Marxist and post-Marxist thinkers would call ideology or Foucault's subjectivation, comes in.

19 Jacques Ranciere's rendering of politics as interruption has been helpful in framing my own understanding. There is a problem however, with Ranciere's idea of politics—in that he sees it in entirely positive terms. His emphasis on the "part that has no part" or his equation of politics with democratic struggle leaves little possibility of understanding how extreme right-wing and xenophobic interventions must be understood as politics.

20 Those interested in that history can usefully consult Jaffrelot (2003).

Select Bibliography

Appadurai, Arjun, "Our Corruption, Our Selves," *Kafila*, August 30, 2011, http://kafila.org/2011/08/30/our-corruption-our-selves-arjun-appadurai/. Accessed November 2, 2015.

Arendt, Hannah, *The Human Condition* (Chicago and London: The University of Chicago Press, 1958).

Bandyopadhyay, D., "Tebhaga Movement in Bengal: A Retrospect," *Economic and Political Weekly* 36, no. 41 (2001): 3901–7.

Basavapunnaiah, M., "On Para 112 of Our Party Programme," *The Marxist* 3, no. 1 (January–March 1985): 28–41.

Basu, Partha Pratim, "Brand Buddha in India's West Bengal: The Left Reinvents Itself," *Asian Survey* 47, no. 2 (March–April 2007): 288–306.

Bayat, Asef, *Life as Politics: How Ordinary People Change the Middle East* (Amsterdam: Amsterdam University Press, 2010).

Bhattacharya, Dwaipayan, "Ominous Outcome for Left in West Bengal," *Economic and Political Weekly* 34, nos. 46–47 (November 20–26, 1999): 3267–9.

Chakravorty, Sanjoy, "Land Acquisition and the Rent-Seeking State," *Seminar*, no. 674 (October 2015): 35–9.

Chatterjee, Partha, "Against Corruption = Against Politics," *Kafila*, August 28, 2011b, http://kafila.org/2011/08/28/against-corruption-against-politics-partha-chatterjee/. Accessed November 2, 2015.

Chatterjee, Partha, *Lineages of Political Society* (Ranikhet: Permanent Black, 2011a).

Chatterjee, Partha, *The Nation and Its Fragments: Colonial and Postcolonial Histories* (Delhi: Oxford University Press, 1995).

Chatterjee, Partha, *The Politics of the Governed: Reflections on Popular Politics in Most of the World* (Delhi: Permanent Black, 2004).

CPI(M), *New Situation and Party's Tasks* (Calcutta: National Book Agency, 1967).

Dasgupta, Biplab, "Sharecropping in West Bengal: From Independence to Operation Barga," *Economic and Political Weekly* 19, no. 26 (1984): A85–A96.

Derrida, Jacques, *Spectres of Marx* (New York: Routledge, 1994).

Foucault, Michel, *The Birth of Biopolitics: Lectures at the College de France 1978–79* (Hampshire and New York: Palgrave Macmillan, 2008).

Jaffrelot, Christophe, *India's Silent Revolution: The Rise of the Low Castes in North Indian Politics* (Delhi: Permanent Black, 2003).

Lefort, Claude, *Democracy and Political Theory* (Cambridge: Polity Press, 1988).

Menon, Nivedita and Aditya Nigam, *Power and Contestaion: India Since 1989* (London: Zed Books, 2007).

Mitchell, Timothy, "The Limits of the State: Beyond Statist Approaches and Their Critics," *American Political Science Review* 85, no. 1 (1991): 77–96.

Mukherjee, Sanjib, "The Use and Abuse of Democracy in West Bengal," *Economic and Political Weekly* 42, no. 44 (November 3–9, 2007): 101–8.

Nigam, Aditya, *After Utopia: Modernity, Socialism and the Postcolony* (New Delhi: Viva Books, 2010).

Nigam, Aditya, "Implosion of the Political," *Journal of Contemporary Thought* 27, no. 27 (Summer 2008).

Nigam, Aditya, *The Insurrection of Little Selves: The Crisis of Secular Nationalism in India* (New Delhi: Oxford University Press, 2006).

Nigam, Aditya, "Rajneetik Samaj, Satta aur Siyasat: Partha (Chatterjee) se Aage Jahan Aur Bhi Hain," *Pratiman—Samay Samaj Sanskriti* (Delhi: CSDS and Vani Prakashan, January-June 2013), pp. 355–69.

Panjabi, Kavita, "Hokkolorob: A Hashtag Movement," *Seminar*, no. 674 (October 2015): 63–8.

Poulantzas, Nicos, *Political Power and Social Classes* (London: NLB and Sheed and Ward, 1978).

Proudhon, Pierre-Joseph, *What Is Property?* Ed., Donald R. Kelley and Bonnie G. Smith (Cambridge, UK: Cambridge University Press, 1993).

Rancière, Jacques, *Disagreement: Politics and Philosophy* (Minneapolis: University of Minnesota Press, 1999).

Rancière, Jacques, *Hatred of Democracy* (London: Verso, 2006).

Rosanvallon, Pierre and Samuel Moyn, ed., *Democracy Past and Future* (New York: Columbia University Press, 2006).

Roy, Arundhati, "I'd Rather Not Be Anna," *The Hindu*, October 2, 2011, http://www.thehindu.com/opinion/lead/id-rather-not-be-anna/article2379704.ece. Accessed November 2, 2015.

Samaddar, Ranabir, *Passive Revolution in West Bengal 1977–2011* (New Delh: Sage Publications Ltd., 2013).

Yadav, Yogendra, Transforming India: social and political dynamics of democracy edited by Francine R. Frankel, 2000, Oxford University Press: New York.

14

The New Conjuncture

Nivedita Menon

There are three strands to the conjuncture that India finds itself in today—Hindu Rashtra, predatory capitalism, and the way in which the pandemic has inflected this nexus.

The term Hindutva is no longer sufficient to describe the ideology that drives the Indian state. Hindutva (Hinduness as political identity) is indeed the ideology of Hindu nationalism, but the emphasis used to be on *samrasta* or gradual assimilation of the non-Hindu other. What has emerged now is the naked face of *Hindu supremacism* in institutions of the state.

A month after the NDA came to power in May 2014, Aditya Nigam and I wrote an epilogue to the second edition of our book *Power and Contestation: India after 1989* (2008), in which we concluded that "for the present, the power of Capital is on the ascendant, and the patrons of Hindu nationalism control institutions of government."[1] Nevertheless, we vastly underestimated the accelerated pace at which the RSS would push the Hindu Rashtra agenda at three levels, especially after May 2019 when BJP came back with an absolute majority on its own, its clout substantially enhanced by the seats of its allies. The first was *institutionally* (within months of the 2019 election victory, amending the Constitution by abrogating Article 370 on Kashmir and passing the Citizenship Amendment Act 2019—CAA); the second was *"by stealth"* (control of media, courts, and state governments by money power, political intimidation and co-option), and the third by unleashing on the ground[2] and in social media,[3] people incited (sometimes trained and sometimes paid) to carry out violence by word and action.

The Current Moment

Consider two scenarios that illustrate the conjuncture of Hindu Rashtra: predatory capitalism and the pandemic.

In April 2020, after the abrupt declaration of a national lockdown to "flatten the curve" of Covid infections, as hundreds of thousands of migrant workers walked long distances to their home states in conditions of exhaustion and starvation, the government took a decision that can make sense only within the surreal echo chamber of capitalism. It approved the conversion of surplus rice available with Food Corporation of India into ethanol for the manufacture of alcohol-based hand sanitizers and also for blending with petrol.[4] It was decided that some of the surplus grain, 5 kg per person, would be distributed free of cost during the lockdown period, but apparently after all the hungry across the land were fed, there would still be "surplus" grain left to be sold in the market, so that private companies could profit from hand sanitizers.

Meanwhile, the discovery that the "namaste" is the more hygienic greeting than the handshake in Coronatimes has fed into the general celebration of "Hindu" culture and civilization that has long accompanied the rise of Hindu Rashtra. (It may be of interest that Dalit politics often insists on the handshake to break the norms of untouchability that still structure Hindu society, of which the namaste is a hierarchical feature, for the "upper" caste will not offer namaste to the "lower" caste.) At every level of Hindu supremacist discourse—members of BJP, social media commentators, saffron clad "sages," and sections of the educated middle classes—there exists a smug satisfaction, all facts to the contrary, that Hindu practices and beliefs protect India from the virus. A BJP leader said, when a Hindu religious gathering was called off by the local administration, that India cannot be affected by the coronavirus as it is home to millions of gods and goddesses.[5] When the PM asked Indians to clap at a particular time to thank frontline workers, there were many who gave this a Hindu spin, claiming astrological features of that moment would force Corona to "run away,"[6] and indeed, "go Corona go" was chanted nationwide by educated people banging on steel plates in the belief that this would drive the virus away. This celebration of "Hindu" beliefs is of course, accompanied by venomous Islamophobia and casteism.

Sanghvad in Action

RSS ideology has been termed *Sanghvad*, which is the particular form that fascism is taking in India. Many argue that this moment is simply business as usual, that most Indians have lived under an undeclared Emergency this whole time—Dalits, Adivasis, the poor, and of course, Muslims. But this would be a mistaken analysis, like an orthodox Marxist analysis that sees no difference between the liberal democratic state and the fascist state because both are capitalist. There is a specificity to this moment that we must recognize, arising from a process set in motion in the 1990s.

Since the 1990s, the RSS has steadily increased its reach over individuals in state institutions, police and bureaucracy. In states in which BJP is in power, RSS has direct control over the state governments. Gradually since 2014 and especially since May 2019, the RSS has established a violent hold over minorities, Muslims in particular, through a nexus between state governments, police and local criminals. RSS members are appointed by the government as public prosecutors in trials relating to anti-Muslim pogroms, to ensure that Hindu accused are acquitted.[7]

Consider that only in the states in which BJP is in power, did the nationwide protests from the beginning of 2020 against the CAA supposedly "turn violent." This is because police are under the control of state governments, except in Delhi, where Delhi Police come under the central government. Fact-finding investigations by citizens' groups and journalists in Delhi[8] and Uttar Pradesh (UP) under a BJP Chief Minister, suggest possible police complicity with RSS activists and local criminals, in incidents of stone-throwing from within anti-CAA demonstrations, arson on public property during protests and so on.[9] In Delhi too, the violence was exclusively in the 7 constituencies (out of 70) that BJP won in the State Assembly elections of February 2020, and police complicity in preplanned violence is strongly indicated.[10]

Such violence that "breaks out" is followed by massive and violent state reprisals on Muslims. Mass arrests, brutal beatings in police custody, and the denial of bail. In UP, the state government levied huge amounts as "compensation" for destruction of state property, mainly from prominent Muslims (also some very poor ones)—including from individuals who were under preventive house arrest during the time the protests "turned violent."[11]

Journalists too have reported on the reign of terror that police have unleashed on Muslims in UP.[12]

Although there is a long history of police brutality and excesses in independent India, and not only against Muslims, as this reading list testifies,[13] I suggest that three features constitute specific transformations to the Indian political system by Hindu Rashtra.

First, the *formal* dispossession and disowning of the Muslim.

The Sachar Committee Report[14] showed that Muslims were even lower in socioeconomic indicators than Scheduled Castes and Scheduled Tribes, historically marginalized communities. There have been pogroms against Muslims before, also mostly conducted by RSS-linked groups but formally, all communities were constitutionally equal.

This formal equality for Muslims has been dropped. The direct targeting of Muslim lives and livelihoods has been mainstreamed. Thus, existing laws against "cow slaughter" have been activated and new laws passed, which provide cover for police and vigilante attacks on all cattle trading. However, the threat of lynching and arrests enables an extortion network by RSS linked groups like the Bajrang Dal, which permits the cattle business to continue, on payment of protection money, as NiranjanTakle found when he did an undercover sting operation in Gujarat.[15]

The government's passing of the law criminalizing "triple talaq" (unilateral divorce by husbands under Muslim Personal Law), which had already been banned by the Supreme Court, is another signal to its supporters and to Muslims that the latter are to be disenfranchised in multiple ways. Already Muslim men are imprisoned vastly disproportionately to their share in the population (as are Dalits and tribals),[16] and this law will add to their number. Desertion of wives is not a religion-specific practice, after all.

The Supreme Court has played its part, ending the long-standing dispute over the demolition of Babri Masjid in 1992, by declaring the demolition of the mosque to have been a criminal act, but nevertheless, handing over the site to the Hindu petitioners, and asking the government to set up a trust for the construction of the Ram temple.[17] Thus, a pliant Supreme Court asked the still nominally secular state to ensure the construction of a Hindu temple, at the site of a mosque demolished by the very forces that run the current government.

There have been a series of similar accommodations of Hindutva by the courts at different levels—orders that protected BJP[18]; stepping delicately back from addressing

Hindu patriarchy[19] while coming down hard on Muslim patriarchy[20]; and penalizing dissenters to Hindutva and to crony capitalism.[21]

The most important landmark in the formal disenfranchisement of Muslims is of course, the CAA which excludes Muslims alone from refugee status, a forerunner to the National Register of Citizens (NRC) that will identify "illegal immigrants." The Home Minister spelt out the "chronology" from CAA to National Population Register (NPR) to NRC, making it clear that the CAA would protect all non-Muslims from being left with illegal status after the NPR and NRC are conducted.[22] After nationwide protests erupted, PM Modi claimed that NRC was not being contemplated.[23] But within three months the government reiterated to the Supreme Court that "preparation of NRC was a necessary exercise for any sovereign country for identification of citizens from non-citizens, and to deport or expel illegal migrants."[24]

What this will inaugurate is the large scale disenfranchisement of Muslims but also of the poor in general, Dalits, and other minorities—removed from electoral rolls, deprived of all status. The very possession of documents is a luxury the majority of Indians do not have—migrant labor; women who upon marriage move to their husbands' villages; the poor who have no means of protecting documents from rodents, floods, fires; trans and intersex children abandoned by their families; queer people who run away from home to escape violence; sex workers.[25]

But not all doubtful citizens will be placed in detention centers. Nor will all of these be Muslims. There simply wouldn't be enough space to accommodate all Muslims and non-Muslims who fail the NRC test. In effect, the NRC will ensure that the entire country will become a detention center, the vast mass of the population excluded from electoral rolls, living in terror and uncertainty, at the mercy of extortionists and blackmailers.

Many of these would simply be collateral damage, because the NRC's target is the Muslim.

Systematically, during the pandemic-related lockdown, extensive arrests, mainly of Muslims, have taken place, of those involved in the peaceful anti-CAA protests. While the protests were ongoing, the entire country was electrified,[26] and it was not only Muslims who were protesting. Arrests or removal of protest sites during that time would have been a huge embarrassment to the government. But once the "public health" claim was made, protest sites were dismantled violently by police,[27] and thousands of arrests carried out. In Delhi, arrests are on the allegation of responsibility for the violence of February 2020, which was in fact, as indicated above, a pogrom against Muslims, planned in advance by RSS-linked organizations. Muslims were the ones largely affected,[28] in their lives and property, but it is Muslims who are being arrested in large numbers.[29]

The lockdown served as a political emergency in which democratic rights have been suspended, and the effect is most devastating on Muslims. This repression continues unabated.

Second, Hindu Rashtra functions through controlled chaos.

Unlike the manufacture of organized "communal riots" in the earlier phases, which had beginnings and endings, what has been unleashed since 2014 is a lynch mob culture, which produces a state of continuous turbulence, threat and terror.[30] Violence can now be sparked anywhere by even one or two activists linked to the RSS, drawing in a larger crowd which recognizes that with impunity it can participate actively, or enjoy the violence and record it. This new kind of violence targets not entire communities, but individuals. Each time therefore, the authorities can say that this particular act was not a casteist or communal incident, but simply an aberrant criminal act. Each one a law and order issue to be dealt with, or ignored, separately.

The impunity unleashed is such that it compensates young unemployed subaltern men for their utter lack of power in the system, and for the crashing economy. They don't need work or income, when they can have the heady rush of stopping a random middle-class man and forcing him to say Jai Shri Ram. In one case the man happened to be a Hindu doctor, and in another, it was a white tourist in Varanasi, but there have been innumerable incidents of Muslims being forced to chant Jai Shri Ram and being thrashed, tortured, killed. Acts of violence against Dalits too have gone up in number and intensity since 2014.[31]

This lynch mob culture taps into deep reserves of justification of violence against Dalits and women in Hindu society, and Hindu supremacist politics has unleashed it from its secret places out into the open.

The pogrom against Muslims in Delhi in February 2020 and in UP in early January was of the older, more established kind—organized targeting of Muslim homes, businesses, persons—systematic, planned in advance.[32] While the older model of sudden systematic pogroms continues, the maintenance of a constant state of controlled chaos and an atmosphere of terror especially for Muslims, is the default condition now. Though not always directly connected with the RSS, this complete breakdown of societal norms is a feature made possible by the RSS takeover.

Third, we see the unprecedented crackdown on dissent, even by private individuals on social media, and the throttling of freedom of expression and critical thinking, in universities. Individuals are mostly targeted through police complaints and court cases by supposedly private individuals, but the fact that police and courts take such complaints seriously[33] is an indication of RSS involvement. In an extraordinary move, the government banned two TV channels for forty-eight hours, for "being critical of RSS" and for "siding with one community" in their coverage of the Delhi pogrom.[34] That is, these channels did not present one of the two acceptable narratives—that "both sides are to blame" or that Muslims were responsible for the violence. But more importantly, "being critical of the RSS" was explicitly stated as a reason for the ban. The order was withdrawn after strong protests from sections of the media, but the heavy hand of the RSS on the reins of India-as-Hindu-Rashtra is very evident. The censorship of opinion is completed by the debilitation of the media, largely intimidated or bought over, so that self-censorship often obviates the need for RSS or government action.[35]

A recent spate of vicious online attacks by Hindu right-wing trolls on antiestablishment stand-up comics, and threats of arrest, has led to public apologies by many of them.[36] The suicide of a young Hindi film actor was weaponized by this troll army and BJP to launch a purge of the Bombay film industry, a space of syncretism, prominent Muslim figures, and one from which strong voices have emerged opposing Hindu Rashtra.[37]

While suppression of dissent happened during the Emergency of 1975–7 too, that was a period of two declared years, and conducted by the state. Now we are over six years down—and counting—into an undeclared war on dissenters (including assassinations)—by the state, by anybody whose "sentiments are hurt," or by armed Hindutva terrorist organizations.[38] While the Emergency produced a polarization into state versus the people, Hindu Rashtra has created a situation of molecular, everyday violence against certain sections.

These three features, each inextricably tied to nationalism, are what mark out Hindu Rashtra from business as usual. Each feature has ways of marking out the nationalist from the antinational, inflected now through the pandemic, and each is about explicitly establishing Hindu supremacy.

Coronacapitalism

Forced labor and data capitalism are the low end and high end of this phenomenon.

The gut-wrenching picture of migrant workers who managed to reach their home state of UP being sprayed with disinfectant, provoked such widespread outrage in India and negative publicity in the foreign media, that the Health Ministry issued a hasty statement that this should not be done.[39]

But this brutality and callousness toward workers and the poor emanates from the very top of this regime—the signal is sent from there, as to who matters and who doesn't. For example, during the lockdown, even as thousands of workers walked long distances home because no transport was arranged for them, precisely in order to prevent them from leaving the states in which they were stranded,[40] the UP government organized buses to bring back students from the state studying outside.[41] Special flights and hospital beds were prepared by the government to bring back Indians stranded abroad.[42]

Meanwhile lakhs of migrant labor were trapped in horrific conditions,[43] prey to rumors and fake news of buses being arranged, special trains being run, to their home states; and when they arrived at bus terminuses and stations in thousands, with their meagre belongings, their little children, they ended up baton-charged in Mumbai,[44] teargassed in Surat.[45] Apart from some state governments (West Bengal, Kerala, Delhi), that took on the responsibility of feeding these hundreds of thousands, it was largely ordinary citizens (many of whom had been active in anti-CAA protests) who stepped up across the country, financially and physically, to set up networks, including NGOs, to prevent mass deaths by starvation.[46] The Central government's contribution to this has been negligible, according to its own reply to the Supreme Court.[47]

The collateral damage of this tragic government-produced crisis was high—deaths due to exhaustion from the march itself, due to police brutality, due to starvation.[48]

During the lockdown, news emerged that indicated rising anxiety about the economic crisis brewing for capital because of labor shortages due to migrant labor going home. In response, in an order dated April 19, the Ministry of Home Affairs issued an extraordinary document, a Standard Operating System for the movement of stranded labour[49] which established:

(i) an outright prohibition on migrant labor, even those tested and found "asymptomatic," from moving out of the state in which they were currently trapped, and on going back to their home states; and

(ii) the recruitment of "asymptomatic" workers in "industrial, manufacturing, construction, farming and MNREGA works" *only in the state in which they are currently located* (stranded), for which they must be "registered with the local authority concerned ... "

This would, quite simply, have been forced labor. After testing for Covid-19, the asymptomatic workers would have been forced to remain within the states they were located and be transported to where labor is needed.

It seems clear in retrospect that the lockdown with only four hours' notice was not inefficiency, but deliberately intended to stop labor from leaving cities.

There was an uproar; the order was not implemented; eventually we heard no more about it. However, attempts by industry in collaboration with the government to force labor to stay where it was needed, continued and in some cases were thwarted by public pressure.[50]

Data Capitalism and the Aarogya Setu App

At the "high end" of the spectrum of Coronacapitalism, there is huge pressure from the government to download Aarogya Setu, a contact-tracing mobile application launched by the Union Health ministry, which will supposedly help users identify if they are at risk of Covid-19 infection.

The Ministry has asked social media platforms to promote installation of the app among their users, giving these platforms a target of minimum downloads of millions.[51] Some departments of government have made it mandatory for employees[52] and some food delivery companies for their delivery partners, to install the app. In short, Aarogya Setu is being aggressively promoted by government and private interests alike.

Bill Gates wrote a letter to the Prime Minister, congratulating him on the Aarogya Setu.[53] Gates's delight in an app that will collect data from potentially the entire mobile phone-owning population of India is not so intriguing. One attempt at least, in the United States, by the Gates Foundation to collect massive amounts of unspecified data via school test scores,[54] was thwarted by parents and school administrations over privacy and security issues.[55]

The Aarogya Setu has been shown to be deeply problematic on a number of dimensions. As a thorough report prepared by Internet Freedom Foundation (IFF) put it, the app is "a privacy minefield and it does not adhere to principles of minimisation, strict purpose limitation, transparency and accountability."[56]

It has now emerged that the Aarogya Setu was not developed entirely by the government National Informatics Centre as has been claimed so far. In response to an RTI query, the government was forced to concede that private partnership was involved, but who these partners are has still not been made clear.[57]

State surveillance is not exclusively a capitalist project. But what is relevant here is the emergence of *data capitalism* globally from the mid-1990s onwards, now a well-entrenched phenomenon. Sarah Myers West defines data capitalism as

> a system which enables an asymmetric redistribution of power that is weighted toward the actors who have access and the capability to make sense of information.[58]

The relentless push by the Indian government toward downloading the app, the data generated by which can be used, shared, and stored in ways about which we know nothing, and over which we have no control, is Coronacapitalism at the high end, as it were.

Meanwhile, Regular Capitalism

The corporate loot behind the saffron banner has been going on since 2014, and has escalated since May 2019—that is, the neoliberal restructuring of the economy and sale of the country's public assets to corporates. In Kashmir, within seventy-five days of the abrogation of Article 370, 125 projects were cleared in just three meetings, diverting forest land for "development" projects, the details of which were not divulged to journalists.[59]

Also within a week of lockdown being declared, the government issued a Gazette Notification changing the domicile rules for Jammu and Kashmir to redefine as resident anybody who has lived for fifteen years in the former state, or studied there for seven years—permitting them to apply for jobs and own immovable property,[60] essentially opening up Kashmir for settlement by non-Kashmiris, an old RSS dream. This decision fulfils the agenda of both Hindu supremacism and predatory capitalism, because land can now be bought by outsiders for any purpose, including commercial.

Since 2014, a one-time expansion of 25 percent given to coal mines in 2012, has been extended twice without taking into account the impact on the environment, and now a new draft policy plans to make such expansions the norm.[61] In the state of Odisha, mining companies are supreme, with fraudulent permissions from village committees being used to legitimize open loot of *adivasi* resources and the destruction of their forests for mining.[62] These are just a few examples. The National Education Policy of 2020 formalizes the ongoing process of making public universities self-financing, and encouraging private capital in education.[63] The public sector in infrastructure is being rapidly dismantled.[64]

During the lockdown, while nonessential projects are on hold, and the Prime Minister demands contributions from the public for the newly formed, opaque, unaccountable, and evidently problematic PM CARES fund[65]; one of the first acts of the Ministry of Housing was to issue a notification to continue with the 20,000 crore rupees project to develop the area around India Gate, called the Central Vista Project. The details of the transformation of this iconic and heritage area are shrouded in secrecy, and the contract has been given to a private firm based in Gujarat.[66] This project is nothing less than a massive capture of public land by "super elites."[67]

The neoliberal agenda is not necessarily linked to Hindu Rashtra, but when it is, the impact is even more devastating. The mythology of the "Urban Maoist-Jihadi network," a deranged script concocted in RSS HQ,[68] blends the twin enemies of Hindu supremacism ("jihadi") and predatory capital ("urban Maoist") to effectively silence opponents of these projects. Among thousands of politically motivated arrests in the last few years are those of journalists, academics, and artistes for supposedly being urban Maoists.

Revisiting the Secularism Debates

Hindu Rashtra is now a state project, and we need to think of it differently from the 1990s. Countering it along the familiar lines of true Hinduism[69] (Mehta 2020) or Left disdain for religiosity of the masses[70] misses the point altogether. Three features are striking in the new conjuncture.

First, we need to recognize May 2019 as a coup d'etat, not an election victory, as suggested earlier. In this scenario, we need to counter fascist transformations of the polity through *state institutions*, with police, courts, Election Commission, and media as pliant instruments in the project. While Hindutva has produced ground level transformations as well, these are temporary, and dependent on the power and reach of the regime. We cannot take for granted any longer that India is a democracy and that elections reflect people's will. Pressure needs to be mounted continuously from parties and nonparty forces, to force institutions to be accountable.

Second, we need to recognize that India is a collection of minorities, not a "Hindu majority" country. The modern project of Hindutva is the current phase of a process that began with the advent of Aryans into this landmass. Dalit Bahujan scholarship and lifeworlds continuously fracture Hindutva attempts to produce a singular "Hindu" identity, through an anti-Brahminical and largely antipatriarchal worldview, which Hindutva tries to delegitimize and marginalize. While all strands of nationalism, including the anti-Hindutva mainstream ones, accepted unquestioningly that a "Hindu" community actually existed, it was only BR Ambedkar who declared that Hindu society is a myth. He pointed out that the name "Hindu" was given by outsiders to refer to all those who lived in this land of the Sindhu river, as they did not have a common name for themselves, and did not perceive themselves as a single community. Ambedkar asserted that "Hindu society as such does not exist. It is only a collection of castes."[71]

Thus the much older term Hindustan, for the land of the Sindhu or Indus river, is not the same as the label "Hindu" emerging in the late nineteenth century, which was given to heterogeneous communities of people supposedly practicing a single religion. That is, there would have been a community following a set of beliefs and practices that were identifiably "Hindu," but not all the remaining communities that were "not Muslim" were necessarily "Hindu" in this way.

Fascinating retellings of popular Hindu festivals emerge from the perspective of Adivasi-Dalit-Bahujan communities, which bring to the surface older histories that have long simmered below the skin of mainstream savarna Hindu society. Ambedkarite intellectual Kanwal Bharti reminds us that the myths behind almost all Hindu festivals involve the defeat of Asuras by Devas—whether Dussehra, Diwali, Onam, or Holi. These Devas, Bharti identifies as Brahmins, and the defeat of the Asuras is the defeat of anti-Brahminical and pre-Brahminical ways of life and religious practices—in forests, and outside centers of established kingdoms. Very often this defeat is by trickery—Mahabali by Vamana, Ekalavya by Dronacharya—and by the co-option of willing elements in these non-Brahmin societies—Vibheeshana, Prahlada.[72] The incorporation of pre-Aryan female and nonhuman deities into the Vedic pantheon as wives and children of male Aryan gods is a centuries-old phenomenon that has been tracked by scholarship for a while now.[73]

By Independence it had become clear that "Hindu" could not be defined in any way that referred to common practices or beliefs. The Hindu Marriage Act of 1955 and the four other Acts that codified Hindu personal law therefore, defined "Hindu" as people who are *not* Muslim, Christian, Parsi, or Jewish, thus bringing under the umbrella of Hinduism a wide variety of practices, many of which had emerged as heterodox critiques of Hinduism, such as Jainism, Buddhism, and Sikhism.

Lately, Lingayats, who had for long been subsumed under Shaivism/Hinduism, have reasserted an old claim that they are not Hindus. This claim is at least eight decades old, as they had asserted their separate identity even while the Constitution was being drafted. Lingayats are followers of the twelfth-century social reformer Basavanna, who rejected the authority of the Vedas and Upanishads, caste, idol worship, and the authority of Sanskrit for Kannada.[74] The claim of Lingayats not to be Hindu is unacceptable only to the politics of Hindutva, not to ordinary people who come under the umbrella term "Hindu." Hindutva is the modern politics of the nation-state, in which it is essential for it to establish that "Hindus" are a majority—the foundation of its national culture. This myth is sustained by the legal definition mentioned above. Once Lingayats get a separate identity, it would lead to many other communities demanding the same, and then Sanatan Dharma would just be one among many minority religions on the subcontinent. It is no coincidence that two of the people assassinated by a Hindutva organization were Lingayats who challenged the "Hindu" identity—Gauri Lankesh and MM Kalburgi; and two others were rationalists—Narendra Dabholkar and Govind Pansare.

What then is the difference between Hindutva and Hinduism? In one familiar formulation, "Hindutva" is the modern political ideology that tries to produce and control a nation-state predicated on one identity, "Hindu," as the only pure Indian one, while "Hinduism" is a set of diverse religious beliefs and practices. However, we need to radically break from this understanding. What we see from the development of the Hindu identity since the late nineteenth century is that "Hinduism" is merely the label that enables the assertion of an eternal identity, one that is in the majority in India. The term also functions to discipline the heterogeneous practices of castes and communities—such as Mahishasura worship, meat eating, alcohol as religious offering—into the rigid North Indian upper-caste version, and this disciplining is key to the Hindu nationalist project of consolidating "Hinduism." Not even a fraction of people brought under the label of Hinduism identify with what Hindutva calls Hinduism. So in effect, Hindutva *is* Hinduism, but this refers to a minority community among other minority communities.[75]

Rejecting the claim of Hindutva that Hindus are the majority requires Left, secular, and feminist politics to engage seriously with Dalit Bahujan scholarship and lifeworlds, and to learn from these.

Third, the Dalit within Hindutva. A fitting illustration of the layers in the project of Hindu Rashtra is offered by the fact that UP's first detention center for "illegal foreigners" is set to open, to be housed in the former Dr Ambedkar Hostel for SC/ST students, built under Mayawati's tenure as Chief Minister of UP. Since BJP came to power at the center, no SC/ST students have been allotted this hostel and the building have been vacant.[76] It has become clear that not even for the consolidation of the "Hindu" community for Hindu Rashtra, can the deep hatred for Dalits in *savarna* imaginations be uprooted. The rapes of Dalit women and humiliation of Dalit men by "upper" castes have gone up exponentially in UP, the most brutal instance of Hindu Rashtra—a 47 percent increase between 2014 and 2018. This is the settling of scores after a period of Samajwadi Party and Bahujan Samaj Party rule in UP, that had kept the Thakurs and Brahmins in check.[77] This means that any Left secular counter to Hindutva has to be simultaneously a Dalit-Bahujan politics.

A concrete example of such a politics is provided by the CPI (ML) Liberation which won 12 of the 19 seats it contested in the recently concluded Bihar State Assembly elections (all its candidates were Dalit-Bahujan). This, despite months of propaganda through "terms such as … 'terrorist sympathisers', 'China-funded Maoists', 'tukde-tukde gang' among others," as Jignesh Mevani points out. Mevani says that the party has successfully changed "the grammar of anti-caste politics in the region" by making "material resource-based issues as the forefront of its anti-caste politics."[78]

Conclusion

The breathless interregnum of the pandemic seems to be lifting. The country has exploded with protests of farmers over new farm laws,[79] and over the rape and murder of two Dalit women, one in Hathras,[80] another in Delhi.[81] The Bihar elections referred to above seem to indicate again capitulation of the Election Commission to BJP,[82] but also the coming together of a vibrant left-of-center coalition of parties and forces. Although Hindutva is undoubtedly the new normal since 2014, it is not going uncontested.

Notes

1 Menon Nivedita and Aditya Nigam, "Epilogue," in *Power and Contestation. India after 1989*, 2nd ed.(Hyderabad: Orient Blackswan, 2014). (First published in 2008).

2 Mohammad Ali, "The Rise of a Hindu Vigilante in the Age of WhatsApp and Modi," *Wired*, April 14, 2020. https://www.wired.com/story/indias-frightening-descent-social-media-terror/.

3 Swati Chaturvedi, *I am a Troll: Inside the Secret World of the BJP's Digital Army* (Delhi: Juggernaut, 2016).

4 PTI, "FCI's Surplus Rice Stocks to be Converted into Ethanol to Make Hand Sanitisers," April 21, 2020. https://www.livemint.com/news/india/fci-s-surplus-rice-stocks-to-be-converted-into-ethanol-to-make-hand-sanitisers-11587408039897.html.

5 Navya Singh, "COVID-19 Cannot Harm India as It Is Home To 33 Crore God & Goddesses': BJP Leader Kailash Vijayvargiya Makes Bizarre Claim," *The Logical*

Indian, March 18, 2020. https://thelogicalindian.com/news/bjp-leader-coronavirus-remarks–2017.

6 Falah Gulzar, "Did Modi Actually Ask Indians to 'Clap' to Battle Coronavirus? Indian Tweeps Ask for More Efforts to Tackle covid-19," *Gulf News,* March 22, 2020. https://gulfnews.com/world/asia/india/india-did-modi-actually-ask-indians-to-clap-to-battle-coronavirus-indian-tweeps-ask-for-more-efforts-to-tackle-covid-19-1.1584876234756.

7 Ashish Khetan, "Delhi Riots: Is the Centre Importing the 'Gujarat Model' to Subvert Prosecution?" *The Wire,* July 20, 2020. https://thewire.in/communalism/delhi-riots-is-the-centre-importing-the-gujarat-model-to-subvert-prosecution.

8 Shivam Vij, "The Delhi Pogrom 2020 is Amit Shah's Answer to an Election Defeat," *The Print*, February 26, 2020. https://theprint.in/opinion/delhi-pogrom-2020-is-amit-shah-answer-to-an-election-defeat/371558/.

9 Karwan-e-Mohabbat, 2020.

10 Hannah Ellis-Petersen and Shaikh Azizur Rahman, "Delhi's Muslims Despair of Justice after Police Implicated in Riots," *The Guardian*, March 16, 2020. https://www.theguardian.com/world/2020/mar/16/delhis-muslims-despair-justice-police-implicated-hindu-riots.

11 The Polis Project, "Disproportionate and Illegitimate State Violence: A Report on the Police Violence in Uttar Pradesh against anti-CAA Protestors," January 28, 2020. https://thepolisproject.com/disproportionate-and-illegitimate-state-violence-a-report-on-the-police-violence-in-uttar-pradesh-against-anti-caa-protestors/#.X5-rboVR3IV.

12 Hannah Ellis-Petersen, "'We Are Not Safe': India's Muslims Tell of Wave of Police Brutality," *The Guardian*, January 3, 2020. https://www.theguardian.com/world/2020/jan/03/we-are-not-safe-indias-muslims-tell-of-wave-of-police-brutality.

13 EPW Engage, "Investigating Police Brutality: A Reading List," 2019. https://www.epw.in/engage/article/investigating-police-brutality-reading-list.

14 Rajinder Sachar, "Social, Economic and Educational Status of the Muslim Community of India. A Report," 2006. https://www.mhrd.gov.in/sites/upload_files/mhrd/files/sachar_comm.pdf.

15 Niranjan Takle, "Secrets of Gau-rakshak—Niranjan Takle Talks about Cattle Smuggling," 2019. https://www.youtube.com/watch?v=1TdcrvqTjGk.

16 Shemin Joy, "Majority Prisoners in Indian Jails are Dalits, Muslims," *Deccan Herald*, January 1, 2020. https://www.deccanherald.com/national/north-and-central/majority-prisoners-in-indian-jails-are-dalits-muslims-790478.html.

17 India Today Web Desk, "Ayodhya Ram Mandir Case Judgment: Supreme Court Rules in Favour of Ram Lalla. 10 Highlights," *India Today*, November 9, 2019. https://www.indiatoday.in/india/story/ayodhya-ram-mandir-case-supreme-court-judgment-top-10-highlights-1617304-2019-11–09.

18 News Desk, "Justice Muralidhar, Who Ordered to Register FIR against Kapil Mishra, Transferred," *HW News*, February 22, 2020. https://hwnews.in/news/national-news/justice-muralidharan-ordered-register-fir-kapil-mishra-transferred/126592.

19 Nivedita Menon, "Law versus Faith, Female Activists versus Male Devotees and Other Strange Creatures at Sabarimala," *Kafila*, February 6, 2019a. https://kafila.online/2019/02/06/law-versus-faith-female-activists-versus-male-devotees-and-other-strange-creatures-at-sabarimala/.

20 Shreya Munoth, "SC Verdict on Triple Talaq, a Legal Reading: Judgment Welcome, but Doesn't Address Sex Discrimination," *Firstpost*, August 23, 2017. https://www.firstpost.com/india/supreme-court-verdict-on-triple-talaq-a-legal-reading-judgment-welcome-but-fails-to-address-institutional-sex-discrimination-3963863.html.

21 PTI, "SC Rejects Gautam Navlakha & Anand Teltumbde's Anticipatory Bail in Bhima Koregaon Case," *The Print*, March 16, 2020a. https://theprint.in/india/sc-rejects-gautam-navlakha-anand-teltumbdes-anticipatory-bail-in-bhima-koregaon-case/382114/.

22 Pia Krishnankutty, "Mitron, Aap Chronology Aamajhiye—This Is How Amit Shah's Line has Gone Viral," *The Print*, March 13, 2020. https://theprint.in/politics/mitron-aap-chronology-samajhiye-this-is-how-amit-shahs-line-has-gone-viral/379823/.

23 Gyan Varma, "No Discussion Held to Introduce NRC: Modi," *Mint*, December 22, 2019. https://www.livemint.com/politics/news/no-discussion-held-to-introduce-nrc-modi-11577033574834.html.

24 Samanwaya Rautray, "NRC Must to Identify Non-citizens: Govt to SC," *Economic Times*, March 17, 2020. https://economictimes.indiatimes.com/news/politics-and-nation/nrc-must-to-identify-non-citizens-govt-to-sc/articleshow/74680527.cms?utm_source=contentofinterest&utm_medium=text&utm_campaign=cppst.

25 Special Correspondent, "Anti-CAA Umbrella Widens," *The Telegraph*, January 3, 2020. https://www.telegraphindia.com/india/anti-caa-umbrella-widens/cid/1732855.

26 nrcprotest.in.

27 Furquan Ameen, "Police Evict Shaheen Bagh Protesters amid Lockdown Measures," *The Telegraph*, November 2, 2020.

28 Hannah Ellis-Petersen, "Inside Delhi: Beaten, Lynched and Burnt Alive," *The Guardian*, March 1, 2020a. https://www.theguardian.com/world/2020/mar/01/india-delhi-after-hindu-mob-riot-religious-hatred-nationalists.

29 Sumedha Pal, "Delhi Violence: Arrests Continue," *News Click*, March 16, 2020. https://www.newsclick.in/Delhi-Violence-Arrests-Continue-Locals-Muslim-Youth-Being-Arbitrarily%20-Targeted.

30 Rahul Tripathi, "NE Delhi Violence: There Were Warning Signs before Rioting Began," *Economic Times*, February 27, 2020. https://economictimes.indiatimes.com/news/politics-and-nation/northeast-delhi-violence-there-were-warning-signs-before-rioting-began/articleshow/74328478.cms?utm_source=contentofinterest&utm_medium=text&utm_campaign=cppst.

31 Sheikh Saaliq and Adrija Bose, "Documenting Violence against Dalits: One Assault at a Time," *News 18*, 2018. https://www.news18.com/news/immersive/documenting-violence-against-dalits-one-assault-at-a-time.html.

32 Tripathi, "NE Delhi Violence."

33 Soniya Agrawal, "Assam Lecturer Posts Remarks against RSS-BJP, Modi on Facebook, Lands in Jail after Protest," *The Print*, March 1, 2020. https://theprint.in/india/assam-lecturer-posts-remarks-against-rss-bjp-modi-on-facebook-lands-in-jail-after-abvp-protest/373526/.

34 Krishn Kaushik, "Govt Bans Two TV channels: 'Critical of RSS, Siding with One Community,'" *The Indian Express*, March 6, 2020. https://www.msn.com/en-in/news/newsindia/govt-bans-two-tv-channels-critical-of-rss-siding-with-one-community/ar-BB10QVHu.

35 Vindu, Goel and Jeffrey Gettleman, "Under Modi, India's Press Is Not so Free Any More," *New York Times*, May 6, 2020. https://www.nytimes.com/2020/04/02/world/asia/modi-india-press-media.html.

36 Express News Service, "Three Stand-up Comics Post Online Apologies for 'Hurting Sentiments'," *Indian Express*, July 16, 2020. https://indianexpress.com/article/india/three-stand-up-comics-post-online-apologies-for-hurting-sentiments–6507903/.

37 Nivedita Menon, "Hindu Rashtra and Bollywood: A New Front in the Battle for Cultural Hegemony," *South Asia Multidisciplinary Academic Journal* (forthcoming).

38 S. Yogesh, "Hindutva Terror: Story of the Common Link Between the Four Murders," *News Click*, August 20, 2018. https://www.newsclick.in/hindutva-terror-story-common-link-between-four-murders.

39 PTI, "Spraying of Disinfectant on People 'Physically and Psychologically Harmful': Health Ministry," *Economic Times*, April 18, 2020b. https://economictimes.indiatimes.com/news/politics-and-nation/spraying-of-disinfectant-on-people-physically-and-psychologically-harmful-health-ministry/articleshow/75226204.cms?utm_source=contentofinterest&utm_medium=text&utm_campaign=cppst.

40 PTI, "Centre Asks States to Stop Mass Exodus of Migrant Workers; Amit Shah Speaks to CMs," *Economic Times*, March 27, 2020c. https://economictimes.indiatimes.com/news/politics-and-nation/centre-asks-states-to-stop-mass-exodus-of-migrant-workers-amit-shah-speaks-to-cms/articleshow/74852309.cms?utm_source=contentofinterest&utm_medium=text&utm_campaign=cppst.

41 Shoaib Daniyal, "Why Was a Special Exception Made for Kota Students to Return to Uttar Pradesh during the Lockdown?" *Scroll.in*, April 20, 2020. https://scroll.in/article/959648/why-was-a-special-exception-made-for-kota-students-to-return-to-uttar-pradesh-during-the-lockdown.

42 Shishir Gupta, "Special Flights, Hospital Beds: Centre Preps to Fly Back Indians Stranded Abroad," *Hindustan Times*, April 25, 2020. https://www.hindustantimes.com/india-news/special-flights-hospital-beds-centre-preps-to-fly-back-indians-stranded-abroad/story-G4r4rZGNGgT4RyN3GqOA4K.html.

43 Geeta Pandey, "Coronavirus in India: Desperate Migrant Workers Trapped in Lockdown," *BBC News*, April 21, 2020. https://www.bbc.com/news/world-asia-india–52360757.

44 India Today, "Mumbai: Police Lathi-charge Migrants as Thousands Defy COVID-19 Lockdown, Gather at Bandra Station," 2020. https://www.youtube.com/watch?v=b0XoOhMozWA.

45 Kamal Saiyed, "Migrant Workers Stopped in Surat; Police use Teargas after Stone-pelting, Detain 96," *The Indian Express*, March 31, 2020. https://indianexpress.com/article/coronavirus/surat-lockdown-police-migrant-labourers-violence-coronavirus–6338852/.

46 Shrishti Negi, "Food for the Vulnerable People: How YUVA's Campaign Is Helping Feed Migrant Workers In Mumbai," *News 18,* April 15, 2020. https://www.news18.com/news/lifestyle/food-for-the-vulnerable-people-how-yuvas-campaign-is-helping-feed-migrant-workers-in-mumbai-2578675.html; Pooja Singh and Karthikeyan Hemalatha, "Anti-CAA Protesters Shift their Focus to Feeding the Needy," *Mint*, April 10, 2020 https://www.livemint.com/mint-lounge/business-of-life/amid-lockdown-caa-protestors-distribute-food-to-migrants-workers-across-india-11586353174017.html.

47 Mukesh Rawat, "In 13 States NGOs Fed More People than Govt During Coronavirus Lockdown," *India Today*, April 9, 2020. https://www.

indiatoday.in/india/story/in-13-states-ngos-fed-more-people-than-govt-during-coronavirus-lockdown-1665111-2020-04–09.

48 Vikas Rawal, Manish Kumar and Jesim Pais, "India's Villages during the COVID-19 Pandemic," 2020. https://coronapolicyimpact.org/2020/04/07/indias-villages-during-the-covid-19-pandemic/.

49 GoI Order 2020 Order no. 40-3/2020-DM-I (A). https://www.mha.gov.in/sites/default/files/MHA%20Order%20Dt.%2019.4.2020%20with%20SOP%20for%20movement%20of%20stranded%20labour%20within%20the%20State%20and%20UT.pdf.

50 Christin Mathew Philip, "Under Fire, Karnataka Does U-turn, Will Resume Trains for Migrants," *Times of India*, May 8, 2020. http://timesofindia.indiatimes.com/articleshow/75614188.cms?utm_source=contentofinterest&utm_medium=text&utm_campaign=cppst.

51 Mugdha Variyar, "Coronavirus: Govt asks Social Media Platforms to Promote Aarogya Setu App," *CNBCTV 18*, April 13, 2020. https://www.cnbctv18.com/technology/coronavirus-govt-asks-social-media-platforms-to-promote-aarogya-setu-app-5664061.htm.

52 PTI, "Prasar Bharati Makes It Mandatory for Staffers to Install COVID-19 Tracking 'Arogya Setu' App," *Economic Times*, April 15, 2020. https://economictimes.indiatimes.com/industry/media/entertainment/media/prasar-bharati-makes-it-mandatory-for-staffers-to-install-covid-19-tracking-arogya-setu-app/articleshow/75158606.cms?utm_source=contentofinterest&utm_medium=text&utm_campaign=cppst.

53 HT Correspondent, "Bill Gates Lauds India's Covid-19 Tracker Aarogya Setu," *Hindustan Times*, April 23, 2020. https://tech.hindustantimes.com/tech/news/bill-gates-lauds-india-s-covid-19-tracker-aarogya-setu-here-s-how-you-use-the-app-story-3CC54mLz4x0RAzDxPTjMzI.html.

54 Rugh, "How Murdoch, Bill Gates and Big Corporations Are Data Mining Our Schools," *The Indypendent*, April 30, 2013. https://indypendent.org/2013/04/how-murdoch-bill-gates-and-big-corporations-are-data-mining-our-schools/.

55 Natasha Singer, "InBloom Student Data Repository to Close," *New York Times*, April 21, 2014.

56 IFF, "Is Aarogya Setu Privacy-first?" 2020. https://internetfreedom.in/is-aarogya-setu-privacy-first-nope-but-it-could-be-if-the-government-wanted/.

57 Aparna Banerjea, "Aarogya Setu App Developed in Govt and Private Collaboration, Clarifies Centre," *Mint*, October 28, 2020. https://www.livemint.com/technology/tech-news/aarogya-setu-app-developed-in-govt-and-private-collaboration-clarifies-centre-11603892923776.html.

58 Sarah Myers West, "Data Capitalism: Redefining the Logics of Surveillance and Privacy," *Business & Society* 58, no. 1 (2017): 20.

59 SabrangIndia, "Post 370 Abrogation, August 5, the Forest Advisory Committee of J & K has Cleared 125 projects on Forest Land," *Sabrang*, October 19, 2019. https://www.sabrangindia.in/article/post-370-abrogation-august-5-forest-advisory-committee-j-k-has-cleared-125-projects-forest.

60 Scroll Staff, "J&K: Those Living for More than 15 Years Now Eligible for Domicile under New Rule, says Centre," *Scroll.in*, April 1, 2020. https://scroll.in/latest/957868/j-k-those-living-for-more-than-15-years-now-eligible-for-domicile-under-new-rule-says-centre.

61 Aesha Datta, "Magic! How the Government Stretched a 'One-time Measure' to Bypass Environment Checks for Coal Mines," *The Economic Times*, June 16, 2019. https://economictimes.indiatimes.com/prime/environment/magic-how-the-government-stretched-a-one-time-measure-to-bypass-environment-checks-for-coal-mines/primearticleshow/69780902.cms.
62 Chitrangada Choudhury, "Mining at Any Cost: The Odisha Government's Continued Dismissal of Adivasi Rights," *The Wire*, May 16, 2016. https://thewire.in/rights/mining-at-any-cost-the-odisha-governments-continued-dismissal-of-adivasi-rights.
63 Nivedita Menon, "NEP 2020: Elitist and Corporatized Education under Hindu Rashta," *Kafila*, September 9, 2020. https://kafila.online/2020/09/08/nep-2020-elitist-and-corporatized-education-under-hindu-rashtra/.
64 K. Hemalata, "3 Years of Modi Government: Country for Sale," *Newsclick*, May 18, 2017. https://www.newsclick.in/3-years-modi-government-country-sale.
65 Reuters, "Modi's 'PM CARES' Coronavirus Fund Slammed as Donations Pour in," *Al Jazeera*, April 8, 2020. https://www.aljazeera.com/news/2020/04/08/modis-pm-cares-coronavirus-fund-slammed-as-donations-pour-in/.
66 Amil Bhatnagar, "UP's First Detention Centre for Illegal Foreigners Set to Open in Ghaziabad," *Indian Express*, September 16, 2020.
67 Alpana Kishore, "2020 PM's house on Rajpath: How a Super Elite is Capturing Delhi's Land," *Newslaundry*, March 16, 2020. https://www.newslaundry.com/2020/03/16/pms-house-on-rajpath-how-a-super-elite-is-capturing-delhis-land.
68 Organiser Web Desk, "Group of Intellectuals and Academicians Submit Report on Delhi Anti-Hindu riots to Home Ministry—Exposes the Forces behind the 'Dharna to Danga' Model," *Organiser*, March 11, 2020. https://www.organiser.org/Encyc/2020/3/11/Group-of-Intellectuals-and-Academicians-submit-report-on-Delhi-anti-Hindu-riots-to-Home-Ministry.html.
69 Pratap Bhanu Mehta, "Ayodhya's Ram Temple Is First Real Colonisation of Hinduism by Political Power," *The Indian Express*, August 5, 2020.
70 Yogendra Yadav, "Secularism Gave up Language of Religion. Ayodhya Bhoomi Pujan is a Result of That," *The Print*, August 5, 2020. https://theprint.in/opinion/secularism-language-religion-ayodhya-bhoomi-pujan-ram-mandir-kashmir/475307/.
71 B.R. Ambedkar, *The Annihilation of Caste*, 1936. https://ccnmtl.columbia.edu/projects/mmt/ambedkar/web/readings/aoc_print_2004.pdf; 6;2.
72 Kanwal Bharti nd, "Holi:Ek Mithakiya Adhyayan," (Hindi) *Streekal*. http://www.streekaal.com/2016/03/festivals-holi-mythology.html.
73 Lyn Gatwood, *Devi and the Spouse Goddess: Women, Sexuality, and Marriage in India* (Delhi: Manohar Publications, 1985); and Kosambi, D. D., *Myth and History* (Bombay: Popular Prakshan, 1962).
74 Gauri Lankesh, "Making Sense of the Lingayat vs Veerashaiva Debate," *The Wire*, August 8, 2017.
75 This theme of Dalit Bahujan counternarratives to Hindutva has been explored more fully in Nivedita Menon, "Counter-narratives to Hindutva Claims. Beyond the Eurocentrism–Indigenism Binary," *Economic and Political Weekly* 54, no. 38 (September 21, 2019).
76 Amil Bhatnagar, "UP's First Detention Centre for Illegal Foreigners Set to Open in Ghaziabad," *Indian Express*, September 16, 2020.
77 Aditya Nigam, "Hathras and beyond: The Upper Caste Counter-revolution," *Kafila*, October 8, 2020. https://kafila.online/2020/10/08/hathras-and-beyond-the-upper-caste-counter-revolution/.

78 Jignesh Mevani, "With Bihar Success, CPI(ML) has Smartly Blended Radicalism and Pragmatic Politics," *The Print*, November 12, 2020.

79 Ashish Mital, "Farm Laws: Claims and Reality," *The Indian Express*, October 9, 2020. https://indianexpress.com/article/opinion/farm-laws-claims-and-reality–6717662/.

80 Billy Perrigo, "The Fatal Gang Rape of a Young Woman Is Forcing a Reckoning in India over the Caste System," *Time*, October 15. https://time.com/5900402/hathras-rape-case-india-violence/.

81 Wire Staff 2020, "Caravan Reporter Allegedly Assaulted By Police, Detained in North Delhi", *The Wire*, October 16. https://thewire.in/media/caravan-reporter-allegedly-assaulted-by-police-detained-in-north-delhi.

82 Manish Kumar, "'Money, Muscle, Deceit Couldn't…' Tejashwi Yadav Slams PM, Nitish Kumar," *NDTV*, November 12, 2020. https://www.ndtv.com/india-news/tejashwi-yadav-pm-narendra-modi-nitish-kumar-could-not-stop-rjd-from-emerging-single-largest-party-despite-using-money-muscle-power-2324298?pfrom=video-read.

Select Bibliography

Agarwal, Poonam, "EC Misleads Public with Bogus RTI Reply on VVPAT Count," *The Quint*, July 22, 2019. https://www.thequint.com/news/india/election-2019-vvpat-count-ec-misleading-rti-reply.

Agrawal, Soniya, "Assam Lecturer Posts Remarks against RSS-BJP, Modi on Facebook, Lands in Jail After Protest," *The Print*, March 1, 2020. https://theprint.in/india/assam-lecturer-posts-remarks-against-rss-bjp-modi-on-facebook-lands-in-jail-after-abvp-protest/373526/.

Ali, Mohammad, "The Rise of a Hindu Vigilante in the Age of WhatsApp and Modi," *Wired*, April 14, 2020. https://www.wired.com/story/indias-frightening-descent-social-media-terror/.

Ambedkar, B. R., *The Annihilation of Caste*, 1936. https://ccnmtl.columbia.edu/projects/mmt/ambedkar/web/readings/aoc_print_2004.pdf.

Ameen, Furquan, "Police Evict Shaheen Bagh Protesters amid Lockdown Measures," *the Telegraph*, November 2, 2020. https://www.telegraphindia.com/delhi/police-evict-shaheen-bagh-protesters-amid-lockdown-measures/cid/1758705.

Banerjea, Aparna, "Aarogya Setu App Developed in Govt and Private Collaboration, Clarifies Centre," *Mint*, October 28, 2020. https://www.livemint.com/technology/tech-news/aarogya-setu-app-developed-in-govt-and-private-collaboration-clarifies-centre-11603892923776.html.

Bharti, Kanwal n.d., "Holi: EkMithakiya Adhyayan," (Hindi) *Streekal*. http://www.streekaal.com/2016/03/festivals-holi-mythology.html.

Bhatnagar, Amil, "UP's First Detention Centre for Illegal Foreigners Set to Open in Ghaziabad," *Indian Express*, September 16, 2020.

Bhatnagar, Amil, "UP's First Detention Centre for Illegal Foreigners Set to Open in Ghaziabad," *Indian Express*, September 17, 2020. https://indianexpress.com/article/cities/delhi/ups-first-detention-centre-for-illegal-foreigners-set-to-open-in-ghaziabad-6599013/.

Bhatnagar, Gaurav Vivek, "India is Locked Down for COVID-19 but Modi Govt Presses ahead with Central Vista Project," *The Wire*, March 24, 2020. https://thewire.in/government/central-vista-dda-land-use.

Brass, Paul R., *The Production of Hindu-Muslim Violence in Contemporary India* (Delhi: Oxford University Press, 2003).

Chaturvedi, Swati, *I am a Troll: Inside the Secret World of the BJP's Digital Army* (Delhi: Juggernaut, 2016).

Choudhury, Chitrangada, "Mining at Any Cost: The Odisha Government's Continued Dismissal of Adivasi Rights," *The Wire*, May 16, 2016. https://thewire.in/rights/mining-at-any-cost-the-odisha-governments-continued-dismissal-of-adivasi-rights.

Daniyal, Shoaib, "Why Was a Special Exception Made for Kota Students to Return to Uttar Pradesh during the Lockdown?" *Scroll.in*, April 20, 2020. https://scroll.in/article/959648/why-was-a-special-exception-made-for-kota-students-to-return-to-uttar-pradesh-during-the-lockdown.

Datta, Aesha, "Magic! How the Government Stretched a 'One-time Measure' to Bypass Environment Checks for Coal Mines," *The Economic Times*, June 16, 2019. https://economictimes.indiatimes.com/prime/environment/magic-how-the-government-stretched-a-one-time-measure-to-bypass-environment-checks-for-coal-mines/primearticleshow/69780902.cms.

Ellis-Petersen, Hannah, "Inside Delhi: Beaten, Lynched and Burnt Alive," *The Guardian*, March 1, 2020a. https://www.theguardian.com/world/2020/mar/01/india-delhi-after-hindu-mob-riot-religious-hatred-nationalists.

Ellis-Petersen, Hannah, "'We Are Not Safe': India's Muslims Tell of Wave of Police Brutality," *The Guardian*, January 3, 2020. https://www.theguardian.com/world/2020/jan/03/we-are-not-safe-indias-muslims-tell-of-wave-of-police-brutality.

Ellis-Petersen, Hannah and Shaikh Azizur Rahman, "Delhi's Muslims Despair of Justice after Police Implicated in Riots," *The Guardian*, March 16, 2020. https://www.theguardian.com/world/2020/mar/16/delhis-muslims-despair-justice-police-implicated-hindu-riots.

EPW Editorial, "Anger, Aspiration, Apprehension," *Economic and Political Weekly* XLIX, no. 21 (May 24, 2014).

EPW Engage, "Investigating Police Brutality: A Reading List," 2019. https://www.epw.in/engage/article/investigating-police-brutality-reading-list.

Gatwood, Lyn, *Devi and the Spouse Goddess: Women, Sexuality, and Marriage in India* (Delhi: Manohar Publications, 1985).

Ghatak, Maitreesh, Parikshit Ghosh and Ashok Kotwal, "Growth in the Time of UPA: Myths and Reality," *Economic and Political Weekly* XLIX, no. 16 (April 19, 2014).

Goel, Vindu and Jeffrey Gettleman, "Under Modi, India's Press Is Not so Free Any More," *New York Times*, May 6, 2020. https://www.nytimes.com/2020/04/02/world/asia/modi-india-press-media.html.

Gulzar, Falah, "Did Modi Actually Ask Indians to 'Clap' to Battle Coronavirus? Indian Tweeps Ask for More Efforts to Tackle Covid-19," *Gulf News*, March 22, 2020. https://gulfnews.com/world/asia/india/india-did-modi-actually-ask-indians-to-clap-to-battle-coronavirus-indian-tweeps-ask-for-more-efforts-to-tackle-covid-19-1.1584876234756.

Gupta, Shishir, "Special Flights, Hospital Beds: Centre Preps to Fly Back Indians Stranded Abroad," *Hindustan Times*, April 25, 2020. https://www.hindustantimes.com/india-news/special-flights-hospital-beds-centre-preps-to-fly-back-indians-stranded-abroad/story-G4r4rZGNGgT4RyN3GqOA4K.html.

Hemalata, K. "3 Years of Modi Government: Country for Sale," *Newsclick*, May 18, 2017. https://www.newsclick.in/3-years-modi-government-country-sale.

HT Correspondent, "Bill Gates Lauds India's Covid-19 Tracker Aarogya Setu," *Hindustan Times*, April 23, 2020. https://tech.hindustantimes.com/tech/news/bill-gates-lauds-india-s-covid-19-tracker-aarogya-setu-here-s-how-you-use-the-app-story-3CC54mLz4x0RAzDxPTjMzI.html.

IFF, "Is Aarogya Setu Privacy-first?" 2020. https://internetfreedom.in/is-aarogya-setu-privacy-first-nope-but-it-could-be-if-the-government-wanted/.

India Today, "Mumbai: Police Lathi-charge Migrants as Thousands Defy COVID-19 Lockdown, Gather At Bandra Station," 2020. https://www.youtube.com/watch?v=b0XoOhMozWA.

India Today Web Desk, "Ayodhya Ram Mandir Case Judgment: Supreme Court Rules in Favour of Ram Lalla. 10 Highlights," *India Today*, November 9, 2019. https://www.indiatoday.in/india/story/ayodhya-ram-mandir-case-supreme-court-judgment-top-10-highlights-1617304-2019-11-09.

Joy, Shemin, "Majority Prisoners in Indian Jails Are Dalits, Muslims," *Deccan Herald*, January 1, 2020. https://www.deccanherald.com/national/north-and-central/majority-prisoners-in-indian-jails-are-dalits-muslims-790478.html.

Kaushik, Krishn, "Govt Bans Two TV Channels: 'Critical of RSS, Siding with One Community'," *The Indian Express*, March 6, 2020. https://www.msn.com/en-in/news/newsindia/govt-bans-two-tv-channels-critical-of-rss-siding-with-one-community/ar-BB10QVHu.

Khetan, Ashish, "Delhi Riots: Is the Centre Importing the 'Gujarat Model' to Subvert Prosecution?" *The Wire*, July 20, 2020. https://thewire.in/communalism/delhi-riots-is-the-centre-importing-the-gujarat-model-to-subvert-prosecution.

Kishore, Alpana, "2020 PM's House on Rajpath: How a Super Elite is Capturing Delhi's Land," *Newslaundry*, March 16, 2020. https://www.newslaundry.com/2020/03/16/pms-house-on-rajpath-how-a-super-elite-is-capturing-delhis-land.

Kosambi, D.D., *Myth and History* (Bombay: Popular Prakshan, 1962).

Krishnankutty, Pia, "Mitron, Aap Chronology Samajhiye—This is How Amit Shah's Line Has Gone Viral," *The Print*, March 13, 2020. https://theprint.in/politics/mitron-aap-chronology-samajhiye-this-is-how-amit-shahs-line-has-gone-viral/379823/.

Kumar, Manish, "'Money, Muscle, Deceit Couldn't … ' Tejashwi Yadav Slams PM, Nitish Kumar," *NDTV*, November 12, 2020. https://www.ndtv.com/india-news/tejashwi-yadav-pm-narendra-modi-nitish-kumar-could-not-stop-rjd-from-emerging-single-largest-party-despite-using-money-muscle-power-2324298?pfrom=video-read.

Lankesh, Gauri, "Making Sense of the Lingayat vs Veerashaiva Debate," *The Wire*, August 8, 2017.

Legal Correspondent, "Supreme Court Issues Notice to Election Commission on 'Discrepancies'," *The Hindu*, December 13, 2019. https://www.thehindu.com/news/national/sc-issues-notice-to-poll-panel-on-discrepancies/article30299992.ece.

Mehta, Pratap Bhanu, "Ayodhya's Ram Temple Is First Real Colonisation of Hinduism by Political Power," *The Indian Express*, August 5, 2020. https://indianexpress.com/article/opinion/columns/ayodhya-temple-ram-i-will-not-find-you-there-6539473/.

Menon, Nivedita, "Counter-narratives to Hindutva Claims. Beyond the Eurocentrism–Indigenism Binary," *Economic and Political Weekly* 54, no. 38 (September 21, 2019) (2020a).

Menon, Nivedita, "Hindu Rashtra and Bollywood: A New Front in the Battle for Cultural Hegemony," *South Asia Multidisciplinary Academic Journal* (forthcoming).

Menon, "Law Versus Faith, Female Activists Versus Male Devotees and Other Strange Creatures at Sabarimala," *Kafila*, February 6, 2019a. https://kafila.online/2019/02/06/

law-versus-faith-female-activists-versus-male-devotees-and-other-strange-creatures-at-sabarimala/.

Menon, Nivedita, "The 'Massive Mandate' Of 2019 and the Role of the Election Commission," *Kafila,* July 6, 2019. https://kafila.online/2019/06/07/the-massive-mandate-of-2019-and-the-role-of-the-election-commission/.

Menon, Nivedita, "NEP 2020: Elitist and Corporatized Education under Hindu Rashta," *Kafila*, September 9, 2020. https://kafila.online/2020/09/08/nep-2020-elitist-and-corporatized-education-under-hindu-rashtra/.

Menon Nivedita and Aditya Nigam, "Epilogue," *Power and Contestation. India after 1989*, 2nd ed. (Hyderabad: OrientBlackswan, 2014). (First published in 2008).

Mevani, Jignesh, "With Bihar Success, CPI(ML) Has Smartly Blended Radicalism and Pragmatic Politics," *The Print*, November 12, 2020. https://theprint.in/opinion/with-bihar-success-cpiml-has-smartly-blended-radicalism-and-pragmatic-politics/542520/.

Mital, Ashish, "Farm Laws: Claims and Reality," *the Indian Express*, October 9, 2020. https://indianexpress.com/article/opinion/farm-laws-claims-and-reality-6717662/.

Munoth, Shreya, "SC Verdict on Triple Talaq, a Legal Reading: Judgment Welcome, but Doesn't Address Sex Discrimination," *Firstpost*, August 23, 2017. https://www.firstpost.com/india/supreme-court-verdict-on-triple-talaq-a-legal-reading-judgment-welcome-but-fails-to-address-institutional-sex-discrimination-3963863.html.

Nair, Ravi, "ECI's Stance on Data Discrepancies: No Right to Question?" *News Click*, June 13, 2019. https://www.newsclick.in/ECI-Elections-2019-Votes-Discrepancies-EVMs.

Negi, Shrishti, "Food for The Vulnerable People: How YUVA's Campaign Is Helping Feed Migrant Workers In Mumbai," *News 18*, April 15, 2020 https://www.news18.com/news/lifestyle/food-for-the-vulnerable-people-how-yuvas-campaign-is-helping-feed-migrant-workers-in-mumbai-2578675.html.

News Desk, "Justice Muralidhar, Who Ordered to Register FIR against Kapil Mishra, Transferred," *HW News*, February 22, 2020. https://hwnews.in/news/national-news/justice-muralidharan-ordered-register-fir-kapil-mishra-transferred/126592.

Nigam, Aditya, "Hathras and beyond: The Upper Caste Counter-revolution," *Kafila*, October 8, 2020. https://kafila.online/2020/10/08/hathras-and-beyond-the-upper-caste-counter-revolution/.

Nigam, Aditya, "So Who Has Won the Election?" *Kafila*, May 16, 2014. http://kafila.org/2014/05/16/so-who-has-won-the-election/.

Pal, Sumedha, "Delhi Violence: Arrests Continue," *News Click*, March 16, 2020. https://www.newsclick.in/Delhi-Violence-Arrests-Continue-Locals-Muslim-Youth-Being-Arbitrarily%20-Targeted.

Pandey, Geeta, "Coronavirus in India: Desperate Migrant Workers Trapped in Lockdown," *BBC News*, April 21, 2020. https://www.bbc.com/news/world-asia-india-52360757.

Perrigo, Billy "The Fatal Gang Rape of a Young Woman Is Forcing a Reckoning in India Over the Caste System," *Time*, October 15. https://time.com/5900402/hathras-rape-case-india-violence/.

Philip, Christin Mathew, "Under Fire, Karnataka Does U-turn, Will Resume Trains for Migrants," *Times of India*, May 8, 2020. http://timesofindia.indiatimes.com/articleshow/75614188.cms?utm_source=contentofinterest&utm_medium=text&utm_campaign=cppst.

Rautray, Samanwaya, "NRC Must to Identify Non-citizens: Govt to SC," *Economic Times*, March 17, 2020. https://economictimes.indiatimes.com/news/politics-and-nation/nrc-must-to-identify-non-citizens-govt-to-sc/articleshow/74680527.cms?utm_source=contentofinterest&utm_medium=text&utm_campaign=cppst.

Rawal, Vikas, Manish Kumar and Jesim Pais, "India's Villages during the COVID-19 Pandemic," 2020. https://coronapolicyimpact.org/2020/04/07/indias-villages-during-the-covid-19-pandemic/.

Rawat, Mukesh, "In 13 states NGOs Fed More People than Govt during Coronavirus Lockdown," *India Today*, April 9, 2020. https://www.indiatoday.in/india/story/in-13-states-ngos-fed-more-people-than-govt-during-coronavirus-lockdown-1665111-2020-04-09.

Rugh, "How Murdoch, Bill Gates and Big Corporations Are Data Mining Our Schools," *The Indypendent*, April 30, 2013. https://indypendent.org/2013/04/how-murdoch-bill-gates-and-big-corporations-are-data-mining-our-schools/.

Saaliq, Sheikh and Adrija Bose, "Documenting Violence against Dalits: One Assault at a Time," *News 18*, 2018. https://www.news18.com/news/immersive/documenting-violence-against-dalits-one-assault-at-a-time.html.

SabrangIndia, "Post 370 Abrogation, August 5, the Forest Advisory Committee of J & K Has Cleared 125 Projects on Forest Land," *Sabrang*, October 19, 2019. https://www.sabrangindia.in/article/post-370-abrogation-august-5-forest-advisory-committee-j-k-has-cleared-125-projects-forest.

Sachar, Rajinder, "Social, Economic and Educational Status of the Muslim Community of India. A Report," 2006. https://www.mhrd.gov.in/sites/upload_files/mhrd/files/sachar_comm.pdf.

Saiyed, Kamal, "Migrant Workers Stopped in Surat; Police Use Teargas after Stone-pelting, Detain 96," *The Indian Express*, March 31, 2020. https://indianexpress.com/article/coronavirus/surat-lockdown-police-migrant-labourers-violence-coronavirus-6338852/.

Scroll Staff, "J&K: Those Living for More than 15 years Now Eligible for Domicile under New Rule, Says Centre," *Scroll.in*, April 1, 2020. https://scroll.in/latest/957868/j-k-those-living-for-more-than-15-years-now-eligible-for-domicile-under-new-rule-says-centre.

Singer, Natasha, "InBloom Student Data Repository to Close," *New York Times*, April 21, 2014. https://bits.blogs.nytimes.com/2014/04/21/inbloom-student-data-repository-to-close/#:~:text=After%20parents%20in%20Louisiana%20discovered,student%20data%20from%20the%20database.

Singh, Navya, "COVID-19 Cannot Harm India as It Is Home To 33 Crore God & Goddesses': BJP Leader Kailash Vijayvargiya Makes Bizarre Claim," *The Logical Indian*, March 18, 2020. https://thelogicalindian.com/news/bjp-leader-coronavirus-remarks-20217.

Singh, Pooja and Karthikeyan Hemalatha, "Anti-CAA Protesters Shift Their Focus to Feeding the Needy," *Mint*, April 10, 2020. https://www.livemint.com/mint-lounge/business-of-life/amid-lockdown-caa-protestors-distribute-food-to-migrants-workers-across-india-11586353174017.html.

Sinha, Bhadra, "Sharjeel 'Radicalised' by Books He Read for Thesis on Partition, Delhi Police Chargesheet Says," *The Print*, September 20, 2020. https://theprint.in/india/sharjeel-radicalised-by-books-he-read-for-thesis-on-partition-delhi-police-chargesheet-says/506598.

Statement, "Lok Sabha Elections 2019—Calling The Election Commission to Account: Statement By Retired Civil Servants, Veterans, Academics and Concerned Citizens," *Kafila*, July 3, 2019. https://kafila.online/2019/07/03/lok-sabha-elections-2019-calling-the-election-commission-to-account-statement-by-retired-civil-servants-veterans-academics-and-concerned-citizens/.

Takle, Niranjan, "Secrets of Gau-rakshak—Niranjan Takle Talks about Cattle Smuggling," 2019. https://www.youtube.com/watch?v=1TdcrvqTjGk.

Tew, Yvonne, "Stealth Theocracy," *Virginia Journal of International Law* 58, no. 31 (2018): 31–96.

The Polis Project, "Disproportionate and Illegitimate State Violence: A Report on the Police Violence in Uttar Pradesh against anti-CAA Protestors," January 28, 2020. https://thepolisproject.com/disproportionate-and-illegitimate-state-violence-a-report-on-the-police-violence-in-uttar-pradesh-against-anti-caa-protestors/#.X5-rboVR3IV.

Tripathi, Rahul, "NE Delhi Violence: There Were Warning Signs before Rioting Began," *Economic Times*, February 27, 2020. https://economictimes.indiatimes.com/news/politics-and-nation/northeast-delhi-violence-there-were-warning-signs-before-rioting-began/articleshow/74328478.cms?utm_source=contentofinterest&utm_medium=text&utm_campaign=cppst.

Tripathy, Harshvardhan, "How New India Developed Its Own Lynch Culture in Just Five Years," *The Citizen*, March 30, 2019. https://www.thecitizen.in/index.php/en/NewsDetail/index/2/16590/How-New-India-Developed-its-Own-Lynch-Culture-in-Just-Five-Years.

Variyar, Mugdha, "Coronavirus: Govt Asks Social Media Platforms to Promote Aarogya Setu App," *CNBCTV 18*, April 13, 2020. https://www.cnbctv18.com/technology/coronavirus-govt-asks-social-media-platforms-to-promote-aarogya-setu-app-5664061.htm.

Varma, Gyan, "No Discussion Held to Introduce NRC: Modi," *Mint*, December 22, 2019. https://www.livemint.com/politics/news/no-discussion-held-to-introduce-nrc-modi-11577033574834.html.

Vij, Shivam, "The Delhi Pogrom 2020 is Amit Shah's Answer to an Election Defeat," *the Print*, February 26, 2020. https://theprint.in/opinion/delhi-pogrom-2020-is-amit-shah-answer-to-an-election-defeat/371558/.

West, Sarah Myers, "Data Capitalism: Redefining the Logics of Surveillance and Privacy," *Business & Society* 58, no. 1 (2017): 20–41.

Yadav, Yogendra, "Secularism Gave up Language of Religion. Ayodhya Bhoomi Pujan Is a Result of that," *The Print*, August 5, 2020. https://theprint.in/opinion/secularism-language-religion-ayodhya-bhoomi-pujan-ram-mandir-kashmir/475307/.

Yogesh, S. "Hindutva Terror: Story of the Common Link between the Four Murders," *News Click*, August 20, 2018. https://www.newsclick.in/hindutva-terror-story-common-link-between-four-murders.

Index

Aam Aadmi Party (AAP) 151, 175, 193, 248–9, 253, 261, 263
Aarogya Setu App 283
abhaydan (gift of fearlessness) 61
abolitionism 33
  village-level 33
Adhikhari, G. 81, 83
adivasis 2, 15, 193, 203, 278
Agamben, Giorgio 143–4
Ahmad, Muzzafar 81
AIADMK 255
Allied Expeditionary force (Russia) 80
All-India Spinning Association (AISA) 64
Ambedkar, B. R. 65, 285
Andrews, C. F. 35, 37
Anna Hazare movement 245–6, 248–9
Anti-Corruption Movement 1
Anti-Indenture Emigration League and Coolie Protection Society 34, 36, 39–40
anti-indenture movement
  elitist opposition 33
  Gandhian politics 32
  historiography 31–2
  Kunti's resilience 32–3
Appadorai, Arjun 263
Arab Spring moment 1, 259
Arendt, Hannah 8, 55, 261
Arrighi, Giovanni 9–10
Arya Samaj 36
Arya Samajist missionary 33
Atlantic slavery, abolition 31, 34

Bach, wife of Mohammed Beg 34–5
Badiou, Alain 10
Bahujan Samaj Party 171, 249, 287
Bailey, F. G. 186, 188
Bajrang Dal 264, 279
Banerjee, Mamata 152, 203, 253–4
Banks, R. W. 37
Basava, Kalyana 166
Basu, Bhupendranath 35, 38
Bhagwati, N. H. 127
Bharatiya Janata Party (BJP). *See also* Modi, Narendra
  absolute majority in 2019 277
  anticorruption movement 263
  Bihar elections 287
  Bombay film industry 281
  corona pandemic and 278
  lotus symbol 172–3
  under Narendra Modi's populism 255
  politics of land acquisition 199, 207
  State Assembly elections 2020 279
  2014 election 193
  Varun Gandhi and 151
Bharti, Kanwal 285–6
Bhattacharjee, Buddhadeb 265–7
Biju Janata Dal 253
Bill, Lokpal 245, 247
Bollywood, New Cinema of the 1970s 233
Bolsheviks 79–80, 84, 242
Bose, Subhas Chandra 65, 113
Bourdieu, Pierre 5, 142
Bradle, Benjamin 79, 81
Brechtian theater 84
Britain. *See also* British rule
  1926 General Strike 82
British Indian Association 33
British rule 51, 60, 102, 108, 110, 112, 128, 242
  absolutism 84
  anti-imperial resistance 76
  charge of "seditious speech" 77
  Indian Mutiny of 1857 223
  proceduralism of law 160
  revolutionary nationalists 242
Buck-Morss, Susan 7, 10, 241

Campbell, J. R. 78
Castoriadis, Cornelius 7–8, 241
Chatterjee, Partha 6, 13, 121, 134, 150, 211, 225–8, 231–2, 235, 262–3, 266, 268–9

Chattopadhyaya, Virendranath 73, 77
Chaturvedi, Benarsidas 34
Chauri Chaura 55–9
 implications of collective power 59
Chenoweth, Erica, *Why Civil Resistance Works* 51
Chief Election Commissioner (CEC) 142
 appointment of 146
Chokhani, Ramdev 39
Citizenship Amendment Act (CAA) 151, 277–80, 282
civil liberties 122–33, 149–50
Cold War 4, 9–12, 74, 81, 87, 236
collective egoism 59, 61–3
collective power 51–66. *See also* satyagraha
colonialism 3–4, 7, 12, 103, 113, 226, 232, 234
communism
 collapse of Soviet Union 13
 Comintern, circulation of 75
 conspicuousness 81–7
 European incarnation 73
 manifestation 77
 modification 3
 Muslim/Islam and 79–80
 religion and 80
Communist Party Historians Group 79
Congress party. *See also* Gandhi, Indira; Indian National Congress; Nehru, Jawaharlal
 dominion status 76–7, 86, 124–8
 election pamphlet (1957) 166–7
 first election 146
 Gandhi's political thinking 52–3, 55, 57–8, 62–4
 Lahore conference 74
 1957 election 166
 1967 election 149
 1977 election 150
 Open Hand symbol 168–70
 political opponents 123
Constitution of India
 Article 324 147
 Article 324(1) 148
 Article 325 145
 Article 327 147
 Article 329(b) 148
Coronacapitalism 282–4
Covid-19 212, 277, 283
CPI(M) 241, 265–8
CPI (ML) 233, 287

dalits 2, 15, 32, 39, 42, 76, 86, 171–2, 184, 191, 193, 249, 253, 255, 262–4, 278–81, 285–7
Dalmia, Vasudha 84
Das, Veena, *Critical Events* 229
Dawes Committee 101
Defence of India Rules and Orders 133
democracy
 appraisive concept 141
 in Asian countries 259
 erasure of politics 1990 262–5
 Nehruvian Era 165–8
 politics and 262
 present trends 259–60
 twentieth-century forms 141, 260–1
democratic politics
 contradiction 12–15
 expanded forms 5
Derrida, Jacques 260
Devji, Faisal 61
Dhar, P. N. 232
Dravida Kazhagam (DK) 130, 253, 255
Dreyfuss trial 86
Dutch imperialism 80–1
Dutt, Ramesh Chunder 102
Dutt, R. P. 55–6, 58

East Punjab Public Safety Act 129, 133
Einstein, Albert 82, 85
election. *See also* Election Commission of India (ECI); election time; first general election
 EC's role 171
 free and fair concept 159–61, 165, 167–8
 judicial apparatus and 169–70
 local social pressures 161
 Model Code violations 142–3, 147, 149–50, 171–5
 petitions 166
 post-1990s era 170–5
 visual images 165–8
Election Commission of India (ECI) 142–3, 146–53
 powers of the Parliament and 148

election time
  citizen's as voters 145
  competitive character 143
  democratic property 141–4
  enumeration of voters 147
  legal exceptionalism 143–4, 151
  model code of conduct 147–53
  specificity and polysemy 142
Electoral Registration Officer (ERO) 152
Emergency Powers (Press) Act 1931 130
English Act of 1848 77

fascism 3, 10, 227, 246, 263, 278, 285
feminism 1, 2, 4, 6, 233, 269, 286
first general election
  constitutional right to vote 145
  procedural certainties 144–7
Foucault, Michel 1, 270
  idea of governmentality 268–9

Galiev, Mirsaid Sultan 80
Gallie, W. B. 141
Gandhi, Indira 149–50
  assassination 170
  Congress Party and 229
  Emergency of 1975–7 168
  film industry reforms 233
Gandhi, M. K.
  all-India campaign of mass civil disobedience 52, 76
  arrest after salt march 63
  aversion to mass democracy 59–61
  collective or corporate power, criticism on 59–61
  and the Congress party 55–6
  decentralized village democracy 60
  frustration with unruly crowds 56
  interest in the minority 61
  Satyagraha in South Africa 32, 62
  self-mastery model 59
  suspension of NCO 56–7
  swaraj or Indian self-rule 51–2
  theory and practice of satyagraha 53
Gandhi, Rahul 204, 207, 209
Gandhi, Rajiv 226
Gandhi, Sanjay 230
Gandhi, Shanta 79
Gandhi, Sonia 151, 203, 206–7
Gandhi, Varun 151

gang rape 223, 225
Gates, Bill 283
German Communist party or KPD 81
Ghadr movement 79, 82
Gilmartin, David 6, 142–3, 148
Girni Kamgar Union (red flag) 76, 82, 85
Gopalan, A. K. 127–9, 132–3
Gramsci, Antonio 54, 182, 209, 227
Great Indian Peninsular Railway 82
Guha, Phulrenu 233
Guha, Ranajit 56–7
  "Discipline and Mobilize" (essay) 56

Habermas, Jurgen 161–2, 170
Haig, H. G. 77
Hardinge, Lord 35
hartal (a work stoppage) 64–5
Hassan, Nurul 234
Hasting, Warren 126
Heidigger, Martin 163
Hind Swaraj 51, 59, 108
Hindu festivals, myths 285–6
Hindu Marriage Act of 1955 286
Hindu-Muslim unity conflict 60, 63
Hindu Rashtra 277–82, 284–5, 287
Hindutva 279–80, 282, 285–7
  Dalit within 287
  and Hinduism 286
  non-Hindu assimilation and 277
  right-wing formations 183, 193
  savarna 285, 287
  social agenda 255
Hobsbawm, Eric 9–10, 75
Home Rulers 33
Howes, Dustin 61
Hui, Wang 11
Hutchinson, Lester 82

indentured workers. *See also* Marwaris of Calcutta
  abolitionist strategies 40
  affidavits 40–1
  as "*coolies*" 31–2
  female 32
  national debate 35
  quarantined 36
  situation of 33–5
  social order of late colonial India 39
India Against Corruption (IAC) 65, 260

India in twentieth century. *See also* Southern India
annual national wealth 99
anticorruption movement 259
armed struggle 241–5
civil society revolts 245–9
communism 73
distribution of wealth 111–12
everyday politics 269–71
general strikes 76
governmental authorities 250–2
historiographical construct 9–12
mass struggles 260
new middle class 231
people's sovereignty 160
politics *vs.* civics 249–53
populism 254–6
region-based parties 264
threat to the sovereign individual 162
transition to capitalism 200
visual realm 163
Indian Emigration Act of 1922 31, 43
Indian National Congress 33, 74, 76–7, 113, 123–4, 127, 151
Lahore conference in 1929 74
Indian nationalism 102, 236
historiography 56
Indian Passport Act 125
Indian Penal Code (IPC) 77, 87, 151
Indian People's Theater Association (IPTA) 79
Indian railway workers oppression 81, 85
Ironside, General William Edmund 80

James, Langford 74, 76–7, 80
Janata Party 149
election petition 169
Jayalalithaa, J. 254–5

Kejriwal, Arvind 248, 253
Khambata, K. J. 101–3, 108, 113
Wealth and taxable capacity 103
Kiernan, Victor 79
Kumar, Kanhaiya 87
Kunti's allegations
Fiji government's investigation 33
letter to the *Bharat Mitra* 32, 34

Lakshmi (Marwari lady) 37–8. *See also* anti-indenture movement
land acquisition
Bhatta-Parsaul agitation 204
contemporary politics 200
countermovement 202–4
major industry associations 206
neoliberal growth model 208–13
new contentiousness 203
original bill 204–5
procedural hurdles 206–7
R&R provisions 204–5, 208–9
Social Impact Assessment (SIA) 208
state-led development 201–2
urban population 250–1
Land Acquisition Act (LAA) 199, 202–4, 208, 212
Laski, Harold 74, 78–9, 85–6
Latour, Bruno 11
League against Imperialism and for National Independence 73, 77
League of Imperialism 77
Lefort, Claud, *The Political Forms of Modern Society: Bureaucracy, Democracy, Totalitarianism* 8
Left Front (LF) 203, 265–8
liberalism 53, 75, 226, 262
idea of power 261
Lingayats 166, 286
spiritual authority of Basava 166
Luce, Henry R. 2

Macdonald, Ramsay 85
Madras Maintenance of Public Order Act, 1947 123–4, 127
Maganlal Doctor, Manilal 34
Maintenance of Internal Security Act (MISA) 132, 236
Majid, Abdul 82
majoritarianism 5, 53, 60–1, 63, 65, 87
Malabar Rebellion (Moplah Revolt) 57
Maoism 241, 245
Maoists 87, 203, 210, 227, 242–5, 255, 264, 284–5, 287
Marsden, A. 34
Marwari Sahayak Samiti (Marwari Relief Society) 36–7

Marwaris of Calcutta 36
  abolitionists strategy 38–9
  anti-indenture movement 37
  stalwarts of 39
Marx, Karl
  Communist Manifesto 73, 75, 78
  Paris Commune 73, 261
Marxism
  class leadership 56
  collective action theories 58
  Gandhian satyagraha and 55
  logic of rule 265–7
  mass action models 56
Mayawati 254
  2012 UP Assembly elections 174
  BSP's campaign 171–2
  criticism of EC paternalism 172–3
  dalit background 172
  elephant symbol 172–4
Mazumdar, Vina 233–5
Mbembe, Achille 181
Meerut trial 6
  anti-imperial opposition modes 78
  communism's role 73–4, 79–80
  constitutive ironies 78–9
  and Muslim insurrection 80–1
  notion of conspiracy 86–7
  place-bound phenomenology 80
  prosecution's exhibits 74
Mehta, Uday 61–3
Mishra, Kapil 151
Mitchell, Timothy 11, 100–1
Modi, Narendra
  2014 election 193, 249
  comparison with Indira Gandhi 235–6
  Covid-19 pandemic 212
  Hindu vote bank 184
  legislative assembly election in 2007 151
  nationalism 228
  on National Register of Citizens (NRC) 280
  populist government 255
  reelection in 2019 225, 235
Mooney trial 86
Mukherjee, Syama Prasad 129
Munzenburg, Willi 73, 77
Muslim League 33
Muslims
  Ali ka Panja visual religious symbol 69–70 (*see also* Open Hand)
  Babri Masjid demolition 279
  CAA and 280
  hierarchical placement 15
  Mufassils and 80
  Open Hand controversy 168, 172
  political society and 253, 255
  RSS and 278
  slum clearance in Delhi 169
  in UP 279
  violence against 151–2, 281
  vote bank 168, 182, 184, 190
  Ziyauddin Bukhari *v.* Brijmohan Mehra 168

Naik, J. P. 234
Nambyar, M. K 127
Narayan, Jayaprakash 133, 232, 236
Narayan, R. K. 145
  "The Election Game" (*The Hindu*) 144
National Emergency 224. *See also* Gandhi, Indira
  Caesarist thesis 227–8, 235
  contemporary history 225–9
  as critical event 229–31
  failure of 249–50
  as a productive space 231–3
  puzzled approach 230
  scholars' reflections 225
  as a watershed 231–3
  women's studies and feminism 233
National Planning Committee 113
National Population Register (NPR) 280
National Register of Citizens (NRC) 280
national wealth 99–114
  distribution of wealth 111–12
  1919 Government of India Act 107, 112
  1924 Economic Enquiry Committee 110
  poverty measurement 102, 109
nation-state 3–5, 12, 77, 100–1, 122, 132–3, 254–5, 286
Naxalites 242
NDA 268, 277
Nehru, Jawaharlal 52
  caste politics 188, 190
  at Congress of the Oppressed Nationalities 77

Gandhi's correspondence 58
on Meerut Trial 86
neoliberal populism 5, 200, 208–9, 211–12
parochial politics 163
party symbols 165–8
neoliberalism 14, 201, 228, 231, 233, 260, 262, 264
market ascendancy 12
Nehruvian development 3
twentieth century claims 9
Niebuhr, Reinhold 54, 61
1919 Government of India Act 107, 112
1924 Economic Enquiry Committee 110
Non-Brahmin movement 33
Non-Cooperation/Khilafat Movement (NCO) 51–3, 83
demonstrations 58
nonviolence
affective dynamics 54
confusion of strength 58
current trends 65–6
Gandhian rules 64
mass-scale mobilization 53
participation advantage 51
people power 51–2
spiritual language 56
theory of action 53

Occupy Wall Street movement 153, 248, 259, 266
Oliver, Kelly 41
Open Hand 168–70, 172
Operation Barga 266

Pan-Islamists 79, 82–3
Patel, Vallabhbhai 65
Patnaik, Naveen 253
Pearson, W. W. 35, 37
peasants 2, 32, 43, 55, 57, 73, 76–7, 80–3, 85–6, 124, 202, 227, 241–2, 250, 265
People's Liberation Guerrilla Army 243
Petrovskaia, Elena 7
Podoroga, Valerii 7
political action
democratic values 64
negative entailments 54
nonsovereign freedom 62
three guiding concerns 54–5
political imaginary
concept 7–8
law and legalities in South India 121–34
political violence 57. *See also* Chauri Chaura
morality of 58
politics. *See also* India in twentieth century
earlier notions 182
negative meaning 181
populism
Nehru's 200, 208–9, 211–12
postideological moment 260–2
under Narendra Modi 255
poverty
improper distribution of wealth 110
measurement 102, 109
political question 260
rural settings 64
Prakash, Gyan, *Emergency Chronicles: Indira Gandhi and Democracy's Turning Point* 236
Prasad, A. 81
Pratap (Hindi Newspaper) 34
Prayag Mahila Samiti (Allahabad Ladies Club) 39
Preventive Detention Act 123–4, 127, 129, 132
Protection of Civil Rights Act (1955) 131
Protector of Emigrants in Calcutta 37–8
Public Safety Acts 123, 125
Punjabi Suba movements 129

Quit India Movement 127

Rajadyaksha, Ashish, *Indian Cinema in the Time of Celluloid: From Bollywood to the Emergency* 233
Ramasamy, E. V. 255
Ramesh, Jairam 204, 206–10
Ranade, Mahadev Govind 102
Rancière, Jacques 42, 74–5, 262, 264–5, 270–1
les sans-part 42
Rao, K. Chandrasekhar 253
Rashtriya Swayam Sevak Sangh (RSS) 232, 236, 277–81, 284
Reddy, Y. S. Jaganmohan 253

Reichstag Fire trial 86
Representation of the People Acts (RPA) 145, 151, 165
  Chapter III 148
The Right to Fair Compensation and Transparency in Land Acquisition, Resettlement and Rehabilitation Act of 2013 (LARRA) 199–212, 264, 267–8
right-wing Jana Sangh (Hindu) 236
Rolland, Romain 85
Roosevelt, Franklin Delano 85
Rowlatt Act 121
Rowlatt Satyagraha 52. *See also* Chauri Chaura
Roy, Arundhati 243, 263
Roy, M. N. 55, 73
Ruhr crisis 101
Russell, Bertrand 80, 85
Russian Revolution 73, 81

Sacco-Vanzetti trial 86
Sachar Committee Report 279
Saklatval, Shapurji 74
Salt Satyagraha 62–3
Sanadhya
  collection of photographs 34
  Fiji Mein Mere Ekkis Varsh (1914) *(My 21 Years in Fiji)* 34
Sanghvad 278–82
Sarkar, Tanika 76
satyagraha
  action theories 53–5, 63
  constructive mode 64
  defining feature 63
  as disciplined action 62–4
  perils and possibilities 51–3
  riots and property destruction 52
satyagrahi 61, 63, 128
Saxena, N. C. 206
Schmitt, Carl, *The Concept of the Political* 8
Second World War 76, 123–4
Self-Respect Movement 255
Sen, Amalendu 41
Sen, Amartya 3
Sen, Sukumar 142–3, 154
Seshan, T. N. 143, 149, 171
SEZ Act 208
Shah Commission 169, 225
Shah, K.T. 101–3, 108, 113
  Wealth and taxable capacity 103
Shani, Ornit 142
Shankar's Weekly 145
Shinawatra, Thaksin 249
Shinawatra, Yingluck 249
Shirras, George Findlay 106–10, 112
  Science of Public Finance 105
Shops and Establishments Act 125
Shroff, Babu Onkarmull 37–8
Simon, Sir John 82–3
Singh, Bhagat 65
Singh, V. P. 270–1
Singur-Nandigram Moment 267–9
Skaria, Ajay 61–3
socialism 10, 12, 79, 82, 86, 113, 227–8, 242, 259
  East European 264
Southern India
  first Indian Civil Liberties Conference 123
  formation of a civil liberties 124–6
  law cases 122
  MMPOA, use of 123–6
  public safety legislation 124
Soviet Union, collapse of 264
Spratt, Phillip 79, 81
Stamp, Sir Josiah 102, 104–7, 109–10, 112
Stephan, Maria J., *Why Civil Resistance Works* 51
Subramaniam, P. S. 146
Swaminathan, T. 150

Tandon, Rambihari 39
Tarlo, Emma 225, 229
  Unsettling Memories: Narratives of India's "Emergency" 229
Tawney, R. H. 74, 85
taxation 101, 103–8, 110, 113
Telangana Rashtra Samithi 253
Thurman, Howard 65
Trivedi, R. K. 150
twentieth-century, political thinkers 54

UK antinuclear campaigns 63
Unlawful Activities Prevention Act (UAPA) 236
untouchability 61, 63, 129, 131, 278

Untouchability Offences Act 131
US civil rights movement 63
Usmani, Shaukat 82–3, 85

Vajpeyi, Ambika Prasad 40
Venkatappayya, Konda 58
Verma, S. P. Sen 143, 149
VHP 264
vote bank. *See also* election; election time
    from 1950s–1970s 185–9
    from 1990s and after 189–92
    cartoons 183–4
    caste politics 189
    dominant common sense 182–5
    Hindu hegemony 183–4, 190
    Mandal upsurge 189–92
    Muslims bloc 190
    patronage relationships 185
    in rural setting 186, 188
    South Asian term 182
    urban environment 191
    Wikipedia on 182–3
voting. *See also* vote bank
    central principle 161
    charge of "undue influence" 166
    pictorial party symbols 162–3
    undue influence 169

Wells, H. G. 74, 85
Worker's Welfare League 74

youth 184, 245, 249, 270

Zasulich, Vera 82
Zedong, Mao 227, 242. *See also* Maoists